may

D1433673

3 0120 02549116 0

So Who's Your Mother?

By the same author

EYE OF THE DAY
MY FATHER LAURENCE OLIVIER

So Who's Your Mother?

AN AUTOBIOGRAPHY

TARQUIN OLIVIER

Foreword by Philip Ziegler

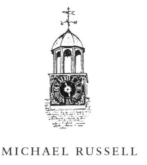

MICHAEL RUSSELL

© Tarquin Olivier 2012

The right of Tarquin Olivier to be identified
as the author of this book has been asserted by him
in accordance with the Copyright, Designs
and Patents Act, 1988

First published in Great Britain 2012
by Michael Russell (Publishing) Ltd
Wilby Hall, Wilby, Norwich NR16 2JP

Page makeup in Sabon by Waveney Typesetters
Wymondham, Norfolk
Printed and bound in Great Britain
by MPG Books Group, Bodmin and King's Lynn

All rights reserved

ISBN 978-0-85955-322-3

FOR MY FAMILY AND FRIENDS

Contents

Foreword

To be the son of a King is always an awkward business, whether the monarch in question is orthodoxly royal, athletic, theatrical or what you will. Tarquin Olivier's father, Laurence, was every inch a King, agreed by most to be the greatest actor of the twentieth century and, by his prodigious energy and enthusiasm, principal creator of the National Theatre. Add to that a mother who was herself a leading actress and to have Noël Coward, Ralph Richardson and Sybil Thorndike numbered among your godparents, and it will be obvious that Tarquin started life labouring under a considerable burden.

He solved his problem by doing his own thing. He loved travel and indulged it prolifically: first during his national service in Germany, then with Quentin Keynes in an expedition following in the steps of Dr Livingstone This gave him a high level of dedication to Third World development. Then he went on an adventurous two years travelling by himself around South-East Asia, and finally into jobs that took him around the world. This is far more than a travelogue, of which he has written one already: it is an exploration of his personality and a rounded portrait of a remarkable life. His passion for travel permeates almost every page.

To be a successful traveller – provided, that is, you wish to escape the comfortable but suffocating embrace of luxurious international hotels – it is necessary to be resourceful and a good linguist, to have an insatiable interest in the lives and thoughts of other people and to be good at making friends. The last is particularly desirable. Tarquin arrived in Caracas knowing nobody. His only introduction proved abortive. Within a day or two he had been invited to stay at the home of a professor from the university and was lent a white tie and tails to attend a ball at the Country Club. After ten days he was driven to the airport, 'followed by several cars of well-wishers who wanted to see me off. That had been the most unexpected ten days I had ever had. A week earlier I had not even *seen* any of them.' Except for the white tie and tails his experience would have been very similar and his pleasure equally great if he had been visiting some backwoods village in a remote corner of Indonesia. To feel at home wherever you are is a rare and enviable trait. Tarquin enjoyed it in spades.

Another attribute desirable for a happy, or at least an interesting and eventful life is a healthy interest in the opposite sex. Tarquin got off to a good start when he fell in love with Judy Garland at the age of six – not the celluloid image most of us had to content ourselves with but the real thing. She plucked an eyelash from his cheek and told him that if he made a wish and then blew the eyelash away, his wish would come true.

Tarquin has greatly enjoyed his life. Fortunately he knows how to communicate that pleasure. The reader will enjoy it too.

PHILIP ZIEGLER

Acknowledgements

As a young man I had no idea what I wanted to do in life until 1958, when during a long vacation from Oxford University, aged twenty-two, I retraced Dr Livingstone's second journey to the Zambezi. The expedition was led by Quentin Keynes, so my first debt of adult gratitude goes to him. That experience awakened in me an ambition to contribute to Third World development. For that to be satisfied I had to undertake a prolonged search with a number of dead-end frustrations.

During my final year at Oxford my father Larry and Vivien Leigh's marriage was foundering. I was shattered by that even though it had been threatening for years because of her mental health problems. I felt I had to get away. I knew that never again would I be able to spend any real length of time being footloose and fancy-free, so I took a Messageries Maritimes boat from Marseilles to Manila. I spent nineteen months wandering round South-East Asia and had a number of experiences which I thought illustrated the people's ways of life and patterns of thought. I described these in the book *Eye of the Day* which was published after much rewriting in 1964. Fifteen years later I was based in Hong Kong looking after the Asia and Pacific regions' business for the security and banknote printers The De La Rue Company Ltd. I revisited the places I had written about and sought out the people I had known. Such rediscovery has been a constant enhancement of my life.

My second book, *My Father Laurence Olivier*, was published in 1992. Its aim was to set the record straight about him, my mother the actress Jill Esmond, and Vivien Leigh, my three main influences. Those two books were focused mainly on other people, with me as a participant. This new memoir overlaps them a few times for the sake of continuity; but a life of experience in eighty countries does provide a wide and bright enough spectrum to be worth recall.

I would like to thank my father's widow Joan Plowright for permission to quote from his letters and indeed her own to me, and also to my stepsister Suzanne for letting me quote from her mother Vivien's letters. She and I went through so much together with her mother's manic depression and ever since she has been a wonderful and supportive friend.

When assembling photographs there were no suitable ones of me and Larry, except from home movies. I much appreciate the assistance of the British Film Institute's archive establishment in Hemel Hempstead for letting me use their equipment to isolate the relevant 16mm frames in those movies, and also to TKone Film and Video in Covent Garden for enlarging and sharpening the images from colour film to stills in black and white.

I am extremely grateful to Philip Ziegler who is writing the most authoritative biography of my father. To assist him I gave him a copy of the first draft of this memoir and he responded with such enthusiasm that I asked him if he would like to write the Foreword, which he has been gracious enough to do.

Above all of course is my publisher Michael Russell. As soon as I saw his publishing list, with so many names of those I knew or cared about, I longed for him to publish this book and will always recall the pleasure I felt when he agreed. Since then his detailed attention and wide variety of editorial points has concentrated my mind wonderfully, a lesson in itself.

When my parents were alive I called them 'Mummy' and 'Daddy'. Here I refer to them as 'my mother' or 'Larry' which is what everyone always called him. On a more personal level, writing this memoir has been the most fulfilling vote of thanks to so many people I have known, yielding pleasure to me on many fronts and for that I am eternally indebted to Zelfa, my wife of twenty-two years, whose idea it was.

At first I thought of calling it *An End in Itself*, which is what I think life should be, but I was told that as a title it was too indefinite. I was then prompted to use my own rather imperious first name. I tried *By the Nine Gods*, a quote taken from the opening of Macaulay's *Lays of Ancient Rome*:

> Lars Porsena of Clusium
> By the nine gods he swore
> That the great house of Tarquin
> Should suffer wrong no more.

After trying it out on friends, we – especially Zelfa – felt it was too portentous. So I challenged her to think of something better, hence the question which I must have been asked more often than almost anybody. Even my children are asked 'So who's your grandmother?'. When Zelfa suggested *So Who's Your Mother?* it seemed a natural choice, and one which might raise a smile.

One

In the beginning was Apple Porch, an old cottage four miles west of Maidenhead. My maternal grandmother was Eva Moore, a star of her era. She had acted in more than eighty plays, and as leading lady opposite Henry Irving, the first actor ever to be knighted. Her husband was Henry Vernon Esmond, an actor manager and playwright who had had thirty of his plays produced in the West End. He died when my mother was fifteen. Their friends included W. S. Gilbert, Herbert Tree, Anthony Hope, Clemence Dane, Rudyard Kipling, John Gielgud, Somerset Maugham, Ivor Novello (who lived two miles away in Burchetts Green), and those who became my godparents: George and Mercia Relph, Noël Coward, Ralph Richardson, and Sybil Thorndike. Eva received several fan letters from Queen Mary. She and Harry Esmond were theatrical royalty.

Their town house was in Chelsea: 21 Whitehead's Grove. After Saturday performances in West End theatres they took the train to Maidenhead, and went the four miles to Apple Porch by pony and trap. Later they bought a steam car which could just manage five miles before having to be refilled with water. The arrival of their first Daimler was a relief.

They built on a servants' wing to the cottage, four more bedrooms, two studies, and a long drawing room which led to a sun parlour. It was badly designed, a most awkward house. After we sold it in 1955 it became an old people's home and has now been completely rebuilt. Outside were two acres of herbaceous garden and several apple orchards. The view still spreads down the fairways of Temple Golf Course and over the Thames Valley. On a clear day you can see Marlow.

In 1925 my mother Jill Esmond was seventeen and played Sorel, the juvenile lead in Noël Coward's play *Hay Fever*, her third West End appearance. I have a first edition of the play where the hand-written dedication reads 'To Jill, from the great God Coward', and five kisses. I saw the play with Edith Evans and later with Celia Johnson. Only when I read it did I realise that the part of the leading lady, Judith Bliss, was modelled on my grandmother Eva, a star actress, trying to become country gentry; and the excruciating house in the play was suggested by Apple Porch. The dialogue between Sorel and her brother goes:

Sorel – Where's Mother?

Simon – In the garden, practising.

Sorel – Practising?

Simon – She's learning the names of the flowers by heart.

Later on their mother says she has been pruning the calceolarias.

My mother was a fine actress, much sought after, had mature literary tastes, was a good tennis player and a party girl. She had a sense of humour and was fun. So was Larry. They met at the Royalty Theatre at rehearsals in John Drinkwater's play *Bird in the Hand*. Although he had neither her literary background nor her maturity, she knew *he* was the man she wanted to marry. All her friends immediately took to him, especially Noël Coward. Larry was like a man drunk even when sober, a wonderful mimic, raconteur, with electrifying changes from gay and amusing to mock serious. An actor's actor. Eva so took to him she couldn't help calling him 'Harry', her late husband's name, instead of 'Larry'. And he called her 'My darling Mum'. His own mother had died when he was twelve, which had traumatised him.

Earliest memories are seldom as comforting as Laurie Lee's, who wrote about them in his book *Cider with Rosie*. His were of getting into his mother's bed in the morning. When she got up he rolled into the valley left by her warmth. To him that seemed the whole point of life.

My own first recollections are of hell. In the frozen winter of 1940 I was smitten with meningitis, still dreaded as a potential killer disease, but then all too often fatal. Meningitis is a swelling around the brain. When it inflames it exerts pressure within the head and down the spinal column. It causes unbearable pain, and in my case an agonising paralysis which twisted and curved the spine inwards, for six tortuous weeks.

This was horrific also for my mother, made doubly so because it coincided with her divorce from my father. He had been Vivien Leigh's lover since their film together, *Fire over England*, in the summer of 1936 two months before I was born. The doctor advised my mother as sympathetically as he could that my chances of full recovery were poor. He had to reveal to her that it was quite possible that the aftermath would be insanity or deafness. Blindness. A lifetime of physical handicap of some kind. My actual survival amazed him. He said that with young children you can so often be wrong. When you think they'll live they die, and when you think they'll die, they live.

The after-effects in my case were only physical. It took years for my sway-backed spine to straighten, helped in my teens by rowing. My legs were less satisfactory. The thighs were disproportionately short and remained so. From finger tip to finger tip I measure six feet, but my height is only five foot eight. The Achilles tendons were so shrunk that I walked on the balls of my feet. Steel-soled shoes were of some help; after a few years I managed to place heels first to the ground when walking, but when running I still can't. On the tennis court I sprint around like a ballet dancer on tiptoe.

It was only after my mother's death in 1990 that I understood the disease had caused *her* a longer lasting hurt. All my life, subliminally, I had associated her hands with that almost deadly pain, so I never liked her touch. I avoided it, which must have been upsetting for her; but we were always each other's best friends and her last words to me were: 'Thank you for loving me as much as you do.'

The doctor said that I should immediately be taken away from England and the Blitz because any explosive bang could destroy my mind. My mother took me and my governess, a strong healthy girl called Joan, to New York. She rented a tiny apartment at the Franconia Hotel on the West Side: the wrong side. She had twice been a great success on Broadway: in 1928 in *Bird in the Hand,* and in 1931 in *Private Lives* with Noël Coward, Larry and Gertrude Lawrence. That was then. Now she was nobody, with £10 allowance to take from England for herself and for Joan, and £5 for me. In the New York world of show business a friend in need was a friend to be avoided. Jessica Tandy, an equally hard up actress, moved in with her daughter Susan Hawkins, daughter of the actor Jack Hawkins who was a British officer serving in Burma. The two actresses shared the rent.

Larry and Vivien paid us a visit in New York when they were on their way back to England, he to join the Fleet Air Arm. I had gazed at their photographs in newspapers and was excited. It seemed extraordinary to see them in our tiny place: we were unworthy of their fame. Joan had put me to bed so that they could not see my tortured walk. They sat next to my feet. Vivien was so beautiful I could hardly believe it.

Once they were gone I expect that my mother, Jessica and Joan sat down and had a nice drink. Jessica had a humdrum job in the British Consulate. My mother ended her radio programme explaining what things were like in war-torn England, and took her chances by going to Hollywood, not overtly touting for work but pretending to have a holiday. As Jill Esmond, she had a fine reputation on screen and had been the lead in a number of successful films, including *Skin Game* directed by Alfred Hitchcock.

The five-day journey by train across America was split between two hostile railroad companies with a stop in Chicago and a wait of several hours. We went for a bracing spring walk along Lake Michigan. I ran as best I could with my steel-soled shoes. I skipped and jumped and fell into the lake. The water felt like icicles. Joan leapt after me, grabbed me and scrambled to the roadside. She took off my trousers and underpants and tried to squeeze them dry. She looked round and saw a parked Greyhound bus. We followed her over to it. She hung my clothes over the exhaust which was still warm. An ingenious solution, but so livid was I with the humiliation that I disowned her, and my mother, waddling off into the crowd, morally superior, disdainful, self-righteous and entirely ridiculous, but at least alone, my buttocks pink as peaches.

In Los Angeles Joan Crawford, the film star at the height of her film career, rang to say there was a bungalow available next to her house in North Cliffwood Avenue, with a large garden. There, within a few days, we settled down. One night we were adopted by a marmalade cat. He came into my bedroom and lay on my chest. He purred, which was new to me, and had a calming influence. It actually made me want to go to bed, to have him with me.

I went to Brentwood Town and Country School, off San Vicente Avenue, a wonderful co-educational school with about eighty children aged from four and a half years old to eight or nine; T-shirts and jeans for boys, cotton frocks for the girls. We all sat together in class and played in the sizeable grounds with swings and roundabouts, lots of brown grass and an old horse called Traveller we took turns to ride. The owners were the Dyes, whom we called Auntie Catherine, head teacher, and Uncle Ben, head of admin. When their son John was killed in the Korean War they renamed their school the 'John Thomas Dye Foundation'.

One of the girls was Gary Cooper's daughter. Her name was Maria. She invited all of us in her class to her birthday party. There were as many governesses and matrons as children. Birthday parties abounded. Everyone came to my own fifth birthday and left a ton of presents, even a scooter.

A special man came to give me physiotherapy, with various exercises and strange contraptions. He had me pick marbles up with my toes. Co-ordination was a problem. If anyone threw a ball for me to catch I would bring my hands together after it had passed me and hit the ground. Oddly, I was apparently good at boxing. My mother and Joan took me for long walks to help my Achilles tendons. I trudged in the heavy steel-soled shoes along trails in the Santa Monica Mountains. I had a recurring dream of their long shadows, ahead of my short one, and my never being able to catch up.

An orthodontist peeked into my mouth, measured the jaw and said there was a further deformity from meningitis. My lower jaw had not grown. Platinum rings were fitted tightly round top and bottom molars with little hooks on the outside. Every night they were joined with tight rubber bands to pull forward the lower jaw, while a permanent band all round the inside widened it. The orthodontist's name was Dr McCoy and the rings were his invention, and named after him. This could have cost a fortune but he fell in love with my mother and never sent a bill. He was a fan of hers and that was enough.

Judy Garland appeared in *The Wizard of Oz* and I fell rapturously in love with her. I wanted to become an actor so as to be close to her in MGM studios. My mother liked the idea. If I were in a movie that was shown in England, my father could see how I was shaping up.

My first part in 1942 was in *Eagle Squadron*, an MGM propaganda movie to encourage America to join Britain in the war. This was before Roosevelt felt it possible to rescind the Neutrality Act. It showed the Battle of Britain, using Pathé's actual news clips of the RAF dogfights against the Luftwaffe, an entire nation's fate being decided by multiple combats between individuals. Several dozen American airmen joined up in the Battle of Britain, as indeed did many more Poles, whose country had been occupied by Germany. Robert Stack played the leader of the American airmen in *Eagle Squadron*. As a US officer on the South Downs of England he had to rescue me from the debris of falling fighter planes. When he picked me up I had to punch him in the face, tell him I hated him, and make the rudest possible noise with my tongue sticking out. There cannot have been many harder starts to a movie career. I liked him so much.

My mother was in six films that year, all at Twentieth Century Fox. My heart was sidelined for a moment from fantasising about Judy Garland when I played Roddy in *Two Tickets to London*, a six-year-old son of Jeanne, a French beauty played by Michèle Morgan. One scene required a large number of retakes. I was tucked up in bed and she had to hug me and give me a big kiss. With her perfume, her soft fair hair, earrings and exquisite ears, I was overwhelmed. Over and over I forgot to say 'Good night'.

My mother helped me learn my lines every evening after supper, which I enjoyed. It was the only time I was really with her, rather than Joan who looked after me and had the genius of making every problem disappear. As for the acting itself, with the camera you must never look at, and the concentration of every man in sight, all in such sharp focus, everything filled me with a unique sense of vitality. On the other hand, the waits between takes were interminable. While the lights were re-jigged for different angles I had to be given lessons in English and arithmetic by a teacher I did not take to. When not actually in the lights I felt I was nothing.

The British colony in Hollywood heard of my passion for Judy Garland. I had sent her a bouquet and she had sent me a signed photograph, all hand-delivered by MGM messengers. A reception was held, with her most generous and understanding permission, for 'Miss Judy Garland to meet Master Tarquin Olivier'. It was arranged by Ben Webster, an old actor well known to my parents, and his formidable wife Dame May Whitty, whom they always referred to as Dame May Titty. She had acted with my mother and my grandmother.

A suit was bought for me of beige linen, a new shirt, my first tie, which to my irritation Joan said made me look grown-up. We parked in a grand drive with trees high overhead. The house was above a hilly garden with flowerbeds and rhododendrons. I was introduced to Judy Garland. I held up my hand to hers. I felt her hand gently clasp mine. I saw her face and could not speak, my throat seized up. It was terrible, like being concussed. She led me away from the ogling grown-ups. We had a lovely stroll and my voice came back.

She invited me to stay the weekend with her husband, a fair-haired and good-looking young composer called David Rose. They were the first young couple I had ever seen who were madly in love. Their eyes were not only for each other but embraced everyone around them, a quality she retained for the rest of her life, the more so when singing, dancing or acting, or all three at once. He had just made a recording of a piece he had composed called 'Symphony for Strings'. They played it at full pitch on their gramophone, with its *pizzicato* vitality and sweeping violins at their most melodious. I think that with me she was wondering what it would be like to have a boy of their own.

David had a model coal-burning steam engine, about two feet high, with tracks running all round the garden. It puffed. It was real, the only concession to comfort being a three-foot extension to the funnel to shunt the smoke above the driver and passengers. A tunnel went through a cliff and beyond there was the panorama, far below, of Los Angeles and the Pacific Ocean, all the way to the horizon.

One day as we sat on the sofa she looked into my face and saw an eyelash on my cheek. She stretched out her hand, with her scarlet fingernails, and retrieved it on her slim forefinger.

'First you must make a wish,' she said. 'When you have decided what it is, and not before you're quite quite sure, why, then you blow.'

I remembered the five-day rail journey all the way from New York, the steam train with the sound of its glorious trailing, exhausted whistle, and putting on two extra engines to help with the climb up the Rocky Mountains. I thought of David's model engine, the view over to the distant coast, the Pacific Ocean. I wished I would travel the whole world. I blew and the eyelash disappeared from her fingertip.

The wish came true.

She introduced me to her niece Honeybunch, a pretty girl about my age who said she would like to take me to church with her family. I had never been to church. I asked about the service and what one was supposed to do and she gave a vivid account. The best of it was singing the hymns. She loved that. She said she always got the tunes okay, just like show business, but could never remember the lyrics.

We moved to Pacific Palisades, the far side of Mandeville Canyon, beyond a polo field and riding school. The plateau was planted with lemon groves. The roads had Italian names. Our house, 1535 San Remo Drive, was two-storeyed red brick with a front and back garden. We rented it from the daughter of the German writer Thomas Mann, winner of the Nobel Prize, who lived in the large house opposite. Other houses were within walking distance and I went round to introduce myself to everybody, as was the American way with neighbours, and they called me 'Sussex' because of my accent.

Every Saturday morning Thomas Mann came over to us, wearing his Homburg hat and carrying a cane. He had been an admirer of Jill and Larry's. He would ring our doorbell, doff his hat to my mother and say: 'Good morning, Mrs Olivier. Stamps for Tarquin.' I still have a complete set of used Hindenburg stamps, a page of unused Hitler stamps and many others he gave me with engraved views from all over the world.

When I was seven my governess Joan decided that her duty lay in England, for the war effort. My mother cried and cried. All her life she was incapable of living alone, so we were joined by her mother, Eva, who came all the way from England. This meant that I was no longer the centre of attention, giving rise to a jealousy I could not contain. I became unbearable, deliberately pasting rude notices round the house, leaving drawing pins on Eva's dining chair, and being impossible to everyone. The schoolteachers became upset at my behaviour in class.

With my mother having Eva for company rather than my governess, the conversation at mealtimes changed from mundane household talk to educated and knowledgeable exchanges, dramatic story-telling and wit. Eva scotch-taped maps of all the war zones across her bedroom walls. She and Jill discussed the campaigns in North Africa, the Philippines, and Burma where Jack Hawkins was still fighting the Japanese. I had a dream in which all the land and the soldiers were purple; so I knew we were in Burma. That was the colour of Eva's map. There was discussion of concentration camps, and prisoners of war in Europe, a number of whom we knew. Every week we packaged up and posted our offerings to them; mainly tins and chocolate, while for friends in England we added nylons, loo paper and hairpins.

I was making some progress in reading so my mother tried to get through to me by correspondence, sometimes in verse:

TARQUIN
In the morning, if you wish to clown,
Don't forget to don your dressing gown.
Your feet, so lily white and fair,
Put into slippers, of which there is a pair.
Don't get cold, or sit upon the floor.
Please use that bump which passes for your brain,
And if it's wet don't rush out in the rain.
Your cold is over, disappeared and gone,
So do your best to keep quite well and strong!

The school suggested that for six weeks of the summer holidays my behaviour might benefit, and my mother be relieved, if I went to the Golden Arrow Camp in the High Sierras.

This topic came up when I was going for a walk with Thomas Mann. 'Camp?' he asked. 'What sort of camp?'

I replied nonchalantly: 'Oh, you know, a concentration camp.'

[8]

I thought they were places where you went in order to think very hard, a sort of seminary.

He stopped in mid-stride, walking stick unplaced. 'I don't think you will be going to a concentration camp.'

'It's the only sort I've ever heard of.'

'Even so.'

We had many walks together. The reason I remember that one is because of the elements of disagreement. Other landmarks in the mind come from my being puzzled by something. One afternoon outside the drugstore in San Vicente Avenue I saw a pretty girl in jeans. Her backside had been patched with red tartan. 'Look at that,' I said to a hobo passing by, 'those patches. Very interesting.'

He said it would be more interesting without them, which was of course beyond my comprehension. The memory is indelible.

The Golden Arrow camp was at an altitude of 11,000 feet, mountains towering above and reflected in a big lake. We carpentered every day, which became a lifelong hobby, learnt archery, water-skiing, shooting with 2.2 rifles, and clambered around rock climbing. Our leader in Tent One, for the youngest, was a teenager. The first thing he made was a paddle to beat us with. He never used it. We slept in our bunks outside and gazed up at the largest constellations we had ever seen, crystalline, never a minute without a shooting star.

At home my mother and Eva had a succession of live-in household servants. The one I liked best was Jean, chirpy, overweight, a terrible cook and she hated cleaning. She taught me 'art'. She bought some fine long-handled paintbrushes, tubes of oil paint and a bottle of turpentine. She painted roses on bottles and showed me how. This kept me quiet. We ran out of bottles so I went in search of some. Beyond us, past Thomas Mann's house, there was a long road lined with guava trees, lemon groves crowding behind them. High up there was a house on a hill and by the entrance there was a line of dustbins. I opened the first, like the cartoon Top Cat, and found priceless empty bottles of all shapes and sizes, clean and shiny. I stood them in line on the road, totally absorbed.

'What *are* you doing?' It was a pleasant lady's voice.

I straightened up. She was beautiful, fine ankles, high heels, a simple summer dress and perfect figure. I explained that I was an artist and wanted the bottles to paint on.

'You sound English. What's your name?'

'Tarquin Olivier.'

'Good heavens. I knew your mother and father.'

'What is your name?'

'Barbara Hutton.'

She led me up the drive. I told her my family news, and where my mother and I lived just down the road. She took me to the swimming pool and introduced me to her husband Cary Grant. As a Hollywood star he had known my parents. He said this called for a celebration. He flicked his fingers. A maid came over wearing a lace apron and a doily on her head.

'A glass of rum for Mr Olivier.'

My mother renewed her friendship with them. Barbara had a son called Lance by her previous husband, a Swede. He was a big boy, a year older than I. He was a great climber of trees and a bit of a bully. He had asthma. He was allowed to hit me but I wasn't allowed to hit him. Disagreements were one-sided, led nowhere and quickly fizzled out, but that didn't make me a pacifist, merely disgruntled.

My mother wanted me to have some idea of what was going on in England during the war. There, unbelievably for me, children had hardly any toys. She had her friends in London send us poorly printed booklets, with coarse paper, showing how you could make your own toys from corks, matches and pipe cleaners. Barbara Hutton was fascinated. She sat at table with me, a row of corks and the rest, as she followed the instructions on how to put together a horse. She was fun to be with, possibly the richest woman in the world and heir to the fortune of F. W. Woolworth, who had been behind the very first skyscraper in New York in the 1920s, as soon as elevators had been invented.

Long after the war – years later in the 1960s – when my mother and I were holidaying in Venice, we met up with her, now often divorced. She said that her years with Cary Grant had been her happiest. With his huge film star earnings he was the only one who had had no need of her wealth. The only problem was his hours of work, starting at crack of dawn and coming home only just in time for dinner. She became bored and surrounded herself with continental European friends. He was still a cockney at heart and was put out by this. All remained well when they were together, until one of his terms of endearment struck her like a thunderbolt. He had kissed her fondly and asked: 'How's my little fat podge?'

She went on a 'coffee diet', clung to her French friends, showed only French movies, and made him, Hollywood's leading man, feel inferior and out of place in his own home. He tried to talk her out of this, but she was horrified, in her thirties that her waist was bigger than it had been when she was eighteen. She became obsessed with that nonsense. Eventually he left. His had been her only true love, she told us.

In Pacific Palisades she and Cary invited my mother to a black tie dinner. That was a problem. She had only one evening dress and did not like it: a long olive green skirt and a leaf-designed top. She tried it on and asked what I thought. I said it looked common. She frowned, but agreed.

'What's the most common thing about it?'

'The buttons.'

She cut them off and Eva replaced them with pearl earrings. This made her feel much better. She told this story at the party and made them all laugh. There were some French people there and she was quite capable of chatting with them because she had had a French nanny.

Our closest friend was the star actress, an exceptional cool fair-haired beauty, referred to in London as the 'English Rose': Gladys Cooper. She had kept her name and at the start of her career worked to lose her cockney accent, often with my parents' help. Luckily she retained her wit and down to earth quality.

Her third husband Philip Merivale had just died of a heart attack. He had had a son, Jack Merivale, by a previous marriage, equally good-looking who forty years later became Vivien Leigh's end of life companion. Gladys became my Granny Gladys. She had me to stay when my mother was filming, in her large wooden house, overlooking the golf course across the end of Mandeville Canyon. She had a red setter dog, a pet white duck called Romeo, and her daughter by a previous marriage called Sally Pearson, a teenager.

I had the run of the place. There were twelve battery chickens, separated in wire cages, each with a sloping wire floor. Their eggs ran down to a runnel for collection. They were fed and watered automatically. It seemed to me unnatural and the sounds they made were piteous so I opened them up and lowered them to the gravel. They hated the feel of dirt and pebbles between their toes. They wailed, picked up each foot in turn and examined it in horror. It took Gladys ages to recapture them.

It was a typically hot summer and I wandered around in bare feet. The volleyball I was playing with ran into the road so I chased after it. The melted tar squashed between my toes, hot but not hurting so I forgot about it; until Gladys saw me walking over her Persian carpet. That was quite a scene, but far worse was my throwing a stone over a hedge. It happened to hit Romeo on the head. He gave a terrible squawk. I rushed round and saw him scamper into the kitchen. I arrived just in time to see him showing his head to Gladys. It did have a speck of blood. It was an accident. The filthy looks at me of a fifty-year-old leading actress together with her injured duck were punishment enough.

She had a large double bed which she let me share one night. I became a sort of doomsday machine. I pawed with my toes, scrunching them like a cat. When fast asleep my feet would seek out a target and lo and behold it was Gladys. There was no stopping them. She got out of bed, crept round it and secretly climbed in the other side, my side, now vacated; but not for long. The monstrous sleeping me went into reverse, groped over and went for her on the other side.

Before she died at her house Barn Elms, near Henley, in 1971 I wrote her a long letter of reminiscences, about the chickens, the duck and the tar on my feet. She lived a little longer so I went down to see her. A number of young admirers were there. She produced a cigarette and three of them dived over with gold lighters to light it. My letter had touched her. However I had made one important omission. She said I had forgotten that I was the only male ever to kick *her* out of bed.

I was in a few more films. Our favourite American friends were the actress Margaret Sullavan and her husband the top agent Leland Hayward, and their children Brooke, Bridget and Bill. There were many others but for conversation there was no comparison to Europeans, Jean Wright and her twin daughters, a number of others and the Danish de Kauffman family: Axel de Kauffman was a prince and had been privy to his government's intelligence secrets. Denmark was occupied by the Nazis. The winter of 1940 had been exceptionally cold. He, his wife, three little daughters and a few friends, carrying as much documentation as they could, escaped on foot across the frozen sea one night, a dozen miles of uneven ice from Copenhagen to Malmö in neutral Sweden. They travelled on to London where he gave the files to the Foreign Office and continued with his family out to California.

The years of my early boyhood in California were golden. I had a mare called Whinney who was so fat I could ride her bareback. After twenty minutes climbing the Santa Monica Mountains you were far away, beyond the yuccas, into the great wine-growing valleys, where the far end was marked by a huge water butt. At night we could hear the coyotes yelling which reminded us to bring the cat in. Everything was so ordered that we never bothered to lock the front door. Rationing was scarcely an inconvenience. Petrol was limited per car. We wanted more petrol so we bought another car, a jalopy with a dicky-seat. One chore we had was the result of all the tinned food which was part of our diet. We had to hammer the empty tins flat and hand them in. We had no idea what the 'war effort' really was. At school we were all Democrats. During Roosevelt's campaign for his fourth term of office we linked arms and galumphed round the school yard shouting: 'Roosevelt, Roosevelt, booey to Dewey.' Everything was so safe that I walked the three miles to school, blue jeans, T-shirt, and lunch box, with great care crossing the road over to the polo fields, past the riding stables and Whinney, and up to San Vicente.

I would not say my mother and I were lucky that I had had meningitis, but one good consequence for my recovery throughout the war was being in sunlit California. That was all over. The passion which lasted was the love of music, all from an evening at the Hollywood Bowl. I started piano lessons with Miss Perry, a loving but formal teacher with a veiled black straw hat. Eva's influence was crucial. As soon as she saw I had some sort of gift she stopped Miss Perry trotting me through the typical children's pieces and started me on music with emotional content: Mozart, and C. P. E. Bach's 'Solfeggietto', an exciting piece which lasted about a minute. It was through playing the piano that I felt my life belonged to me as an individual, alone on a piano stool, giving a performance.

Two

We set sail back to England in June 1945, a month after the Armistice with Germany was signed. The 40,000-ton liner *Franconia* was still painted battleship grey, as was the whole of our slow-moving convoy across the Atlantic. She had been used as a troopship and had a single twelve-inch gun on her stern. On the horizon all around us were destroyers. One of them was attacked by a U-boat and we saw the upshot of depth charges, but heard no news of the result. The enemy must have fled. We understood that a number of German submariners were fighting on, refusing to believe that their Führer had killed himself.

The Americans on board were as easy as ever. The English were cliquey. Eva, my mother and I had to share our cabin. The first evening a friendly fat woman handed an apple up to me in my bunk. She said I was a lovely boy. As soon as she left the cabin my mother and Eva complained about being thrown together with a cockney. It took some time for me to accept the cast-iron English class system as it was. Our compatriots seemed to have little barriers round them. None were entirely happy about returning home. They did not know what to expect, no matter how long the letters they had received from family and friends. They might be considered renegades even though the government had requested that mothers with children should, if they could, live overseas, so as not to be a burden on their hard-pressed nation.

Liverpool was swathed in cloud. The docks had been patched up from bomb damage but the surrounding blocks of flats were left shattered. Some of them, four or five storeys high, above collapsed rubble, had the remains of walls which showed where the stairs had been, the different wallpapers from floor to floor and the backs of fireplaces and chimneys, soot blackened. On the ground grew blitz weed, masking the rubble with its profuse mauve blooms.

In London we stayed with a cousin in Clarendon Road, W11. Even among friends we felt foreign, my mother especially. I had never known her comfortable in her own skin, probably the aftermath of Larry, but here in her own country where everyone else had such an unhealthy pallor, and for the most part wore frayed clothes, her nervousness and never-ending cigarettes had changed her. She found it impossible to get work in the theatre and took a small part in a film with Rex Harrison, called *Escape*.

She took up charity work in the Actors' Orphanage and the Theatrical Ladies' Guild. It was difficult for her to build bridges with friends, after their untold and untellable losses and suffering, the deaths on the front and at home from the Blitz, the crowded shelters overnight. Our days were spent queuing with shopping bags and ration books. At least that brought us together with everyone.

We rented the coldest house, in Campden Hill Gardens. She hated living alone and her sense of displacement was made worse by her divorce from Larry and his fame now rocketing with the worldwide raptures over his film *Henry V*. For many he had come to symbolise *the* England, with the Shakespearian lines of 'We few, we happy few, we band of brothers'. I was dying to see the film but she could not bear to go with me. I think this was because she was afraid of breaking down with emotion. So I went with the son of our daily woman Alice. His name was John and we became friends. We were bowled over by the movie, so clean and colourful and exciting in the enormous Kensington Odeon. It made me hugely proud. I went round saying I was his son, even though I had yet to meet him in England as a schoolboy.

During the war, like so many in the profession, Vivien had made exhausting tours to visit the troops. While he was in Ireland making *Henry V*, she was with other actors entertaining in North Africa. She wrote to him:

Dateline: Bone, Algeria, 13 July 1944

I don't think I've told you about what General Montgomery said when he came to see us. He was v. charming and said we had no idea of the importance of the work we were doing and that we were a 'battle winning factor' which I must say was jolly thrilling coming from him. I haven't written to you all this last week my darling because the heat has been something indescribable. People who've been here for years say there's been nothing like it. When I've got back at night I've just fallen on my bed and lain there in a bath of perspiration. I've got v. v. brown, which is nice. The bathing in Tripoli was sheer heaven. Our first night there after Cairo we went to a Roman amphitheatre and gave the shows and played to 17,000 men. I have never enjoyed anything so much, even though during the daytime performances 50 flies settled on one's face and neck and flew in one's eyes. The sight of all those boys sitting in such a lovely relic of the past was beyond words exhilarating. It was perfect for speaking too.

At the end of the war Larry bought Notley Abbey, a majestic medieval pile, endowed in the fifteenth century by Henry V, and occupied by Cardinal Wolsey when he was building Christ Church, Oxford. The ancient house, the gardens, orchards, and woods, and the little River Thame, all breathed romance.

There, in the years to come, their friends and guests were theatrical and cinema royalty from England, America and the Continent, several cabinet ministers like Walter Monckton, John Profumo and Duncan Sandys, leading Labour lights Hartley Shawcross and Arnold Goodman, the literary people, the owner of the *Telegraph* Michael Berry and the formidable Lady Pamela, F. E. Smith's daughter, Garrett Moore, later Lord Drogheda, head of the *Financial Times*. Kenneth Clark of 'Civilisation', the composer William Walton who wrote the music for Larry's Shakespeare films, and the conductor 'Flash Harry' Malcolm Sargent. Then Lady Alexandra Metcalfe and Lady Diana Cooper. Larry and Vivien were wonderful hosts: England's most glamorous acting couple ever.

In 1944 Vivien was still exhausted from her tour. Larry tried his best to make her rest but there was excitement in the air, of victory just round the corner. She had conceived his child. She felt there was nothing she could *not* do. This was the seal of divine approval on their love which had started illicitly, two months before my mother had given birth to me. She took the part she had set her heart on: in the film of *Caesar and Cleopatra*. It was too much for her. During a violent scene when she had to chase and beat a slave she collapsed. She had a miscarriage. The loss of their baby had fearful moral overtones for both her and Larry. I think it was her miscarriage followed by a six-month-long recuperation from the TB which followed that led to her mental problems. Between times of her being her normal divine self she sometimes descended into bouts of manic depression and over the next dozen or so years this developed into a mortal danger for both of them.

She and Larry had a romantic little house in Chelsea: Durham Cottage, 4 Christchurch Street, SW3. near Burton Court. They decided, during her illness, that it would be quieter for her to stay at Notley, an hour's drive into the Vale of Aylesbury. He went to her almost every night in his beautiful Rolls, lucky to be allowed the petrol. She had never been a sleepy baby. While confined to her bed, with almost military discipline she read her way through the whole of Dickens, Trollope, Scott's Waverley novels and much more. At least that was more restful than keeping her friends up all night in Chelsea.

My mother gave a cocktail party planning for Larry to come. There were Tony Guthrie, his favourite director with his wife Judy, Leo Genn who had played the Constable of France in the film *Henry V* and who was there in service dress, just back from Allied Occupied Europe; and my mother and Larry's dearest and only lifelong friends George and Mercia Relph, both of them part of the wildly successful Old Vic Theatre Company which Larry had set up with my godfather Ralph Richardson at the New Theatre. Leo Genn had been at the liberation of one of the concentration camps. With his deep velvet voice he described the unimaginable horrors of the holocaust, the clearing up, and the rescue of the starved bodies which still clung to life. In the dumbstruck silence the phone rang. My mother picked it up. Her face fell and she ended by saying 'Maybe another time', which we all heard.

It was Larry. He said Vivien had had another relapse and he had to go down to be with her at Notley.

Some weeks later Larry came round to Campden Hill Gardens for tea. I rushed downstairs to open the door. He was not dressed as Henry V, nor as a flying officer in the Fleet Air Arm, but fairly stylishly in a grey flannel suit and garish Garrick Club tie. My mother was in a summer frock and high heels, which I much preferred to her being in slacks.

I gazed up at my estranged parents looking at each other. Their affection was real and shared, but neither of them could have known the overtones and undertones and half tones of what the other felt. She traced her forefinger down a deep scar on his upper lip. It had been cut while filming *Henry V*. A horse had charged too close and the camera had hit him full in the face. She said how much more important that scar made him look: this made him blush.

Attention was turned to me in my jeans, sneakers and T-shirt. I took him up to my room. He was pleased to see the pictures on my shelf which he had sent of himself, in armour and in his brass-buttoned uniform as an RNVR naval officer. He sat on my bed. He asked if I would like him to read something to me, so I took down a copy of *Boy's Own Annual* and opened it at a story of four naval officers marooned in a lifeboat, under attack from a U-boat. He read it thrillingly, making it frighteningly real.

Then he was off to Vivien and Notley.

As I had done in California, I started to explore the neighbourhood, but got nowhere. I rang doorbells and after three or four hostile receptions I realised that in London I wasn't wanted. A month or two later, after my toys had arrived from America, I tried again at the house opposite where there was a girl my age. I introduced myself to her mother. She hissed that I was a nosey parker. I went home in confusion and complained to my mother. She tried to explain the class system as then practised. It made no sense to me; I thought we were just people.

She said that *she* and her friends were ladies while Alice was our daily woman. Being a lady did not mean that you shunned hard and dirty work if it had to be done and there was no one else to do it. You went and did it well. Only a 'near' lady would be too proud for that. I was still unclear precisely what she meant. Now in the year 2011 we have a cleaning lady, and I am married to a woman.

In 1945 my mother and I stayed at Apple Porch the rest of that summer. I loved the Berkshire countryside, living beside Temple Golf Course and having a Bechstein grand piano to play; no feeling of isolated loneliness there with the grim, seemingly irremediable destruction of so much of London. Nearby there lived a pretty girl called Virginia. Her father had been killed while flying for the RAF and her mother had married his best friend, a medical doctor who had served in the Navy. There really was nothing nicer than exploring the golf course and the woods, with a pretty girl my age in a flowery cotton frock. She was the first one I showed my lead soldiers to – a row of ten guardsmen in scarlet tunics and bearskins. She didn't laugh when I said that I longed to be like that.

Vivien's recovery became established and Larry rehearsed her in Thornton Wilder's play *The Skin of Our Teeth*. She was an electrifying comedienne and given rave reviews for her part as the skittish maid Sabina. Larry introduced us and we drove off to Notley for the weekend, me in the front with him, Vivien in the back with George and Mercia.

The medieval house was in a valley, beyond the River Thame and a millstream. It was grander than any I had ever seen; stone, with cinqfoil windows and mossy tiled roof. The only rooms decorated at that stage were the bedrooms – the servants', Larry and Vivien's, one of the guests' – and downstairs the dining room, and the library where we sat in evening dress before dinner. Vivien's sophistication was perfectly stated. The butler Alan and the maid behaved naturally in their roles. As well as George and Mercia there were Tony Bushell, an ex-Welsh Guards major and associate producer for *Henry V*, and his girlfriend Annie Serocold, living together in the gardener's cottage. Vivien wondered whether I ever wished I had brothers and sisters. I said no, otherwise I would have been sent to an early supper with siblings instead of being with *them*.

Larry gave me half a glass of white wine with the fish and a half glass of claret with the grouse. Delicious. Unfortunately I woke up half way through the night to be sick. Luckily no carpet had yet been laid in my room. Even so, it was not very nice for Larry to clear it up. He didn't want to leave it to the butler: a perfect gentleman, I thought, equivalent to being a lady.

Larry said he wanted to have a chat; the throwaway word that can indicate something portentous. The huge drawing room was totally empty except for the full grand Steinway which I had been playing. He led me into the library and I sat in an armchair opposite him as he leant back into the sofa, smoking. He threw the cigarette into the fireplace, interwove his fingers and cracked them away from him, nervously. Eventually he drew breath:

'I have some things I must say before you go to boarding school.'

I immediately hoped he would reveal the mysteries of sex.

'Well, of course,' he said, 'you know all about sex.'

I nodded gamely, dying for more.

What he had to tell me, he said, was far more important. As my father, he loved me. Whatever I did, whether I behaved most terribly, or even committed murder, he would be displeased, maybe horrified, but I must remember that whatever happened he would always love me. From time to time we might not get on very well. I might drive him barmy or detest something about him. Many people did. His beloved audience. That could be mutual. But whatever happened, however we might otherwise feel, he would always love me.

He sat back. 'Christ, I need a drink. Given the circumstances,' he smiled fondly, 'I won't ask you to have anything more serious than a juice of some kind.'

Then the others came in, joined him at the drinks table and chatted.

Nothing prepared me for the total change of character I had to adapt to. All my life I had been a boy, at ease in mixed company of many kinds so long as they did not freeze me out as had our neighbours in

London, and I had loved going to a Californian co-educational school in jeans and T-shirt. I now had to become something I had never been before: a *little* boy, with long grey socks, short grey trousers and a school cap.

My mother and I had lunch at The Ivy with the headmaster of Cottesmore School, Michael Rogerson, and his wife Marion. He had been a captain in the Army. He was now looking for new staff to join the school when it returned to Hove in the New Year. Meanwhile we were evacuated to North Wales. He said he would start me in the second form. He was tall, with a kind narrow face, and she too was handsome, with high cheekbones. We liked them.

When the time came I tied my tie, put on the school uniform and long blue mackintosh, and at last the dreaded cap. At Paddington Station all the mothers and a few fathers stood on the platform in their best, trying not to look desultory, not to let down their sons; about eighty boys. The grown-ups all wore hats and the boys school caps. Strait-laced is the phrase which leaps to mind.

The journey by steam engine to north-west Wales took fourteen hours. From Barmouth station the school buses took us away from the windswept beach and up a very steep hill to Cors-y-Gedel Hall. We new boys were shepherded into a freezing room, our names called out by a master, and we were told what set we were in: Scotts, Haigs, Clives or Drakes. I was a Scott, my school number was '51' and I hung my cap and mackintosh on that peg. This gave me a feeling of identity.

We were shown up the heavy oak staircase to our dormitories. There were five other boys in mine, our school trunks at the end of each bed. I recognised my eiderdown, and the wooden tuck box with my name on it, all sent in advance. We immediately knew where we were, put our suitcases on our beds and clattered downstairs to the dining hall. It was freezing, despite a huge wood fire. We felt we belonged together.

From Cors-y-Gedel on a fine day, all too rare, we could see Mount Snowdon. Our local hill was called Moelfra, round-topped, high above the sheep-cropped grass and rocky streams. We played rugby football three afternoons a week. Life was a struggle. For the other three afternoons we went 'wooding'. Great trees had been felled and we boys had to cut through them with double cross-cut saws into eight-inch thicknesses for the games master to cleave into logs. The only heating in the school came from three huge fireplaces. Coal still went to the war effort. We all ended up in a sweat which cooled and dried as we went inside and one third of us went for a bi-weekly bath supervised by Nurse.

The only other females were Welsh maids, and the scripture teacher Miss Joly whom I described in a letter home as a 'stern Christian'. One day when I was being maddening she hit me in the face with a Bible which gave me a nose-bleed. She said she was sincerely very sorry, told me to go to nurse and then lie down. Nurse asked what happened and I said I had had a fall. Miss Joly wrote an abject letter of apology to my mother and said my not having sneaked on her made her and the staff like me. The Welsh maids spoke little English, all sing song. They could not begin to pronounce my French name Olivier so they called me 'toe face'. It didn't stick.

Cottesmore School introduced me to chapel: daily morning service with lessons, psalms and hymns; two on Sunday, with all the boys singing, and hearing the masters' bass voices. It made me feel how we were unified in the presence of the Lord, a new concept for me..

Michael Rogerson made the inspired purchase of Buchan Hill Estate, near Crawley in Sussex. It was a Victorian gothic mansion with the heaviest stone roof in the county, immense grounds, a large lake and rhododendrons up the drive, and a long tunnel of rhododendrons to one of the boundaries. It had been built by a man who had made his fortune from ostrich feathers. From that moment Cottesmore went from strength to strength. I sent my son there and he has sent his, and his daughter. The new headmaster is the third generation of Rogersons.

My mother's court case was held for her to win back her residence in the house she had leased, a large St John's Wood property. It had been rented to some Czech refugees who refused to move. She won and they had to leave. Months were then devoted to cleaning the place, redecorating, taking the furniture from storage and bringing life back to the garden: her favourite pastime. It became one of the best herbaceous gardens in London, delphiniums comparable to the Chelsea Flower Show.

We went to Henley Royal Regatta, not far from Apple Porch. The old actors Beau Hannen and Athene Seyler invited us to Leander Club, the Mecca for oarsmen, he in his blazer, white flannels, pink cap and socks. Athene was plain as ever and my mother was nicely dressed but nervous among the rowing gentry indulging in afternoon tea. She still felt guilty at having been out of England during the war, like a renegade, despite having been told to leave for the sake of my health. When the teapot needed more hot water she tried to be helpful, picked up the wrong jug and out poured milk. Her awkwardness was so sad. We were rescued by a pretty waitress who changed the pot. As she walked daintily away Athene leant confidingly towards me and said, 'My Beau has fallen in deeply love, with that delicious young waitress's bottom.'

I looked at it twinkling away under the black silk skirt and saw what Athene meant.

'Luckily,' she added, 'he never sees mine.'

There remained the small matter my parents had yet to agree upon. With the dislocations of war, divorce, evacuation and Larry's work being so demanding they had not put me down for a public school. Larry grandly consulted the Labour government's Minister of Education who felt bound to recommend a state school. Failing that he should send me to Eton. My mother shamed him into sending me to Eton, where his cousin had been and mine was going – both Oliviers. Through a friend's contacts I was squeezed in to the house of Mr E. P. Hedley, a devotee of the theatre who fancied himself as an actor. So I took my Common Entrance a year earlier than normal and passed, to become the youngest boy in the school and the shortest bar one.

Deadly Hedley, a humourless and self-righteous man, was sensitive enough to realise that both my parents had taken against him from the start. He had been a classics scholar at Eton, then King's College, Cambridge, then back to Eton as a teacher of classics. His poor sight had prevented him from being called up. His deep set eyes were magnified by powerful horn-rimmed spectacles. His presence induced guilt. He gained satisfaction from reducing a roomful of thirteen-year-old boys to abject tears of unworthiness. He took one class through *As You Like It* and they hated it. Despite his education being the best that money could buy he was not an educated man. He did not read, had no appreciation of music and seemed not to see as far as any horizon. His wife, on the other hand, was attractive, easy to talk to on a wide range of books, and many varied subjects. She would have been a far better housemaster than he.

On the football field my shrunken Achilles tendons still made me run on tiptoe, but eventually the boys stopped saying 'Ha ha, look at Olivier running'. For summer I decided against cricket and took up a sit down sport: rowing. I became a stylish sculler and won quite a few races, but never the final. The Thames, overlooked by Windsor Castle, was an escape into nature, with the swans and ducks and all aspects of life on the riverbank. That was where I was happiest. Also I had luck with my piano teacher. My grandmother Eva had suggested I learn

Debussy's 'La Fille aux Cheveux de Lin'. The Precentor, Dr Sydney Watson, asked me to play something so I played the Debussy. He was most surprised. He stammered that I should play something else, so it was 'Solfeggietto'. Both pieces so out of the ordinary for young boys that he decided to teach me himself. My first term I learnt Debussy's 'Deux Arabesques'.

During the summer holidays Larry and Vivien took me and her daughter, my stepsister Suzanne who was three years older than I, to the South of France. There we joined Vivien's first husband Leigh, a lawyer with a dry sense of humour. We stayed with his sister who had married a wealthy Frenchman. Their classic Midi mansion was called l'Oulivette, surrounded by its own parklands, on a hill overlooking Cannes, the Mediterranean and the Iles de Lérins. It had high rooms, and patios for the master bedrooms. A hundred yards away there was a cottage beneath umbrella pines which I shared with Susie, now one of my closest friends.

Every morning Leigh, Larry and Viv went to market to buy a picnic lunch while Susie and I sat testily in the back of Leigh's car. They found a small wooden fishing boat, skippered by a local fisherman called Edmond, and we would go out to the islands for lunch. Larry had bought me a bikini. It had shocked me in the shop, trying it on, incredibly brief, but so were everyone else's on the boat. I spent much time trying out my French with Edmond.

My mother and I went to Apple Porch for Christmas with Eva. Every night at six we would sit in Eva's morning room and listen to the BBC news. As the tones sounded six times she would say: 'You're late, Jill,' and my mother would give her a whisky. As we listened, Eva would comment: 'The world's in a terrible state.' She was a grand old lady who had lived a great life creatively, from the time she fled her middle-class home to go on the stage and be disowned by her parents. Whenever a public holiday approached she used to say, as if she were Queen Mary: 'Oh I do hope the weather is fine. For the people.'

After Christmas my mother and I went skiing in Grindelwald, starting a sport which became my favourite. We teamed up with an avuncular old friend called Teddy Clarke who was looking after two Gibson brothers, both at Eton, Clement in the same class as me. He and I became best friends.

Music was becoming more and more important, not only the piano where I was learning more passionate pieces, but also as a chorister in the Lower Chapel choir. With love in my heart and nowhere to put it, music became a refuge. For schoolboys any show of emotion was taboo, but in Chapel it was accepted. However, as choirboys we were not angels. Sex was in our minds. I invented a game to help us while away the sermons and readings from the Bible. If we were using a psalter all you had to do was signal over to the boys opposite the number of the psalm and the verse. During a more than protracted sermon I came across a gem. I caught the eyes of the others, signalled the text and feverishly they looked it up. It read; 'For the Lord hath proved me and seen all my works.' I pointed between my legs. They almost burst with laughter.

A term later I was Keeper of the Lower Chapel Choir, carried the Cross at the head of the procession and had to become more serious. I composed the music for the canticles: the Magnificat and the Nunc Dimittis. During the chapel's weekly practice under Dr Watson all the boys had to learn the new tunes. Daddy Watson, as we referred to him, said that it had long been the case in College Chapel for the canticles' tunes to be composed by boys, but this was the first time for Lower Chapel. I managed to look calm and no one guessed it was me. Hearing them sing my tunes so lustily was exciting.

By the summer of 1952 I was in College Chapel with the senior boys, and tall enough to wear Eton tails rather than the idiotic short Eton jackets we called bum freezers. For the holidays my mother and I were invited to Denmark by our old wartime friends from Los Angeles, the de Kauffmans, to stay at their log cabin compound near Gilleleje, north-west Rutland. Their daughter Inge was now aged just sixteen, still with her platinum blond hair, exceedingly curvaceous but with the unfortunate addition of a tall blond boyfriend. However he did not stay long. After a family dinner she and I put to sea in a canoe. The Aurora Borealis was at its most brilliant, pulsating across half the night sky. When we paddled there were bursts of phosphorescence at every stroke. I was learning to smoke. She leant back to hand me a cigarette. I leaned forward to take it and we suddenly turned turtle, straight into the water. I surfaced to hear her laughter. It was glorious, even pushing the canoe to shore. We took off our wet clothes and shoes and strode back to the house in our underwear: innocence and desire.

Then we went to Normandy, this time with Eve Brierly, who had come to live in our top floor flat. She was an elderly, etiolated French lesbian, which I never suspected at the time; such is nature's protection of the young, for my mother had become bisexual: anything for company. Larry had ruined her for serious relationships with men. We stayed near Cabourg in a village called Le Hom. There was plenty of French speaking which I began to enjoy. The beach was wide and windswept. I built a sandcastle with tunnels and runnels for red golf balls to run down. I was joined by a granddaughter of the Rodier fashion house, called Jacqueline. We got to know her family who had a cottage overlooking the beach.

That winter in London I had dancing lessons and went to the Hyde Park Hotel for my first ball, given by Adrienne Allen (she had played in *Private Lives* in London before it went to New York with my mother in her role) and her husband Bill Whitney. There were about sixty of us teenagers, all delivered by our parents, also in evening dress, who came to collect us much later. The girls were ravishing, shy in their new ballroom gowns, necklaces and earrings, and we danced. The hit musical in London was *South Pacific* and after the show its star Mary Martin came to sing to us, in cabaret.

When my mother drove me home she was blushing with pleasure and I asked why. She looked slightly coy. She said she had been standing next to Mary Martin's husband, a most attractive man and they had chatted. He had given her bottom a little pinch. I expressed alarm. She said she enjoyed it. It was a nice pinch. I wondered if she had been wearing a girdle.

I wrote to Larry:

I had the most wonderful Christmas at Apple Porch to which I invited Virginia, my English girlfriend. She is not as good-looking as Inge de Kauffman but that cannot be expected. She is very nice and a little younger than I am. At the moment she is a little taller too. We are very devoted and are keeping up a fulsome correspondence. I think the reason for this is that on Christmas night, when I was saying goodbye and nobody was looking I shared what mistletoe was for. I enjoyed this very much and look back on it with much pride as it took a lot of nerve as it was my first experience of anything in that line.

I was fifteen and a half. The letter goes on to describe Jacqueline in France. My persistence in writing to Larry was starting to yield returns. His response was a classic.

Just as a spur to my already smarting conscience there arrives today your second angelic letter. You are a dear chap to keep writing to me so sweetly. I am enjoying so much your descriptions of all …
My *dear* boy! The international spirit you show in your choice of

girlfriends is very laudable, though I fear it may be a severe tax on your diplomacy as time goes on. Such hazardous procedure may well endanger world peace, or are you training for the diplomatic corps? Otherwise I'm afraid such a very ubiquitous love life may well consign you to a naval career! French, English and Danish. I'll try and pick one for you in New York shall I? And one from Jamaica – a nice black job if we go there to visit Noëlie [Coward] on our way home.

Every now and then poor Vivien showed very publicly her symptoms of manic depression: nervous breakdowns at a time when it was an incurable sickness and mental illness was ill understood. It led to rebounding and confounding mood changes, some very serious, to the enraptured attentions of the press. Again and again, page after page, photographs and exaggerated shock stories. The boys at school expressed their understated sympathy, but those newspapers, day after day … It was awful.

After all our letters it was natural for Virginia to come and stay in the old-fashioned shabby calm of Apple Porch. Her family had known my mother's for two generations. She was intelligent and fun. One day as we sat in the spring sunshine she placed my hand on her breast and life changed gear – but only that one gear. It kept us happy for hours.

Apart from the piano and rowing, my last couple of years at school were transformed by my modern tutor, Oliver Van Oss. He was of Dutch extraction with strong cheekbones, rounded nose, deep dark eyes and black hair. He was a modern linguist of distinction. I felt at ease with him. I once asked whether, during the war, he had ever been a spy. His crow's feet creased with humour: 'No.' 'Why not?' 'I did try but they said I looked too like one.'

All the boys liked him. He was a tremendous worker and wonderfully perceptive. My mother found him a bit daunting when she had her first chat with him, but she was enthralled by his assessment of me. His knowledge of all the arts was stimulating and we debated it all with him during our weekly sessions, about a dozen of us in his study. He did from time to time ask after Larry and Viv's problems, when alone with me, while correcting something I had written. This helped. Hedley never did, and he couldn't bear Van Oss. He dismissed him as a dilettante, which is the best quality to engage the interest of boys. He knew what was good and his horizons were wide.

Notley had become amazing. Vivien organised the decorations with the help of Sybil Colefax of Colefax and Fowler and made it the loveliest place I had ever seen. Every school holiday I had a weekend or two there, always arriving with a suitcase. Never a corner which was actually mine, except for the Steinway. The place became known for Larry and Viv's hospitality and entertainment. The newspapers got that right when they described it as 'legendary'. There were surprisingly few actors among our usual guests; only those few who really were close friends. The theatre world was more burdened with envy than any other; acting was a profession where genuine friendships were rare. Their real friends were for the most part from other professions. Vivien always encouraged me to play the piano, especially to William Walton and Malcolm Sargent, an excellent way of learning how to handle nerves when performing.

With guests on all sides Larry had little time for me except for our single afternoon walks together, and on the tennis court playing very mixed doubles and laughing till we ached. In the mornings I went to their room for breakfast on a tray while they had theirs in bed, avidly reading the Sundays. Not the news, just the critics: Harold Hobson in *The Times* and Kenneth Tynan in the *Observer*. Their reactions, even at that delicate hour, were stentorian, filled with vicious and uproarious sarcasm about the reviews, the plays and the actors themselves. Larry's language knew of no restraint and he made me and Viv laugh painfully, *in extremis*. He was ridiculously, gloriously funny.

Clement Gibson and I went to Grindelwald again with Teddy Clarke, who had made his money in Argentina, some of it through the beef of Fray Bentos where the Gibson family were prominent.

Then there was a day unlike any other day. We were lunching in the restaurant of the Hotel Bahnhoff, not the most electrifying establishment. The best thing on the menu was Rösti potatoes, a Bernese gift to civilisation. Then, at the far end of the restaurant there arrived a vision of such purity and beauty that I knew in *less* than a heartbeat, that my life had changed. I put my napkin down, rose to my feet, hurried out into the lobby and rushed upstairs to the room Clem and I were sharing, and brushed my teeth. I was smitten, bowled over, pole-axed, or whatever the unworthy words are to describe the emotion which I felt I had not only discovered but invented, and I thought it was marvellous.

Her name was Jenny. That was a love which was to flourish for five years. We danced a bit, had a day's skiing, hardly spoke a word and when she left I gave her a beautiful silk scarf. She placed in my hand a scrap of square ruled paper with her address. So started our letters, hers in English, mine in French. They became daily.

This surge of desperately untried love combined powerfully with what was the spiritual height of my religious passion, and the only way

I could express it was on the piano. There, things were rising to a higher level. I had won the junior and the senior piano competitions and became able to move the people who were listening to me. As I sat facing the keyboard with the audience on my right I could sense the direction the emotion came from, and then feel it expanding, growing and it became as if my hands no longer existed, awareness of the delineated notes beneath my fingers reached another plane, as if nothing existed between the actual sounds and the hearing of those who were listening. When I played at Notley after dinner, if things went well the feeling of emotion came from all of them; except Larry. He had unequalled power to move huge audiences. He did it for a living, matchlessly, night after night. He knew what I was experiencing and was like a star looking down affectionately upon me, his little piece of earth. He knew I could perform, but that was in my genes. I was not a natural musician. I couldn't even sight-read a hymn. He knew that emotions could feel sacred, but they were not the be all and end all.

Even so I did so want to excite him. For my final school concert, which I longed for him to attend, I learnt the 'Revolutionary Study', written by Chopin when he was twenty-one, in an overwhelming nationalistic rage at the Russian seizure of Warsaw and the partition of Poland, land of his birth, between Russia, Austria and Germany in 1831. It is a hell of piece, virtuoso by any standard, often played by professional soloists as a final encore to wrap up a piano recital. It was brave of Dr Watson to entrust me with it.

Every weekday I practised it for half an hour on my way back from sculling on the river. My hands were very strong. There is a tremendous climax built up on page two, with the left hand doing impossible leaps and convoluted runs while the right hand chords crash higher and higher. At the summit, top of page three, they give a yell of such rage and tragedy as is seldom equalled on the keyboard. Now my purpose was to excite my father. I thought the way to *get* him would be, for that climactic chord, to throw my head back theatrically, look up at the ceiling and blindly bring my right hand crashing down – accurately. This I practised over and over. I knew that for any performance to work you had to take risks, no matter how humble the medium, even reading the lesson in church. Without risks it is not a performance, only a bore, no matter how perfect the delivery. But what I was aiming for was not just a risk. It was near-suicide.

Unfortunately Larry could not come that Saturday night of the School Concert. In my self-centred state it didn't even occur to me that he might be acting. But my mother, Eva and Virginia were there and School Hall was packed. I had second billing, the best, after the Eton College Musical Society, lamely accompanied by the School Orchestra, worked their way through something quite dull. So I made my entry at the end of desultory applause, cast the tails of my coat behind me over the piano stool and sat down. As soon as all was still and seeming to crackle with expectancy I started.

After only ten seconds I realised that I was playing it faster than ever before. This was terrifying. I couldn't stop and restart. That would have been terrible. Adrenaline came roaring to my rescue. I forgot about my hands and gloried in the sounds. It was my heart that was playing. Yes, the climax built up at impossible speed. Yes, there came the violent crescendo and I only just remembered in time to gaze upwards at the ceiling, as if seeking a place in space, and from a great height I axed the chord. It worked. It was wonderful.

As I took my bow I remained in a vice-like trance, locked into music as if transcendentally. For an encore I played Debussy's 'Clair de Lune', a piece everyone knew. My interpretation was to play it as if it represented the four seasons, starting with springtime. The warmth of summer comes and this leads to the gathering together of all the cascading sadness of falling leaves. The reprieve of the original spring is in the sharp guise of frozen winter, an octave higher. Not much to do with moonlight but a lovely context. At the end the cheers burst out all round and it seemed that a line had been firmly drawn over the schoolboy part of my life that was now at an end.

Three

For National Service I wanted to fulfil my childhood dream of serving in the Coldstream Guards. The War Office Selection Board had to decide who was officer material, and selection by the regiment was by no means guaranteed. We stood outside the gates of the Guards Depot at Caterham, Surrey, carrying suitcases and feeling awkward, mostly in grey flannel suits, about seventy eighteen-year-olds, virtually all from public schools. We were waiting at the edge of the great barrack square, looking down three long ranks of guardsmen in battledress, boots gleaming, rifles at the slope, the Adjutant facing them, a drummer boy behind him. The Adjutant flicked his wrist, the side drum struck out with a crack and the whole parade took a sharp pace forward. As the drum cracked into a roll the men snapped to eyes right and took their dressing in thunderous tiny steps. The drummer quietened as their lines reached perfection. They stood, facing smartly to the right. The Adjutant flicked his wrist again, the side drum rapped out and they faced the front like lightning. So that, we realised, was what was to become of us.

There was a bellow from a sergeant. Two guardsmen rushed out from the Guard Room and told us to follow them. They marched so fast we had to run to keep up. About twenty of us Coldstream recruits were in the first barrack hut, Scots and Grenadiers in the second, the Irish, Welsh, the Life Guards and Blues in the third. We Coldstreamers were in the charge of Lance Sergeant Brough, a magnificent man who had been sixth in Mr Britain at the age of sixteen. Like most other ranks in our regiment he was a Geordie, from Newcastle. Our barrack room was under the orders of a guardsman whom we had to call 'trained soldier', who slept in the corner next to my friend from Eton, Duff Hart-Davis, whose delicate duty it was to wake him up at Reveille by placing a lit cigarette between his lips. We were the lowest of the low, mere recruits.

These men, the regulars in the other ranks, had hard eyes. Several of us were stopped and asked bluntly 'Are you in love, are you courtin'?' Unlike them we looked out on the world as a friendly place. Some of them said we looked like poofters, the whole ruddy lot of us. Our trained soldier was paid to be unpleasant. Our boots had to be polished to look like 'fookin' glass', the floors scrubbed to be 'fookin' white', everything had to be 'fookin' immaculate', to the degree of making me wonder whether he could ever respond to finer things. I showed him a picture in my copy of *Life Magazine*, of a Madonna and Child. I could see he was actually moved and asked what he thought. He struggled and then selected a word which was precisely accurate: 'Fookin' immaculate.'

Almost all of us passed the War Office Selection Board's assessment. Those who failed had to stay on at Caterham and move in with the other ranks, while we went on to weapons training and field exercises at Pirbright. At the Adjutant's suggestion we gave Sergeant Brough a farewell dinner, a rousing and splendidly tipsy time. I thought he would never stop singing 'Hallelujah, I'm a bum ...' That was the end of our Coldstream platoon. We proceeded north to the Infantry Officer Cadet School at Eaton Hall, the Duke of Westminster's palatial country place near Chester. We were combined with three times our number of others from line regiments. With them our standards of drill deteriorated. The Regimental Sergeant Major, a Coldstreamer, yelled out his despair: 'If you don't get a shaggin' move on, I'll rift you round till your legs is wore down to your arses; then I'll put you on a charge for arsin' about on the square.'

Most of the time we attended lectures, took copious notes and memorised scores of technical and organisational facts. Our lives outdoors were devoted in the main to the infantry platoon as a fighting force, chiefly in the attack. The one great defensive exercise was given the deserved name 'Marathon'. This had us in opposing camps on top of a mountain referred to as 'the Bickerton Feature'. We had to dig in, facing each other over a mile wide valley and spend three nights patrolling and being patrolled against. According to the programme we would then march the dozen miles back to Eaton Hall. However, that January it snowed and became the coldest winter of the century. To warm us up we were ladled plenteous supplies of rum. Our senses of humour were unfrozen.

The captain in charge of my squad gave me a wonderful report, saying that I was a very determined young man. When I was accepted by the Coldstream I was given No. 1 Platoon, of No. 1 Company, of the First Battalion, stationed in Chelsea Barracks. With three other freshly minted second lieutenants, solitary brass pips on each shoulder, we were trained in sword drill, and in carrying the colour for changing the guard at Buckingham Palace. We did public duties in scarlet tunics and bearskins. It gave us a feeling of style and pride. In later months when we were posted to the British Army on the Rhine there was a noticeable difference between the guardsmen who had done public duties in London, and those who had joined after our transfer to Germany. When on field exercises the new arrivals had nothing like the pride nor the discipline.

In London the Fifties were a decade of unmatched elegance: the New Look – high heels, narrow waists, full breasts and hips – hourglass figures, day dress lengths below the knee, stockings and suspender belts, entirely delicious. That decade, before the Pill, provided the final gasp of the Coming Out Season. Those of us National Service officers based in London were few in number and much in demand for the debs, the cocktail parties, dinners, white tie and tails extravaganzas in London's ballrooms, and for weekend country house parties with huge marquees. With my own officer's servant to look after me life was like Czarist Russia; effortlessly spoilt, the only social duty being the care-fully hand-written thank-you letters, trying to sound genuine.

One evening in the officers' mess, still in battledress, I was sitting on the fender with my brother officer Martin Lutyens, a contemporary since Eton days. We were both debs' delights, wondering what to wear. He put my problem into verse: 'Heads dinner jacket, tails tails, Macbeth's son's nightly quandary.'

This was the end of the age of innocence. We heard that one debs' delight had taken a deb to bed with him. This outraged us; what a rotten thing to do. Our limited sense of adventure confined us to clinches. Taxis, then with rear windows the size of rear-view mirrors, were a favoured field of play. Abbreviations describing men abounded among the girls. NSIT – not safe in a taxi. A few men were dubbed SSITPQ – suspiciously safe in a taxi, probably queer. Most of us were MTF – must touch flesh. Life was beguiling and simple. Now, fifty years later, our days and nights appear to have been absurd, flippant and disconnected from the real world. And so they were.

Life with Larry and Vivien was terribly stressed at that time with her on another of her manic depressive 'highs'. Noël Coward's diary (published in 1982 by Weidenfeld and Nicolson as *The Noël Coward Diaries*) records:

The Olivier situation is worsening by the hour. Graham [his part-ner] and I drove down to Stratford with Cecil Tennant [Larry's agent] on Tuesday. He is deeply perturbed and wanted to discuss the whole business. We went to the opening night of *Titus Andronicus*. Larry was wonderful ... and Vivien not very good ... She was in a vile temper and perfectly idiotic. Larry was bowed down with grief and despair and altogether it was a gloomy little visit.

Last night I dined with Tarquin 'on guard' at St James's Palace. It was a perfectly sweet evening. Three very young officers and one slightly older. Lovely manners and good old shabby, traditional glamour. Tarquin is bright and attractive although too small. He obviously is worried about Vivien and Larry. He's been to Notley a good deal and seen it coming. I do so hope, if only for his sake, that another rip-roaring scandal can be avoided.

One weekend at Notley the guests were Tristram Hillier, who painted an impressive picture of the grand old abbey beyond the River Thame, and Quentin Keynes who became a lifelong friend. Among his forebears was Charles Darwin as a great-grandfather; Sir Geoffrey Keynes the famous surgeon was his father and his uncle the economist Maynard Keynes. He had led an expedition to South West Africa and Angola in search of the giant sable antelope. In the rutting season he had come across a herd, isolated between two remote rivers. The antelopes were all off guard, watching two stags locking their curved six-foot horns in a show of strength, their haunch and neck muscles bulging with the strain. He was able to go close enough to take the first ever photographs of those noble creatures. They were published in the *Illustrated London News*. On his way home he went to Spain to meet the Condé de Yebes, who had shot a giant sable and transported it home to be preserved by taxidermy. After their meeting the Count suggested to Quentin that he make his own way down the terraced garden. There was someone there he might find interesting. So he left the *palazzo* and trod down the old stone steps. He came to a terrace with a fountain, perhaps even with cupids, a chaise longue beside it. There, her cigarette at the end of an extra long holder and lying in a negligée, was Vivien Leigh. She invited him to Notley. I found him fascinating and hoped one day to accompany him on one of his expeditions, I started writing to him about my adventures while on night patrols with my platoon.

I had been writing to Jenny constantly. Her handwriting was childish, but I had been once-in-a-lifetime smitten two years before in

Grindelwald. She and her foster-mother Marie-Rose had come to visit me at Eton. Jenny had high heels, a modest summer frock over her long legs and perfect figure; her face welcomed the whole of life, fine long eyebrows which curved to her temples, high cheekbones, and soft wide blue eyes. Her voice was mellifluous. Her foster-mother, on the other hand, was clad in black like a spider, was tight-lipped, supremely possessive of Jenny, archly Catholic and *petit bourgeois*. Yet she had a low voice and did her best to be pleasant, for the sake of 'ma petite fille'.

At that time of constant emotional and spiritual highlights I had to have a mild operation on my sinus. The left antrum, the passage from the bridge of the nose through the cheekbone and under the eye, had become clogged and the mucous was going rancid. The specialist in Wimpole Street gave me a general anaesthetic. Gas. The experience caused a profound and extraordinary change in my views on life, dying, and death itself.

The anaesthetist made me lie on the operating table with my hands down behind my back to keep my arms still. A nurse spread a white sheet up to my neck. The gas mask was lowered. The specialist stood waiting beside his tray full of instruments. I breathed in. My lungs filled slowly and for some reason expelled the gas at speed. Slow in and sudden expulsion, in a perpetuating rhythm. I sensed I was going down a dark tunnel, and at the end of each outward breath there arose flashing lights. They repeated again and again at every breath, becoming brighter and brighter, and in the background behind and all around was an atmosphere of harmonious feelings. Each flash made them more wonderful, more filled with goodness and love: the ultimate orgasm.

Next thing I heard was the two men having a conversation about trades unions.

The 'dark tunnel' and its accompaniments have been described by people at the point of death, for example by drowning, who have been saved at the very last second. I had just experienced it. Now there was nothing for me to fear about death. Fear of pain before dying, certainly, and the whole range of agonies and the deterioration of physical and mental health, but death itself? None. A perfect ceasing to be.

Strasbourg was a day's train journey from our barracks in Krefeld, near Düsseldorf, down the Rhine with a change of trains at Karlsruhe. I went for a long weekend in late November. The city was looking its grimmest, the huge Strasbourg Cathedral forbidding. The taxi driver spoke neither French nor German but a thick local dialect common to many Alsatians. Many times he had to ask the way to '*rue Schiller*'. He eventually found it off a road skirting the upper reaches of the Rhine. It was a large house. No sooner had I paid the taxi than Jenny came bounding out of the front door, arms outstretched, fair hair flowing.

Her foster-mother Marie-Rose introduced me to her foster-father, Jules, a tiny grey man with glasses as thick as bottle bottoms who reminded me of Arthur Askey. They led me down a passage lined with coat hooks. It was a primary school with little rooms and desks, the walls plastered with childish drawings, empty and peaceful over the weekend. They insisted I have a bath after my 'long' journey and showed me into Jenny's bedroom; narrow, with a single bed under shelves full of books, a single window, a desk and a potted philodendron. She was to take the spare room, isolated the other side of her parents' double bedroom.

Once bathed and changed and in the drawing room I was made to feel that I was in a long lost home. As Jenny went to prepare dinner, Marie-Rose set out our relationship as if she were laying a table, everything in full view and just so. Her daughter was in love with me. This suited her very well as a parent while I was in England, and even now while I was in Germany. It meant that the boyfriend was not a daily occurrence, living nearby, perhaps on the prowl. Her daughter, like her, was a devout and practising Catholic and was constantly praying for my happiness. Her husband, she said dismissively, was not Catholic. He was Russian Orthodox. Not the same thing at all. The school, for eight-year-olds to twelve-year-olds, with forty or so children, was a gold mine. They were very well off.

So after she had defined her daughter's love, their faith and wealth, I wondered if I could ever fit in. I hoped that love would conquer all and was relieved when dinner was ready.

The next time I went was over Easter. We took the train to Paris and stayed at a modest hotel in the Place de la République. I had never been to Paris before. That brilliant spring, as Jenny and I crossed the Louvre Courtyard above the Place de la Concorde she pointed to the Champs Elysées, a shimmering and wondrous mirage of cars toiling up to the far off Arc de Triomphe. My jaw dropped in wonder. She said: 'Ceux qui n'ont pas vu Paris n'ont rien vu.'

French was a language which started to consume me. I no longer had to think ahead before saying anything. My gestures and facial expression took on a mimicry of the people. Jenny took me up the Eiffel Tower, then across the city to the heights of Montmartre, and the glowing white Sacré Coeur with its domes narrowing into points. Inside the incense-tainted gloom we bought our candles, lit them and placed them among ranks of others. We knelt and prayed – she to the Holy Virgin. Mother Nature had wrapped my love in puritan robes. Very faith-affirming.

Next day the four of us took a bus to Versailles. Marie-Rose regaled us with the glory of French history, the treaties signed in the Hall of Mirrors, the divine dictatorship of Louis XIV, and who had done what to whom in the Petit Trianon. Jules listened obediently. She was a historian while he, despite his incomprehensible accent, taught English. Jenny and I had only thoughts for each other, which got on her foster-mother's nerves. Marie-Rose was sour the rest of the day, disapproving all through dinner at La Thermomètre restaurant in Place de la République. At the hotel she hastened to the lift, Jules in her wake, and up they went, leaving us alone at the foot of the stairs. Jenny was upset about her 'petite mère'. I put my arms round her and we kissed. She floated upstairs. Next day we took separate trains, they to Strasbourg and me back to soldiering.

That winter I was made battalion skiing officer, told to take my platoon to Winterberg in the Harz Mountains, and teach them to ski. With white skis and white denims we trudged to the nursery slopes. After they had learned how to stem turn and stop I challenged them to a race; they poled down the hill as fast as they could while I skied back-wards, facing them, goading them. After a few days they could do Christianias, jump turns and were game for anything. At the end of each day on the slopes my platoon sergeant paraded them in three ranks, skis and poles held upright. He stamped smartly in the snow and asked permission to fall them out. 'Yes please, sergeant,' I said limpidly.

During the spring of 1956 we went to Senelager for more varied forms of battle training, including combined platoon and tank attacks, and all the way up to Brigade exercises in the countryside with the Scots Guards and Grenadiers. Whenever we marched anywhere as a platoon my men sang. The variety was wide, from 'The Lord is my shepherd' to 'Oh, Sir Jasper, do not touch me she said, as she lay between the sheets with nothing on at all at all'. That was much better. At each repeat the remaining last word was omitted. At the penultimate stage, in perfect rhythm and the right beat in the bar they sang 'Oh, Sir Jasper,' then six strides in dead silence, and the final set of 'Oh' with seven silent strides. This puzzled the Germans we passed. So different from the Wehrmacht. We were fit and enjoying peacetime soldiering at its best.

Back at barracks there wasn't really enough to keep the men occupied. The officers' mess was not scintillating. Few of them read and there was little social life outside apart from shooting geese or duck with a few hospitable Germans. I started German lessons at the Berlitz school but as the German teacher's only other language was Spanish, as a medium of instruction it was not worth the candle. So we played poker. Time wasting. Krefeld was uninspiring. Half an hour away was Düsseldorf where we enjoyed the restaurants and looking into the shops.

Brussels was two and a half hours' drive away so four of us decided to go to a night club there, far enough away for indiscretion. After a day of seeing the sights and a good long dinner we parked outside a neon lit house which looked interesting. We asked a local about it. He shrugged, like a Frenchman, and said it always gave satisfaction. We went in, were immediately greeted by a uniformed concierge, given seats in a waiting room and served 'champagne'; from the right kind of bottle but there the resemblance ended.

He announced the arrival of four beautiful young companions and brought in four more glasses and another bottle for them. In they traipsed; four rotund, part-worn, shop-soiled women whose breasts were only a burden. We were certainly not interested in them nor they in us. After an hour's conversation, so as not to hurt their feelings, we thanked them for their company and prepared to leave. Perfect gentlemen. The bill was presented. It was enormous, for their 'company' and alleged champagne. Between the four of us we hadn't enough money. Perfect idiots. I was the only one with traveller's cheques.

At a quarter to midnight, leaving my three brother officers as hostages, I was escorted by two plump harridans either side of me in mink. We stood on the pavement. They hailed a taxi. The only place where cash was obtainable was the railway station. I will never forget the expression of the cashier as he looked up from his ledger at me, then saw my bodyguards. He blushed and looked down, pulled my traveller's cheques towards him, examined my passport, and counted out the Belgian francs as the ladies clung to my elbows. He turned away as he handed everything back. I stuffed the empty cheque book, the cash and passport into my pockets, then they marched me back to the taxi to return to my chivalrous brother officers. As we collated our cash to pay them off a phrase ran through my mind for the first and, I'm happy to say, last time: 'They took all our money.'

I joined Jenny and her parents for ten days' summer holiday in St

Raphael. In 1956 it had a line of pretty two-storeyed houses with gardens, overlooking a narrow coast road, the beach and the Mediterranean. The staff of our shabby little hotel were intimately French with their Marseille accent, slang and a dismissive shrug at anything that was not perfect. My pillow was stuffed with straw. Above the bed was a sign saying 'C'est formellement défendu de pousser des cris d'extase'.

Wherever we walked the street photographers snapped away. Next day we would collect the pictures – at first of affection, shy in brief clothing, swimming things. A bikini, then proudly holding hands defiant with happiness, and eventually together touching from upper arms down to clenched fingers. We swam, water-skied, played tennis, but spent most of the time sprawled on the beach, silent, with an occasional sigh. By the end of the week we were engaged. I gave her a gold ring with a facia, the plan being to have our initials engraved: TJ, or even JT which could stand for 'je t'aime'. She gave me a LIP watch and we looked forward to a long engagement.

After National Service I went up to Christ Church, Oxford, reading philosophy, politics and economics. My main tutors were the philosopher Oscar Wood, the historian Robert Blake and the renowned economist Roy Harrod. I had a room in Peckwater Quad, looking out at the great Library, pitch black and magnificent with soot before it was restored to its original honey-coloured sandstone. I shared it with a tall Old Wykehamist, Nicholas Mills. We both decided to row for the House in the Long Distance Eights. That led to the first time I had been a proper member of a team. At football, with my ridiculous feet, I had always been useless, but on the river, after being mildy successful at Eton but only as a sculler, I now became part of the ultimate team sport: in a racing eight.

Rather than go direct to Strasbourg for Christmas I made a detour via Krefeld. I had heard of the bond between officers and men and wanted to find out about it. At Krefeld station I telephoned the Adjutant. He said that I was welcome to stay in the mess, but that evening was the Guardsmen's Ball in the gym. He put me through to the Regimental Sergeant Major. His measured gruff voice said: 'Wonderful to hear from you, sir, welcome back to the family.'

After dining with the officers, me in a suit, they in their blues, we wandered across the parade ground to the gymnasium, which poured forth thunderous rock 'n roll music. Inside was teeming with other ranks in battledress and almost as many local girls. I was soon surrounded by men from my platoon, offering me whisky, beer, anything, and wanting to know all about life at Oxford as a student. We reminisced about Changing the Guard at Buckingham Palace, marching through the streets of London to guard the Bank of England, and the many and varied patrols, attack and defence exercises in the fields, forests and hills of Germany. My faith in human nature was reconfirmed.

In Strasbourg all was well. Jenny and Marie-Rose said that it was Jules's birthday and that, for the sake of drollery they were pretending to have forgotten. He went round with a long face all that day, unaware of the mighty preparations for dinner. When all was revealed as a surprise and the champagne was opened he poured it down. Like a greedy child he tucked into the meat and vegetables. He even followed the meal with a big cigar which gave him a choking fit. Then he had a stomach-ache. He lay down and it got much worse. He insisted that a doctor be called. He said the pain had spread to his heart and that he was dying. He held Jenny's hand. She was worried about his continual coughing because his feeble eyes showed such strain.

The doctor arrived.

Jules said it was his heart.

The doctor took off his overcoat, jacket, and in his shirt-sleeves loosened Jules's trousers and unbuttoned his shirt. He gently felt the little man's chest and stomach. He said it was a simple case of over-eating.

'C'est le coeur,' insisted Jules. 'Je sais.'

The doctor assured him that it was nothing to do with the heart, 'which is there', he prodded with his finger. 'While the stomach goes from here to there.'

He opened his medicine bag and took out some suppositories. 'Take one of these when I've gone.'

I helped the doctor on with his overcoat and he said a formal farewell. Meanwhile Jenny had cut out one of the suppositories and was trimming it with nail scissors. Jules took it from her, put his hand behind his back and in a trice inserted it, buttoned up and sighed.

'C'est le coeur,' he said again. 'Je sais.' He closed his eyes and drifted into a peroration, stating that Jenny was the only one who loved him, how Marie-Rose never had. That had to be accepted.

I turned to Marie-Rose sympathetically. She shrugged, 'He says that every time he has a birthday. Yes. That has to be accepted. I am his wife. I let him take me from time to time. I wish he weren't so clumsy.'

A hell of a birthday.

We went to Grindelwald and my usual skiing friends were at the Hotel Bahnhoff, including Clement and the avuncular Teddy Clarke. They had been there when I first met Jenny and were enchanted by her. She had then been chaperoned by a couple from the *haute bourgoisie* of Strasbourg. With her foster-parents it was different. They didn't fit anywhere. They were not skiers and not even walkers. They spent most of the day in bed watching television, complaining how exhausted they were. They made no effort to join my friends. Jenny and I had to sit apart from the others with her two parents, as if in Coventry. My mother had written to ask Teddy about them. He wrote back that the foster-mother was the ultimate in *petite bourgoisie* and there was nothing to say about the foster-father except that he was a nonentity who just looked hideous, while Jenny was divine.

Larry wrote to Marie-Rose a spoof letter. In retrospect I realised how funny it was but at the time I was mortified. It began, 'I am apprised by my son of the delightful circumstances concerning your daughter.' It continued with many a camp twist of Edwardian affectation. Marie-Rose put together an excellent and witty reply in classical French, assuring him of her depth of gratitude for his most gracious letter which had given her so much pleasure as she did enjoy laughing. She matched point for every phoney-sophisticated point. I felt almost proud of her.

In spring she and Jenny came to London to stay with me and my mother in St John's Wood. That was a disaster. Larry came over to meet them. Marie-Rose took him into the music room for a private conversation. Some time later they reappeared. She went over to Jenny on the window seat and Larry took me to one side saying he wished he was better at French. He told me that Marie-Rose kept insisting that Jenny stole in order to make me happy. I coaxed the actual words out of him. He had muddled 'prier' for 'prendre'. Jenny spent hours *praying* for me. 'That sounds even worse' he said.

Only a few days later it hit me that Jenny and I really weren't meant for each other. 'Nous partons demain,' her foster-mother said, and they did. The farewell was deadening.

That August was my twenty-first birthday. Vivien was overseas so my mother and I went together to Notley. Larry and I played vicarage tennis. In the evening we were joined by nine or ten of their mutual friends, including George and Mercia, Glen Byam Shaw and Angela from Stratford-upon-Avon, and others I knew and liked. Larry gave a very touching speech to my mother's good health. I wondered if they would still have been married had Vivien not appeared, love her though

I did. Without her he would never have bought Notley. Her earnings were huge and her style more than matched that glorious place. She and Larry did seem so right together and in the eyes of the world. Strange having my mother there. She looked ill at ease and I felt very lost without Jenny. We had agreed not to write to each other. It was over. It was a long time before I really loved again.

Back to Oxford. For my second year I had taken the rooms Anthony Eden had had on the top floor of the Old Library. It was above the fifteenth-century cloisters and faced south, to the ruthlessly Victorian-gothic Meadow Buildings. Vivien had lent me some paintings, my mother a baroque mirror, and my upright piano fitted in nicely. I had the place to myself and could practise in perfect freedom.

For my twenty-first birthday present grandmother Eva had paid for a sculling boat to be made for me by Sims of Putney. In the New Year I stroked the Christ Church torpid for the second time. Sculling went well and I won the New College Sculls easily, in the final beating a heavyweight Oxford blue by 17 seconds.

I was always short of money and only dined in Hall. One day I treated myself to buying a long-playing record of Brahms's First Piano Concerto which I had never heard, and a pot of blue hyacinths. The sun streamed into my room. The music's knotted muscularity and passion stirred me profoundly. With the glorious smell of the hyacinths and after the final mighty cadence of a rising arpeggio ending the first movement I felt a surge of happiness, the first since Jenny.

I went all out for training, pumping iron to build up my back and shoulder muscles. At Eton my only significant race had been the final of the junior sculls when I was easily beaten by one John Mead, a big man whose thigh muscles protruded dauntingly at each stroke. He was now at Merton College. We drew each other in the first round of the Oxford Royal Regatta Challenge sculls, over a short course of about half a mile. At the halfway point we were level and I wondered whether I would ever be any good. No one could have trained harder.

As we came to the boathouses I put everything I had into a sudden sprint and took fully a length off him. He now could not see me. Mercilessly he pulled back closer and closer with every stroke. He sprinted but I held him off, just, to win by half a length. Had the course been fifty yards longer he would have won. The final was easy. By the boathouses, way ahead of my opponent, I heard the commentator saying: 'That's the way, Larry's boy, give the girls a thrill.' Bloody man.

But later when I was handed the trophy, of silver sculls etched in arabesques on a bed of Oxford blue velvet, one of the teenage onlookers said 'Well done Larry's boy,' and that I rather liked.

Every Saturday night after dining in Hall I cycled up to Little Clarendon Street where my piano teacher the composer Bryan Kelly lived with his boyfriend John Webster, the organist at University College. They shared a flat above a butcher's shop. John was a friend of Mary Wilson, the poetess, married to Harold who was a lecturer at Univ as well as being leader of the Labour Opposition in Parliament. He used to join us for the sickliest of all drinks, gin and orange, very bad for my rowing training but it was only on Saturdays, and so did the great Wystan Auden, Regius Professor of Poetry. We discussed everything from poetry to the entire reassembling of civilisation, entirely in keeping with the university's ethos.

Round about midnight we would hear the butcher getting to work in the basement, hacking his carcases. This was a sign for Wystan to take off his patent leather shoes, tie the laces behind his neck, peel off his silk socks and trudge back all the way to Christ Church in bare feet. He would be back at work by six in the morning. Hence perhaps the deep lines on his face. Maurice Bowra said they made him look like a wedding cake left out in the rain overnight. I took my mother there one evening after we had dined at the Randolph Hotel where she was staying. She shone brilliantly with Harold and Wystan, one of the best evenings of all.

Every term I and others were invited to dine by Tom Boase, President of Magdalen College, in his private rooms. He was later to become University Vice-Chancellor. Once he had been Larry and Vivien's dinner guest at Notley, he told me, and as the butler was helping him with his coat, he heard Larry saying: 'He's a don at Oxford, but he's quite all right.' A great comfort, he said. The unfulfilled love of his life was Peggy Ashcroft, who had in 1935 been Juliet to Larry's Romeo. Once again Maurice Bowra's repute as an Oxford bitch was well earned: 'Tom Boase is a man of inestimable public qualities, but alas, no private parts.'

I lost the first round of the University Sculls to the President of the University Boat Club, Ronnie Howard, by two seconds over the full mile and a quarter course. He was so surprised he bought me an ice cream afterwards. Next day he gave a very close race to John Mead, who broke the long-standing record time by a full six seconds.

I wanted to win a university event. David Edwards, son of the rowing sage Jumbo Edwards, agreed to have a crack with me at the University Double Sculls. Mead stroked the other boat with a not very distinguished partner behind him. We should have won easily. Unfortunately something happened to the boat we were used to. There was no time to adjust the outriggers of its replacement. They were far too low for me, making it extremely difficult to get my hands away at the end of each stroke, and by the end of the race they caused abrasions on my wrists. We lost. I was furious.

This was too much. I took David to a pub and we each sunk three pints of Worthington E. Back at Christ Church I pointed out that the Cathedral was under scaffolding. With my interest in medieval architecture I had been up it several times. I insisted that David join me.

The ladders and tread boards were firm under our feet as we climbed. On top of the cathedral, to the east, and a distance away, were the stone mullions rising above the far end of the roof. There was a long flat lead encasement about a foot wide ahead of us, with the roof sloping steeply down either side. I accurately trod along that way. God sometimes looks after the drunk. We reached the end. We hauled ourselves up the West Front and stood triumphantly, surrounded by the most glorious views of the whole of Oxford; every tower and spire, the dome of the Radcliffe Camera, all the way round to Magdalen Tower and Christ Church Meadows.

Years later when he was married David named his son 'Tarquin'.

Four

My letter-writing to Quentin Keynes, describing the Army patrols I had led in Germany, had the desired result of him asking me to join his African expedition that summer. 1958 was the centenary of Dr Livingstone's Zambezi journey. We, with a young American called Dave Coughlin, were going to take a Union Castle liner to Cape Town and retrace the great man. Quentin was thirty-four, six foot two, fair-haired, with an aquiline nose and blue eyes, made the more piercing by his slight stoop. He had been a maverick since the age of sixteen when he climbed the roof of the family house in Hampstead, and refused to come down until his parents agreed that he didn't have to go back to boarding school. He turned away from the usual paths of high achievers. He sought out remote parts of Africa, became an explorer, amateur filmmaker, a safari leader. Every winter he made his money by lecturing and showing his films, which he narrated viva voce, to schools and various societies in Britain. He also drove all across America doing the same. I persuaded him at the Earls Court Motor Show to buy his first Jensen sports car. Every summer he went on safari with a posse of young men; no guides, no tents and certainly no guns. From his father he inherited a passion for collecting historical manuscripts and books, mainly about Africa. That was his genius. Fifty years later, after his death, his collection was auctioned by Sotheby's for a total of more than three million pounds, paying for the school fees of many young relations. He had a philosophy which was attractive even if impractical without inherited wealth: if you really want to do something strongly enough, then life will allow you to do it.

Coincidences were part of his character. In 1957 he bought the ultimate explorer's letter, left by Dr Livingstone at the mouth of the Zambezi in a bottle. It read:

> Kongone Harbour
> 25 May 1859
>
> To ...
> Commander of Her Majesty's Ship ...
>
> Sir,
> We have been at the Luabo Melambe and Kongone mouths of

the Zambezi since the 18th in hopes of meeting one of H.M.'s cruisers with salt provisions for our crew, but none appearing we presume our letters to the Admiral and to the Captain of any Man of War that might be on the coast have suffered detention, or it may have been incompatible with other duties to comply with our request. We leave the Luabo tomorrow morning, and before going deposit this letter in a bottle ten feet Magnetic North from a mark (+) cut on the beacon of the island of this harbour.

Livingstone then describes the discovery of a magnificent inland Lake Shire, and the advisability of keeping this a secret from the Portuguese, who were colonising Mozambique, until the announcement was made by Her Majesty's Government. This letter gave Quentin the idea for our expedition.

We carried with us many other documents, Livingstone's published writings and journals and Baines's original map of the Victoria Falls which Livingstone had discovered in 1845.

The atmosphere in South Africa was difficult when we arrived in July 1985, even in comparatively liberal Cape Town. We dined with a friend, so-called 'English speaking', as opposed to the Afrikaners who were still referred to as Boers. He actually agreed with their policy of apartheid as the only way white farmers could save themselves from having their throats cut. Many considered rural Africans to be savages, while the rest were servants, errand boys, or workers in ill-dressed groups. Many whites thought that even university-educated Africans could easily be subject to violent passions; hence the tension latent behind the dour quietness of African servants, referred to universally as natives, even by themselves. One was not supposed to say 'please' or 'thank-you' to them, though of course we did. Several times I got on to a bus for blacks and they asked me to leave. 'Non-whites' and 'whites only' were translated as 'net blankes' and 'nie blankes' which was easy to muddle. The Africans did in fact have the vote when South Africa was granted independence in 1923 by the British, so long as they could write their name, had an income of £50 a year or a house worth £75. In 1936 they were disenfranchised by the Afrikaners. With recent Independence the African National Congress took over with a full franchise and black rule. Since then it has to be admitted that more than 3,000 white farmers have been murdered.

We gave a number of interviews to newspapers, especially Afrikaner ones, about our Livingstone Zambezi Expedition. This created good-will and opened doors. One night after dinner with one of our contacts we three returned to our long-wheelbased red Land Rover, parked under a streetlight. A native was wandering round it. Quentin thought he looked suspect so we gingerly got in. The native put his head through the front window, Quentin's side, smiled and said 'hello' in a deep voice.

Quentin took a deep breath and shouted 'Petrus!!!'

He flung open the door and danced around the man, waving his arms, spluttering and laughing, all teeth and wide-eyed for joy. I have never seen him so excited. This was the man Quentin had taken on board in Ovamboland, South-West Africa, on his quest for the giant sable. He was the only English-speaking native there, and now he was thrilled to see his old master again. He was handsome and had a cropped head. He had seen newspaper reports, pictures of us, our Land Rover, and noted the number. He had come to South Africa to make money so that he could return to Ovamboland and set up a shop, a trade usually carried out by Indians, a situation he disapproved of. He wanted to join us, and to make things even better he had become a car mechanic. This was irresistible. He became a crucial part of our expedition. A truly Quentin coincidence.

We spent two days buying camp beds, blankets, lanterns, mosquito nets, loo paper, firelighters and for cooking, a kaffir pot which with its lid in place looked like an iron football on three legs. We bought jerry cans, enough for sixty-five gallons of petrol which cost only £9.05. My mother had given us a large medicine chest, complete with a chrome syringe and needles, pills and serums for everything – for her peace of mind, she said.

Quentin's leading contact was Major Piet van der Beyl, the United Party's Shadow Minister for Native Affairs. We went to the Legislative Assembly, an understated building of about 1920 with sub-tropical gardens and views beyond of Table Mountain and Lion Rock. We were shown into the visitors' gallery and watched the debate below. The National Party Prime Minister Dr Verwoerd, who had codified the original apartheid policies for separation of the races in South Africa, was making an impassioned speech in Afrikaans, banding about the words 'propaganda' and 'bantu', the word Afrikaners used for black Africans. We saw our Major and sent a note down to him by white messenger. He was about fifty, tall, with finely bred features and a suit of studied elegance. He read our note. took out a pen, held a fastidious hand on a piece of paper and started to draw something. We guessed it was a map. He waited for the session to end and we met him in the lobby. He apologised for the delay and said the Prime Minister had been attacking him.

He showed us round the building and into the Senate. It was rather dark and smelt musty, not so much empty as dead. With irony he said. 'I see the Senate has risen.'

A few days later we headed east to his 300,000-acre farm 'Fairfield House', near Bredasdorp. His family had been in South Africa for three hundred years. His wife was a dark-haired English beauty. They had a whitewashed classic Dutch colonial house with curved gables. He showed us his collection of guns, a pair of Purdeys, a room with the heads of lions, buffalos and many antelopes. He was followed by an adoring Great Dane which on its hind legs would have been as tall as he. There were dozens of caricatures, a photograph of him rowing for Cambridge and the framed document of Germany's surrender of South-West Africa in 1917 which had been handed to his father.

There was a small herd of a rare antelope on his estate: bontbok, which he was keen to show us. In his open Volkswagen we hurtled across the veldt in a shuddering test for the car's suspension. He was a ferocious driver and all the while he regaled us with his politics which he considered liberal. To summarise: his neighbours may be white, coloured or native, whatever, he would raise his hat to them, but he considered that non-whites were different in likes, moral philosophy, outlook and smells. Physical contact was wrong. He would not like a black in his club, nor as a son-in-law. However feudal he sounded, the Africans on his estate looked us straight in the eye in recognition. This was a pleasant change from the suffocated looks in Cape Town, under the shroud of apartheid.

On a mountainside of wild herbs and flowering aloes we saw five bontbok grazing. We stopped fifty yards away and they looked over at us, their coats reddish-grey with patches of white and chic little horns. Quentin filmed them. Van der Beyl said a bit of a chase would do them good so we headed for them. They ran, jumped with their delicate legs high in the air as they hurtled up a slope that was too steep for us. We stopped and looked at the evening sun, the reddening brown earth and rolling green hills with a few high cactuses like pillars, in the distance a wagon with a team of bullocks driven by an African, and a large herd of sheep.

The Garden Route took us to Port Elizabeth where we turned north, away from the Indian Ocean, to Grahamstown. There we met Professor Smith, a reserved and learned man who had identified a great fish, the coelacanth, caught near the Comoro Islands. He kept one in a coffin-sized bath filled with formaldehyde. The creature was rectangular, five and a half feet long and a foot wide, one of the earth's very oldest – 170 million years – and the first to have articulated forelimbs with elbows and small fins on the end of them. It was nicknamed 'Old Four Legs', the seaborne precursor to all limbed creatures.

Our onward drive was the first to give us the feeling of being a team on our own. Petrus sat behind us with all our kit crammed up to the roof behind him, all wedged down by our Dunlopillo mattresses. Next to him was the medicine chest, a typewriter, all our books and maps. We three sat in the front, the middle man with the gear lever between his knees. That main highway was then only two lanes wide, with gravel shoulders. Whenever a car came the other way we slowed down and waved to each other. Every hundred miles or so we stopped, refuelled, drank from our canvas water bags, peed, and Petrus had a cigarette. Then we changed places in the front seat. We had left Grahamstown early and climbed to the top of a high hill in second gear. We looked down on clouds lying over a valley ahead. At around nine o'clock they vaporised and we saw a huge plain surrounded by mountains. We coasted down and after fifteen miles climbed the next mountain range with little cumulus clouds above it.

Every twenty miles or so there was a little town at a crossroads, two or three shops, maybe a small inn with a notice about a forthcoming dance, a Standard Bank, estate agent, Old Mutual Assurance and then more miles of road, eventually with the towering rock Drakensberg Mountains and Basutoland.

On the border above a corrugated hut flew the Union Jack. A Basuto official came out, unsure which way to put on his hat. We told him we were from England and he waved us through without checking anything. We drove on to the ramshackle capital Maseru and stayed in a hotel made of round brick-built *rondavels*. The windows had blazingly coloured curtains of local fabric. The dinner was good and the African serving girls efficient and friendly, so different from South Africa, like equals. One of them asked whether we had much trouble with elephants in England, and was England bigger than America. We went outside and stood in the freezing porch to admire the crisp full moon. The watchman asked; 'Is the moon *very* big? As big as London Town?'

Johannesburg was preceded by huge mounds of yellow slag cast aside from goldmining. After the hundreds of miles we had driven through, land that was for the most part empty, the city's high-rise buildings seemed out of place. Now it was our red Land Rover which was the odd kid on the street, covered in dust and with canvas water bags flapping from the side, amid the fleets of well waxed saloons.

We had to drive on to Pretoria, the administrative capital, to obtain permits for Petrus to accompany us outside South Africa. Major Piet van der Beyl had briefed the Civil Service and after a couple of days we were given an appointment with a Mr Lindique of Internal Affairs, in the imposing Union Buildings Secretariat. He was tall and daunting. He had powerful deep-set eyes, with jutting forehead, nose and chin. His suit was scruffy blue worsted. His voice was quiet, and he spoke softly with a heavily Afrikaans accent. He did not shake hands but bowed. The fingers of his right hand were mangled. Straight away he advised that normally it would take three weeks to obtain a permit for Petrus. Quentin showed him some of our press cuttings in nationalist Afrikaans newspapers and he was impressed at the amount of support expressed for the Livingstone Zambezi Expedition.

He looked Petrus up and down, examined his native pass. He went behind his mahogany desk and we all sat down, except for Petrus who stood behind us. He telephoned the police in Cape Town and read out one of our newspaper articles in Afrikaans. The police confirmed that Petrus was a good man. He then questioned Petrus in Afrikaans and was satisfied. He arranged for him to have a passport with exit visas for Mozambique and Angola. No visas were needed for the two Rhodesias and Nyasaland. (Now Zimbabwe, Zambia, and Malawi.) As he said farewell he added that he was taking a bit of a chance: 'Oim tiekin aye beet of aye chornce.' What he had done was remarkable. Petrus was given a white man's passport, with no mention of race.

On Sunday 20 July 1958 at eleven in the morning we left Pretoria. We felt our real journey had started, along undulating scrubland beneath a dark blue sky with bright white clouds. Our altitude was 3,000 feet. Far ahead were the Zoutspansberg Mountains. We stopped on the gravel shoulder for a quick snack. Dave being an American, and I, having had my boyhood in the States, had peanut butter sandwiches. Quentin howled his disapproval and had his strawberry jam the other side of the Land Rover.

The pass through those unfertile mountains was narrow. There were hardly any other cars, the few trees stunted, the fields of maize barely alive. By mid-afternoon we were through the pass, reaching down towards the lower slopes. There was an African village of mud *rondavels* thatched with straw, and the world's most prehistoric-looking trees, like pachyderms plonked on their rumps, spaced like a convoy of motionless ships: great baobabs with trunks and branches shaped like pyramids, as if swollen by elephantiasis. They looked as if they were upside down, their roots jutting high into the sky. In later journeys I saw them as far north-east as Tanzania, and in Senegal on the extreme western point of the entire continent they grow on a slope which comes to an abrupt end at the Atlantic, the rough sea pounding black cliffs. Baobabs to my mind delineate the heart of black Africa.

This dreamy quality was with us all the way to the customs post at Beitbridge. Two Afrikaner officials waved us into their office: 'Whites Only', so Petrus stayed in the Land Rover. They were amazed to see his passport, said they had read all about us, stamped everything and wished us 'Tot sins'. Over the border the British Rhodesian official likewise, with a 'Cheery bye'.

We drove through a huge ranch, our headlights catching high trees on either side. Two magnificent kudus leapt across the road, their long corkscrew horns laid back, their eyes terrified, then some zebras; not noble, more like ponies in striped rompers. We camped, and heard them making singing noises. After we had gathered enough dead branches and made a fire Quentin sat on his stool, advising Petrus on cooking with the kaffir pot, 'Now add some salt.' One of his favourite activities. For the first time we set up our camp beds, laid out our Dunlopillo mattresses, pillows and woollen blankets, climbed into our pyjamas, took it in turns to clean our teeth, Petrus included, and hit the sack. At dawn it took us two and three-quarter hours to get up, wash, rekindle the fire after finding more dead wood in the bush, cook, eat, pack, refuel and leave. Clearly we would have to do better than that.

Salisbury was on the up and up. There was no apartheid legislation. It was unnecessary. The splits between the races were incontrovertible. The only blacks in the club were behind the bar, as is still the case in the southern United States. The whites were all settlers, as in South Africa but much more recent, many of them very big men. They wore shorts, long socks and sandals, and usually a short-sleeved shirt, its pocket with a packet of Matinée cigarettes. They were considerate and helpful. Every skyscraper had been built in the previous seven years. The rate in building investment was one million pounds a month. The city had a vigorous spirit.

Even the most educated Rhodesian whites spoke with curious vowel sounds. The 'ah' sound became 'awe', as in 'How now brown cow, grizing on the green green grorse'. And 'a form is a plice where kettle are kipt'. (Cattle are kept.) The suffix 'min' can be added anywhere as a sign of familiarity; as Macbeth would say: 'Is this a digger, min, that I see before me, min?' and Lady Macbeth would reply: 'Yes, min.'

We filled out our camping inventory from Salisbury's wonderful shops, salespeople for the most part black or Indian, customers mainly Indian or white, and drove off north. Granite boulders call kopjes rose up on all sides above the rich vegetation. At the Mozambique frontier post a Portuguese welcomed us. No customs, no search, a friendly stamp on our passports. It seemed the Portuguese ambassador in London had set news buzzing about our expedition.

Near the provincial capital of Tete there remained the walls of a seventeenth-century Portuguese fort, overlooking the mighty Zambezi. The river was fully a mile wide, brown and smooth. It had built up its volume over the fifteen hundred miles from its source. Now in the dry season it was at peace.

The town itself was of dinky two-storey concrete houses painted in pastel colours. There had once been some gold mining, long since exhausted. The Intendente of the whole Tete region, Mr Peralto, made us feel under-dressed in our khaki, with his long blue trousers and white shirt. He had been to Oxford and Cambridge to study British colonial administration before his recent promotion. The hierarchy went: Governor, Intendente, Inspector, Administrador (equivalent to a District Commissioner), Secretario, Chefe de Poste and, lastly, *aspirante*. He delegated a driver, a well-educated African, to lead us in his jeep upstream to an old Mission called Buroma. The driver had passed his exams and become a '*civilizado*', giving him all the rights of a European; an enlightened Portuguese policy, all too rarely put into effect.

We drove between lush fifteen-foot-high *mopane* trees, like young beeches. There were wide shallow lakes filled with flowering lotuses, and waders with spindly legs and toes on floating leaves, dipping their beaks into the water. The surrounding trees showed signs of being flooded to a height of five feet, with mud stains on their trunks and dead grasses stranded in their branches.

Buroma had beautiful 1885 colonial buildings and a gabled church on higher ground set well back from the riverbank. The White Fathers welcomed us, led by Father Martin, a Jesuit. The White Fathers were an organisation of missionaries founded in 1868 in Algiers. There they had had to be accepted by Arabs, so they donned white robes and Arab headdress for work all over Africa. In Europe they wore black. For many decades they prospered. Lake Tanganyika was once described as a large expanse of water surrounded by White Fathers. Since African independence they have been disbanded for lack of support from Europe and the dangers of unprotected life there. At Buroma they put us up in a large room. Quentin had the double bed, Dave and I used our camp beds and Petrus to our shame had to sleep in the Land Rover.

We changed, then went into the whitewashed refectory. We stood at the long wooden table as the twelve of them softly spoke grace in unison, the only food visible being bread and water. We sat and Africans helped us to delicious soup made with oleaginous mixes of cabbage, followed by helpings of game birds, vegetable, cheese and heavy red wine. They were all keen historians. Father Martin was blunt in claiming that the British had tried to take the glory for discoveries which had really been Portuguese. He showed us a book written in Livingstone's day by José Luis Lacerdo claiming that the Victoria Falls had been discovered by Portugal years before 1845. If so, I suggested, they had kept it very quiet. Exactly, he said, just as Livingstone had given instructions that his alleged discovery of Lake Shire in 1859 should be kept secret from *them*; as if they had not already known about it. Throughout history, he said, England had played grand-mother's footsteps with Portugal, in India long after they had settled in Goa, in Malacca where the Dutch and then we had pushed them out, and we had struggled to catch up by creating Hong Kong only a few hours along the coast from their colony of Macau. He was concise, articulate and good-humoured.

Our next stop was a hundred and sixty-five miles west along the Zambezi, a tiny place called Chicoa, where the Chefe de Poste was Señor Ariano. The village had one good house for him and his wife, and a couple of outhouses for their servants. There were three or four shops. The earth road was needlessly wide, seemingly designed for centuries to come, leading from nowhere to nowhere. demarcated along its edges with whitewashed stones. Ariano had no resources other than his fair-mindedness as a magistrate and his common sense. He was respected for settling the myriad conflicts of interest arising in any rural community. His wife gave lessons in the local language to those who were interested, mainly children. They did their best with no visible support. Sweet people, their favourite phrase being '*mas o meno*', more or less. Nothing too serious.

Jill Esmond, author's mother, 1952

LEFT Author's maternal grandfather, the actor manager and playwright Henry Esmond, at Apple Porch, 1900; RIGHT his wife Eva (Moore), pictured here with Henry Irving's son

Apple Porch 1913: l. to r., author's grandmother, grandfather, mother Jill and uncle Jack

In California, 1942: LEFT the diminutive boxer, with a view to the right of Yakaloma desert; RIGHT his mother Jill

Brentwood Town and Country School, 1943: author front left eyeing girl on the top right

Author's father as Henry V, 1943 (inscribed to author foreground right)

Author's father with Vivien Leigh, 1952

Eton, Fourth of June, 1952: author with his mother

Author with his father, 1952

Author stroking the Christ Church First Torpid, 1957

Christ Church First Eight at Henley, 1957: l. to r., Jumbo Edwards (coach), John Edwards, Gavin Sorrell, David Edwards, author, Peter Barnard, John Lewis, David Badcock, Bill Rathhbone

In Livingstone's footsteps, 1958: LEFT Quentin Keynes; RIGHT Livingstone's monogram

The baobab with Petrus looking into the high cave-like hollow

The country became more beautiful. Lotus lakes gave way to sudden closed thickets of jungle, with strong creepers tumbling from a canopy of trees of cathedral height. We stopped, got out and gazed upwards in the diffused light, and down at the dark patches of mildewed under-growth, thick damp leaves, pungent smells, the great trees' roots cradled in decay, as if the whole balance of nature had stuck. A hundred yards further on there was lively dappled light and birdsong.

We camped on the Zambezi which was now only half a mile wide. There was a flat rock on shore. We threw off our clothes and dived in. We shouted at Petrus to join us. He undressed behind the Land Rover, then ran into the river, arms waving, his head thrown back and mouth wide open in a rictus of happiness. When we were back drying ourselves with our towels he was still dancing around in a state of nature. This went on a bit long and Quentin took out his camera, hoping that modesty would tempt Petrus back into his clothes, to get on with collecting dead wood for the campfire. Quite the contrary. He gave high leaps like a gazelle and Quentin took an excellent shot of him in mid-flight.

After we had eaten dinner Petrus said he had noticed that we had been 'cut', all three of us. He wanted to explain to us why he had not been 'cut'.

'Mass Quentinkeynes,' he began, 'I tell you I went to the doctor to be cut.'

'Really? Why did you want to be cut?' Quentin sipped some water.

'Because Mass Jesus Christ was cut. The missionaries taught me. But in Ovamboland none of the boys are cut. And if one of them comes who is cut and he bathes and everybody looks at him, and the girls, and they point at him and laugh, and he hides himself.'

'What about in Cape Town?'

'The doctor in Cape Town didn't cut me.'

'What happened?'

'Well, sah. Other day morning I went to the doctor and tell him I want to be cut. He say am I sure, and I say yes, man. I am sure because Mass Jesus Christ was cut. So the doctor makes me take off my clothes and lie on a bed in a very cold room. Air condition. He goes into his room to get his things. I shiver. He comes back and looks at me. He lifts my man with his finger and thumb. Then I see he holds a *very* big knife in his other hand. I sit up. Are you going to cut me with that thing, I say. Yes, he say, it is very very sharp. Then I look at the knife and see it is sharp, then I look at my man. I begin to think; no, man, I don't want to be cut, no man, not like that. And I put on my trousers and went away from him. He was smiling but I left fast.'

'How about Cape Town. Do the girls laugh at you there?'

'In Cape Town there are many different people and they all bathe together and nobody laughs.'

We had been told by the White Fathers of a village called Chafombo where there was a Chief Chapoto who had a car. He had paid them a visit in Buroma. We wanted to find out more. Just before the Southern Rhodesian border there were vehicle tracks leading south into the high grasses, between intermittent trees. Some had branches ripped off which put us on guard against elephants. The broken branches became more frequent and we saw traces of green paint on a tree trunk. Then another. We started to use the trail of broken branches as our guide. More green paint. In an hour we came to a hilltop and in the valley beneath there was an old green car, stopped and rusted beside a poor kraal of *rondavels*. We headed down to it and got out.

The car was a complete wreck. Petrus managed to lift up the bonnet.

'Very very sick,' he said.

A sweet old man came out of the kraal. He told us in hesitant English that he was Chapote's cousin and that the chief was in the mountains hunting elephant.

The huts were rudimentary and some of the straw roofs collapsing. Chickens limped around aimlessly. It was unbearably hot and dry, pervaded with the sweet smell of rotting food remains. He showed us into the *shamba* where many of the tired maize plants had been torn up by elephants. Two old women were rummaging for some moth-eaten cobs. He spoke of the terrible lack of water, and showed us a dried up river bed. The only source of water was a hole dug in the sand, where two feet down there was a puddle with a broad green leaf growing in it. He said how the children often died and there was no doctor for hundreds of miles. We asked why they carried on living in such a place.

His face wrinkled sympathetically. 'We are all born here and so were our fathers. It is our place, sir.'

Back in the kraal he offered us eggs, both with soft shells. We offered him a few coins but he said it was far too much. We insisted and he accepted with tears in his eyes. We asked if he had a bucket. He brought one and we filled it with water from our jerry can. He cupped his hand and had a sip.

He said that in the mountains there was a wild tribe called 'Madana'.

They wore skins and string 'from the trees'. They were armed with spears, but did accept the occasional elephant hunter so long as they could share the meat. Chapota's village was one of the poorest we saw and the old man said there were many like it.

It is fair to wonder why the Portuguese had done so little to develop Mozambique; for water a well-digging programme at the very least would have saved thousands of lives. It was such a huge country, and so very far away from Lisbon, itself under-resourced, subjected to the dictator Salazar. However it must be said that they had maintained peace, a great improvement on the internecine wars so constantly described by Livingstone, and peace nowadays is no longer a concept which leaps to mind when considering Africa.

We had been warned that crossing the Zambezi would be difficult. The far side was joined by a great tributary, the Luangwa, which flowed between Northern Rhodesia with its little town of Feira, and Mozambique's village of Zumbo. The Zambezi River's edge in this dry season was a quarter of a mile out, beyond level sand. There was a broken down jetty but no sign of a ferry, only a contraption of four dugout canoes strung together. We ignored this and blew our horn, hoping to attract attention in Feira. A boat with an outboard motor headed our way, the breeze dancing in wavelets against its prow. It was driven by a smiling Portuguese *aspirante* called Luis Lacerda.

He took us and our night things on board. Being in the centre of that river revealed its grandeur, so huge that our gaze seemed to follow the curvature of the earth before it turned a far distant corner. As we approached the landing place we passed some hippos wallowing in the shallows, their huge pink and black heads breaking the surface, their eyes looking unfriendly and intruded upon, nostrils distended then snapping shut as they submerged. Once on land we heard them resume their base throbbing barks, their hums resonating with contentment.

Luis's straw house had a sitting room with a fire where he cooked our dinner: cabbage soup, fish he had caught in the river and his garden vegetables. We went to our beds replete.

At one in the morning I had a most vivid dream. I awoke with a start and prodded Quentin in the next bed, pointed, and said in a panic: 'Quentin. There's a hippo!'

He awoke. So did Dave. I then realised I was looking at a window and not a hippopotamus. This made them both laugh, outright, and they had not stopped before I went to sleep again.

There was no ferry. Eight Africans laid heavy planks across the four dug out canoes and hammered them in so as to fit the spread of the Land Rover's wheels. We emptied it totally to reduce weight and Quentin drove it on to the Heath Robinson contraption. There was no alternative. The canoes gave a little but held, with six inches free board. It was early. We thought that so long as the river remained flat calm all would be well. The Africans pushed off and the raft with our red Land Rover was under way. They paddled. We watched from the bank. One of the Africans shouted that a canoe had sprung a leak. Four of them disappeared under the Land Rover and tried desperately to patch up the canoe. There was a lot of shouting. A breeze lit the surface of the water. The Land Rover was a hundred yards out, the canoes out of control, starting to revolve in the strengthening breeze. The men baled out, paddled harder and eventually made it across. We loaded everything into Luis's boat, and went over to his house.

He then took us upstream to Feira to meet the British District Commissioner. The DC's wife told us he was on tour, walking on foot round his region. It was normal practice for every DC to make a yearly tour of his region on foot, with some African staff, so as to pick up all the gossip and monitor the progress on the projects agreed upon: school building, road development, installation of running water from wells, and agriculture. He had five white men on his payroll. His wife seemed happy, bringing up her small children in the bush. They had a swimming pool which was a stunning pale blue, and electricity. Their housing was properly built of concrete and wood, and their office, called the *Boma*, was being replaced with a much larger concrete building under construction, complete with vault, generator, fans, lights and so forth. Her husband was fluent in all the dialects. Schooling was being introduced to secondary level and in the recent budget there was provision for a big mechanical road leveller. His own main task was the administration of justice, the maintenance of peace and management of his staff.

That day, learning about the British Colonial Service, became a key day for me. I had found out what I wanted to do for a living. The desire for self-sacrifice, so common in the young, clasped me. I wanted to be of service, as these people were, to Africa. They were totally different from the white settlers who went there for the sake of enriching themselves, no doubt being of immeasurable help in advancing the locals, but mainly for their own good. The concept of actually being of service to Africa had a greater appeal for me than anything I had considered.

With the Land Rover still unloaded Quentin sped us next day to a mission called Miruro, several miles away. We roared up a steep murram road and there, in the middle of miles and miles of stunted bush was a whitewashed church and refectory. It had been built by the Germans in 1910, seven years before their African colonies had been taken away from them; Uganda, Tanzania, Southwest and Togo. Now the mission was in the hands of the White Fathers, utterly remote. That this tiny pinpoint in the wilds had been selected for the sake of religion seemed to have given the place a divine sanction, alone in the wilds.

Padre Jesus and his companion Padre José had fifteen Africans in their care, all learning Portuguese, keen to pass school certificate so that they would qualify as '*civilizados*'. The students were bright as buttons in their bush shorts and shirts, whether writing essays in the refectory, hoeing the vegetable garden or irrigating it from a nearby spring. To live like that, teaching your faith, surrounded by the unpeopled wilds of African nature, seemed a wonderful calling.

Five

We drove more than 13,000 miles on our expedition, the last month with just Quentin, Petrus and me because Dave had to return to college in the States. The rhythm of our days was largely the same. Quentin said there was nothing he preferred to driving across the wilds of Africa. With each other for company we hardly made more than brief acquaintances with anybody else. Despite his experience over the years I would not say that he was an expert on the people, their history, culture, nor indeed the animals we saw, filmed and photographed. He did have a passion for all of this, but only in the manner Rousseau described: he *sensed* everything. His supreme interest was in collecting Victorian explorers' letters, their books, everything written about them, and the first pictures published of big game.

We went to the great Zambezi Delta, up to Mozambique Island, via Nampula to Nyasaland, then drove up the length of Nyasaland, across Northern Rhodesia to the source of the Zambezi at Kalene Hill, followed it round into Angola and back eastwards to end at the Victoria Falls and Livingstone.

There were quite a few highlights. First the light-hearted ones, involving pachyderms.

On 12 September while going to Fort Jameson, Nyasaland, we drove through a little known area called Lukusuzi, a place elephants went to have their young. The bush trees were much higher than normal, up to fifty feet, wider spaced and nearly leafless. Many of them had been pushed over by elephants, some across the road which had not been used for two years.

There was a shallow valley spreading away to our left. In the front wing-mirrors we could see plumes of the dust raised behind us, drifting down into it. Half a mile away there was a herd of ten elephants, with a few very young ones. We stopped, left the Land Rover and walked towards a granite kopje, a hundred yards short of them. We climbed it, settled down and took some telephoto shots. One of the babies was so young he was still hairy. The image of a family at peace. A big bull rose on his hind legs and with his left forefoot leant against a sizeable tree, its trunk about ten inches thick. He lurched a few times and the roots yielded. Its crown crashed to the earth and the herd ambled towards it, not all that impressed, and plucked a few leaves.

The bull paused. I watched through the binoculars as he raised his trunk, like a periscope pointing in our direction, the nostrils tasting the air. They were downwind of us. We had thought our scent would blow over them. It hadn't. The bull trumpeted and three of them charged. The creatures were so huge they seemed to move in slow motion, trunks trailing over their shoulders, ears held back as they gathered speed. The rest of the herd hastened away.

We fled, leaping down the kopje, and sprinted towards the Land Rover, a diminutive rectangle of red. I waited a moment for Quentin who was bad on his feet and he whizzed past me. As I ran I turned and saw the three bulls, heard their massive soft feet only eighty yards away. The adrenaline made me feel like Mercury, a winged man, effortless. My mind carried vaguely related misgivings – of my father in the Garrick Club years later being asked what his son was doing, and him replying that I had been trampled to death in Africa by elephants, and his friend being intrigued. Well at least it was different.

I turned again and they were only half the distance away and just then a sudden change occurred. What was it? It was the wind. It had swung round and blew from behind us. I heard the trees bending before it. Our scent shifted and the bull elephants followed a false direction. Their poor eyesight and the wind had now saved us. We kept running running running until we slapped into the Land Rover as if it were life itself. For days our lungs ached.

We camped outside the Luangwa Reserve near a large pool. The flat muddy bank had the spoor of rhino. We wandered round to collect dead branches. Petrus lit a fire while I did all the unpacking and Quentin selected the tinned food for dinner. As we ate we heard an elephant trumpet twice, not a frequent sound but here they were testy because of their young. It put us on edge. Then we heard some hyenas. We laid our beds right beside the Land Rover in case elephants disturbed us, taking care to close all the doors and windows so they would not be attracted by the smell of the fruit we had bought. We stacked the fire as high as we could, put on pyjamas and went to bed.

At dead of night a deafening scream twenty yards away was countered by a colossal bellow. Two bull rhinos crashed into each other and the fight was on. We were instantly in the front seat, door closed, Petrus behind us. Outside, bushes were being flattened, water splashed, then thudding hooves stopped abruptly and there was silence, except for their stertorous panting. That faded and after a minute of nothing we grew self-conscious huddled together in pyjamas. We went back to bed. That happened three times and after such a disturbed night we slept until seven.

As Petrus cooked breakfast over the embers we strolled in pyjamas and bare feet. There were some dry old elephant droppings. I picked one up; it was round, five inches in diameter and two and a half inches high, rather like tinned components made of crushed straw and twigs.

A crash just ahead of us was such a shock that we found ourselves with neither effort nor decision springing up some thorn trees. It was a bull rhino, upwind of us, looking bleary-eyed and hung over, but then they always do. He had not seen us. His fat bum bucketed away – at a dainty trot for a ton-plus creature.

That was all very well. Our Pavlovian jumps had launched us up thorn trees with spikes an inch long, our feet and hands were badly scratched, pyjamas caught up and torn all over the place. There was no Pavlovian serpent to scare us down to the ground with a leap, so in a state of pain and fear, we picked our descent, assisted by much filthy language.

In Northern Nyasaland there was the Scottish mission at Livingstonia, on a high plateau 3,000 feet above the brilliant waters of Lake Malawi. Far across its shimmering surface were the Livingstone Mountains. He had never been there but he would certainly have approved the mission. Ever progressive, the Scots had built Central Africa's first hydro-electric power house in 1901. They fed us, gave us baths and bedded us. Nothing like it after weeks of life in the bush. Their generosity put us on our best behaviour. They directed us to the District Commissioner at Rumpi and he pointed us to Lake Kasuni where there were twenty-four hippos.

We arrived there in the evening. The air was drifting with smoke left over from the dry grass being burned off, black all the way to the horizon. Africans do this in the dry season so that young green shoots sprout for their cattle to eat without needing water. In the middle of this burnt out plain was a mile wide lake surrounded by a hundred-yard strip of soggy emerald green grass where we camped. We could see the tops of the hippos' heads and backs half a mile away, hear their puffing and deep bass barks and their reverberant humming.

In my diary I wrote:

Monday 8 September, 8832 [to show the miles we had driven so far] At night. The others are in bed asleep. The fire is alight and I am at a table writing by a paraffin lamp. The air is cool and soft, crickets shrilling intermittently. A grass fire glows in the distance. The night is clear and moonless, the lake is still, but all along our side of it the hippos are lapping at the sodden grass. They are quite near. The far side of the lake the natives are having a party, beating drums.

I got into pyjamas and went to bed. The hippos seemed to be coming nearer. I could hear them belch and fart. Perhaps the sound was more defined at night. In a state of enchantment I fell asleep.

I awoke with a start at 4.55 to hear the hippos champing very near – it seemed like fifty yards. It was completely dark and the grass fire in the distance had died down. Quentin sat up as well and we both strained to see how close the hippos were. We heard them breathe. The more we tried to see the less we saw, and the grunts, sighs and chewing came nearer and nearer. Quentin thought we should go the other side of the Land Rover but Dave and Petrus were still asleep and we couldn't leave them.

It grew lighter and we could just see them returning to their lake. When we got up and went to look we saw their huge messy footprints were only just over thirty yards from us. Had they, with their extended family, been alarmed by us at night, or in daytime come to that, we would probably have been killed. More people are killed by hippos than by any other creature in Africa.

The Kariba Dam between Northern and Southern Rhodesia was under construction to create an extensive lake, control the unmanageable flooding of the Zambezi and generate massive hydro-electric power. South Africa persuaded Portugal to do the same in Mozambique, building a dam at Kebra Basa, as Livingstone had called it, now Cabora Basa. There the second longest river in Africa surges through a twenty-mile narrow defile. A feasibility study was under the guidance of two young Portuguese engineers to determine the positioning and specification of the project to create a lake forty miles wide and 180 miles long. We wanted to see the gorge itself, which was fourteen miles away from the 'Missao de Fomento a Povoamento do Zambeze'. The engineers did warn us that the road was tricky, indeed for many miles invisible. They gave us a man who had walked the trip but never been in a car.

He sat on the bonnet next to Petrus. They spoke a lingua franca called 'lapa-lap' which Petrus had picked up during our week in Salisbury. They pointed out to us the faint tyre marks of a Portuguese jeep. There were many dried up drifts where flash floods had hurtled, some so steep that we had to hack a way down with hoes and a spade. A car was exceedingly rare there and attracted Africans from far and wide when they heard the engine in the silent dry heat. They clapped their hands and waved, and sometimes even helped us push. When they did we gave them cigarettes. They were always full of questions.

Elephant grass ten feet high loomed ahead. The guide walked in front and divided it as if swimming the breast stroke. The entire world disappeared on either side of us between the towering green stems. An hour later (about half a mile) there was a clearing and an exceptionally deep drift. I went out to recce among the trees and dry creepers.

A sharp tingling struck my back. I scratched and it got worse. Much worse. Unbearably. I tore off my shirt and rolled on the rough ground and the piercing sensation spread to my chest and arms. I rushed back to the others but they could see nothing. It attacked my legs like a million ants stinging. I thought I would go mad. From the medicine chest I poured witch hazel over myself but it made no difference. I lay on the ground again and rolled over and over as it crept into my eyes and hair. Then after ten never-ending minutes it went away. Our guide said they called it 'ulili'. Microscopic hairs blow from a sausage-sized bean when disturbed. The Portuguese call it 'monkey beans' and Livingstone 'cow itch pods'. An indication of the explorer's stoicism was his only complaint that they were 'annoying'. An understatement beyond belief.

We peered down the drift and saw it was filled with dangling pods, no hope of avoiding them. That crossing was sheer hell for all of us. Our guide, suffering like the rest of us, said that parents would send their children through them if they were naughty.

A few hours later we had to cross a flowing river five yards wide, two feet deep, with a bottom of mud. 'Lungil' said the guide: soggy. We decided to face the problem the next day, collected dry wood, put out our beds and Petrus cooked. The guide said it was excellent lion country, supposing that we had rifles. The only weapon we had was a bread knife and the security of a camp fire. There were no roars that night, only the intense trilling of the cicadas high in the trees.

We had somehow to make a bridge. A hundred yards away we came across an entire African village of eleven huts which had been gutted by fire. The stakes were still strong so we gathered them in armfuls, relaying loads over to dump them in the river and pile them up. We had breakfast, packed, refuelled and Quentin drove across our bridge, reached the other side and ground up the bank. He promptly turned round. We thought he was mad. He drove back over it in an exercise of glee. It worked each time.

Further ahead the mountains closed around us and we had to go round immense boulders. One upward slope was so steep that in low gear ratio, the engine tugging with the strain, it felt as if we might roll over backwards. The trees hung over our windscreen with their white bark vertically above, and the occasional flowering cactus like bunches of thorny organ pipes. The road ended. We took some picnic things in baskets, Quentin's cameras and thermoses of water, and set off on foot. The only sound apart from us was the hoarse coughing of baboons.

Out of the blue fifteen Africans arrived, their shorts in shreds, saying they wanted to help us. We said we preferred to carry our own things. They could so easily have run off with them. They told Petrus they had never seen white men before. He assured us we could trust them so we parcelled out our things, glad of the relief. We followed them down a steep dry riverbed between the shoulders of a gorge. Our skin was softened by continuous sweating, our finger nails black from scratching the detritus from *ulili*-tortured flesh, limbs and bodies bloodied from thorny creepers.

We faced the Zambezi at an elbow of deep calm water fifty yards wide, with a welcoming stretch of sand. Upstream was the end of a cascade and below us we could see the river tearing off in a torrent. Where we stood was calm in the concentrated high noon of heat, reflected down on us from more than a hundred feet of white rock cliffs on all sides, scoured clean by floods. The trees above them were choked with the dead branches torn away upstream by raging floodwaters and deposited up there in the months of long rains.

We tucked into lunch. The Africans accepted some fruit from us and sat discreetly away. We undressed and threw ourselves into the river, isolated by the rapids from the danger of crocodiles. Getting clean again was a relief. Even the itching stopped. Afterwards we lay to dry and the Africans roared with laughter. I suppose we lay there for an hour, exhausted, and slept. When we awoke there was no doubt we had caught the sun. Our chests were pink. An African called over to Petrus and spoke seriously to him. He had said that we, having changed into a pink colour, should stay there with them until our colour changed back, otherwise the white girls would not have us.

Now to our original purpose: retracing Livingstone. In volume one of his 'Zambezi Expedition' journal he wrote:

16 September 1858. We wooded at Shiramba, about four miles above the spot pointed out as the great house. All is deserted now and we saw no living thing except a small brown antelope. While the men were cutting down a lignum vitae I walked a little way to the Southwest and found a baobab which Mr Rae and I, measuring at about three feet from the ground, found to be seventy-two feet in circumference. It was hollow and had a good high opening into it. The space inside was nine feet in diameter and about twenty-five feet high. A lot of bats clustered round the top and I noticed for the first time that this tree has bark inside as well as out.

Elsewhere he commented about the baobab's unique ability to protect itself by growing bark when hollows develop through age, unlike the beeches of Burnham. Yet again he drew attention to his fascination for baobabs: 'though it possesses amazing vitality it is difficult not to believe that this great baby-looking bulb or tree is as old as the pyramids.'

We mentioned this journal entry to the Intendente at Tete. He knew all about the tree and told us that Livingstone's initials were carved in the hollow. He gave us detailed directions how to find it, which took us half a day. There were so many baobabs, huge old ones, and we examined every one, none with a hollow. Then ahead of us we saw a vast array of swollen upper branches reaching into the sky, seemingly the height of Tower Bridge. The tree loomed larger and larger, its smooth grey whale-sized branches at ungainly angles, vast knuckles bursting into stubby short ones and with small walnut-sized leaves, in magnificent defiance against flood, drought or the passage of time. We approached with deference.

It did have a hollow. The proportions we measured were precisely the same as Livingstone's had been a century earlier. The cave-like hollow was still about twenty-five feet high. Perhaps he had camped there, alone with his British team of men and his Africans, because his wife Mary was recuperating from fever in South Africa and was not to see him again until a couple of years later in Tete. Inside many initials had been carved, one dated 1890. We looked carefully at each and took photographs but there was no 'D.L.' Perhaps the Intendente had exaggerated. There was no mistaking this extraordinary tree.

We had a rather sad lunch and went inside the cave-like hollow again to have a last look. Quentin pointed at something three feet above ground, carved in the bark. It was a monogram four and a half inches high, blackened with age. We called Petrus and Dave to come and have a look.

In England Quentin went to see Professor Frank Debenham who said this was the most important Livingstone find for many a year, which Quentin quoted in an article in the *Daily Express*. He claimed to have discovered it and never acknowledged any guidance from the Intendente. Perhaps a weakness integral to explorers. However he did persuade the Portuguese to build a proper wrought iron fence round the tree with a historical note and a gate. Livingstone had also carved his initials in the bark of a tree on an island in the middle of the Victoria Falls, but with the growth of that tree they have become indecipherable.

The three greatest changes since Livingstone's time are first and foremost the abolition of slavery. His books illustrate the grotesqueness of that human tragedy, the piteousness of men, women and children in their dozens in leg irons, yoked together in their tens of thousands, by Arabs sometimes using one tribe to capture another for sale in the Middle East.

The second, in 1958, was peace. A hundred years before the Zulus from South Africa used to present themselves to the Portuguese colonists in full battle order, in ranks carrying spears and shields to demand tribute. And there were the constant outbreaks of violent hostilities between the local tribes set on proving their manhood. In 1958, before African independence, peace was absolute. It would have been possible for us to traverse the whole continent on foot, unarmed. Will that blessed situation ever return?

Thirdly, and sadly, was the difference in activity levels in the countryside. Livingstone's books are filled with etchings of Africans building boats, attacking wild game, refurbishing houses, making weapons or pottery, skinning an elephant, fishing, hoeing their *shambas*, playing an orchestra of xylophones, gongs or pipes of Pan and drums. It is still possible from the shapes on the hills and mountains in the background of these pictures to identify exactly where they were done in real life today, and to compare what was with what is. In 1958, nothing to compare; the people left behind looked less healthy than they had. The desertion had been by buses with sides painted 'Lonrho' or 'Ulere' over-stuffed with Africans wishing to seek opportunity in towns hundreds of miles away. Leaving behind emptiness.

On our way to the Indian Ocean coast we paid our respects at the tomb of Livingstone's wife Mary, near Marameu. She had succumbed for the final time to malaria. She had rejoined her husband on the Zambezi at the end of January 1862, the height of the rainy season, on the Luabo mouth, the southern end of the hundred-mile-long Delta, together with a dozen or so intrepid men, mainly from the Universities' Mission, and two other wives. They were held up for months in feverish conditions of downpour, a constant frustration in tropical Africa which not only immobilised movement but destroyed health.

Livingstone had become increasingly fired up: 'I have a very strong desire to commence a system of colonisation of the honest poor [selected from Britain]. I would give £2,000 to £3,000 for the purpose. Colonisation from a country such as ours ought to be one of hope and not despair to parts of the wide world where every accession is an addition of strength.'

He received rebuffs from London to any and every such ambition. They pointed out the fatal experiences they had had long before when trying to settle the Central American coastline of Darien. But he persisted, his vision becoming more vivid, of Christian colonies, the spread of arts and civilisation, the cultivation of cotton and the disappearance of the slave trade. Hope rose further in the person of Bishop Mackenzie. He had gone with a friend to rescue the captured slaves who were the husbands of local women left behind. They managed to free them, but on their way back to the coast their own canoe was upset and sank with their medicine chest. Both men were smitten with fever and died.

Livingstone wrote in despair to the Bishop of Cape Town: 'The blow is quite bewildering, the two strongest men so quickly cut down, and one of them, humanly speaking, indispensable to the success of the enterprise. We must have the will of HIM who doth all things well … I shall not swerve a hairsbreadth from my work while my life is spared.'

He and his wife returned to Shupanga, in mourning. Then she became ill and died, vomiting every quarter of an hour, which prevented any medicine from taking effect. Dr Stewart wrote: 'He was sitting by the side of a rude bed formed of boxes, but covered with a soft mattress, on which lay his dying wife … and the man who had faced so many deaths, and braved so many dangers, was now utterly broken down and weeping like a child.' She was buried with her headstone under an enormous baobab in Shupanga, where a Franciscan friar in 1889 founded the Mission of Immaculate Conception.

We were now nearing the Zambezi Delta and beginning to wonder whether we would find anything concerning the letter which Livingstone had left in a bottle and which had led Quentin into setting up our expedition. About this, and in happier days, Livingstone wrote of shooting water buffalo, seeing a flock of flamingos and many white ibis walking along the sandbanks. His companions collected eggs of pelicans and gulls. Acute hunger prevailed at Tete which made the locals keen to follow him in the hope of finding food. He wrote: 'Their willingness I look upon as the effect of the influence of the gracious spirit in their minds, and I hope it is a pledge that He will bless me in opening that country too and O may it be for the promotion of divine glory!'

His religious devotion was formidable. Retracing his footsteps and reading his accounts of a century before induced a sense of wonder at the man.

In returning to Luabo he became more earthly. He wrote; 'Without seeing a man of war it is probable that my letter may have been detained too long at Quelimane and that the vessel of which we heard at Melambe was the Lynx, returning from the Cape after the Mozambique voyage. We expect to hear tomorrow at Mazaro if there is mail for us by her.'

We did spend a number of days in the Delta, courtesy of Sena Sugar Estates, on one of their paddlesteamers transporting barges stacked high with sugar cane to be processed in their mills. By speedboat we traced the outlet to the sea which Livingstone had indicated, but a comparison of earlier maps with the ones we now had showed that the shape of the islands had altered beyond recognition. We could learn nothing more about Quentin's letter-in-a-bottle.

In southern Nyasaland we came across a story illustrating the bloody-minded side of Livingstone. The DC of Chikwansa and his wife were enjoying their teenagers being at home for the school holidays. She was a qualified nurse which added to the benefits he brought as a magistrate, with staff for road development, agricultural extension officers, primary school building programmes and all the usual activities associated with being of service to Africa. The ADC to the local chief Kasis was a young Englishman called Tony Hammond who was also a historian. He had come across three descendants of the Makalolo bearers who had been with Livingstone.

We went to meet them. All three had finely bred features and were focused, unlike the locals who were rather plain. Their grandfathers had outraged Dr Livingstone a hundred years before. They had gone hunting, but on a Sunday, the Holy Sabbath, when the missionary doctor was holding a service. They came back with a zebra they had shot for the pot. He summoned them to appear before him. He said they had violated the Sabbath. They were no longer worthy of serving him. There was no question of forgiveness. They had to go. Yes, GO: all the way back to their homes in Bechuanland (now Lesotho) a thousand miles away. Since the good doctor was in his own opinion fair-minded he gave each of them a rifle and ammunition for their protection.

So they left him and started walking. They headed south. However, once over the nearest hill they sat down. In keeping with African tradition towards travellers they were made welcome and offered water and things to eat. They found the local girls attractive. The feeling was mutual. They decided to stay, much prized for their firearms. Their descendants are still proud of their Zulu background. Livingstone could from time to time be a misery.

The upshot of Livingstone's Zambezi exploration was mainly in the great response to his graphically illustrated book. The effects were immeasurable, though any thoughts he had once had of finding a navigable means to cross the whole of central Africa had to be cast aside.

His third and final journey found him much further north on the east bank of Lake Tanganyika. There he was sought by the Welsh born Stanley, sent by the *New York Herald Tribune*, who found him at Ujiji on 10 November 1871. Stanley's astonished words: 'Dr Livingstone, I presume?'

In addition to his treating the heathen for their health and trying to convert them to Christianity, he became caught up in the craze among his contemporaries for discovering the source of the Nile. This had captured the imagination of several great explorers, the English Sir Richard Burton, John Speke, and Samuel Baker. Even though Speke had gone a second time to Lake Victoria in 1860 and followed the Nile flowing out of it all the way to the Sudan, Livingstone was convinced that so mighty a river must have a source further removed from the sea. He returned to Lake Bangweulu in early 1873. He became so weak in that swampland that he could no longer ride a donkey. He was so thin that only two bearers were needed to carry him, slung in a hammock from a single pole.

The village where he died was in north-eastern Northern Rhodesia. We started that journey from the site of Kariba Dam, under construction, for the world's largest man-made lake. Africans had said that the spirit of the Zambezi River would cause catastrophic destruction for the whole undertaking. They were nearly right. In the winter of 1957 the most terrible floods on record tore through the coffer dam. It was being built to surround the main structure of conjoined giant thirty-square-foot piles of reinforced concrete set to rise several hundred feet. That was unprecedented and then again a year later Mother Nature gave a repeat performance. For the two to occur concurrently defied the rhythms of nature. When we were there in 130-degree heat we wandered along the base of that fantastic project, and explored the machine halls being hewn from the escarpments for the provision of immense hydro-electric power.

We left there at five past seven on Tuesday 23 September for a drive of 560 miles up the North-East Trunk Road, of well-impounded earth. We were to meet Dr Livingstone's grandson at his home in Lubwa. He was also a Scottish missionary doctor, Dr David Livingstone-Wilson. His hospital was spick and span, supported by charity but I was so exhausted by the drive I made no entry in my diary about any discussion.

Next day we went to stay with a 75-year-old Sir Stewart Gore-Brown at Shiwa Ngandu. He had built a three-storeyed Italian-style palazzo of homemade brick, round a big courtyard with arches and flowerbeds. He had bought the land at the end of the First World War and made a fortune from lime oil. Then the citrus became blighted and he changed over to timber. He showed us the village he had built for his staff, accompanied by his manservant Henry who was a cut above them. He had taken Henry to London, fully suited and Homburg-hatted, just like himself.

Sir Stewart described how to reach the place where Livingstone had died: Chitambo's village. The rains there at that time would have only just ended so the place would have been swampy. With us in September it was dry.

In his book *The Way to Ilala* Professor Frank Debenham wrote: 'To my mind the most moving incident in the story of the last few days is one which brings vividly before us the desperate hope of this indomitable man, that the end of his search [for the source of the Nile] was near, a search which had now, for him, almost taken on the guise of a Quest for the Holy Grail.'

Livingstone had asked the elders of Chitambo's village whether they knew of a hill which was the source of four rivers. They knew nothing of it. There his spirit gave out. He died, discovered by his bearers on his knees in an attitude of prayer at his bunk bed. The Zulus cut out his heart and buried it there, in Chitambo's village, for it to remain in Africa. The spot is marked with a fifteen foot high memorial plinth with a large Cross on top and a plaque which reads:

THIS MONUMENT
OCCUPIES THE SPOT
WHERE FORMERLY STOOD THE TREE
AT THE FOOT OF WHICH
LIVINGSTONE'S HEART WAS BURIED
BY HIS FAITHFUL NATIVE FOLLOWERS.
ON THE TRUNK WAS CARVED
THE FOLLOWING INSCRIPTION
'DR. LIVINGSTONE MAY 1, 1873'.

His Zulu bearers carried his body all the way to the shore. With devotion such as that it is a pity we have no record of their names. His coffin was shipped back to England and buried in the central aisle of Westminster Abbey. Only one grave has a more exalted position: that of the Unknown Warrior. The brass lettering set in the black granite of Livingstone's grave reads:

BROUGHT BY FAITHFUL HANDS,
OVER LAND AND SEA,
HERE RESTS
DAVID LIVINGSTONE.
MISSIONARY,
TRAVELLER,
PHILANTHROPIST.
BORN MARCH 19, 1813
AT BLANTYRE, LANARKSHIRE.
DIED MAY 1, 1873
AT CHITAMBO'S VILLAGE, ILALA.
FOR 30 YEARS HIS LIFE WAS SPENT
IN AN UNWEARIED EFFORT
TO EVANGELIZE THE NATIVE RACES,

TO EXPLORE THE UNDISCOVERED SECRETS,
TO ABOLISH THE DESOLATING SLAVE TRADE
OF CENTRAL AFRICA,
WHERE WITH HIS LAST WORDS HE WROTE,
"ALL I CAN ADD IN MY SOLITUDE IS,
MAY HEAVEN'S RICH BLESSING COME DOWN
ON EVERY ONE, AMERICAN, ENGLISH OR TURK,
WHO WILL HELP TO HEAL
THIS OPEN SORE OF THE WORLD."

Six

My final year at Oxford I shared a flat with an American Rhodes Scholar, Lance Farrer, from Princeton University, at 1 Crick Road, towards North Oxford. Philosophy, politics and economics I enjoyed to the full. The tutorials were lively and challenging.

My special subject was economic development in Third World countries. Roy Harrod thought this a good choice because I had actually had some experience of developing countries, almost a calling in that direction. The trouble was that neither he, nor my other economics tutor, had been to such places, to experience life in the bush, in villages, to take the pulse of the population at large. Their algorithms and graphs and charts tabulating theories were irrelevant, in my view. It is impossible to compare the prospects for advancement of the educated Chinese of Singapore with any country in sub-Saharan Africa. But that was the flavour of the age, applying uniform mathematics to disparate peoples.

A prime example of such academic fatuity was the MIT man at the very top of academe, Walt Rostow. Norman Stone wrote about him fifty or so years later in *The Atlantic and Its Enemies*, page 211, showing how experience has altered our approach. He describes Rostow as an extremely interesting man who wrote a characteristic book, now seeming rather naïve: *The Stages of Economic Growth*. It identified a moment of industrial take-off, when countries saved enough of their GDP to foster investment and thence an industrial revolution, and development economics went ahead, with the assumption that squeezing the peasants would mean investment for big industry. Roy Harrod referred me to many learned journals with expositions of similar nonsense, a few of them by himself.

When it came to the Finals Exams my heartfelt opposition did me no good at all, causing me to get a third class degree instead of the second everyone expected me to get. Roy Harrod wrote sympathetically to me, knowing how I felt, but it was clear that my emotion had taken over. Philosophy and politics and other bits of economics I enjoyed to the full, and the tutorials with Oscar Wood, the historian Robert Blake and others were lively and challenging. There was a place for me in the

Christ Church First Eight so I grabbed the opportunity even if I was only rowing in the sharp end at two.

Most Saturday nights and Sundays I spent at Notley with Larry and Vivien. Their marriage was pulling itself to pieces. Her problems with manic depression were bewildering and tragic, yet between times her company and her beauty were spellbinding as ever, and he was at such moments desperately in love with her and torn by it. At other times she would invite guests he didn't like and then embarrass all of us, lecturing him about various trumped up failings of his, on and on, whining 'Larry Boy, you're not truthful.'

There was nothing anybody could do for them. If I stayed around too long it would irritate them. They were becoming a danger to themselves and each other. I felt that their final bust-up, which was only a matter of time, would break my heart if I were there, and that the best thing would be to get the hell out of it. I thought I would undertake a journey the like of which I would never be able to do later in life. I chose South-East Asia, rather than India because the people looked happier and cleaner. Alone this time, so that I would get to know the local people rather than any travelling companion. 'One's company' as Peter Fleming wrote. It would deepen my understanding of developing countries.

My plan was to spend a year in South-East Asia, six months in People's China and then, after becoming immersed in the Orient, slowly head westwards, from Siberia and across the immensity of Russia, hoping to recognise each stage of the approaching advent of Europe. Mao's China and the Soviet Union were the trickiest when it came to introductions.

Our Russian friend Moussiah Soskin was most helpful. He had organised the Soviet jockeys' participation in the Grand National at Aintree. He introduced me to the head of the Soviet Trade Delegation, Mr Kamensky and his wife. I took them to Stratford to see Larry in *Coriolanus* and spend the weekend at Notley. Then my mother and I had them for dinner. For companionship we invited Dickie and Sheila Attenborough. He was already a well-known film star and my mother was chairman of the Welfare Committee of the Actors' Charitable Trust which he headed. He arrived on time and parked his sleek Rolls-Royce right outside our garden gate. Then a large and crude Soviet barouche grumbled to a halt behind it.

Dinner went well. Dickie sat next to the puddingy Mrs Kamensky. Her husband sat beside Sheila and paid a most charming compliment to her beauty. She sweetly said that she was not actually looking her best; she had had a baby only three weeks before. He bowed his head so low, below her breasts, that he was within kissing distance of her slim tummy. We were all delighted, especially Mrs Kamensky whose bosoms were generous enough to feed an army. Dickie immersed us with his own left-wing views of the world and there were no problems.

Over coffee we discussed the Soviet exhibition of paintings at the National Gallery: Soviet realism depicting daily tasks. Mr Kamensky agreed that they were unimaginative. I asked him to come and see a large abstract painting in my bedroom. It was called 'The Visitation', by Raymond Hitchcock. He was intrigued and asked me to explain it. I said it represented the Holy Virgin as a tower of thickly applied white, confronted by the Angel Gabriel as an upright rectangle of shimmering gold, and between them the glowing yellow and scarlet of the Holy Spirit being communicated to the Mother of God. He said it was hardly suitable for Soviet workers. I said, and he responded to my introductory smile, that I had never had a Soviet worker in my bedroom. As he left he gave us a bottle of Sovietskoye Shampanskoye. We tried it a few days later. Parts of it were clear.

Next week he gave me some important leads in the Chinese Embassy and wrote to his opposite number in Peking, describing my hope of spending some days in the glorious people's communes and sharing with them their way of life. He wrote in Russian of my being the son of Laurence Olivier, 'husband of Vivien Li'. Moussiah Soskin gave me an introduction to the largest landowner in the Soviet Union, maybe even the world. He owned hundreds of square miles in Siberia and had the title 'Master of the Forest'. So I set about learning Russian, listening to audio discs and having lessons.

The preceding winter my mother and I had met Faubion Bowers at the first night party after Arnold Wesker's play Roots. It was the first time we had seen Joan Plowright in a leading role and we were most impressed. We had seen her in the John Osborne play where Larry had triumphed as the Entertainer and she had taken over the part of his daughter from Dorothy Tutin. Faubion was married to Santha Rama Rau, author and playwright, resplendent in a sari and daughter of the Indian Ambassador to Washington. He was an American hybrid of European and Cherokee, once a concert pianist, and a linguistic genius who had been official interpreter in Japan for General MacArthur. Faubion and Santha had travelled in Asia together writing their books.

His was a masterpiece called *Theatre in the East*: from India, through South-East Asia to China and Japan. He said that if I wanted to meet any of the many people he wrote of, all I had to do was say that he had recommended it. His introduction to Tom Benitez in the Philippines was of tremendous help. With that family behind me he said I could meet anyone in South-East Asia, from Presidents down.

The week before I left for Manila Larry joined me and my mother for dinner at 31 Queen's Grove. I said how impressed I had been by the Wesker play, in particular with Joan Plowright. He agreed, in a curiously disengaged way. We immediately sensed that there was more behind his distant though positive appraisal of her acting. Then he dived into the subject which most concerned him. Vivien and he could never, ever live together again. They had hurt each other too much. The repeated returns of her manic depression for fourteen years was killing both of them. The effect of the mental sickness was to make her hate, really hate, the thing she most loved: him. And to judge by her manifestation of hatred she must, on that score, have loved him to excess. Specialists were advising that if they carried on together, one or other, or both of them, would end up dead.

I knew this was coming and had dreaded it for years. The irreconcilable horror had now reached its peak. One of the reasons for my faraway travel plan was in all sincerity to get away from that and I told him so. He was strongly opposed. He admired my spirit of adventure but deplored every other aspect. How would I survive? Who would look after me? Why the hell should someone not take some unknown advantage of me. It was an unconscionable waste of time. My mother, on the other hand, supported me as she had from the start. She had always quoted Somerset Maugham in *The Summing Up*, where he wrote that the best thing an aspiring writer could do was to cut all family restraints and see the world. 'Oh to be twenty-three', which I was, and my mother had always hoped I would be a writer.

Larry was nothing like as well read as she and had to give ground to her intellect: one of the problems of their marriage, I suspect. In fact he used to complain that the only reading he could do was 'bad plays', on the hunt for his next production. Well it was a beastly conversation, upsetting, and made far worse by his news about Vivien. I could not accept that his love for her was over and done with and said so. He said that of all the people in all the world I was the one more than anyone else who had so often witnessed the irremediable situation they faced. That was that. As for my Asian aspirations, he had no comment other than to say it would be extremely risky and a waste of everything I had been educated for.

One of my problems was that I still did not know what I wanted to do. With independence forthcoming all over Africa it was obvious that I could not join the Colonial Service. To work as a civil servant in the Overseas Development 'Ministry' would have driven me mad. I was artistic but with no talent identified that was worth anything. I had to find a suitable way of working in the developing countries. Before anything else I wanted to learn more about the world. I went on at some length. I can't say that he took his leave of us with any paternal feeling. The last thing my mother said to him was: 'You have forgotten what it is like to be young. Go on. Go home to the next play. That's all you understand or care about: the end of the second act.'

My first letter home was written on board the *Cambodge*, to my mother. It ended: 'I have been so very happy during the last few months with you. I have so loved sharing my excitement with you. You have been loving and imaginative. I so hope that we shall keep the friends we have made during this time, particularly Faubion and Santha.'

The 25,000-ton French liner went from Marseilles to Port Said, where I climbed a pyramid, Aden, Bombay where we went to the Elephant Caves, Sri Lanka, Saigon and after four weeks we docked in Manila. The passengers were mostly married French couples, colonial school marms, and nuns who sat around in clumps, according to their different religious orders. The few Indians and Sri Lankans disembarked halfway there.

On arrival in Manila harbour I met the most welcoming people. Passport and Customs controllers came on board and said there had been articles in the newspapers about me. They waved me through with broad smiles and I tottered down the gang-plank with my heavy suitcase. I was met on the hard by Tom Benitez and his driver who took the suitcase and led us to the air-conditioned limousine. Tom was tall and impressive. He had served in Washington. He had recently founded a new political party with two of the most highly respected elder statesman, intending to fight the election then at its height. They were Senator Recto and Senator Laurel, renowned for their integrity. Their main ambition was to break away from graft and corruption. That problem was endemic. Editorials competed in terms of sheer relish at their never-ending exposures, from the Presidency down to local bureaucrats, of bribes and criminal dealings.

Tom's wife Nena was away, taking the Bayanihan National Philippines Dance Group on tour in America, so he had me stay with her parents. They had a family compound with a large bungalow for themselves and three smaller ones for their three sons and young families. Next door was a much larger house, the Residency of the Japanese Ambassador, which they had sold. The lawns were mown as finely as golf greens. The rooms were shielded from direct sunlight and the décor had a Spanish influence.

My first venture was in the far north of Luzon, the Mountain Province. Canon Simpson, Dean of Christ Church, had given me an introduction to some Episcopalian missionaries and their man in Sagada was Revd George Harris. On the way I visited a sugar estate in Pampanga. That area had been subdued some years earlier by Maoist terrorists called Hukbalahap, determined to destroy capitalism. This was neutralised by the only great Filipino President in anyone's lifetime, President Magsaysay. He actually bested corruption by strong leadership, and introduced land reform. I met one of the estate managers and asked his opinion. He said corruption had returned in force, but at least his men did not work *for* him; they worked *with* him. Together they had formed a co-operative in which they all had a share.

The capital of the Northern Province was Baguio, originally a US Army hill station with large villas, spreading gardens, high fir trees, a clubhouse, playground and a lake. The journey further north, to Sagada, was in a broken down old bus with pigs tied on the roof between all kinds of baggage wrapped in rattan. Under the seats were baskets full of clucking chickens. The passengers were Igorot people from the Mountain Province. The women wore long-sleeved shirts and skirts down to their bare feet, the man in T-shirts and jeans. When the slope uphill was too steep we all tumbled out, then went back past the suspension base which was completely flattened by weight even without us on board, and we pushed wherever we could get a hold. This bonded all of us, and it became easy to start up a conversation. Travelling by bus is much the best for that.

What the Igorots had created and maintained for centuries is one of the world's greatest landscapes: the Ifugao rice terraces, as many as eighty rising in series one above the other, like the drawers of an enormous wardrobe of earth, water-filled, each one brimming with vivid green shoots of rice. Out in the open when at work the adults wore loincloths, the mature men and the women topless. Their enormous toes were permanently spread open to keep them from slipping in the mud.

Father Harris and his wife were from North Dakota so they were used to isolated communities. They had two small daughters. The Igorots had helped build the church. No scaffolding had been necessary. The men just leant poles against the walls and gripped them with their huge toes, leaving both hands free to apply cement. At the evening service they sang the hymns accurately in unison. As a departure Father Harris had taught them to sing one of Bach's chorales in four voices. He took each one separately, the old men starting with the bass; then the tenors, and he combined the two. He did the same with the older women and then the younger ones. When eventually they were sure enough of the notes he brought all four voices together and they were all bowled over by the beauty of it. Within a few months his introduction of singing was a major factor in the success of his mission. At the end of every service as they left there was the soothing and redemptive sound of their bare feet lisping on the stone.

When the Igorot children graduated to Baguio High School, maybe even university in Manila for the very bright, they seldom returned. Their houses were primitive stone, hardly a man's height, crammed together in the small spaces of flat ground. For lavatories there were sunken pens occupied by pigs which ate the faeces. There was usually a hefty stick on the side to keep the pigs at bay. When the elderly retired they spent their declining days hollowing out a four-foot length of thick tree-trunk, for their bodies to be lowered into in the foetal position and then stacked with hundreds of others in a high cave, overlooking the land of their birth.

One of the Liboro uncles, Angél, was running for election as governor of Mindoro Province, a large island with great sugar estates and no land reform, a night's ferry journey south of Manila. I went with his nephew Tato Liboro, who lived in the family compound. He was a successful attorney and highly literate. His wife was the most beautiful *mestiza*. They had four children and decided that was enough, even though they were practising Catholics. He told me of one of his confessions.

Tato knelt at the confessional grille and the censorious priest had asked: 'Birth control?'

'Yes Father.'

'That is a very terrible sin.'

'Yes Father.'

'A mortal sin.'

'Yes Father.'

'How many times have you practised it?'

'Plenty of times, Father.'

While Uncle Angél concentrated on the island of Mindoro, Tato was his electioneer in the tiny island just north of it, called Lubang. It had a few fishing boats, and its main agriculture was rice and subsistence farming. Fourteen years after the Second World War two Japanese soldiers were still at large there. They ignored all the leaflets advising then that the war was over and they could give themselves up in peace and return home, and would they please desist from helping themselves from the local islanders. They only gave themselves up twenty years after that.

During the years of Japanese occupation no new foreign films had been allowed in. The Filipinos made do with what they had. They saw the same films over and over again, including *Wuthering Heights*, with my father as Heathcliff. Even in Lubang.

I was sitting on the ground with Tato and a family who were winnowing rice by hand. The women shredded the ears through a comb made of nails and some younger ones pounded the seeds in a big pestle, casting the light husks on one pile, and the white rice into a large basket. Several pregnant women sat and gawped at me. Tato said that was because they wanted their babies to look like me. I said I thought the fathers had more to do with it but he said that made no difference to them. One very old woman stared more obtrusively. She was chewing betel nut, a stimulus, and expectorated scarlet saliva to one side. Eventually she made up her mind, pointed at me as if her memory had returned, and said: 'Heathcliff!'

Electioneering built up to a climax and groups sang national songs with improvised words on politics. I never really identified the two leading parties' programmes; both were stridently against 'Graft and Corruption'; the differences related to personalities. Tato and Uncle Angél thought they were winning but this was not to be. On election day the opposition distributed banknotes worth two weeks' wages per vote. Once a peasant had accepted the bribe he or she felt bound to honour it. The newly elected governor of Mindoro would of course have to reimburse this unseemly expense from 'Gruff and Collupshun', once in power.

In Manila, at least, Tom Benitez and his party won the constituency seats in Quezon City. There was much discussion about Philippine nationalism but it seemed to me based on rather immature anti-Americanism. I discussed this with Senator Recto and said it was a shame, given the Philippines' good economic performance. He had coined the phrase 'Filipino First'. He challenged me to define nationalism. I said it should reflect national pride and unity in a land of so many hundreds of islands, dozens of languages and such stark contrasts in wealth, and such strong economic prospects. He was kind enough to give me an excellent introduction to Ruslan Abdulgani, Vice President of the Supreme Advisory council of Indonesia.

The journey south to Cebu by sea was beautiful. It was capital of the Visayan Islands, central Philippines. The ferry was a brand new 2,000-tonner. I had a cabin on the top deck. I sat on the roof beside the funnel and gazed at the hilly green islands crowned with coconut palms, girdled with thatched seaside villages of woven pine.

Tom Benitez's American friend Ed Canova met me. He was the local head of the Aboitiz company which owned the ferry, thermal electricity generating companies and much else. He had me shown round the pineapple and sisal plantations. He asked me to give a talk to the Rotary Club about the small farm my father had had at Notley – a hundred acres with 2,000 deep-litter hens, eighty fattening pigs, four large greenhouses, market garden and meadows with eight Jersey cows for their cream. This was intensive mixed farming, efficiently managed by Larry's brother. At Rotary in the Philippines they were unfamiliar with the concept of 'gentlemen farmers' in Wellington boots. The atmosphere was serious, a cross between business-ese and bottom lines. I took them through the four seasons, growth and non-growing, to the marketing. At the end Ed Canova thanked me and said I had agreed to take questions.

I thought it had gone well and was graciously, even patronisingly pleased to invite the first questioner. A hand went up and I said: 'Yes, sir, and what is your question?'

He stood, straight-faced and asked: 'Who's your mother?'

I practically fell off the podium. I grabbed the lectern, recovered, aware that I was hot-necked and beetroot-faced. The fact that I knew the answer had not helped. I replied that she was the actress Jill Esmond who had married my father when they were twenty-three, divorced nearly ten years later when he was with Vivien Leigh. She had brought me up. The terrible feeling I had was of shame. What was that about? In mentioning the three people in the world I adored more than any other, my mother above all. Why the shame? Happily they had other questions.

There were picnics and parties. The prettiest women are to be found in Cebu. Conversation was pleasant, seldom exciting, but this was more than made up for by the Filipino genius at dancing the night through.

Both Faubion Bowers and Santha had written enticingly about the islands in the Sulu Sea. I went to the capital, Joló. It had a tree-covered hill, while the other islands were of white coral only, at low tide barely a yard above the level of the sea meadows. They were completely submerged at high tide, the houses standing on stilts above the placid blue water. One of them, about a hundred yards square with *nipa* huts, was occupied by the ladies of the Sultan's harem; the next by eunuchs to attend to them. Joló itself was alive with kite-flying children, the harbour festooned by even more of them.

The Aboitiz company manager met my ferry. He took one look at me and said I needed a haircut. At his house I saw myself in a mirror and realised that I looked like Beethoven's mother. There was a hairdresser on the fringe of the outdoor market. I had heard of Muslim extremists there hiding scimitars in watermelons and killing Christians. He reassured me. I went into the shop and he left. As the barber cut my hair the window was plastered with dozens of children's faces gawping at me, the strange white foreigner. Security of a kind, I supposed.

Señor Camlón was a pirate and the State had placed a hefty price on his head, dead or alive. Joló city itself was barricaded with barbed wire because of him and his nefarious smuggling from North Borneo. It so happened that his great friend was the Chief of Police. I was beginning to think that this made powerful sense in a place like Joló. The Chief showed me Camlón's anchorage. There were only two boats there at the time, fifteen feet long and shaped like wheelbarrows, with three 50-horsepower outboards lined up on the stern, at that time the most powerful available anywhere. On a robust steel stand they each carried a medium machine gun. The bow had a stout ram at sea level. A year before the police had given chase, but they had no chance because their boats only had two outboards.

The bulk of contraband cargo was in duty-free goods from Sandakan, on the coast of Sabah, for onward delivery to Zamboanga in Mindanao. Occasionally they carried small arms for the Muslim Moro rebels. The Police Chief thought it was better for them to be carried by Camlón's outfit than any other because he at least knew more or less what was happening.

He took me to a two-storeyed house with a restaurant on the ground floor. There was a table with three old wooden chairs and Camlón sitting alone. He looked the caricature of a pirate; not quite striped jersey and earrings, but big white teeth and sparkling eyes, and a complexion like fruit and nut chocolate. Beer was brought in by the prettiest and most enticing gamine I had ever seen. He called her 'Nutty', short for Natividad. Over dinner Camlón repeated the stories the Chief had told me about the police chase at sea. Afterwards Nutty asked me upstairs to dance. The two men looked at me as if to say 'what more could a man want with such a beauty'.

The attic was her bedroom. She put on an old 78 record of Frank Sinatra and came into my arms as light as a feather. Her movements were graceful. After leaning back to give me a provocative gaze she said she really must go to bed because she had so much reading to catch up. I was intrigued and asked what it was. A Filipina who read? Rare indeed.

'Comics,' she said. And that was that.

The Police Chief laughed all the way home.

Back in Manila I stayed again with the Liboros. Someone introduced me to the rowing club and lent me a racing sculler like the one I had had at Oxford. The Pasig River was full of contaminants and looked like an oil slick. I had to keep an eye out for clumps of water-hyacinth floating on the surface. It smelt of stale vegetation and sewage, even opposite the elegant Spanish built wooden Presidential Residency, the Malacañang Palace, and its two neighbouring guest houses.

Further upstream, away from the city centre, were children of the very poor, picking over a miasmic mound of rotting garbage. Some of them jumped into the river to cool down. A line of women pummelled clothes on hard boards with no soap. It was extraordinary that so many preferred life like that, in the capital, instead of in their pretty rural villages surrounded by rice fields and farms.

A party was given for me by one of the leading lights in the art world; Luís Araneta. His house, and especially his garden, were decorated with many impressive antique pieces. A number of couples from leading families were there, some speaking Spanish among themselves, though all were comfortable speaking English.

Their style of life seemed at odds with the country as a whole. Very few of them had seen much of it. Their outlook seemed hardly Asian, more like Latin America with a dozen top families in a hotly competitive oligarchy, while the rest of the people grappled ever upwards with what they could. In fact, although colonised by the Spanish until the end of the nineteenth century, this was done via Mexico. There is a hoary old observation that the Philippines spent five hundred years in a convent, followed by fifty years in Hollywood. Even the phrase Catholic Asians sounds like an oxymoron.

I was shown a documentary film which had won an international prize. In the final climax a live volcano smoked in the background near Legaspi in Southern Luzon, and a Spanish church half-buried in lava closed the sequence, the voice over saying that the deeper you dig in the Philippines the more you come across Spain, Spain, Spain. Yet the country they look up to is the United States, the colonial power which drove out the Spanish at the turn of the century and gave the Philippines independence half a century later. Filipinos know infinitely more about America, where so many go to university, than about their Asian neighbours. At an intellectual level the Philippines is hardly related to them. I did not write about the country in my book about South-East Asia. However, fifteen years later I did have the good fortune to return, many times, and in a fascinating business.

Seven

When my plane landed under heavy rainfall in Djakarta at the end of 1959 I was the only passenger to get off. It was a DC4 from Singapore, going on a night flight to Australia. The steps down to the tarmac were unlit and soaked so I walked down carefully, a typewriter in one hand and a heavy camera case in the other. At the bottom was a soldier with a little machine gun pointing at my chest, motioning that I should precede him through the rain and into the building.

Inside there was a single bulb in the corridor and a door for the gents' loo. I said I wanted to go there, went in and he followed me. As I stood I found it difficult to concentrate with him behind me, gun aimed at my spine. I turned and smiled apologetically, and asked him in the name of progress to point the gun somewhere else. He smiled back and complied.

Four years before, President Sukarno had achieved a moral status internationally through calling together a conference of Non-Aligned Nations in Bandung. It was attended by India's Prime Minister Nehru, Egypt's President Nasser, Marshal Tito of Yugoslavia and dozens of neutral countries which were non-participants in the Cold War. The Non-Aligned movement was formed. This put Indonesia on the world's political map. It was an inspired idea which incorporated a philosophical, economic and political presence. It had to be recognised by the opposing forces of capitalism and Communism. And it was Sukarno, too, who had unified the world's most enormous and disparate archipelago and given all its people the Indonesian language, based on Malay, and some kind of cohesion as a nation.

Things had started to fall apart with various rebellions, based on local culture, interpretations of religion, nascent Communist cells, the persecution of the Chinese middle classes, the expulsion of the remaining Dutch citizens and the spread of corruption. Sukarno still spoke to and for the nation he had led into independence. His rhetoric was everywhere, resonant and wonderfully put together. *Sudara sudara*, my brothers and sisters.

I had been invited, out of the blue, to stay with the Hatcher family. They had read about me in the *Straits Times*. Phil Hatcher had been head of Nestlé in Malaya, which he said had no speck of corruption. He had now been a few months in Indonesia which was awash with it. During the war he had been imprisoned for years by the Japanese in Singapore. Even he, who had 'seen it all', felt the burden of daily stress in Djakarta. He and others called Indonesia the land of unlimited impossibility. He lived a hundred yards from the Presidential Palace, a gleaming white building with Corinthian columns, overlooking a lawn which was being mown by an old man with a stick and little more than a razor blade on one end, sweeping it from side to side. Djakarta was subsisting at a low rate. There were only two traffic lights in the entire city, the trishaw and car wheels were mostly worn smooth. Whenever you parked you had to remove the windscreen wipers to prevent them from being stolen.

Indonesians are wonderful-looking people, both sexes, unlike some Asian countries where the women are beautiful but not the men. At that time most of the women wore their national dress, a long-skirted *kain* made of *batik* cotton and a light floral long-sleeved *kebaya*. Their hair was pulled tightly from their foreheads, hanging down the back of the head with complex braids in a net.

The Philippine Senator Recto's introduction to the number two man in the Indonesian Supreme Advisory Council gave me an entrée to Sukarno's inner circle. Khrushchev, Chairman President of the Soviet Union, made a state visit to Indonesia. The Soviet leader and his henchmen and henchwomen looked unseemly among the elegance of their hosts. They were pallid, hard-eyed and their conversation was riddled with propaganda about the staggering success of Communism, and the exploitation of Indonesia by the imperialist Dutch. There was no gainsaying any of them. No debate could be squeezed between the black or white terms in which they saw the world. This made it impossible for Indonesians to come to any depth of understanding with them, because of the Indonesian practice of *mushjawara*: talking any problem to death. A most democratic and time-consuming activity.

I accompanied a Soviet official and his interpreter in their car from the Central Javanese capital Jogjakarta to Borobudur Temple, the greatest Buddhist monument in the world. It is about eighty yards square of lava rock and represents the universe, the whole structure is topped with a huge bell-shaped *stupa*. Very steep steps lead up six storeys, each level sculpted along each of the four sides with scenes from the Buddha's life. On top there are three circular terraces with ninety-two *stupas*, each a lattice-work of stone with a life-sized Buddha visible inside. This spiritual centre is surrounded by rice fields. Its meditative quality is enhanced by the sound of the ploughmen singing to encourage their buffaloes, songs from the epic Hindu Mahabharata.

The arrival of dialectic materialism in its midst seemed crass. Sukarno led up the steep steps, trim in his Field Marshal's service dress with the Order of Lenin on his chest and his baton firmly held. On his head he wore a black velvet *songkok* which hid his baldness and made him look younger.

Khrushchev, with a pale loose suit hanging round his barrel of a body, laboured behind him. He was sweating and breathless and took many pauses. His rotundity gave new meaning to the word 'girth'. He had to balance his mass on short stumpy legs. We stood at the top, President Sukarno, his two intelligent lady secretaries, the press corps, all waiting for him. Khrushchev eventually pitched up and stood breathlessly to one side. Sukarno tapped each of the six microphones and listened to the corresponding loudspeakers reacting round the quiet crowd below.

Thousands of Javanese stood between the base of the monument and the rice fields. In the silence before the speech we could still hear the ploughmen singing. It was a clear day and unusually for that time of year we could see a dozen miles away the summit of the perfectly formed volcano, Merapi, smoke rising lazily from its crater.

Sukarno's speech dramatised the Indonesian struggle for independence. He was in fine form, lowering his voice to a carefully amplified whisper, then in full volume roaring out the same phrase to tumultuous cheering. He reminded me of Hitler, though his voice had less of a manic rasp, and his gestures were controlled, his eyes quietly hypnotic even when he was in full cry.

'Indonesia from Sabang to Merauke' indicated the spread of the country from the island north of Sumatra all the 3,000 miles across to the far eastern border of what was then the Netherlands New Guinea, still to be released to Indonesia to become Irian Jaya. 'A just and prosperous society.' A constant exhortation, 'We must re-tool the revolution', was his pet phrase for that year.

And on it went, with the crowd's cheers growing. The loudspeakers were switched off. Once again we could hear the ploughmen in the rice fields, their singsong voices rising and falling. Sukarno turned to Khrushchev and asked for comment. The interpreter, who had managed very well so far, relayed the question. Khrushchev shook his head and said he didn't like it. Rather than translate those few bleak words the interpreter sought some elucidation.

He turned once more to Khrushchev and asked: 'What do you think, Mr Chairman President?'

This was translated into Russian.

'What do I think?' Khrushchev demanded rhetorically. 'I think you need tractors.'

This was translated into Indonesian.

Sukarno was stunned. His Soviet guest then proceeded to outline the need for planning. Everything must be planned, every minute of the day, every aspect of life from state education to match all the needs of production. When he had finished Sukarno murmured that that was the life of a robot.

The State Visit proceeded to the blessed Isle of Bali. In the baking midday sun the two Heads of State sat together on a high stand, shaded by gorgeous palanquins. In the street before them paraded streams of bare-footed Balinese dancing girls, their hair folded within itself in two loops, crowned with frangipani blooms, their bare arms undulating in unison, their bodies wrapped tightly in scarlet and gold, their legs in traditional *kains*. Beyond them on the other side of the road was a gamelan orchestra with polychromatic xylophones and every kind of bass gong, emitting sounds ranging from deep reverberation to the thinnest tinsel. Meanwhile we were treated to fruit juices and ice cream.

At the end of that long hot day there was an Indonesian cultural evening at Tampaksiring Palace. In the front row were two high-backed wooden thrones. Khrushchev came in and sat down with his male secretary behind him; Sukarno took his place next to him, and behind him the most ravishing Balinese maiden in white. I was a few rows back with Ganis Harsono, head of the Foreign Office Cultural Section. He had never seen the girl before. And all through the interminable dances, while Khrushchev gave dictation to his secretary, Sukarno turned to her and fed peanuts into her hands, with limpid looks. Everyone knew of his philandering. It was even said he liked to give really important speeches within an hour of making love. She looked Balinese. He was half Balinese on his mother's side so he would have known how to get her, but she was a perfect mystery.

A week later I went to the Sanur coast of Bali to see the Javanese painter Agus Jaya. He had a large wooden bungalow on the beach, overlooking gaily painted fishing-boats, masts laid flat, rolled up in their sails. His wife explained that when he came out of his studio he would remain so immersed in his painting that it would take him a while to focus on anything else – even her.

She showed me a life-size portrait of a naked young woman's back-view, lying in a forest. It reminded me of the similar painting by Velasquez, but without the mirror showing Venus's face. That omission made her even more sensuous. We looked at it for quite a while, unaware that Agus Jaya had joined us, a rag in one hand, apparently glad to have heard what I had been saying. We shook hands and I wondered what would have happened if Sukarno had seen that painting.

'Oh he did,' he replied. 'That's the girl now with him. He went to her village and she agreed for him to take her. It will be some time for her to get over the shame when he leaves her.'

My first time in Bali had been made most memorable by a sweet and loving relationship with a Balinese girl. I wrote fully about Sri, the name I gave her in my book. We had a wonderful month together. We bicycled miles and miles trying to find somewhere we could be alone. Even in the most luxuriant and leafy forests there was no chance. Around every tree trunk peered the face of a grinning child. It was the happiest and most uncomplicated month either of us had ever had. So hard to say goodbye. But I was to see her again fifteen years later.

For several weeks I island hopped eastwards in small wooden ferries, eventually arriving in Timor, which means 'East'. It was far beyond the live body politic. I accompanied an American anthropologist, Clarke Cunningham. He was about thirty, handsome and married to a French girl, as lovely as Brigitte Bardot, who had only just conceived their first baby and was passionately and shamelessly in love. He let me accompany him far into the interior, to a people who had hardly ever been visited by anyone, and never by a doctor.

Their village was a ropey version of traditional poverty, rattan and well-trodden earth. The trees grew high above it, spaced so the canopy just joined. These rag-clad poor people farmed in nearby sunshine: hill paddy, vegetables, and fish in hand-dug ponds. None of them could read or write. Many had eyes cloyed with infection, fed upon by flies. About a dozen of them had twitches and facial expressions indicating mental problems. Wonky faces, wonky walks. There were indeed some devils waiting to be cast out.

I was struck by the thought that these were the conditions prevalent in the Holy Land at the time of Christ. We did wash their faces with mildly salted water to clean their eyes. It seemed that in one or two cases this did restore eyesight they had lost for some time. I applied some antiseptic I always carried and their swollen lids got a bit better. They did not seem to look upon the world as individuals, with their own identity. Most of them just looked lost. I had never seen anything like it in Africa, even in Chafombo's village which every year went for days with no water and was much poorer in every way.

There were three or four seniors among them who remembered aspects of their history they wanted Clarke to record. Those few had special faces, focused, and one looked like Voltaire. They all spoke Indonesian as well as the Timorese language and answered Clarke's questions clearly, day by day, and he noted down how their society was organised. They said some of their children had gone to the Timorese capital Kupang for teacher training. Their time would soon come, and they would truly participate in Indonesia's finest achievement: the development of education.

When I returned to Jogjakarta my Javanese friends could not believe my photographs were of normal Timorese. 'Are these beggars?'

I gave some lectures in the university, courtesy of the American professor of economics. The Indonesian gift for languages is extraordinary. Their English was so good they understood every nuance and laughed out loud at my story about the Cebu Rotarian's question: 'Who's your mother?'

Out and about there were frequent conversations where references to the volcano Merapi were used as an opener, like weather with the English. Yet hardly anyone had climbed it. I persisted with the Department of Volcanology and managed to obtain a permit for a team of American professors to come with me. I had asked a number of students but they didn't see the point. With their inborn Javanese images of spirits and mystery perhaps they did not want to let sunshine in on magic.

So we were five men. We had to drive our two jeeps round to the east side of Merapi, with a volcanologist. He guided us up a tarmac lane, threading through steep hairpin bends, up and up to a height of about 6,000 feet. It was evening. We came to a solid brick hut with a view of the peak. One of the rooms was equipped with barometric and seismological equipment, all perfectly kept, the record books open and up to date.

It was very cold. We had an early dinner with hot food and whisky and got into our camp beds, preparatory to getting up at three in the morning. We would then be able to reach the summit in time to see the sun rising behind other, lesser volcanoes far away. These formed the backbone of Java, making it the most beautiful island in all the world, with its immense spread of rice fields and terraces, the occasional clump of a village under fruit trees and palms. Our guide said that with such a view extending below us we would feel like kings.

We awoke, made coffee, toast, boiled some eggs and bundled on our sweaters and windbreakers, all except for the economics professor. It was sharply cold and I wondered why he chose to remain only in a sleeveless vest. A young colleague told me he wanted us to admire his pectorals and biceps. Before we started our climb he lit a cigar.

No moon. A slight mist reduced the stars. This worried our guide. He led us up and up and up. The slope was precipitous and the path slippery. We had to stop for breath every few minutes. The one who was the only possessor of mountain boots started gasping that his heart was playing up. We stopped and waited until he said he felt well enough to go on. Slowly. The economics professor finished his cigar and stamped it out. Our breathing became shamelessly loud.

After a couple of hours, still in the dark, we came to a stone hut five hundred feet below the crater. It had a hefty door with special seals inside to protect occupants from any poisonous gas from the bowels of the earth. We sat, exhausted, our eyes drained of any spark. The stars were still shrouded and the guide said we must wait. The mist would make it impossible to see any gases coming down the mountainside. The light increased slowly but we were enveloped in mist so the expedition had to be called off and back we went. The trudge down was far more treacherous than the ascent. We were dreadfully disappointed.

A year later I received a letter from one of the professors saying they had put the expedition together again, climbed to the top, taken pictures of the inside of the crater steaming away at the bottom, and turned to hail the dawn. They had all cried three cheers for Ike and the Queen.

In Singapore the editor of the *Straits Times*, Wee Kim Wee, was most impressive. With his iron-grey hair and gentle face he looked possessed with the wisdom of a sage, despite the constant interruptive demands of running a major newspaper. Twenty years later he was Singapore's Head of State. He was quietly spoken and philosophical. He asked me all about Indonesia. I said that Singapore, so clean in every detail, seemed a world away from the vagueness and continuous stress which I had left behind, though with much regret. My eight months all over Indonesia had taught me more than any other such period in my life, and I felt more affection for a foreign country than I had ever known. I used the word 'spiritual' in a number of contexts, especially Javanese, and he understood.

I asked him where he thought the heart of Singapore was to be found. Without hesitation he said 'Chinatown'. I said that I would have to stay there. He said that might be difficult; a diplomatic way of telling me not to be silly. The ostentatious waterfront of Singapore was a thin façade in 1960. Directly behind it spread the populous and narrow streets of Chinatown. People's servants lived there, taxi drivers, shop-keepers, factory workers, clerks and dockworkers, all the cogs and nuts and bolts which connected the big wheels. It was the basic ingredient of Singapore; not so much the heart, perhaps, but the guts.

In between sorties to Malaya I returned five times to Singapore. I gave up staying at the YMCA – no privacy – and took a cubicle in a very poor hotel on the outskirts. Even there I had to fill out a police form with passport and other details. The Emergency caused by the Communist uprising among Malayan Maoist Chinese, led by Li Peng, was only recently over. The British Army, under General Sir Gerald Templer, had infiltrated the jungle hide-outs, ferreted out the terrorists mainly with small arms and patrols, resettled the vulnerable locals in protected new villages, and won the battle for hearts and minds. Malaya and Singapore had each only been independent for a year. The presence of visitors and hotel guests remained under scrutiny.

I had checked in late at night. At seven thirty in the morning the phone rang. It was the Commissioner of Police of Malaya, a well-estab-lished friend: Sir Claude Fenner, who also had the Malay title 'tan sri'. The next title, 'Dato', came later.

'How on earth did you find me here, of all places?'

'We have our means.'

He asked me to join him on holiday in a police launch up the east coast of Malaya.

He was a very big man, huge policeman's feet, powerful and heavily built. He had managed to evade capture by the Japanese and had had a very successful war in the jungle, Force 136. During the Emergency which followed he was one of the masterminds against the well-organised Communists. His wife Joan was Elizabeth Arden's rep-resentative for the Far East. With two young couples we had a wonderful week together on his launch along the east coast.

We came across some Chinese fishermen, their black hair bleached red by the sun, their skin was the colour of mahogany and their four wooden boats silver grey. Claude had served in Quemoy and Matsu on the south coast of China and spoke their kind of Chinese. He persuaded them to let me join them.

One of their boats had a diesel engine and it towed the other three. After an hour they switched off and we drifted in silence. One of them put on flippers, a facemask and dived in. The sea was so clear and calm we could see him, his legs sweeping him further and further down until he was out of sight. Then he reappeared, letting out air bubbles, until at the surface his breath exploded with a yelp. He gave the thumbs up. Fish were there. He had seen masses of them. He hauled himself into the boat. Two others held out a much-worn diver's suit, with metal feet and a glass-windowed helmet which screwed on like a space suit, and helped him into it. His hands were free, the wrists tightly bound.

While they prepared the air hose and pump, the rest of them paddled the boats quietly down the tide, with the current. He crammed his belt with sharp metal pegs, gathered up an enormous net and jumped in. One of the men pumped his air and we watched him sink down at the end of a rope, disappearing to the seabed. There he pegged the bottom of the net, about fifty feet in diameter, into the sand.

When he was pulled back and his kit removed, each side of the main net was hooked on to a shallow surface net with floats. This was to mark the two outside boundaries, spreading out like a hundred-yard-long funnel leading out from the main net. Silence remained the order of the day as they paddled, so as not to frighten the fish away. We were each given two-foot lengths of bamboo, bound with rope with six-foot iron chains on the end. We all got into the boat with the motor. When the feeder nets were fully unwound, the engine started up with a roar and ploughed noisily from one side of the funnel opening to the other. We jumped off like parachutists and swam deep into the translucent sea. We unwound the chains and dangled them at the end of the ropes, shaking them to make an ethereal tinkling sound far below, like altar bells. The thudding engine was way above. The fish were panicked into the main net.

We clambered aboard and grappled up the main net. There were a ton of fish, brightly coloured with pale green fins, a few octopus and one small shark. We scooped and shovelled them into the boats. This simple but effective method of maximising the catch had been taught them during the Japanese occupation.

It was the time of year when leatherback turtles struggled out of the sea and up the beach to lay their eggs. They came at night. They were up to seven feet long and left tracks like a tank in the sand behind them. We came across one of these great ladies, her tail end pointing to the sea. With her hind flippers she dug a hole about two and a half feet deep, scattering sand in all directions, some of it into her eyes which watered with soggy tears. Nothing would disturb her once she started laying, bursts of three or four eggs at a time, like soft ping pong balls.

I heard the story of a French photographer at such a scene in Java, lights all set up and ready to film. Across the sand there appeared a magnificent male tiger, eyes dazzled by the lights. He was hungry. He went for a laying mother turtle and sunk his teeth into her shoulder. She retracted it as much as she could, enough to trap his upper and lower jaw inside the vice-like entrance of her shell. He tried to tug his head free. She weighed at least half a ton. He strained, haunch muscles bulging with the effort, feet pushing through the soft sand.

She continued laying her eggs. When she finished she covered them up with her hind flippers. She managed to turn with her one free front flipper. She moved with extreme difficulty down the beach, the tiger growling and now with the extra strength of terror. The sand became firmer as she entered the water. The tiger tugged and strained and shook. She dragged him further, into deeper water. She drowned him.

Back in Singapore I scratched around the periphery of Chinatown and made no progress. I met the well-known novelist Han Suyin, famed for *Love Is a Many-Splendored Thing*. It became a not very good feature film with William Holden and Jennifer Jones. She was half Belgian and half Chinese and used her non-professional name Elizabeth Comber. She invited me for tea at a hotel renowned for fat ladies eating cakes. She was at the height of her beauty, slim, long-legged, wearing a cheongsam with high neck and slit high up her left thigh, the acme of chic. Her ankles were superb in high heels.

She seemed not best pleased to meet me. Even after each other's news on mutual friends, including her publisher, she remained patronising. As if addressing a child she asked whether I would like an ice cream. I said I would love one, and how much I admired all the different sorts there were in Singapore; why, I saw on the menu they even had caramel and walnut.

She ordered it for me. As we waited I said how taken I was with the clothes of Asian women, how much I admired the flamboyant grace of

Hindu women in saris, how they moved, not so much taking steps with their feet, one by one, more like flowing, their diaphanous scarves wafting behind them.

That was more than she could bear. She cut in: 'If you were a practising doctor, as I am, you would see what most Indian women look like naked. They have big bellies, pendulous breasts, sloppy bottoms, many discolourations of skin. Their saris do a good job of disguise.'

She sat up as she warmed to her subject. 'A cheongsam, on the other hand, forces you to stay trim. Its cut forces you never to relax. You have to sit up straight. And the high neck makes you hold your head to your full height. When you walk upstairs you have to tread carefully, sideways, each foot balanced on high heels, one at a time, and when you stand up from sitting down you must rise, knees together, like a model. A cheongsam presents you with a constant moral, physical and spiritual challenge.'

She then saw that my eyes, over a spoon of ice cream, were smiling fondly. To my relief she found this delightful and laughed. She had sailed into my ambush and liked it there. She accepted my invitation to dinner.

I told her of my efforts to stay in Chinatown. 'Good heavens,' she said. 'You can't expect me to know anyone *there*!'

On my fifth visit to Singapore I chose a particularly grubby hotel, with living standards even worse than I imagined in Chinatown. After several sorties I found a taxi driver who did live in Chinatown. I told him I was writing a book. 'A story book?' he asked. I concurred and eventually, after he had offered me a cigarette and we had had fried noodles together at the outside car park market, he asked me to stay with him and his family.

The address was 40B Temple Street, which they have long since vacated. Parallel to it, now bulldozed and built with high-rise apartments, was Sago Lane, a sort of Death Row, where the very old, too old to stay at home, ended their days, sitting beside their expensive coffins of polished hardwood, several laid out on shelves one above the other.

I asked him about Sago Lane.

'Don't live in Sago Lane.'

'Why not?'

'Because why, because it is very noisy. They play musical instruments, marching in the street all day long. Every time there are funeral processions. They play mah-jong all night. They have death houses where old people go, so they are looked after, but then they die and all the relatives are drinking and gambling. Because why it is very dangerous. They have gangsters. I want you to stay with my fourth brother as our guest, as our friend. You sleep with our family. Can!' He beamed at me.

'I come tomorrow night,' I said.

'Also can!'

They lived on the second floor and rented out one room for an opium den. They closed it down a couple of years later as soon as Fourth Brother had passed his accountancy exams. I wrote all about this in my book but there are two further stories.

Temple Street teemed with people, arms full of shopping and babies. Cars seldom went there because it was so crowded. Every day was market day. The street was choc-a-bloc with precarious trestle tables under awnings, with fruit, fish, vegetables, toys, baby things, dry goods of every kind and at one end the reptile market, with fresh snakes, and small tortoises awaiting slaughter. Bets were placed on how long their hearts would beat after their heads were cut off.

Every morning I looked down from our second-storey window. Opposite was a single man with three small children. He sat in the shade under the arcade over the pavement, next to the monsoon drain, reading his newspaper. When he finished he tore it up, gave a fistful to each of the children. With so much activity nobody noticed three little bottoms over the drain. Then they went back to their father who patted them on the head, gave them their schoolbooks and off they went.

One evening further down the street there had been a fight between rival gangs. Acid had been thrown. The police raided the house, made a number of arrests and the place was vacated, including *its* opium den. Singapore policy on opium was wise. That drug was easy to detect. You could smell an opium den as you passed by. For addicts there was an effective rehabilitation policy. The police did not normally close the places down because opium would be replaced by heroin, a far more dangerous drug and difficult to detect. Their aim was to cut off the sources of opium supply and leave the streets in peace, but after the throwing of acid they had to be one hundred percent thorough and close that one.

For two days all was normal, which is to say the deafening yells of street vendors, the smashing of mah-jong pieces on the trestle tables, the radios blaring the favourite love song: 'I've got the bells of ding-dong, deep down inside my heart.' Fourth Brother hated the song because he had yet to find out what the words meant.

Meanwhile the rats which had lived above the opium den had not been getting their fix. They went into cold turkey. They bounded down the stairs, out of the door, along the arcaded pavements, into the helter-skelter street.

Everyone panicked. Screams of every age and sex. Women leapt on to the trestle tables which collapsed, awnings were pulled down, pressure lamps fell and set them on fire. The rats were horrible hairless creatures with blackened teeth and mad eyes, careering up and down. Even the reptile market was knocked for six and the tortoises waddled down the street, blinking between flying legs. On and on went the maelstrom of rats until they picked up the scent of other opium dens. They scampered up the walls of houses, ours, some of them, until they found their way into the eaves. There they breathed in the fumes with relish and relaxed. Peace.

In Chinatown, unless seriously shaken like that, the interdependence of life in so jam-packed a community imposes a discretion and considerateness of behaviour which you would never guess at, given the boisterous noise.

My second story is about a view of propriety, a difference between East and West, what can and what can't be done. It concerns Larry. One morning I was reading in *Time Magazine* a review of his film *The Entertainer*, based on John Osborne's play. Larry played the lead: Archie Rice, the drink-sodden, down-in-the-dumps, gap-toothed, untalented, music-hall pretend optimist. In the play his performance was rightly hailed as stupendous: poignant, funny, and shatteringly moving. That was the play.

The review of the film was ho-hum. In the middle of the page was a photograph of Larry as Archie, cane in hand, trilby on, a leer, and three unfortunate naked ladies posing either side of him.

Fourth Brother peered over my shoulder and asked: 'Who's that?'
'My father.'
He squinted down at the magazine. 'He doesn't look like you.'
'Not there, he doesn't.'
'And are those his wive?'
'No.'
'How many wive have you father.'
I thought I'd play along with this to see where it led.
'Three. He's just got married for the third time.'
'So you've got three mothers.'
That had never occurred to me, but I let it pass.

'And how many brothers and sisters?'

'None. I am an only child.'

He was horrified. Shocked. He seized the magazine and called out to Sixth Sister, the one who worked in a rubber factory snipping out imperfections from sheets of Ribbed Smoke Sheet One. He told her of his acute embarrassment, what he had made me confess; that my father was impotent, had been for a quarter of a century. Three wives. Must be something to do with him, not them. Such was his commotion that some of the opium addicts came out of their room in their underwear to find out what was happening. I could not get in a word of explanation. The magazine was by now crumpled from him showing everyone the picture, their comparing it with me, and shaking their heads at Fourth Brother's terrible manners, how insensitive.

For a whole week nothing more was said. Then he came to me, all smiles.

'I know who your father is.'

'Well done.'

'Very famous. Everyone know him.'

'That's true.'

His eyes narrowed. 'He's rich.'

'No, Fourth Brother, not really. As a working actor he's comfortable, but not rich.'

'He's a millionaire.'

'Far from that.'

'He's a multi-millionaire.'

'Nothing like it. Never will be.'

'He is!' He whooped with delight. He felt redeemed from his terrible sin. 'Now I understand. So now I know why he have three wive.'

In other words, if you're *that* rich it does not matter if you *are* impotent. I wrote to Larry and told him the story. He said that I must get a new pen, the one I was using was so pale he thought it was the opium, which of course I never touched.

I wrote back:

What fun to have a letter to answer. It makes me feel far closer to you – even though you, you lion, want to put a whole pride of cubs between you and your grand cubs one day to be. I had a letter from Vivien saying that she was starting to feel herself again and even believe that there is great peace and joy for her. I hope I will always be as close to her as I have been.

Sometimes things make me laugh which shouldn't. The idea of having brothers and sisters for the first time when I am a quarter of a century old. No longer do I wish anything but that it should be so. I think I have learned to value your happiness more. I think we *might* recognize each other in the street again. I have lost 25lbs since I last saw you, but the resemblance between us is, I think, still there; except that Han Suyin said I was better looking because my nose was more finely shaped. Wasn't that naice.

In Singapore, Malaya and Thailand I met officials in their various finance and economics ministries to learn how they promoted their many developmental policies, and travelled the length and breadth of the two mainland countries. There were two experiences which still cry out in my mind to be recorded, the first physical and the second metaphysical.

The first was of a kind of which it suffices to say, with discretion, that I remember her well. Beyond description. I slept in late in the southern Thai village of Haadjai, over-exerted, and the first meal I had was lunch. I was sitting under an awning, feeling so unburdened I wondered if my appearance had changed from top to toe.

I saw a trishaw and the divine young girl. She saw me, stopped the trishaw, came over and brought her hands together in the Thai 'wai', which I returned and she sat down next to me. She wanted a Coke. The manager came over, smiling broadly. He spoke English. 'She told me,' he said, 'she liked you very much.' I blushed and said something about how lovely she was. He continued: 'She said you were very good. She and her fiancé are so proud.'

'Her fiancé?'

'Yes. They are saving up to get married. You were good and kind and generous.'

So I ended up feeling that I was not only Casanova, but St George.

The second was in the northern capital of Chiengmai where I studied Buddhism for a month with the Lord Abbot, Pra Maha Suratana, at the Wat Pra Singh monastery. The deal was that I should spend each morning teaching English to their primary school students, using the Oxford English Course. It had a picture of Christ Church on the cover, which was of some comfort. The contents on the other hand were daft. I had to read out each sentence – the first being: 'Have tigers blue eyes?', and they had to repeat it back to me. Their pronunciation was good, but the second sentence must also have made them seriously wonder what was wrong with the English: 'Have I three hands?' We got by, somehow, for an hour each morning. 'No, I have not three hands.'

Really. Oxford.

I stayed in a rest house. At dawn the monks came round with their metal begging bowls. Each household, in order to gain merit, ladled out rice, meat and vegetables, enough for breakfast and the one main meal of the day which was lunch. Thereafter they fasted, smoked and drank incessant cups of tea. They spent time gardening, to 'keep their bodies strong', in the temple intoning for hours in a bass monotone which they said induced emotions of peace, removed from all human desire, and studying the scriptures in Sanskrit, which they called the Pali language, of all the Buddha's teachings. These were massive. During his lifetime he had surrounded himself with leading scholars and dictated his teachings to them so that the record would be accurate and complete. They sounded grave and beautiful when read out.

English translations available in the temple library were piecemeal. There were the do's and don'ts common to every faith, except that Buddhism was more a way of life than a religion. There was no God. The moral code was governed by the wish for self-perfection. At its simplest, the world was a mess and the purpose of life was for everyone to help straighten it out. The reward was to be reincarnated at a higher level, the highest was to become a Bodhisattva to live forever above earthly existence. The sanction against sin was to be reincarnated within the Wheel of Life as something inferior. I found all this attractive but unbelievable.

I was intrigued by the Buddha's teaching on embryology. Through his meditation he was able to divine the development of the human foetus, in the womb, from only six weeks after conception. That was two and a half thousand years ago. He has since been proven correct by modern science. He got the order right: the brain, spinal column, optic and dental nerves and the development of the organs.

More important to me by far was a philosophy I had never seen put into words but had long sensed; he called it the Oneness of Life, all of it, both animal and vegetable. This appealed to me absolutely. I had always felt a strong affinity not only with animals but with trees, fields of wheat, gardens of any kind. Meditating on this single thought brought me great satisfaction. It complemented the philosophy I had learned in Java about the acceptance of life. It changed my outlook.

My letters to Larry always ended with my blessings to him and Joan in all the things they do. I said that 1961 would be the year I would finish my book, now at 35,000 words, and would present him with something he could keep. So it was a shock when he wrote:

Our letters often seem to answer each other as if they touched on the way. Until you really start doing what you have decided to do there will be nothing else to talk about. We are both just swaying gently about like two men just a bit too drunk to have the sense to go to bed. You, I think at the moment seem to be luxuriating at a prospect, standing on a bridge, staring down at your little craft and wondering how and if you will win a race. And I am saying to you with that immaculate decorum for which I am famous 'get into the fucking thing and *row*' ...

You have my dearly loving wishes, as always and forever, your fucking old DAD.

To my mother he had written:

I had a letter from T last week and just between ourselves I'm a bit nonplussed how to answer it. The darling gets seriouser and seriouser, and short of suggesting that he goes to join Schweister in Africa I can't for the life of me think of any livelihood that would content him. 'I want to save mankind ... without any religion' he says. I really do feel a bit anxious. I don't want to write too realistically for fear of making him think he is talking to a philistine and drying him up from me ...

You are so sweet in telling me how you worked at getting him and me closer together, but now I must confess I feel a bit pariah-like.

It did take me longer than most to find a livelihood that combined the three essentials: that it paid enough, that I was good at it, and liked it.

Eight

Returning home after nineteen months in South-East Asia I stayed with my mother at 31 Queen's Grove. The garden was lovely, the delphiniums and wisteria at their peak. She was happier.

Every day from nine until one, and from two to seven, I was incarcerated in my room. I sat at a handsome desk with a view over the pond in the front garden, Queen's Grove beyond, and revised my book on the people I had known the previous nineteen months. Writing did not come naturally to me. In Djakarta I had met an Australian journalist representing the Australian Broadcasting Corporation. His name was Kenneth Henderson. He offered me a job writing news for the Swiss Shortwave Service in Bern, where he was going to set up an international news department. That was to start at the end of September and I looked forward to it. Meanwhile I hammered away at my typewriter, wanting to finish my book first.

My friends in England all had jobs, mainly in the City. Some were fascinated but some frustrated by their distance from whatever it was they were trading, broking or financing. They could not take seriously that I was writing a book and working longer hours than most of them. An Etonian and Christ Church friend, David Gladstone, invited me to his wedding. The bride was April Brunner, a debutante of my 1955 vintage, her parents and mine old friends. The ceremony was in Christ Church Cathedral and the reception was at the Brunners' early eighteenth century Wotton House, a few miles from Notley. I was improperly dressed, the only man not in morning clothes. It struck me that I was becoming an outsider.

Larry came to Queen's Grove to dine. He was full of life, happy in his second year of marriage to Joan Plowright. They had bought a Regency house, 4, Royal Crescent in Brighton, overlooking the Channel, decorated in Georgian style. It had a small garden at the back, and in London they had a flat they kept quiet about, in Roebuck House, Victoria. Larry used to learn his lines on the Brighton Belle train.

Over dinner both he and my mother said my letters from South-East Asia had been a terrible disappointment. All I had written had been descriptions: nothing that indicated conflicts between individual people, the *sine qua non* of drama, fiction, comedy, or any real story development. Nothing like the wondrous stories of Somerset Maugham in *The Casuarina Tree*. Well, I had read them; my main reaction, although admiring the story-telling, was that they must have damaged the reputations of the English managers and colonial servants working there. They did agree that I had found a number of interesting adventures to pursue and I told them of my determination to finish my book about those.

In the evenings in London I looked up the people who had given me introductions and told them about my travels. One of them was an American journalist who worked for Associated Press. He and his wife had me for drinks, and also a beautiful Malayan Chinese actress, Yu Ling, who had a part in the play *The World of Suzie Wong*, which was in rehearsal. We became very fond of each other. She was getting over a relationship with a fashion photographer. She was an old friend of Malcolm MacDonald. He had been High Commissioner for South-East Asia, and masterminded the top military and civilian appointments to defeat Communism in the Malayan Emergency.

I stayed with Vivien in Tickerage Mill, her newly bought country house near Uckfield in Sussex, in a valley with a big pond flowing into the River Uck. She had brought Mr Cook, the gardener, and his wife from Notley and housed them in a nearby cottage, so the grounds looked their best. Her paintings and plush furnishings fitted the modest-sized rooms and she seemed happy to have settled down with Jack Merivale, Gladys Cooper's stepson, a man of wonderful good looks, consideration and refinement but little energy and barely any talent on stage. He would go to bed soon after dinner while she and I sat up with our brandies all hours of the night, tirelessly, conversation meandering. We were as close as ever.

September came. I finished my book before going to Switzerland and gave it to Peter Watt, a literary agent the novelist Pamela Frankau had introduced me to. Yu Ling and I parted sweetly and continued to write letters to each other. Her plan had been to see the play *Suzie Wong* through its tour and into London, then return to Malaya where she had a long-standing relationship of some kind, I didn't inquire too much, with a talented Malay about whom Malcolm expressed reservations.

The Swiss News Department offices were near Zeitglockentum in Old Bern. It had telex machines, for Reuters, United Press International, Associated Press, Agence France-Presse and Deutschland Press Agentür. Whenever any of them, or indeed all of them, had anything to report they would hammer away rowdily. My boss was Ken Henderson, the Australian journalist I met in Djakarta. He had worked on the Swiss Shortwave 'Programme Side' in previous years. He had done very well to convince the Swiss of their need to have an international news service. The country had a fine reputation, still no representation at the UN, and no international voice. My sub-editor was another Aussie, Norman Bennel, who had damaged his nose as a boxer, and an American, Eddie Isenson. The secretary was a 22-year-old Swiss girl called Elspeth.

I became a sort of machine which could read a thousand words of boring French, grasp the import, refine the lead sentence and summarise the story in crystal-clear English. Eddie did the same with German. Norm wrote and sub-edited and Ken approved. We had American medical students to read our ten-minute bulletins. To start with we only broadcast domestic Swiss news – the opposite of exciting: cantonal politics, conferences in Geneva, pollution in the lake. Every day for practice we also wrote dummy international news bulletins. When we got better these were submitted to the Swiss Federal Cabinet. They gained enough confidence in the News Department to let us become the International Voice of Switzerland. Not bad for just four of us, and a triumph for Ken Henderson. Our bulletins were translated into French, Spanish, Portuguese, Arabic and Indonesian.

We moved offices into a brand new building on the outskirts of the city. From my desk the view was of the whole range of the Bernese Oberland, the Munch, Jungfrau and the Eiger: Grindelwald's mountains. This was close to my flat in Kirchenveldt. We finished at 7.15 when the newsreader went down to the studio to broadcast our ten-minute bulletin, and the translators went to work for their own news programmes.

I used to dine alone in a pleasant restaurant, the Burgenzeil; my only chance for reading books. I had a letter from Peter Watt saying that my book 'Eye of the Day' was readable, interesting and certainly publishable. I immediately felt I could do no wrong and lent it to Eddie Isenson to read. He was not all that nice about it but there was something irresistible about his personality, his very hooked nose, eyes which almost completely disappeared when he laughed, and his and his wife Bev's knowledge of photography. He said my book was 'tweeny'. It was not readable; interesting, yes, in parts, but certainly not publishable. Now by that time I had been news-writing in the simplest and most easily assimilated English, to assist the speed of translation, with the kind of rhythm our English newsreaders could best use for emphasis. In something of a sulk I took my typescript to bed with me and re-read it. I felt

I was descending at increasing speed down an elevator shaft without end. I could see exactly how right he was, though I did not come round to agreeing it was 'tweeny' until some years later, because at the time that was what I *was*: 'tweeny'.

I started to rewrite it slowly, in longhand. After dinner I would leave the restaurant and be home at my desk by nine and write until the local church bell struck midnight. Straight to bed, without even finishing the sentence. Up at 6.30, shower while the coffee heated and egg boiled on my electric ring, then back to the book at 7 a.m., becoming immediately immersed until 8.45, ready for the walk to work. I have never felt more productive, writing my book before and after the busy day in the News Department. By that time it was winter so I spent weekends on the skiing slopes.

Larry and Joan had a son, Richard. Larry gave me an air ticket to fly over for the christening. He had become Artistic Director of the Chichester Festival Theatre, under construction, so I drove my mother down to Brighton and then Larry drove us and Joan to Chichester Cathedral. Larry had made Joan change her hat, which miffed her, so I cheered them up with a limerick:

> A beautiful woman from Chichester
> Made all the Saints in their niches err;
> One morning at Matins
> The heave of her satins
> Made the Bishop of Chichester's breeches stir.

The Dean officiated in a bright cope and stole designed by the painter John Piper. It was held together with an orange tile across his chest. As soon as Richard was in his arms the tiny hands grasped and unhooked the tile, which was fastened up again only just in time to avoid catastrophe. I was a godfather. When on behalf of the baby the oath had to be given to eschew the world, the flesh and the devil, Richard belted out a fabulous squawk of resentment.

Back in Switzerland in the New Year I went to see my godfather Noël Coward in Les Avants, sur Montreux. This is the letter I wrote afterwards:

7 January 62
Darling Mummy,
    I have just returned from my weekend with Godfather Noël, exhilarated, flattered and a trifle perplexed. He met me down at

Montreux station just after lunch on Saturday, his face chapped, shiny with grease he had used to counteract the dryness, his ears swollen. We went to a chemist shop to buy something and I noticed how his hands shook as he took the small change off the counter.

We had dinner with Adrienne Allen and Bill Whitney. Bill talked I thought quite interestingly, but on the way home, Noëlie, Graham Payn [his boyfriend], Gladys Calthrop [the theatre costume designer], and Cole Lesley [his general factotum who wrote far the best biography], all agreed that Bill was a terrible bore and wasn't it marvellous of Adrienne to be so good with him. I couldn't help wondering whether I would have found Bill less interesting than I did if I had not become absorbed by Bern.

This morning I went up to N's room for an after-breakfast tête-à-tête with him still in bed. He talked a great deal about what had prompted my voyage to the Philippines and why I had stuck it out. He overwhelmed me with the unexpectedness of all he said when he talked to me. He ascribed tremendous importance to me trying to learn Russian on the boat going to Manila. Understood completely my affection for farmers as well as princes.

He made me feel that I have talent. I told him about reading my manuscript and how unhappy I felt, the letter from A P Watt saying it was good, when I came to realise it was bad. He said so many things about his admiration for you. But most wonderful of all was his saying how marvellous it was to see that you were so obviously my best friend.

I seem to be putting as many superlatives in this letter as he does in his speech. Never mind. He thought I was well balanced, vulnerable and incapable of being cruel. He insisted that if I had talent as a writer I would be absorbed, fascinated, never bored, always busy for the rest of my life.

I told him I hated looking at people from the point of view of a craftsman, the writer, unattached and incorrigibly aware of how I would deal with so and so in prose. He told me not to worry. He closed his eyes, wrinkled up his nose in a puglike grin, eyes pressed watery tight and said, oh my dear boy, if you can write ... you will be violently happy, desperately unhappy, constantly, all your life. And love it.

He said that if Willy Maugham had been nicer he would have been great. But he lacked compassion, was so cynical. I said what about *Of Human Bondage* – that was compassion all right. He said the compassion was there for the wrong reason – self-pity.

We talked of plays. Osborne's, Wesker's, and of his dis-attachment from them. He seemed to have far more awareness of the stories within them – how stale, or bad, or good etc. He has seen so much.

I told him of my affair with Yu Ling, how it had started when she was hurt and fed up with her boyfriend, how happy we had been those few months together in England, and what loving letters she had been writing, even now, after she had gone back to the same boyfriend feeling refreshed and ready for love again. He described to me what a beautiful story that could make.

I had sent him my rewrite of the first few chapters of my book. He had a number of technical points on grammar. Never use the word 'very' unless it is *very* useful. He said that for the purpose of my own survival my journey to South-East Asia was the best possible thing to have done, striking out on my own. 'How silly of Larry not to see the importance of that. Without it you would have felt in his shadow, and now you don't. How wise of Jill.' He thought my writing tended to be too serious.

He wrote in his diary:

Monday 8 January 1962
It has been a lovely holiday and we've painted and lounged – the snow was only really good on one day – and done crossword puzzles and made some very good jokes. Altogether one of the nicest Christmases I have known for years. Yesterday Kit [the American actress Catherine Cornell] and Nancy Hamilton drove over for lunch with Brian and Eleanor Ahern. Tarquin, my godson, was here so we were quite a crowd. Kit was wonderfully good, sad underneath but gay on top. [Her husband Guthrie McClintock had recently died.]

Tarquin is really a bright and sweet boy. Jill rather surprisingly, I think, has been a wonderful mother to him and he quite genuinely adores her. Larry as a father figure has not come off quite so well. Tarquin is vulnerable and, I think, fairly tough. He recently spent twenty-one months in Indonesia living, in acute discomfort, with the natives and working out theories about how the West can ultimately understand the East. Personally I think this unlikely, but in any case he seems to be very dedicated and has written a book on the subject, which he is now rewriting, as well as working nine hours a day doing a news broadcast service in Bern. I do *hope* that he has a genuine talent for writing and that his book is good.

After the winter of wonderful skiing the hills burst into spring and beckoned for picnics. I met a Swiss actress, Linda Geiser, who had the looks of Greta Garbo. She did not ski. Her profession forbad it lest she hurt herself. She was wonderfully well read and made me feel so alive. Desirable, but I felt beyond my reach. Her English was slightly accented, her High German perfect but she said she was frustrated by the lack of variety available for acting in that language. She had decided to change to the English language, and managed to get a small part in Sidney Lumet's film *The Stockbroker*, with Rod Steiger. As a stage actress she still toured in German productions in Zurich or Germany.

Later that summer I met an Austro-Hungarian, Alice, who had been married to an Indian and divorced; a strong healthy girl with eyes as blue as the temple tops of Isfahan, and very fair hair. She lived in Geneva. We sailed on the lake, picnicked on the Mount Salève, and the following winter went skiing everywhere for the weekend.

In October 1962 came the Cuba Crisis. The News Department now had one more writer. The crisis was so overwhelming that we thought it was not good enough for our United States evening transmission merely to be a repeat of our European transmission which went out at 7.30 p.m. our time. The four of us took it in turns to get up at midnight and make our way to the newsroom to bring the lead story up to date. When it was my turn I could hear the alarm bells of the telex machines smashing out at every hit of their typing heads. Inside the office there were yards of paper all over the floor. I tore them off, stuffed them away and replenished the feeds with new rolls of paper so that they would not run out when most needed. Bang bang bang, ding ding ding on all sides, panic in English, French and German. Facts, alleged facts, interpretation, contradictions, emergencies, everything flying around. I wondered how much contradictory information, from every source in the world, was getting through to the White House and the Kremlin where ultimate responsibility lay.

Then at about 1 a.m. there was a despatch on UPI in English: an unconfirmed report that the Soviet destroyers, carrying nuclear warheads for the missiles they had installed in Cuba, had stopped five hundred miles from the coast. Those Soviet missiles, if launched from so close to Washington would make a devastating hit before any defensive missiles could intercept them. At first President Kennedy had warned Khrushchev that if his destroyers did not stop at least a thousand miles from Cuba, then the United States would unleash nuclear Armageddon on the Soviet Union itself, believing that any riposte from that huge distance would be *almost* contained by its own anti-ballistic missile missiles. One did wonder, in those days of nuclear confrontation, while the whole world waited in horror, whether anyone was working on an *anti*-anti-ballistic missile missile.

In a rare instance of British diplomacy having a great effect on the Administration, we learned later that our Ambassador, David Ormsby-Gore, a close friend of Kennedy, advised the President to reduce the flash zone, from one thousand to five hundred miles from Havana. The logic behind this was that it would give the Soviets slightly more than a day of further thinking time, without altering the strategic position. The world knew none of this. So for a full twenty-four hours, from the moment the destroyers breached the one-thousand-mile perimeter, Armageddon was awaited globally. Never has the entirety of mankind been held in such agonising abeyance.

Reading the unconfirmed report from UPI, all alone in that chaotic room, that the Soviet destroyers had stopped, before the world knew, was astounding. The story was immediately denied by Agence France-Presse, in French. I could sense their fury at being scooped, but it was only to be expected that America would scoop whatever the news was in its own back yard. So I lead the updated story for the 3 a.m. newscast with the unconfirmed reports – now several of them. It meant that Khrushchev had blinked. Ken Henderson arrived just in time to take my updated bulletin, go down to the sound studio and read it live in English for the United States and Canada. Next day the newspapers had the story and the world could breathe again.

I went home for a week's holiday in London that summer. I had met Joan Plowright, a new Lady O., for dinner with Larry at Overton's, St James's, the year before. Very awkward it was. Later I saw her in their new Brighton home, happy and delighted, and the funniest raconteur. Her pauses and grunts, her amazing eyes and her timing were as brilliant as Frankie Howerd's.

My Swiss actress friend Linda joined me in Queen's Grove. On the way to Chichester we had lunch with Vivien and Jack Merivale at Tickerage Mill. It was especially lively because John Gielgud joined us. He held forth at a speed even greater than Noël Coward's, tearing into every topic with erudition and tactlessness. If political correctness had yet existed he would have sheared his way through it. He was often unintentionally funny, as when, at the end of an accelerating tirade against certain young actors, the only words we could understand were his last ones ' … and speak so badly'. So we all said: '*What?*' and burst out laughing.

We drove on to Chichester to see the opening play directed by Larry: *The Chances*, a lightweight and highly physical romp with Joan, Keith Michell, John Neville and others. Chichester's octagonal splendour stood in a sloping grass field. There was a festive air outside as everyone wandered round in the evening sunshine, drinks and cigarettes in hand, mutual recognition on all sides. Frequently I introduced Linda to theatre people, all very much taken by her intelligence and beauty, more like Greta Garbo by the minute.

A recorded announcement amplified Larry's voice at his most ingratiating, saying that the play would commence (awful word) in five minutes and ladies and gentlemen were invited to take their seats. Then followed the most mellifluous orchestral music by Handel. We almost danced into the stalls to see the theatre-in-the-round, no proscenium arch, the stage surrounded on three sides by the stalls, and above it and all around was a gallery with balustrades.

Linda was most impressed by the English actors' light comedy techniques, and especially the way the young actors moved, their physicality. We adored Joan in the sauciest role of a lifetime, funny, sexy, enticing and one would never have guessed she had given birth to Richard so recently. Larry and Joan had us for dinner at a nearby restaurant. The atmosphere between them was delirious, fun, fulfilled, and with an almost youthful innocence in their stolen glances. This was different from Vivien who always looked up to him, which he adored. Joan looked at him as an equal, from another generation, yes, and from another tribe but he had fallen in love with the change. I think that was the start of the happiest few years of his life. His marital and paternal status was more legitimate than ever before.

The reviews for *The Chances* were disappointing, for the second play *The Broken Heart* even worse. He said that the last offering, *Uncle Vanya*, would also be slaughtered by the critics; but knew in his heart of hearts that it would be great.

Linda and I drove home to Queen's Grove. Next day I took her to Henley Royal Regatta. Quite by chance her cotton dress was perfectly chosen. It was criss-cross-patterned in black, grey and white squares like the colours of the Christ Church Boat Club. I was wearing the tie. We went to the Stewards Enclosure with appropriate entry medals flapping about and joined Gladys Cooper for lunch at Barn Elms, now Dame Gladys, halfway down the regatta course. Linda marvelled at some of the hats. 'Where,' she asked, 'where in Switzerland can you wear hats like that?'

That night, after bathing and changing, I took her to see *The School for Scandal,* cast with Daniel Massey and his sister Anna, lifelong friends. The play was a wonderful production and we went round afterwards to see Anna in her dressing room. Linda tried too hard, as usual, and said that Gielgud had been right about something, a silly name drop. We returned to Switzerland our separate ways.

Later that month I sent my rewritten draft to Noëlie and went to spend the weekend with him. The actors Alfred Lunt and Lynn Fontanne were there, George and Bethina Saunders, Catherine Cornell and Nancy Hamilton her stout friend. The one I liked the best was Bethina, married to such a hard-faced and imposing George Saunders, so frustrated with not being as important in real life as the roles he played that he cheated. He had milked government funds for non-existent entrepreneurial farms and narrowly escaped prosecution. She adored his sense of humour, which must have taken some doing. She told me that one day she went home from the doctor in tears, and told George she had advanced cancer in both breasts. She was going to have to have them both cut off. She buried her head in his chest, clutched him and shuddered with horrified tears. His response somehow made her laugh. 'Who wants them?'

Breakfast with the Master next day was worrying. He had been examined in hospital for his arteries. The one going into his right leg had a blockage and was shrunken. He might have to have it chopped up and replaced by a plastic tube. He was on the wagon and taking medicine to see if he could get away without an operation. Yet he was highly cheerful and the night before, wagon or no, was far and away the most brilliant of that shining company. Well ... he had read my book and considered it much improved, *very* much improved. Then he, the Master of the English language in all its variety and vicissitudes, his vocabulary of unparalleled riches, paid me the most memorable compliment, the one that means more to me than any I have ever received. He said I was a 'persistent little fucker'.

Malcolm MacDonald was a constant visitor to Geneva, as Chairman of the United Kingdom Delegation for the International Conference on

Laos. He introduced me to organisations based in Geneva with an input to developing countries. I was well received, even by David Morse, the Secretary General of the International Labour Office, but kindly advised that, whatever my exposure to the developing world, there was nowhere for me without a technical qualification. I had been following up this and other leads over a number of weeks, all with the same result. Malcolm said that the head of Britain's Technical Co-operation Department, which was a sort of overseas development ministry, had said the same, even with Malcolm's recommendation. An Olivier, the actor's son, the man had said, Eton, Coldstream, Christ Church – too high falutin' for us.

Meanwhile I had a letter from Peter Watt saying that Hodder and Stoughton had turned down my book. He would now try Hutchinson. I suggested my old friend the publisher Jamie Hamilton, who had expressed an interest. Jamie wrote a long hand-written letter to me saying a lame 'no', for no particular reason, save that friendship should not influence professional decisions and that his wife Yvonne was so angry with him she was threatening divorce. Then Hutchinson said 'no'.

I left the Swiss Shortwave Service with a sense of utter and absolute failure; nineteen months of travel, all those people for whom the book was intended to be a worthy acknowledgement with heartfelt thanks in so many directions, followed by two years of writing and rewriting – it was too much. Taking my leave from Alice was complicated, but she had to accept that I was nowhere near thinking of marriage. It was hard to say goodbye to her.

My mother sensed how miserable I was and drove from London to Bern in her Jaguar so we could have a holiday together, touring in France. After three rejections from publishers there was not much encouragement she could give. We drove through Annecy, Cahors with its amazing medieval bridge, St Emilion, Chenonceau and Blois. She was wonderful company.

Through various networks in London I met the head of the Overseas Development Institute, a larger than life, bombastic and bright man called William Clark. He had been Anthony Eden's press secretary during the Suez crisis and resigned over Eden's failure to set up a Ministry of Information in time of war. His Institute was set up in Macmillan's premiership as a sop to Tory consciences over developing countries. Its secretariat arranged countrywide lectures, put together a superb library of treatises and relevant books, provided a meeting place for experts, and recruited postgraduates to assist the Civil Service in newly independent administrations.

At our meeting he invited me to his mill house cottage in Cuxham, Buckinghamshire, with him and his friend David Harvey who was with the Wool Board. They both became lifelong friends. There he referred to our meeting in London as having started off uptight, and ending even upper and tighter. William was charged with self-mockery.

'Oh God, why am I such a failure? I wonder if what I'm doing is wholly wise. Now he, yes I sent him to run the government of Uganda. I mean Ghana. No, Malawi.' And when a close enough friend accused him of name-dropping he replied: 'Funny you should mention that. The Queen Mother said the same thing only last week.'

He introduced me to Sir Jock Campbell, later to become Baron Campbell of Eskan. He was chairman of Booker Brothers McConnell, which owned and managed almost all the sugar estates in what was then British Guiana: BG, now Guyana. They ran practically everything else as well. He was a vigorous, bright-eyed heavyweight, an Old Etonian scholar, so I had no problem on that score, and he wanted someone to manage the expansion of the cane fields so that Guyanese workers would own their own land and manage it. The estates had long since paid for their birth, provided health, schools, shops, playing-fields, cinemas and at the end of it all they put each worker into a box and buried him. The country was sometimes called Booker's Guiana. The workers had little chance of gaining much sense of responsibility. As independent cane farmers they would have to.

The scheme had been tried in Trinidad by another company. Jock wanted me to do a year's postgraduate research there, learn all about it at the University of the West Indies and get a diploma in Tropical Agriculture. He had been impressed with my experience of Asian peasant farmers and considered this relevant. He had no qualms about my personal background and was making a technical qualification available. We talked about books, music, and various theories of economic development. He agreed that too little attention was paid to sociology, too much in abstract mathematical models across widely different cultures. I realised that at last I was on to something which fitted. He said that as a governor of the University he would put in an application on my behalf.

Meanwhile I met many agricultural and development people and institutions. The Chairman of the Agricultural Engineers Association, Air Vice-Marshal Hopps, wanted me to help his three-man secretariat at the Royal Show in the Midlands. This was Britain's premier agricultural event, covering all aspects of food farming and rural life, receiving up to 100,000 visitors over four days. The grounds were huge, several hundred acres, with lines of tents, prize competitions for every kind of livestock, machinery from small lawn edge-cutters to the largest combine harvesters, appropriately called 'Landlord'. There were numerous refreshment tents and, being in England, a regimental band.

A senior delegation came from the Soviet Union: their Minister of Agriculture, and four technicians. No interpreters. So for two whole days, with my under-nourished Russian, I did my best to introduce them. They wanted to see it all. Luckily the main companies like Massey Ferguson, David Brown and Fisons had their own interpreters for Russian and they did good business. One sideshow fascinated the Soviets: battery hens, only slightly automated, otherwise just like the ones in Gladys Cooper's garden twenty years before. They ordered hundreds.

A colleague came over to me from the AEA tent and said my mother was on the telephone. This had to be important because she knew I was being paid to help and time was not my own. I went over and picked up the receiver, worried about her.

'Wonderful news,' she said.

'Tell me.'

'Heinemann have accepted your book.'

I felt blinded. 'Heinemann ...'

'Yes. They want to publish your book. They're the publishers of Somerset Maugham, Graham Greene, our friend Pamela Frankau.'

Just then, outside, the regimental band started to play 'Bali Hai' from *South Pacific*. Followed by 'A Cockeyed Optimist'. Too much.

I told the Soviets my news, that I was now an author. The Minister could not understand what I had done – travelled alone round Asia, written a book without being commissioned, done it all entirely at my own risk. Of course, I said, why should anyone have any confidence before they had a product? It had taken four years of effort, a chance, the way one has to, with capitalism.

He hated the concept. 'Supposing you had failed?'

I so nearly had.

All was set for me to go to Trinidad that September, 1963. Heinemann's had given me an advance and I used this to pay the University fees.

Nine

Georgetown was the capital of what was then British Guiana (since 1970 the independent Guyana). It could hardly be called a city, being entirely built of wood. I stayed with Senator Tasker, an Englishman, and his wife at their grace and favour house called 'Colgrain'. It had a gallery overlooking the wooden cathedral. He gave a drinks party for me 'to meet the troops' as he bracingly put it. They were almost all English, reflecting their senior staff status, in a country that was mostly East Indian with a substantial minority of Afro-Caribbeans and a few Chinese and Lebanese. They suggested I try the local rum, much the best, they said. My first sip was electrifying, unlike any I had ever tasted. It was also the most powerful. I accepted a second glass. Quite different. Bland and too sweet. Then I realised that the first had been diluted with gin instead of water. They assured me that had never happened before. They were intrigued by the job I had been selected to do and said that I was sure to enjoy the University of the West Indies in Trinidad.

I was taken to a number of Guyanese sugar estates and had free-ranging discussions with the general managers, their staff and their workers in both factory and field. It seemed that none of the locals had any basis – be it religion, patriotism or any traditional outlook – to which an outsider like me could appeal. They had been subject to paternalism for so many generations they had been robbed of ambition. Fatalism had shrouded all desire to enter the world of choice. I could not imagine how I would fit in, but knew that a Certificate of Advanced Studies in Tropical Agriculture would in any event stand me in good stead in the Third World.

The UWI in Trinidad was in tropical parkland overlooked by the northern mountain range which reached a height of 2,000 feet. There were wide lawns and fine buildings. My little concrete room was a bit like a cell, with a wash-basin, small bed and plain table with some shelves. It was part of Canada Hall, an aid project of the Toronto government for tropical agriculture. I was with a couple of dozen English BSc graduates in Agriculture from Wye College, Reading.

There were also three Africans, from Nigeria, the Gambia and Cameroon, together with twenty West Indian postgraduates. Engineering students were housed in Milner Hall. There were only those two faculties, the rest of the University being in Jamaica. I had to work hard to catch up on the BSc graduates' technical knowledge, acquired over three years as undergraduates.

Lectures were held in the mornings. Afternoons were devoted to our theses. Mine was 'The Adoption of Innovations among Cane Farmers'. I randomly selected sixty such farmers from a list of several hundred, each with several acres of land. During the harvest campaign they cut their own cane and loaded it on bullock carts, though a few had tractors, and delivered them for weighing and purchase by the factory. Their houses were spread down the East Coast Highway which ran from Port of Spain to the Atlantic coast. It teemed with vertiginous traffic, dominated by 'drop taxis', mainly Ford Zephyrs, which screeched to a halt if they had room for you. The drivers were mainly black, some of them huge. The journey felt like a toboggan race. At full speed, once you had named your destination, they would dictate the fare, take payment with one hand still on the wheel and give back the change. While overtaking they seemed to try to nudge the other car off the road. The taxis were garish, radios blaring calypsos sung by any number of calypso kings – the Mighty Sparrow, Lord Kitchener, the Great Pretender – to the rowdy and harshly beautiful accompaniment of steel bands.

My cane farmers were mainly Indians, living in concrete houses on stilts. The 'under house' with its floor of beaten earth was where everything happened except sleeping. They all spoke good English, were clean and welcoming, delighted to show me their plots of sugar cane and explain their plans. Rural credit was available. Some of them had cows adored as sacred – 'He helping me with his milk, and with pulling me cart. Fine animal.' They had mortgages and bought tractors on hire purchase. They were far more advanced than the workers in BG. The men who attended to their field drainage did infinitely better than those who didn't, but they were few. Most were content just to get by. Cane is a forgiving crop and they always got something, no matter how dilatory the farming. Unlike tobacco.

I grew fond of them. None of this was stimulating but the lecturers did their best. The main agronomist was an intellectual, a Barbadian called Pat Haines. I also admired Peter Rapsey, an independent English farmer who grew watercress and anthuriums. These he flew to London, their stems inserted into balloons, not blown up but merely to hold water, laid like soldiers in shallow cardboard boxes, to arrive next day at Moyses Stevens. We found we had friends in common and he introduced me to a number of others.

At the University before dinner some of the more serious students enjoyed sitting round the table discussing politics and what was happening on the campus and in the world generally. They liked my idea of starting a news bulletin, a few pages in length. I wrote up the ideas we had discussed, and got their approval before I mimeographed it for distribution. It was at such a meeting that I heard about the assassination of President Kennedy.

I was introduced to a pretty Chinese girl called Marjorie, bright, educated and she danced everything from the slow waltz to the most vigorous Trinidadian shakes. She had just got her first job in advertising as an accounts executive. I bought a part share in a beaten up old car and we drove off to the cinema, for picnics all over the island and had a delicious flirtation. She introduced me to Carlisle Chang, the leading creative artist who had met many of the young talents in London. In preparation for the mighty Carnival of Trinidad, the world's second biggest after Rio de Janeiro, he was designing fully researched Kabuki costumes for more than a hundred young men and women. For himself he was making an outfit of a Japanese frog.

Marjorie also introduced me to the poet Derek Walcott. His Mexican beauty of a wife was charming but he seemed consumed by a macho vigour which was difficult to adapt to.

'What the hell are you doing here?' he asked, eyeing Marjorie.

'I came to see you, to meet you, as an admirer of your poetry.'

'I mean here in Trinidad. Someone like you, with your background.'

'Getting a technical qualification for work in developing countries.'

'But you're artistic. Look at you.'

'Many of my forebears worked in developing countries as colonial servants. Two of them were colonial governors, one the Secretary of State for India. Those days are over, but with independence on every side the developmental needs get sharper all the time. I want to help, within a suitable organisation.'

'Why?'

'I feel I owe it. I've travelled all over Central Africa, in villages throughout South-East Asia. It's payback time. I am pleased that the book I wrote is being published.'

I wonder now whether his winning the Nobel Prize years later has made him less angular. His presence then, and his focus, had a dark quality which reminded me of my father, who could totally disconcert a man with the slightest raising of his eyebrows. Larry would lean back as he did so. Walcott was leaning forward. They were both geniuses in their own single artistic field, each of which addressed the whole of physical and spiritual mankind. Their awareness was daunting.

'Why not something in the artistic realm.'

'I have tried. I was a good schoolboy pianist but nowhere near good enough to earn a living. Neither will my writing. I lack the imagination for fiction. I don't want to be an itinerant travel writer all my life. I haven't the intellect to be a critic of any kind.'

'It must be difficult being Laurence Olivier's son.'

'Of course. Luckily he and my mother are divorced and I am an only son. I say luckily because this means that I have been able to know them each separately, on their own individual terms, and without interruption from siblings. By writing constant letters to him and bullying wonderful replies out of him, his affection has become all-embracing.'

'I envy you. I have seen everything of his that I have been able to see. I wonder if you have any idea of the giant scale of his talent.'

'Yes, I have. I love him. He *is* my father.'

He glowered threateningly: 'He's *everybody's* father.'

Like a number of other creative people he struck me as being in a state of permanent transition, on his way some place. He was not thinking for a minute that provincial Trinidad was that place.

Heinemann wrote to say that they were ordering a reprint of my book before publication. It was going well. They sent me the proposed cover, taken from a photograph I had taken in the rice fields of Bali, of Sri and her family making offerings at a small bamboo altar and being blessed by a priest, the blue sky reflected in the water among newly planted sprigs of rice.

I decided to allow myself £100 for a holiday over Christmas and New Year in neighbouring Venezuela, where I knew not a soul. I left on 23 December, glad to miss the festivities which for me, away from family, would only have been a pretence. I took a Dakota plane through the most extraordinary cloud formations to Maturín, dazzling white pillars thousands of feet high, white cliffs, so thick it seemed they could only be held up by the heat of a furnace, multiplying until they became too heavy, turned grey, and cascaded in gusts of rain to the sea.

After jungle, mangrove and a gradual thinning down to bush the far horizon was of deserted yellow plains. Maturín was a hot crispy waffle of square brown houses of mud on dirt roads, so I took a taxi to Caripito. This was quite large, 30,000 people, and all from a bottom drawer of humanity, expressionless faces, starved dogs, children everywhere uncared for. Poverty and over-population. I went to a Russian film but my lingual capacity was stumped and I had to look at the Spanish sub-titles for help. All the women had their hair curled round the cardboard cores of loo paper. Sleep at my cheap hotel was impossible because of the festive season. Jalopies trailed along the streets dragging sheets of corrugated iron behind them. Anything for noise.

I took a taxi to Carúpano, a historic and civilised Spanish town on the coast with a church and bells, a piazza with trees and flowers and a statue of Columbus. The countryside was mountainous, wild and green, the distances huge, ridge after ridge. After lunch there I went on to Cumaná, a beautiful place, the oldest town of the New World, with an ancient castle. My hotel room had empty bookshelves. The manager said it had been occupied by one of their poets. I had never been to a Spanish country before and my schoolboy Spanish came bounding back. I could converse. It was Christmas Eve and I went to midnight mass. The women now had their hair combed out and wavy: Spanish, little Amerindians and a few negresses all in black veils, men in jeans. The Bishop kept sneezing at all the wrong moments.

I went by bus towards Caracas. This was the first time I had ever entered a country from its poorest end. Off the north coast there was the Peninsula de Araya. It started off with hills of green and became drier and drier. The end looked completely dead and the passengers became depressed at the view of it across the sea. I took a ferry and went to have a look. The activity there was salt gathering. About thirty men, parched and torn, lived in some shacks with a wonderfully healthy German sheepdog, more awareness in its eyes than in any of theirs. The scene reminded me of John Steinbeck's *Cannery Row*.

Back on the mainland the bus climbed higher and higher, and the air became colder, below sixty degrees. Occasionally there were wayside cafés of mud, lit with Pepsi Cola signs, fairy lights, an Amerindian hut, a few truck drivers and a couple of drunks perhaps. Then just after sundown we started to descend.

There, suddenly, was a valley splashed with a sea of city lights – Caracas cradled among mountains, with super highways, skyscrapers, six or seven flyovers arching overhead, elegant and oversized, with a blaze of headlights, street lights, advertisements ... fantastic. Having come straight from the sparse bush my feeling was one of amazement that such a multitude of opulent people had got there first and created so much real estate, all built on respect for a 'promise to pay'.

The bus dropped me in the city. I took a taxi to a cheap Italian bed and breakfast. Ten shillings a night, including aspidistras, and everything too small. In the morning I went to the British Embassy Trade Promotion Centre, just on a whim. I asked the woman if she could help me find a Dr Roldán, a banker whom I had shown round the Royal Show in England the previous July. After a few telephone calls she put me in touch with her head of department. He had a thin neck, large ears and nose, deep lines down the sides of his mouth, spectacles and a cigarette. On his desk was a modern telephone with buttons, through the window a view of mountains. He said his job was to put British industries in touch with Venezuelan agents. A contract for tomato ketchup bottle tops could be worth £80,000 for British exports.

He had been the chief tracing officer in Hamburg after the war. He was confident of finding Dr Roldán. He said it was marvellous what you could do with a little patience, aggressiveness and common sense. He once got a top priority telegram from the Foreign Office saying 'Contact Mrs Novgorod.' Nothing else to go on. Mrs Novgorod in the whole of Germany! He had to drop everything. He tried the Russian refugee net, Schleswig-Holstein, hit on an old boy who had heard of her and gave an address in Frankfurt. Told our head of intelligence there to drop everything. He did. Found the old woman. Location confirmed within ten hours. 'If I could find her in the whole of Germany I expect I can find Dr Roldán.'

Well, he couldn't. It then occurred to me that perhaps I had made a mistake and the man was from Colombia, not Venezuela, but I decided to say nothing.

He told me another story, then arranged for me to be taken round the agricultural research centre of Shell the following Monday, car collecting me at 7.30. He introduced me, by phone, to Dr Eduardo Mendoza, the former Minister for Agriculture, and as important in Venezuela as the Fords or Rockefellers in America.

Eduardo Mendoza asked me to meet him for lunch at the 200 Club. He was my height, dapper, the epitome of neatness, and handsome. His eyes were vigorous and bright. He was very impressed with the University of the West Indies' Agricultural Faculty. He said it had always been his dream to go to Oxford for a diploma in Agricultural Economics. We had long chats about community development. He was modest for such a well-known industrial genius, philanthropist and benefactor of the arts. Next day he had me driven to a sugar estate called Santa Teresa which had a highly developed system for cane farmers. He had hoped that all sorts of others would be at lunch with us but nobody came. He said: 'I want you to apologise me.' Actually it was far better talking to him alone. He gave me a number of articles in Spanish and invited me to go back there at 6.30 to meet a gathering of his friends.

I went back an hour before sunset and took in the view of Caracas, the skyscrapers graceful and exciting. He arrived and apologised again because he had made another mistake. It should have been 7.30, so we had another nice talk. He asked me to accept a piece of advice which he offered in good faith: don't devote any time in British Guiana. The country was about to fall apart. One other memorable line, but less serious, was that there were three ways of losing money: horses, women and agriculture. Horses is the fastest way, women the pleasantest, and agriculture the surest. Everybody arrived, backslapping and Venezuelan *abrazzos,* large men, all of them Rotarians. Their Spanish was elegant and spoken at speed from neat mouths. One of them was Señor Allegaz, president of some film company. I was told that there were three presidents: the actual President of Venezuela, the President Elect, and President Allegaz.

Then Eduardo remembered it was his wedding anniversary and for the third time wanted me to apologise him. I had to tell him that I was overwhelmed by what he had done already, whereupon he fixed up for me to spend the evening with Mr Allegaz, who took me to a national fiesta of peasant singing and dancing, 'assisstado por el señor Presidente de la República, Dr Leoni'. There was delicious food, wine and rather too much whisky. Unfortunately there were long and dreary speeches about *problemas.* Two fat generals convoluted with self-importance were standing behind the President Elect as if to ensure his obedience, their lines of medal ribbons like fruit salad. I met the President. My Spanish was good enough to be coherent but bad enough to make him laugh and misinterpret what I meant. The dresses and jewellery were lovely. Soldiers with little machine guns wandered round in the throng as we stood to watch the dancing which everyone said was *'muy typico'.* Ugly girls in dirty dresses and dull drum beats.

Eduardo's driver had told him about the dump where I was staying and it was decided that I should move, and stay with his brother-in-law, a university man, Professor Requena, who had a nice son my age called Álvaro who showed me round Caracas. The racecourse was the largest in the world, the stand eight storeys high. It had an inside air-conditioned paddock for thirty horses, rows of escalators and halls of marble. In the middle was a sunken garden filled with poinsettias, a lake and swans, with a view of mountains towering several thousand feet on the horizon. There were many structures built by their last dictator Perez Jiménez. The Venezuelans were right to be proud of them, in particular the tunnelled road down to the coastal airport, fifteen miles and a drop of some 2,000 feet.

Eduardo had two daughters. Their boyfriends did not please him so he wanted me to be their escort for New Year's Eve at the country club. He kitted me out in his white tie and tails, from Anderson and Sheppard of Savile Row, my own tailor. He gave me two lace handkerchiefs, one for the breast pocket, one for the trousers. We dined at his house, he in black tie. His daughters were debutantes, with bouffant hairdos showing the clean lines of their ears and necks, dark-eyed Spanish beauties in satin Jackie-O gowns and exquisite jewellery.

At two in the morning we left for the Country Club. Their voices were harsh but how they danced, taking it in turns between sitting with friends of all ages. The young men, several of them, were like the chinless wonders of London.

At dawn we took a car to a restaurant where the girls chose a British breakfast. We were famished. It had been a wonderful night and despite the hour their youth kept them excited and fun to be with. I suggested that as it was New Year's Day they, as good Catholics, should attend Mass. They agreed, still in their ballgowns. We went to a church called Las Mercedes and climbed up the steps. They then, both at once, realised that they had no veils on their heads. So I gave them each one of Eduardo's lace handkerchiefs and laid them on their soft hair, like ferns.

A couple of days later Álvaro drove me down to La Paloma Airport on the coast, followed by several cars of well-wishers who wanted to see me off. That had been the most unexpected ten days I had ever had. A week earlier I had not even *seen* any of them. On the plane I suddenly felt exhausted. When I got back to my little cell in Milner Hall it was an hour before dinner. I decided to have a short nap. I got up at 7.30. Everyone wanted to know where I had been that first day of term. Sheepishly I worked out that I had slept the whole night and the whole day through, the full twenty-four hours.

The conspicuous consumption I had so enjoyed in Caracas was at the behest of men who expressed serious concern for the spreading poverty all round the city, the accelerating population growth, the ever-expanding towns all over the country of spiritless people. They had programmes for resettlement, for distribution of the oil wealth from Lake Maracaibo, for creating industries with suitable jobs, for trying to put some heart into the agricultural sector other than the massive estates. The country and its people were still far from being all of a piece. It was a race against time, and within their own remaining years of life the leaders had to witness that poverty and over-population had won. They were overthrown by a movement which gave rise to the most corrupt, fatuous and incompetent government in their history: Chavez, Castro's chum.

Trinidad had no such wealth in any hands, but for a country of its diminutive size it did have a remarkable spread of interests and the greatest of these was Carnival. It is impossible to describe, the phantasmagorical costumed parades, the jumping up in the streets of Port of Spain for days and nights. Everybody joyful, now exported to London's Notting Hill as well.

I had interviewed thirty cane farmers. The head of their trade association, Norman Girwa, invited me to one of their meetings. Three hundred of them came, mainly East Indians, more excitable than the Afro-Trinidadians. Norman often had to rein them back, or try to, and when he failed it was always a black man, with a rich bass voice, who would stand and with the authority of his manly presence bring the meeting to order after a few gentle words such as: 'What you want say? So hush up. Let another say. Then you say.' And sit down to a murmur of approval. Such qualities were valuable, but when it came to cane farming very few of the blacks were any good. They hated it because they associated it with slavery, made illegal only a century and a half before.

My mother came out for Carnival. She enjoyed it as a spectator while the rest of us jumped up in the streets. Her main purpose was to see what on earth I was up to. I took her to meet one of my farmers and parked at the end of a clutch of typical houses. I asked the whereabouts of Ramcharran Latchman, one of the names on my list. An old man came over and pointed the way. A sexy teenage girl sitting on a gate cried gaily: 'I Lamchallan!'

I replied: 'It's not you I'm looking for!'

The old man nudged me: 'But it's you *she* want!'

We went to the under house and Mrs Ramcharran said her husband would soon be back. She brought some tea. She said she was worried about her mother's arm and took me over to the old lady, who looked up helplessly from her wicker chair. She held out her wrist which was very swollen. I turned it over, looking for an insect bite. I said she really ought to see a doctor. The old lady patted my hand and thanked me. Ramcharran came in covered in soot, holding a machete. He had set fire to his field and was harvesting it quickly, to get his cane to the factory before the juice went off. He bowed and disappeared upstairs for a shower.

My mother lit a cigarette. She said it was the first time she had seen me with such people. She could see how drawn to each other we were but wondered what I could really do for them. Here she put her finger on it. In reality not much. I could observe, make recommendations in a thesis, but I had no authority. They did not want anyone telling them what to do. Cane farming was not a career that gave them much self-respect. They all wanted their children to qualify for something better.

Ramcharran came downstairs, his hair smoothed back, wearing an ironed cotton shirt and trousers. He held a picture calendar which he gave my mother, and joined us for tea.

'Mr Tarquin helping us,' he said.

I was surprised and asked him how.

'You got the sugar factory more interested in us.'

That was true. I had persuaded the manager to have more people working the cane scales at the factory gate so as to reduce waiting time for the cane farmers. No more than that. The manager considered cane farmers as peripheral and tiresome. The estate itself grew almost all its cane requirements.

In January the news from BG was that Bookers had bulldozed 9,000 acres into action for cane farmers. It was recognised that estates were no longer politically desirable and they had to prepare the right sort of people to take over the right-sized chunks of land. They would all be Indians, but with no experience of responsibility. In Trinidad I was fond of them as individuals but deplored their lack of neighbourliness. This was in their culture. A myth illustrates the strength of it: Lord Shiva offered to give a peasant whatever he could possibly want. The peasant asked about the conditions. Lord Shiva said that he would give the neighbour twice as much. The peasant was outraged. How could he possibly accept that. He would rather die. Then, after thinking it over carefully, he begged Lord Shiva to put out one of his eyes, and then both of his neighbour's eyes.

I carried on with my thesis which showed that the cane farmers were quicker over new initiatives than anyone had thought. Then in April I heard from Jock Campbell. He wrote that he could not hold out any prospect for the sort of job he had planned for me. Everything in BG was at sixes and sevens. He finished: 'I do feel personally responsible for having encouraged you to spend this year in Trinidad. And while I hope this will stand you in good stead I would like at least to show our very genuine interest in your career by meeting your travelling expenses to and from Trinidad.'

Just before I left Trinidad my literary agent Peter Watt wrote to say that the American publisher William Morrow were going to publish my book, and that P.A.Norstedt and Soner were translating it for publication in Swedish. Their advances were credited to my account. I flew to New York and stayed in East Fifth Street, the Puerto Rican Quarter, with Linda Geiser, now settled there from Bern with an American girl-friend Denine. Her change of languages was being helped at the Actors' Studio under Walter Berghoff and Kim Stanley.

In July New York was much hotter than Trinidad. She took me to a mad Manhattan party. That was one of the early years of bra-lessness. Some of the dresses were of wool, for the air-conditioned rooms, but knitted with needles the size of broomsticks. The gaps between stitches were an inch across, giving a view of nipples like raisins, not always in alignment. I found myself standing next to a Central American with a sleek Hercule Poirot moustache and hair, polished fingernails, diamond rings and tiny feet. I introduced myself. He said: 'I am my Excellency, the Ambassador from Nicaragua.'

'Your Excellency,' I said, 'what an honour.'

Later I was chatting to an international art dealer and asked how he coped with exchange control in such difficult times: after all some paintings were changing hands for millions. He said he borrowed from the Mafia. I wondered what rate of interest they charged. Five percent, he said. I wondered if I could get in touch with them because that was less than the rates offered by the Halifax Building Society. Oh no, he meant five percent a week.

'Any other disadvantages?'

'Ya. Yer gotta pay them back on time.'

He had just returned from the trip. 'I met this gorgeous doll, tall, fair hair, big blue eyes. So I took him to Paris. We stayed at L'Hotel. Perfect taste. Bathroom with scarlet marble and gold fittings. He loved it.'

I had posted a copy of my book to Faubion Bowers and went to see him. He was thrilled with it. As he opened the door of his flat he said: 'Your bath I have prepare for you', referring to the constant refrain from Fourth Brother in Singapore, especially the first couple of days there when I smelt different from them because of the European food I had been eating. After a few days of Chinese food I smelled the same and got away with only a couple of baths a day. Faubion was completing a two-volume biography of the Russian composer Scriabin. This was to become one of the finest musical biographies ever written. Sadly he and Santha Rama Rau had split up and he no longer saw their son. I took her to lunch in the Museum of Modern Art. She had gained in stature following her successful dramatisation for the stage of E. M. Foster's novel *A Passage to India*. For some reason her and my paths never crossed again. Faubion remained a lifelong friend

The World's Fair was on. I went to the Indonesian Exhibition which had one of the most spectacular pavilions. It even had a full height stone and brick Balinese palace entrance. At reception were Javanese beauties in their national dress. For Americans they were the main attraction. I asked one of them if she knew Didiet Soerjotjorko, the younger of President Sukarno's two secretaries in 1960. The girl said yes and put a phone call through, asking my name, which she repeated. I heard a happy yell from the phone and the girl said; 'Didi, don't shout!'

Didi came down looking lovelier than ever. She showed me every detail of their exhibition and we even watched part of a shadow puppet play because she knew how I had loved them. I invited her out to dinner. She had served in the Indonesian Embassy in Rome and knew of the best Italian restaurant in Manhattan. I asked her to wear her national dress.

I returned to East Fifth Street to bathe and change in the July heat and went to pick her up in a taxi. I could not believe what she was wearing. She was dressed as a Balinese princess, her hair high on her head, woven with leaves of beaten gold leaf, garnet earrings and necklace, and cloth of scarlet and gold wound round her body over a long sleeved *kebaya*, and a *kain* down to her golden Italian high heels. She was excited and happy. In the restaurant the Italian waiters practically fell over themselves to serve us. They could not believe that such an otherworldly vision could speak perfect Italian. When we were finishing our meal two elderly American couples knelt on the floor in front of us, gazed at her and humbly asked the name of her country.

'Indonesia,' she said, which took them back a bit because it had been getting a terrible press, following one of Sukarno's military sorties.

At midnight I took her for a coach and horse ride round Central Park and delivered her home, reminded of everything I had most loved about Indonesia, and puzzling how that wonderful land would ever set itself to rights.

Ten

A year earlier, before going to the West Indies, while discussing possible careers I was advised to meet Mr Prideaux, at the merchant bank Arbuthnot Latham, who was Deputy Chairman of the Commonwealth Development Corporation. He was on the lookout for people like me. A couple of weeks later I went to his City offices, as grim as Victorian mahogany can be. He was courteous, and as a conversation starter we talked about Eton where he had been and his son too, a contemporary of mine. An appointment was made for me to meet CDC's Head of Personnel, Mr Jackman. That organisation sounded superb, offering finance and management in projects of great variety; agriculture of every size and kind, industry, heavy and light, hotels, harbours, railways, airlines, mining and development banks. This was not aid, which I distrusted. This was business, supporting the disciplines of profit and loss, sound balance sheets, with eight years' grace when it came to the fructification needs for certain crops such as palm oil. Unfortunately by the time I met Jackman I had signed up with Jock Campbell.

After the debacle of my aims for cane farming I returned to CDC and they took me on. Start date September. I thanked my lucky stars. Shortly afterwards the Guyanese, who had the best-educated populace in the Commonwealth Caribbean, went bananas and burnt their capital Georgetown to the ground. I felt well out of that. In London I rented an apartment, a tiny single bedroom one at the top of Garrick House, Carrington Street, W1. It was round the corner from CDC Head Office in 33 Hill Street, Mayfair. On my way there I walked up Queen Street, Mayfair, where Heinemann had their offices, with *Eye of the Day* displayed in their window. On my return to Shepherd Market every evening two dear old hookers were smoking their fags, clearly with hearts of gold but little else to offer. Perhaps there were younger ones inside. 'Evenin' love,' they used to say.

Just after publication of *Eye of the Day* I was made a member of the Garrick Club. I was proposed by Hamish Hamilton, the publisher, who had turned down my book and wanted to make up for it, and Beau Hannen the old actor I had first met at Henley Regatta. I was among the few younger members, at the age of 29, and was immediately made to feel welcome. Unlike now, when too many grey professionals have taken over, the place was full of actors, its original purpose, and the atmosphere then was charged with life. My friends enjoyed lunching with me at the peripheral tables. After my recent year in Trinidad a number of them were from the Caribbean. One day an imposing and elderly man stopped me as I was hanging up my hat.

'Now look here,' he said. 'I know your father is a renowned member of this club, but I, and a number of other senior members, would be happier if you didn't introduce so many blackamoors.'

I responded with outrage. 'Sir, I do not know who you are, but I prefer the company of black friends to being accosted by a racist white stranger.'

He trounced off, hurt mainly perhaps at my not knowing who he was: a most eminent judge with sometimes much-criticised authoritarian views, Sir Melford Stevenson. Our confrontation did, however, have a happy ending. Five or six years later I was elected to the General Committee. When it was next replenished Melford joined us. We elected Lord Constantine as an honorary life member. He had been captain of the West Indies cricket team, Jamaica's High Commissioner in London and then the first black peer of the realm. After our meeting Melford came over to me and said: 'Now look here. I think I owe you a drink.'

An old school friend, David Mitchell-Innes, asked me to join him on a sailing trip to Brittany. I asked who else was coming and he said two co-owners, and a couple of girls. I asked could I bring one too. He didn't know I had one. I hadn't. I wondered if there was room. He said yes, why? This was extraordinary. Only in England could anyone ask such a question. I scoured my friends, and friends of friends, with only a couple of weeks to go before weighing anchor.

Joy Pearce, my mother's companion, said her elder son had a friend who was a nun. I harrumphed and she told me not to interrupt. There was a younger sister, eighteen, called Riddelle. Sounded a bit young to me at the age of twenty-eight. I had made no discoveries so far. Joy invited her to dinner. She had been a drama student before being advised to give theatre a miss. She had read my book and warmed to the idea of meeting me at my mother's house. Apparently they had told her exactly what to wear, so I was curious.

The doorbell rang and I opened the door to her. She had the loveliest face, wide blue eyes and eyelashes with a bit too much mascara, a perfect mouth, even teeth and a dimpled smile, her curved forehead swept under a hairpiece with a cascading scarf. Her voice was mellow and a touch conspiratorial. As I followed her into the drawing room I was drawn to her.

Of course I don't remember what we talked about, the four of us. It didn't matter. The beginnings of a slow spell started to enfold me. This was not the heartbeat flash across a crowded restaurant which had happened a dozen years earlier with Jenny, in Grindelwald. Nonetheless those vivid moments leapt up in my recollection, and became a sort of lens I had to look through to see Riddelle, her hand movements, her expressions, unpoised, natural.

Dinner came and went in a flash and afterwards I played the piano. They all sat on the sofa in the music room, under a large Balinese painting I had bought in Ubud. I played restful and romantic pieces. Afterwards we were left alone and we sat at far ends of the sofa. I explained about the yachting trip: three couples, all very sound. She was sure her parents would let her come sailing with me. By that time Mother Nature had taken such charge of my mind that I really thought her resemblance to Jenny was complete. Even then I realised this was an overworked cliché in many romances.

Her parents lived in a sunless flat on the ground floor of Hallam Street, near the BBC. She resembled neither of them. Her mother Patricia was an overweight Catholic Irish woman who went to Mass every day at 6 a.m. Her books were all to do with religion. I wondered what on earth she felt so guilty about. Her saving grace was a throaty chuckle which made her shake like a liquid pillar box. Her husband Pat described himself as a Christian, but her as a bloody Roman. The real irritation was her white Scotty dog, Robert Burns. If you crossed your legs he would growl. Wherever Patricia went to fetch anything she had to pull him, like an anchor being dragged by a ship. Pat had a well-bred sensitive face, complemented with a neatly trimmed Ronald Colman moustache. He was Director of Personnel Services at the British Institute of Management in Marylebone Road. They both smoked, which was a help.

Riddelle and I took an overnight ferry and joined David and the others at St Malo. The trimaran *Highwayman* was practical for cruising. All equipment and sails not actually in use were stowed in the port and starboard hulls, leaving the main hull free for eating and sleeping. She was eighteen feet wide, thirty feet long and the main mast thirty feet high, yawl rigged. Space was found for Riddelle's hat boxes. We set sail. After a not very good dinner I suggested to her that it would be perfectly all right if we shared a bunk so long as we did not get as far as consummation. 'Gosh, I respect you for that,' she said, keen as mustard for whatever else.

I took Riddelle to meet Larry and Joan in Brighton. He was at the front door as we arrived. She rushed out and landed a kiss slap on the mouth and he fell for her at once. Inside we sat in the playroom and Joan brought in Richard, now a splendid four-year-old, and his baby sister Tamsin. Nanny relieved us of them as we went in to lunch. The dining room was Regency at its strictest, made more severe by the Salvador Dali portrait from the film of Larry as Richard III. The style, especially the curtains and swags, were manifestly his taste and Joan looked out of place. They were still happy and in love with their young family. He said that my presence with Riddelle had brought him even greater joy, he was so delighted we had met each other, we seemed so right for each other. Then he apologised for going over the top. We saw him a couple more times in London, between his overburdened business hours and his performance as Othello, which bowled us over.

She came to my tiny flat, called it 'a poppet' and wanted to know when I would ask her to marry her. It was a leap year so that was fair enough. Word spread fast and we were everywhere. Vivien gave a party for us at 56D, Eaton Square. Riddelle was in a long black silk skirt and patterned blue blouse with full sleeves and tight wrists. Her hair had been permed straight back from her forehead and as she saw the beauty of the room she became radiant.

'Darling Tarkey,' Vivien said. 'She's ravishing.'

Riddelle ended up sitting on Noël Coward's knee, arm round his shoulders, questioning him about something or other, which he loved. He described her in his diary as 'a nice intelligent girl and very pretty'.

For the sake of form I tried to organise a meeting of our two sets of parents, any time, any place, but Larry said that as the lead actor *and* the National's Director he had too big a job to take any time off. He did not accept the in-laws' written invitation for drinks, nor did he invite them. Bloody rude. On the phone I tactfully asked him when would it be the least inconvenient time for him to come to our wedding, early January '65, what time, which day? He said 5.30 on the eighth and wanted to know whether I was inviting Vivien. I said of course. He was mightily put out: 'So I suppose you'll be having me sit on the groom's side of the church with my three wives next to me.' He was never at ease with anything approaching Establishment but this was laughable.

'Will Joannie be coming?' I asked.

'No, she's got better taste.'

A week before the wedding Larry telephoned to say he was at Eaton Square with Vivien. She was sitting next to him as he spoke, he said. Did I really want her to come? I said yes, most definitely, and asked to have a word with her. How was I? she asked. I said I was about a hundred miles up. Really, she said, up what? She knew how to break tension and said she would love to come and was so pleased to be asked. Poor Larry, she said, silly boy. Which was perfectly true.

The *Daily Express*'s William Hickey described the wedding:

It was a moment to make a theatrical Knight tremble beneath his make-up. An acute attack of stage fright and on a key line too. Yesterday Sir Laurence Olivier saw his future daughter-in-law, 19 year-old Miss Riddelle Gibson, falter at a crucial stage of her marriage to his 29-year-old son Tarquin.

Standing at Tarquin's side before the altar of St. Mary's Roman Catholic Church, Cadogan Street, Chelsea, she had got as far as saying: "I Riddelle take thee Tarquin to my wedded husband ..."

There was a long pause and the bride was heard to sob out loud. After nearly a minute the priest, Monsignor Patrick Casey, prompted her with the words 'To have and to hold.' And nervous Riddelle, once a drama student at the Guildhall School, haltingly managed to follow him. The bride's voice again broke down at the final words '. . . and thereto I plight thee my troth.' Her face was stained with tears.

But when the couple emerged from the vestry after signing the register young Mr Olivier was wearing a brilliant smile to match his brilliant brocade waistcoat. And as he kissed his bride at the top of the aisle her smile was even broader.

It was a strange time of day for a theatrical family to arrange a wedding. Dusk. Only a couple of hours before curtain-up. And for Sir Laurence it was quite an emotional day altogether. Two of his ex wives were there, though his third wife, the present Lady Olivier, actress Joan Plowright was bathing their two young children at their Brighton home while the flashbulbs exploded.

Sir Laurence arrived at the church in a grey Humber with his first wife and mother of the groom, Jill Esmond. They were married for ten years. His hair was now as silver as hers. They have kept on good terms all these years and he warmly guided her into the church by the arm. Miss Vivien Leigh, his wife for a score of years and stepmother to Tarquin during his youth, came with her actor friend John Merivale. From beneath a brown velvet Garbo hat which almost made her anonymous, she said theatrically: 'Any time is a good time for a wedding.'

The 270 wedding guests represented our finest acting talent but it was difficult to pick out the full cast in their penguin wedding suits.

The bride's mother Mrs Patrick Gibson took an Oscar as the most thespian figure in sight. She wore a black velvet hat decorated with enormous ostrich feathers which waved wildly around her face. 'Doesn't Vivien Leigh look lovely,' she whispered to a friend.

Riddelle and I led the procession out of the church, followed by the bride's mother and my father, then my mother and Pat Gibson. Patricia later told me what then happened. After a series of flash camera bursts and the bright lighting from BBC television news, the chauffeur held open the car door for her and Larry. She stooped and sat down, joined in the back seat by Larry. The door closed and they were alone, being chauffeured slowly away, never having met before going into the vestry. Her stoic self-control was detonated by her fury at Larry's behaviour.

'You have the worst manners I have ever come across. If you were Prime Minister you would have accepted our invitation for drinks, not even supper, knowing how busy you are. Just drinks. And you never invited us.'

Larry patted her hand which she sharply withdrew.

'Now dear,' he started. ...

'Don't you call me "dear". That's the most provincial approach I ever heard. How dare you.'

And she kept this going all the way to the Anglo-Belgian Club in Belgrave Square, so she told me.

As the car came to a halt he tried again. 'I do so hope that one day we can meet again.'

She snapped back: '*That* won't be necessary.'

It took a toll on him. Weeks later a number of friends said they had no idea how much taller I was than my father. However at the reception he did enjoy himself with so many of his dearest friends. Vivien stayed only a short while for my speech, which I loved giving; a captive audience I could actually look at face to face, unlike playing the piano. Never had I done that before and I could see his and everyone else's enjoyment. He was much taken with Yu Ling. He had never before been charmed by a lovely Chinese. In fact the following day he telephoned my mother and asked was it really true that she had been my girlfriend?

When we had changed and were leaving for our honeymoon everyone lined the staircase and balcony. Riddelle was in a smart purple tweed suit and round fur hat. They all looked down at us and sang 'For he's a jolly good fellow'. The car took us all of two hundred yards to the London Hilton.

We had a room service dinner and turned on the nine o'clock news. After an assortment of stories, the threat of a major strike in the steel industry, and more bad news about the Americans in Vietnam, the dulcet voice said: 'Meanwhile in St Mary's Church, Cadogan Street was the marriage of ...' and there we were standing in the doorway of the church, looking absurdly young and happy.

We honeymooned on the Mediterranean coast of Spain.

In London we took a flat in Lancaster Gate. The drawing room was large even if the furniture was an afterthought and the bed became a sofa in the daytime. There was plenty of room for friends to sit around and the front hall worked quite well for dining six people. For my work it was a twenty minutes' walk across Hyde Park to CDC in Hill Street. Riddelle got a temporary job in Queensway; nothing more settled than that because we expected an overseas posting.

In Head Office I was given a small portfolio of investments to monitor, and became representative of the Swaziland Sugar Association for the monthly discussions to do with the Commonwealth Sugar Agreement, which was chaired by Jock Campbell. This was in preparation for negotiations on quotas, prices and future plans. My Controller of Operations said my career would benefit if I qualified as an accountant, an Associate of the Cost and Works Accountants: ACWA. That course of action on my part was as far out of character as I have ever targeted.

At home when we were alone together, between going out and having people in, I realised that we had very little to talk about. She did not enjoy reading. She was put out whenever I picked up a book. 'I don't think you like me tonight, Tarquin,' she would say. 'In fact I don't think you like me at all.' Now that was a joke and we always laughed whenever she said it because she knew how much I loved her. Curiously she never minded my studying accountancy Part One – Bookkeeping, Statistics and so forth.

I wished we had lived together before marrying. But that was not yet done. It should be essential, a requisite. I found myself in a deep quandary and one which I could not discuss. We had only just married. I worried about our future together. Had I made a fatal mistake? How can anyone not enjoy reading? I had never come across that. We had decided to wait before having babies so as to get to know each other better. That was sensible. But even with the attentions of the best gynae-cologist, with our bodily cells pounding for procreation, it was only to be expected that Nature would laugh at us. I remember walking home along the pavement of Lancaster Gate when my eye was attracted to a fallen green leaf from a plane tree. I stood and focused on it. For some reason it assumed a very odd significance. I knew instinctively what had happened. Despite the precautions a baby was assured the following January.

When the news was confirmed we became effusive, ecstatic. So was everyone else. 'I love you too much,' she kept saying. It was quite an awakening.

We stayed a weekend with Larry and Joan at 4, Royal Crescent, Brighton, to which they had now added number 5. Parked outside was the most beautiful royal blue open Rolls-Bentley. The gleaming chrome grille, bumpers and over-riders were aggressively masculine. The skins of the seating were soft, stretched and tanned. It was a hermaphrodite car, created to please all save the envious.

'Yes,' Larry said, 'I was so fed up with that fucking National I felt that if I didn't buy it I'd shoot myself.'

He was very proud of it. With their two children there and heaps of congratulations to us for our own expectations it was an idyllic day beside the sea, windswept under bracing sunshine. Larry looked so happy.

Eleven

Our overseas posting with CDC was to Tanzania, a five-year-old sugar estate and factory: Kilombero Sugar Company, two hundred miles inland from Dar es Salaam. We landed in Nairobi on our way and took a week's leave. We stayed with Malcolm MacDonald, now British High Commissioner after being Governor and handing Kenyan Independence to Jomo Kenyatta. He had moved from Government House into a pleasant Shell Company house for senior executives in the northern Nairobi suburb of Karen. This obvious step downwards gained him everyone's increasing respect for his generosity of spirit. There was a swimming pool and a large garden which he was remodelling with flower beds in curves rather than its martial straight lines.

The first evening Riddelle and I sat opposite each other at one end of the large table with him at the head. He ate nothing. His last meal of the day was tea. Lunch was his only real meal. He would go to bed at a normal time, around eleven, and be at his desk, spruce and clothed by five in the morning, with breakfast at nine. Riddelle was radiant in her early pregnancy, looking her best in a summer dress.

After our breakfast we rented a car and drove out of Nairobi, past the big game park and into the Rift Valley. There were small herds of Thomson gazelles leaping around and on the far horizon there rose Mount Kenya. We had seen it the day before, far below us from the cockpit of the VC10 airliner. We came to the high escarpment above Lake Naivasha, the water shimmering pink at one end with flamingos.

We stayed near the lakeshore with the Hopcrafts. They had a brick and wooden bungalow and a large farm, with nice houses for their workers. They said everything had settled down after the terror of the Kikuyu rebellion a few years before. They had been spared because of their employment policies. Their great hope was President Kenyatta. They had cattle and, thanks to Kenya's height above sea level, temperate crops such as wheat. Enlightened people, in love with the country and admirers of the Kenyans.

We drove off to Nyeri to stay in Treetops Hotel, where Princess Elizabeth and Prince Philip had been when King George VI had died.

There she heard for the first time the words: 'God save our gracious Queen': the start of her lifetime's pilgrimage. A dozen years later the original building had been replaced with a solid two-storey building, above a large pond, which was visited every evening by elephant, wild boar and the occasional lion.

Back in Nairobi, Malcolm explained that he had a formal dinner that night: a British delegation. He sighed conspiratorially: 'Led by the British Officer Commanding the Middle East. Can you imagine the fatuity of such a title? Even *before* Suez. And next to me will be his lady wife. I do hope she reads a bit. I shall have no food myself because I never do for dinner. I shall have to pretend enjoyment. I'll spare you that.'

We dined in our room. There was a knock on the door. It was a footman in a fez with a tiny envelope on a silver salver. The back of the visiting card inside said in Malcolm's hand: 'You lucky things.' I took out one of mine and Riddelle wrote on the back: 'Bottoms up', and sealed it in an envelope. We imagined Malcolm's discreet apology to his lady of honour as he turned to the footman, sat back and opened the message and said: 'No reply, thank you.'

Riddelle and I went to meet CDC's Regional Controller, Peter Wise, responsible for many tens of millions of pounds worth of investments in East Africa. With the bureaucratic love of initials he was known as RC. Unofficially as RC-tarcey. He had a neat head, shaven hair and a lumpish body, not all of a piece, but his mind and deliberately low-pitched voice personified authority. He had served CDC in the East. His wife Norinne was part Afghan. It was she who drove us frighteningly fast to their house on the outskirts of Nairobi, far from the more sought after areas. This was typical of CDC, always with an eye to economy. Its employees were more driven by passion for development than by considerations of pay. The one redeeming feature from my point of view was that when the occasion eventually arose they would pay two-thirds of my children's boarding-school fees. The provision of school fees was for twenty years to be the foremost constraint on anything I did.

Kilombero Sugar Company was in dire straits. It was overlooked by majestic mountains, and between them poured the Kilombero River, source of all irrigation. Floods burst its banks for the first time in history as the big factory was being built and all work was stopped. That river behaved with the same wilfulness as the Zambezi had during the construction of Kariba Dam. After six and a half thousand hectares of cane were planted half of them were smitten with a fell disease which dried them up. World famous cane scientists failed to identify it so they made up the name 'Yellow Wilt'. The diseased canes had to be burnt, ploughed in and the planting process repeated with different cultivars. The shareholders were CDC, the Netherlands Overseas Finance Corporation and the International Finance Corporation, an affiliate of the World Bank. The original Dutch Managing Agency was removed and a general manager appointed instead, a brilliant Dutchman, Mr Wevers. The thirty senior staff were Dutch, except for the chief accountant, a Yorkshireman, and me. The company had no senior representation in the faraway capital, Dar es Salaam, with no telephone link, and only a fluky radio system. At IFC's insistence a new managing agent was appointed, over Mr Wevers's head: Holland Vereinigings Amsterdam – HVA. Its chief executive resided in Dar. This put Wevers in an impossible position.

My job was to be assistant to practically everyone, company secretary, chief accountant, staff personnel manager, all under the heading of administrative assistant to the General Manager. My direct responsibility was the financial administration of the hospital, staff housing, all insurances, the company's enormous stores, the guest house and a myriad odds and ends inevitable in the day-to-day management of a large project. Wevers was a technical genius and under his leadership the company morale was excellent. Once a month he and I attended meetings in Dar. As soon as he was back on the estate everyone sensed his presence. His strong Americanised personality attracted instant and undivided attention. He really did care about the staff. Being so demanding it was lucky for them that he had charm. The Africans nicknamed him Bwana Bonn, after President Nyerere had had a difference with Germany over its aid programme and had said he would not be dictated to by Bonn. This determined man could not bear being overruled by HVA and he left, suddenly. The senior HVA man on the estate took over, decent but uninspiring.

Senior Staff housing was excellent. We had a large garden, a delightful gardener who did all the heavy work, and a cook housekeeper which was a more difficult job to fill. After a couple of failures we found Germanus, an intelligent man, just married. He lived beyond the back of the garden in a little concrete house with a couple of rooms for him and his wife, and one for the gardener. It was only his lack of education that held him back. He taught himself English. There was a school for the Dutch senior staff and an African school which was in my portfolio. I started a monthly newspaper and invited contributions. These came in thick and fast. I had to have them translated for the sake of ensuring propriety. Some of them were interesting and some bizarre, especially the verse. One poet described a pretty girl's breasts as being like coconuts. He said it sounded beautiful in Swahili. The *Kilombero Times* became a sounding board and an education for everyone.

Riddelle settled well into estate life, liked the Dutch and the Africans, the Staff Club, swimming pool and tennis courts. Our best friend was a nearby cane farmer, Major George Pletts, an Englishman with a heavily accented South African wife called Jean, and their teenage son David. She was, as they say in the colonies, a real character. She once said: 'If ma husbind doesn't like ma brists, he can lump them.' They lived ten miles away beside a beautiful mountain stream with hundreds of butterflies.

I started work at 7 in the morning, the same time as all the field staff, had an hour and a half's lunch break at home, then went on until 6. Saturdays, mornings only. It was stressful, especially when the chief store keeper was killed in a car crash and I had to take over the nitty-gritty of that as well. He had left everything in a fearful mess. The relationships between people were interesting but hardly memorable. Getting to know the wives added insights into the employees themselves, how often the women's views of their husbands' responsibilities were wildly different from their men's. It added more dimensions to the way I saw my colleagues.

Our son Tristan was born on 23 January 1966 in the Estate Hospital, just after I had had air-conditioning installed in the senior staff ward. Riddelle opted not to have any painkiller and perform *au naturel*. It was agony even to watch but she said my being there was comforting. She did very well and he was a splendid baby. This fulfilment of nature cloaked our relationship.

For local leave we set off for Nairobi for me to sit the ACWA Part One exam, which I passed, with Part Two six months later. Our Peugeot 404 had big spiral springs for the front wheels and bounded over the roughest roads at sixty m.p.h. As we went north the gentle slopes carried us up to the Masai Steppe: flat lands with tall grasses waving in the cooler air. We drove by several groups of statuesque Masai warriors, scornful of any other way of life, with their spears, earrings, dyed reddish flesh, long loping strides and their herds of cattle.

We stopped the car and went for a stroll to stretch our legs. Tristan was five months old, asleep in his basket on the back seat, all his gear piled round him. There was a muff beside him with some bells inside. Whenever we drove over big bumps the bells tinkled comfortingly. So we left him and wandered, hand in hand and outward bound, the sky streaked with alto-cirrus clouds. The clouds straight ahead of us were different. They were not moving, not even fractionally. Then we understood: we were gazing high up at the snow-clad summit of Mount Kilimanjaro. We both felt we should be kneeling in the presence of greatness, rising 19,000 feet straight up with no foothills, to two-thirds the height of Everest.

From Nairobi we headed west to Keekorok Game Reserve. It was soon after the rains and no other car had yet got through. We were the first. At the camp our cabin had three little birds perched in a line along the roof, singing in a kind of harmony. We hired a Land Rover and guide and saw the usual game. We stopped by a large pride of lions and their cubs. They paid us no attention, bored by harmless Land Rovers. Riddelle breast-fed Tristan, put him over her shoulder and he burped. The lions leapt to their feet, ears spiked, eyes suddenly alert. Had a young buck strayed into their midst?

One evening before sundown the guide stopped and we watched a couple of black rhinos, a young one nearby. He said something was about to happen. It did. The bull mounted the cow. As his erection developed she squirted him with vaginal juices. His penis straightened like an elbow, and eventually the tip like a wrist, growing to the length and thickness of a man's arm. He pushed heftily nearly all the way, with the whole weight of his huge body. A minute or two later it was over and he hopped his front feet back to the ground. Riddelle exclaimed: 'That was wonderful!' and our guide laughed. He said that in thirty years he had only once before seen rhinos mating.

We drove to Ngorongoro Crater Lodge, an old-fashioned wooden hotel overlooking the huge crater of an extinct volcano, miles across and filled with game. Our room was cold but it had a fire blazing away in the grate. Next day we drove down to the eastern Serengeti Plains to see Olduvai Gorge. It was very difficult driving over irregular surfaces of granite. Tristan's bells tinkled all the time. We came to a halt and walked down into the ravine, about 300 feet deep, carrying him into the dried up gorge. There Dr and Mrs Leaky had worked from sunrise to sunset with their brushes, separating tiny chips of bone from fragments of dirt. These were all accumulated and composed into a humanoid skull. They also pieced together the earliest hand capable of holding tools – two million years before – and much else from the 400 pieces they assembled. This was confirmation of mankind's African Genesis.

While standing there with our baby we saw a lioness wandering across the other side. There was no vegetation, just rock and dried up earth. She was desperately thin, her belly as close to her spine as a greyhound's, and not like a lioness's. She did not turn towards us and we were relieved.

After fifteen months, despite the domestic bliss and Riddelle conceiving again, leaving the estate was a relief. CDC set up an office in Dar es Salaam under a Representative for Tanzania, Arthur Lewis, who had been Minister of Finance of Zambia when it was still a colony. He, as Rep T, reported to Peter Wise and I worked as his executive assistant. The timing could not have been worse. The United Kingdom was having problems with Southern Rhodesia, which had made its Unilateral Declaration of Independence under the minority white leader Ian Smith. All talk was about NIBMAR – no independence before majority African rule. Tanzania's President Nyerere broke off diplomatic relations with Britain. The consequence for us was that CDC could not make any new investments in Tanzania. All I could do was study accountancy, keep the office books and portfolio manage our existing investments. Arthur made me alternate director for fourteen companies. I attended their board meetings all over Tanzania, often flying over Kilimanjaro and seeing its two extinct black volcanic craters surrounded by snow. There were strained discussions with fellow ex-patriot businessmen whose companies were being scrutinised with a view to nationalisation. Arthur was bringing in an already approved commitment to invest in three game lodges in the Serengeti. We also had a commitment to Permanent Housing Corporation of Tanzania, overseen by Jack Lyle of the Treasury who was years later to feature significantly in my work.

Our apartment belonged to the British High Commission, which was now the British Interests Section of the Canadian High Commission. There was no room for Germanus and his wife, so they had to find a place in one of the miserable, but new, National Housing Corporation estates. We took them to the sea which they had never seen. They were amazed, and laughed at the Indian women fully clad in saris wading far out towards the reef. Whenever an airplane flew overhead Tristan would point towards it and cry out 'Am! Am!' Germanus could not believe that a plane was big enough to carry us home so we took him to the airport. Really if only such a man with his mature and pleasant personality had been properly schooled he could have gone to university and had a fine career.

That Easter Riddelle amazed me with a surprise present. She had created two straight line drawings in the style of Mondriane, with felt-tipped pen, and had them framed. This cheered us both. During lunch break we collected butterflies and her birth pains started while we were catching them. She gave birth to our daughter Isis. The Ocean Road Hospital had a top gynaecologist and a room for European mums. 'A boy then a girl,' the African nurses said. 'How did you do it?' Riddelle's room was on the ground floor, no air-conditioning, with the doors and windows wide open for ventilation. It was clean but hardly sterile, overrun with chickens which went discreetly outside to lay their eggs.

For Isis's christening lunch our High Commissioner lent us the official silver plates and platters engraved with sovereign status. Twelve of us. All Europeans. It was the only time ever that I failed to make friends with the locals. Me, of all people. We invited them and they never showed up, some excuse about not being hungry. They never invited us. CDC did not matter to them because we had nothing further to offer during the embargo on investment and Nyerere's absurdity in breaking off diplomatic relations. We were not wanted.

As a breath of fresh air William Clark came for a few days for his Overseas Development Institute. He found my boss Arthur Lewis most enlightening. These two very different characters were at one in their developmental views: Arthur, with his CBE and membership of the Commonwealth Parliamentary Association, was a pallid little man of great knowledge who looked like a church mouse. William in contrast was booming with over-confidence, exposition after exposition, often mocked, but influential in high places. One morning he and I took baby Tristan into the sea and sat down in the shallows. A fish settled a couple of feet from our knees, It had a brown sausage-shaped patch towards its tail. 'Oh dear,' said William. 'What *has* happened to breakfast? How one *can* tell what time of day it is.'

Tristan's baby laughter added to ours.

'Oh, isn't it a lovely day,' said William. 'Oh, good old God.'

His Institute had appointed three young men to assist in various Tanzanian ministries. 'I wonder', he said, 'what they are doing and if it's wholly wise. Well, that's what I came to see.'

Then we heard of the unexpected death of Vivien. Larry had always insisted she have her incipient TB attended to. With Jack Merivale this had been overlooked and it killed her. Hers was a rare version of that disease which had been on the sidelines of her health for so long. Her manic depression was now under control thanks to the development of new drugs. The way was set for her to have a healthy old age with a quality of life she enjoyed. Her dying like that was shattering.

Before we left I opened a bank passbook for Germanus with three extra months' pay. '*Mingi* money,' he said. And we gave him the baby clothes Tristan and Isis had grown out of. Six months after we had returned to London he sent a photograph of himself and his wife, and their baby boy wearing the floppy blue hat Riddelle had made for Tristan, whom he had called Bwana Simba: Mr Lion.

The end of my first tour of duty was like leaving a limbo, so little achieved, save for the birth of our family. However, ten years later, after Kilombero had been taken over but still not paid for by the government, the IMF made a study. The company, still managed by HVA, was in profit. National consumption of sugar had doubled. IMF finance more than doubled the company's size. The Kilombero River was dammed up in the mountains, creating a lake to guarantee year-round irrigation and prevent any repetition of flooding. In retrospect at least there is the satisfaction of knowing we had played a part in keeping it going during its worst time, and that it had all led to success.

We stayed for a week in CDC's leave house in Hill Street Mews in London W1 and gave a party for friends. I was set on buying a house, determined never again to pay rent. Robin Mills said his brother Nicholas, my old room-mate at Christ Church, had a house on the market: 31 Queensdale Road, Holland Park, W11. It took six weeks to raise a mortgage and complete: a three-storeyed house in a terrace with a small south-facing garden. The neighbours were Robin Mills, Rudolph Agnew who became head of Consolidated Gold Fields, a BBC features writer, the deputy editor of *Punch*, and Peter Yates the film director. I paid £14,500 with £5,000 help from my mother. She called it a beastly little artisan's house. I referred to it as 'our little dump'. We were both wrong. It's now worth more than a hundred times as much.

CDC's Head Office at 33 Hill Street, Mayfair; was made up of three Victorian terraced houses thrown together with misaligned corridors. The entrance had a uniformed commissionaire and the front-of-house rooms were high-ceilinged and made into stylish offices with velvet curtains. The other offices with linoleum floors were drab. My boss was Peter Meinertzhagen. He had been a Regional Controller and now had the grey-sounding title of Co-ordinator of Operations: Deputy General Manager by any other name. For eighteen months I reported to him as

Acting Secretary of the Estimates Committee. 'Acting' because I was not qualified as an accountant. I had only passed ACWA Parts One and Two. I had to summarise the quarterly reports produced by all the CDC regional offices. More than one hundred companies. Where our investment was only in debentures that was a brief exercise. Where we had shareholdings, management responsibility or wholly-owned direct projects I had to produce summary cash flows, highlight the weaknesses and suggest solutions to key points, all derived from the multifarious reports submitted by the regional offices.

The CDC General Manager was William Rendell, known and even addressed as GM. He had been Controller of Finance during the era of Lord Reith who had rescued CDC from financial ruin caused by unwise investments and lack of sound procedures. It was now extremely sound. He had iron-grey hair, thick brows and deep eyes, a *retroussé* nose, his mouth pursed but with generous full lips. He took in everything he saw as if seeking things out, as if looking for burglar alarms. If he rang any internal telephone the recipient received a definitive ring tone and the response was an automatic: 'Hello, GM.' His Executive Management Board sounded rather like the cabinet of President Lincoln. When eleven votes were cast against a motion, Lincoln raised his hand, the only one to do so, and said: 'The ayes have it.'

I liked Peter Meinertzhagen. He agreed that if we had been working together in the colonies we would be inviting each other home for dinner. He accepted our invitation. He arrived in a suit and his wife in a way-out lace top with flowing white sleeves. 'Hi,' she said, 'I'm Dido.' 'Hi, I'm Riddelle.' She was lovely. We had a fine time and they invited us back.

The other leading lights were the Head of Engineering and the Agricultural Adviser, both lively and experienced, their departments supporting plantations and industries all over the Commonwealth Caribbean, Africa and South-East Asia. The Controller of Finance, like them, was also enlightened and well-read. However it seemed that any indication of excitement was discouraged. They were referred to as H. Eng, Agr. A and C. Fin. In fact outsiders on being introduced called him 'Mr Fin'. Head Office (always called HO) had three expert solicitors. Mostly it was staffed by operations controllers and their dogsbody accountants: my constant associates. Few of them were comfortable in their own skin. Over lunch they were solemn. It was not appropriate to raise a laugh or be controversial. Enthusiasm was frowned upon. Where I would have liked to say a project was amazing, they would say it was not uninteresting. They loved the use of double negatives. Not inappropriately. They lacked freedom of spirit. With my constant crunching of numbers I felt my breadth of vision, which had narrowed in Dar while keeping the books, narrowed even further; but the strength and effectiveness of CDC was a constant inspiration. The looseness of overseas aid as a concept had never attracted me, with all the opportunities for corruption in the recipients' hands. CDC imposed balance sheet disciplines with all the commercial disciplines of finance and management.

The journey to work was pleasant enough, from Holland Park tube station to Marble Arch, then a quick walk down Park Lane, turning left at the Dorchester Hotel into Hill Street. Riddelle's father gave us a big dining table and eight chairs which the British Institute of Management was throwing out. My mother gave us some red velvet curtains saved from Apple Porch. I bought a large Princess Bokhara carpet (more likely Princess Manchester) and our dining room looked baronial. Riddelle did everything well. It was a pleasure to sit at the head of table for our dinner parties which were all successful save for two. We had invited a Scottish friend I had known since California days, who had married a black Jamaican. His parents disowned both of them. She was beautiful and intelligent, and was assistant to the head of the Commonwealth Secretariat. She knew how the world wagged and the workings of the City. Our male guests were fascinated by her conversation and also her cleavage, modest, but her black flesh interested them. Their wives were also in evening dress but their minds were drab, and the world of business was not theirs, nor was the City. They sulked.

The other disaster was when we had the writer and actor Emlyn Williams, a famous wit, and at the same time the journalist, night club owner and MP, a personality who did voice-overs for bloodhounds advertising dog food: Clement Freud. There were other actors there as well but the antagonism of those two, both renowned raconteurs, shut us all into icy courtesy.

This was before pampers saved civilisation. Nappies governed the day. I helped when at home. The square yard of soft cloth you folded into a kite shape, then placed the baby in the middle of it on your knees, and fastened the three ends together with a huge safety pin, avoiding the wriggling flesh. Every evening we filled, used and emptied the washing machine and hung the damn things the length of the bathroom. We shared the cleaning and other chores. Most evenings I was carpentering. Bookcases, shelves, clothes cupboards full length or smaller, radiator covers, her dressing table, covered with a mirrored surface, food racks, a garden table, and a great deal of painting. Luckily Nicholas and Sue Mills had installed curtains in the drawing room and bedrooms and they were fine.

Everyone thought we were fortunate with our lovely house and family, but Riddelle was restless. She did not like me giving the babies their baths and wanted to do everything herself, turning her back on me in many ways. Mother Nature's balm had disappeared. Isis was no longer in babydom. I went to ask Larry's advice. That was between acts when he was playing a French butler in the Feydeau farce *A Flea in Her Ear*. His costume was extraordinary, a square cut striped waistcoat, high collar and foulard, his face made up with hard lines to contrast the comedy of his role. I was stunned by his incongruous looks during our intimate conversation. He smoked his cigarette as if everything were normal, in that get up. He wondered if it would help if I pretended to have an affair. Perhaps a better compromise would be for her to take the children to stay with friends, to be joined by me later. The following year we tried that.

Twelve

In the summer of 1968 I was asked to do a feasibility study in Cyprus on behalf of Hallway Hotels, one of CDC's subsidiaries. Its chief executive was a colourful character called Eric Hall. He had set up and managed a hotel in Zambia which was the first to accommodate whites and blacks on equal terms. This had attracted CDC. He said he thought I would thrive in his hotel business, so I accompanied one of his accountants to Nicosia.

Archbishop Makarios was President, always in Greek Orthodox robes. There was a truce between the Greek and Turkish Cypriots after years of war had divided them. From my bedroom window in the Ledra Palace Hotel I could see the Turkish Star and Crescent flying above sandbags and barbed wire. The Old City of Nicosia was mainly Turkish and so was the north, plus the wired off Turkish enclaves along the south coast. All the rest was under Greek Cypriots.

The accountant took me to the Treasury and introduced me to Mr Solomides, the relevant authority for hotel development. The most interesting introduction was to an elderly English architect of repute, married to a twenty-year-old with a tiny baby. The accountant left me with them.

The architect's first chosen site was a very poor area on a hill overlooking Nicosia. This was ideal. The land was cheap, the householders dying to sell up and enjoy the cash. He was arrogant and theatrical with windswept golden hair and a big gold signet ring. I followed his Bentley in my hired car. He took me to Akrotiri, a valley overlooking the sea, with dried up little rivers and smooth pebbles of every colour, as if waiting to be broken up and placed into mosaics. This, his preferred site, was idyllic. It was also in the middle of the British Sovereign Base Area with a sign warning that when the red flag was up the land was being used as a firing range. I ruled that site right out. We went up Mount Troodos and sat under a vine trellis in one of the villages to have lunch. Then he left me on my own.

I decided to drive all round the island. The first thing which struck me was how the beaches were cordoned off for the exclusive use of the

Greek Cypriots. The Turks were forbidden. In fact their enclosures had security gates and watchmen. I asked several of them, at a number of such enclosures, what on earth was happening, what were they thinking of doing. They all said 'Nothing', their eyes helpless and hopeless. Their fields were overgrazed, the hens wretchedly thin.

I drove round to Paphos where St Paul had stayed two millennia before on his way to be tried in Rome, his right as a Roman citizen. It was ideal for a sizeable tourist hotel by the beach. Then on to the western end there was a promontory called Vouni. Spread over the top of it were the remains of a Roman castle which had been occupied by Othello and Desdemona. I could imagine Larry and Vivien in the roles (if only she had been) – I could hear their voices, her preference for the south-west side with its vistas of little bays far below, while he would have preferred the view with the slopes of Troodos sweeping down into the great valley, leading north-east all the way across to the Pentedactylos range above Kyrenia: the land he ruled, the Mediterranean beyond.

The tops of the Troodos range were grown with a forest of conifers, redolent of Big Bear in California. That timber could have made splendid log cabins, with swimming pools for summer and the ski slopes for winter. On the north coast Kyrenia, with its fishing harbour overlooked by little restaurants, was crying out for development, sparingly done. I wrote up my ideas while still in Cyprus, my room overlooked by the Turkish Cypriot flag and sandbags. Being there was a constant reminder of the Greek passion for *Enosis,* union with Greece, and the Turkish rejection. I recommended a long delay before considering any investment.

At Nicosia airport I carried bulky rolls of maps and plans. I bumped into my godfather Ralph Richardson, his trilby at a high angle.

'Mah dear chap,' he cried, 'how splendid you are. Are all those scrolls scientific? Are they geographical? Are you planning an invasion?'

He had heard that Cyprus had beautiful villages and beaches and wondered about buying a place. 'Very pretty,' he said, 'but far away and I don't think I would really like to live here.'

He travelled first class and I was at the back of the plane. At Heathrow, in the cold of England, Ralph had flung a tweed cape round his shoulders. While waiting at the luggage carousel he made a riposte which only he could have delivered. We were chatting when a man minced towards him, wearing a suit of a fabric which could have been designed for Odeon cinema seats, and a bookie's peaked cap.

'Excuse me,' he said perkily, 'are you Sir Ralph Richardson by any chunce?'

Ralph drew himself up and looked down at him, his head slightly shaking as it always did.

'Yaas,' he said. 'By chance ... I am.'

The man vanished.

Peter Meinertzhagen and Eric Hall agreed with my recommendation to leave Cyprus well alone. I dived back into being Acting Secretary of the Estimates Committee, now familiar in numeric terms with the foibles of many kinds of business. It did seem as if the original estimates themselves could be done more efficiently. I did some research into computers. Early days at the time. I worked at it over a number of weeks and Peter Meinertzhagen saw that many hours could be saved but HO accountants hated the concept. A decade later, of course, you could hardly move for all the computers everywhere.

Riddelle took the children to stay with friends of hers in Eire: Kinsale, County Cork. With her, any absence from me always gave rise to the most electrifying welcomes. This was a whole week. Her welcome was rapturous. She couldn't take her eyes off me that first evening but by next day she was back to her moody normal. Her friends were Honour and Paddy. He bred pigs which he sold to the local abattoir. Honour told me Riddelle had kept saying she wanted to be free, she wanted to be free, and she had tried telling her that with two small children she couldn't be. She and Paddy were a delightful Anglo-Irish couple, their house as elegant as they were when out of working clothes; proper country people with the pig farm out of sight over the hill; large white pigs, just like Larry's at Notley.

When out riding I noticed that none of the iron gates opened properly, making you have to dismount. Paddy was more than happy for me to heave each one over to the workshop and spot-weld it with a template to hold the broken hinges together. After a few days we could open every gate from horseback. This gained his confidence and I broached the subject of computerised farm planning. He leapt at the idea. He had been hoping to expand his pig breeding several times over but was unsure how. I put him in contact with Farm Planning and Computer Services and within a few years he had tripled his output. His management accounts had become less of a pain, more of a doddle.

Judy Garland had had a wildly successful season in 1964 at the London Palladium which my mother and I had been to see. She was immensely fat then but it made no difference to the audience. Everyone took her to their hearts, her all-enveloping personality, her legendary status and her matchless voice. We went round to her dressing room afterwards and she was so happy to see us. She said I looked far too young even to think of writing a book.

In 1969 I went to see her with Riddelle when she was singing at The Talk of the Town. This was also a stunning success but she had become so thin her thighs were no bigger round than her knees. Even so the power of her voice was almost too much. In her dressing room after the show she was delighted to meet Riddelle and asked us to come to the British Film Institute on the South Bank where she was having a retrospective of her old movies. That night *A Star Is Born* was being shown. As she went behind the curtain to get ready we chatted with Mickey Deans whom she had just married; a fine-looking thirty-year-old pianist and disc jockey with a pleasant bass voice. There were also two Catholic priests in dog-collars. I could not help thinking that was a bad sign.

Riddelle and I drove over to the South Bank and went into one of the BFI cinemas. A couple of dozen others took their seats as Mickey Deans played some gentle popular songs on the piano until we were all settled down. We sat right behind him and Judy. They were stroking each other rather sweetly and she turned to tell me she really had found the right man. As soon as the lights were dimmed and the film started her concentration on the screen was absolute. She commented on how wonderful all the extras were, so authentic.

At the intermission the lights went up and we all made our way out. Riddelle and I walked along the riverbank, under the globe-shaped street lamps on dolphin stands. It was one in the morning, calm, with London asleep between the golden face of Big Ben shining over the Palace of Westminster and the floodlit dome of St Paul's Cathedral above the City. I commented to Riddelle that I knew what was happening: Judy was viewing her work as a prelude to saying goodbye to her life. Within a fortnight she was dead.

At last we got our overseas posting to Jamaica with me as executive assistant to the Regional Controller, Gordon Firmston-Williams. He was an Old Harrovian, blimpish and with a reputation for not getting on with people, especially his staff. However I was glad to be going back to the tropics where the climate and the life style suited Riddelle. I could rent 31 Queensdale Road, make it self-financing, and repay my overdraft. A further delight was that my great-uncle, Sydney Olivier, had twice been Governor of Jamaica in the early nineteen hundreds and had written two enthusiastic books about it. The Jamaicans had taken to him. There is an Olivier Road around the northern part of Kingston, and the Olivier Shield for inter-schools football. He was one of the founders of the Webbs' Fabians and served in the first Labour government. He became Secretary of State for India and was given a peerage.

I left England six weeks ahead of my family so as to organise housing. My predecessor had been a bachelor and lived in a dump. In London Riddelle got in touch with our rich friends and together with her they had the time of their lives. She turned them into dance fanatics at Annabel's almost every night. It became a way of life. She was as energetic on the dance floor with them as she and I had been when first together. She was free.

For my first week I stayed with Gordon and his wife Joan who had been crippled with polio. She shunted herself round in a wheelchair, drove his Jaguar with élan and was lovely to be with. I could not understand why she had married such a bore. For openers he wanted me to write his three- month report on all the Caribbean projects. As a trained journalist I quickly put together Gordon's three-month report and this got things off to an excellent start.

CDC's rent allowance may have been enough for my predecessor, but not for a family of four. Eventually I plumped for a sizeable house with an acre of garden in Havendale Heights, off Stoney Hill Road, with a small house for a maid, but unfurnished, so I bought beds, a wrought-iron and glass dining table and six chairs. The rest I decided to make myself: the sofa and chairs in the drawing room.

Jock Campbell and William Clark had given me introductions: to Edna Manley, widow of Norman Washington Manley, one of the founders of Jamaican Independence and mother of Michael Manley, Leader of the Opposition; to some of the leading journalists and writers; to the chief Bank of England representative, and others. I decided to keep these new friendships to myself because none of them knew Gordon. He was a recluse.

I drove round the island and stayed with an English-born farming family. They had a seven-foot bath made of wood which Sydney Olivier would have used when he stayed there. A major CDC project was on the north coast: Ocho Rios had four high-rise holiday apartment blocks under construction called Turtle Beach, overlooking a bay of sand reclaimed from the sea, awaiting the construction of a large holiday village with lots of shops which, when complete, would enhance land values ready to be sold lucratively to a Sheraton or Hilton.

Noël Coward lived nearby in a house called 'Firefly', overlooking Puerta Maria and Oracabessa, just down the road from Ian Fleming's house 'Golden Eye', which Noëlie called 'Golden Ears Nose and Throat'. I had lunch with him and his secretary Cole Lesley ('Coley') on a Sunday, after they had been to Mass for fun. After a few strong bull shots they described the locals in their Sunday bests, all with shiny black faces and the little girls with angelic pigtails, the women with dark straw hats with veils. During the liturgy in Latin the priest kept seeming to say 'Oracabessa Puerta Maria, Oracabessa,' and they had had to control their giggles.

Noël said they both loved cooking but in that heat they often stood over the stove with no clothes on, except for an apron. While Noël was attending to a sauce the doorbell rang. It was the vicar. Noël told him it was a crucial moment for the sauce he was stirring, he would only be a minute and turned back to the stove. When he returned, the vicar had gone.

Riddelle arrived exhausted with Tristan and Isis, now aged four and nearly three. They all loved the house and garden, the kitchen was stocked, the beds made, high chairs by the dining table, and I cooked their favourite food: steaks for us and chopped roast chicken for them. The previous occupant had left me with a lovely yellow Labrador called Tammy, the gentlest of creatures. We had never had a dog before and the timing was perfect for the children. We found a nice maid called Celeste.

Every morning on my way to work in downtown Kingston, near the harbour, I dropped Tristan off from my Ford Cortina at Hillel School. Riddelle collected him for lunch in her Ford Prefect, both cars thanks to loans from CDC. She settled down with my new friends far better than she had in London. With Celeste in the house and a gardener she had plenty of time to spend on her pictures. She had moved on to composing sprightly animals of cut out felt, pictures of flower arrangements, all beautifully framed for sale. She started to follow the constructivist school using three-dimensional objects. I brought round the owner of the John Peartree Gallery. He was critical of her constructivist pieces. The rest he liked, their precision and sense of abandon, and wanted to give a showing in his gallery.

At work I was made responsible for CDC's Jamaican portfolio, apart from being Gordon's dogsbody. The Kingston developmental background was considerable. The town was next to the original harbour which had been too shallow for large modern ships. The dockyards and warehousing, the stevedores and violent crime made a widespread mess of the place. CDC financed the Matalon Group to create a huge land reclamation scheme to one side for a large acreage of foreshore reclaimed to accommodate light industry. With the core taken from the seabed the newly deepened water became a modern harbour. There was ample space for warehousing and the rest of it.

There was a shortage of land for low-cost housing needed by the burgeoning population, so further reclamation was made the other side of the bay, with an elegant causeway and bridge across to it. Each prefabricated house was made from pre-cast cement walls, already embedded with electric wiring and plumbing. There was plenty of room between each so that owners could build on patios, more rooms and plant gardens and trees. Within a few years Portmore had become attractive, made possible by CDC's mortgage finance company. Further land was constantly being created, using a dredging barge with a giant revolving drill which sucked up the sea bed with tons of water pumped by pipeline to the land being created, which would then take months to dry out.

My largest project was to be the Kingston Beach Hotel, on Portmore, the jewel in that particular crown, beside a reclaimed beach of white sand and a view down Kingston Bay and across the city to the glorious Blue Mountain. Put like that it sounds irresistible and so everybody thought except for me. That was to be my downfall. Let me explain.

The bay was like a horseshoe with Kingston at the base. Palisadoes Airport was at the far left-hand point. The hotel guests would be driven miles along the isthmus, turning in towards the capital. They would go through the most unattractive part of it, which offices were moving away from, even CDC, in preference for New Kingston which was a few miles inland. The hotel guests would skirt the industrial area and head towards Portmore, along the causeway, over the bridge, and eventually, after nearly an hour, reach the hotel, at the top right-hand end of the horseshoe. This was just under the flight part of aircraft coming in to land. The second shortcoming was that by 11 a.m. every morning there was a rushing wind sweeping in from the sea and across the beach towards an extensive dry area beyond Portmore which became extremely hot and created an updraft, sucking in the gale. It was almost impossible to sit outside because of the sand blowing in your face. A third problem was that the sea water was filthy from all the shipping, which gave the white sand beach no chance. So much for geography. The statistical fact was that there was no room for a further 200-bedroom hotel. There were too many hotels under construction,

The Minister of Tourism's Permanent Secretary paid Gordon a visit and said they were most concerned. He was a big intelligent brown Jamaican like most of my friends. Confronted by Gordon's refusal to do other than think well of his favourite project, the man exclaimed: 'Dat damned ting goin' to be a lemon!' Gordon replied that the investment was already a commitment. That was true, but it could have been cancelled. No wheelbarrows or piling hammers were at work on site. I was still engaged in negotiating the building contract with Cementation but it was obvious that nothing could change his mind. Even the Regional Finance Officer rejected my doubts: 'it would be good for Portmore' became a mantra.

So I had to let the contract to Cementation. I called up the capital for this direct CDC project to be managed by Hallway Hotels, and redid the fifteen-year cash flows on the preposterous assumption of 65% occupancy. Frankipile jack hammers arrived within a couple of months and there started that spectacle which always excites me, the sheer muscle involved in creating foundations at the start of a major construction. A year later the hotel opened and within five months everyone in CDC could see that it was about to go belly up. It did. Bankrupt. A terrible and foreseeable waste of money and very bad 'for Portmore'. By that time I had been sacked for opposing the project. Sacked before being proven right. Not wholly wise.

Gordon grew fond of Riddelle and the children. They had us for lunch. He was sweet with his crippled wife, picking her up in his arms and lowering her into their swimming pool. We sat round after bathing with gins and tonics in our hands, feet in the water. Isis went over to him and pointed to his belly which rested on his thighs. 'Gordon,' she said, rather surprisingly for a 3½-year-old child, 'you've got a tummy like a bosom!'

At home I was busy making furniture. I had the merchant saw the timber into the lengths I wanted so all I had to do was chisel out mortice and tenon joints. The single chairs were ordinary but the sofa pleased us. It was long enough for us to sit at opposite ends and touch our feet together, the arms behind us boomerang-shaped to wrap round our backs, ending with a six-sided surface to put our glasses on. We chose lovely materials for the cushions. In the street I found a large empty spool for carrying cables, six feet in diameter, and rolled it home. One of the gardeners I passed asked: 'Man, you gotta licence for di wheeled traffic?' I used one round surface to make a pouffe covered with a soft mattress and the other for a patio table.

All that was tactile and sensuous between us remained in perfect order, but not the rest. The stress at home was more wearing than at the office. Ever since Isis started going to school the mercies of Mother Nature had lost their fond embrace of Riddelle. Our very different characters were confronted by reality. One morning she passed out while in a dentist's chair. He rang and advised me to take her to hospital. On a return visit there after work I had collected her wedding and engagement rings from home and put them on her finger as she slept. She had had related problems before but this was the worst.

While she was recuperating and I was alone with the children there was a staggering thunderstorm, seeming to blast the rain down in uninterrupted sticks. The flashes of lightning frightened the children. The thunder shook the house, so I invented a game. At each flash we would breathe in and then, as the crash followed, we would shout 'Hurray!!!' Tristan and Isis were instantly thrilled, full of chatter over their dinner when the storm died down, and as good as gold in their bath.

As always, our absence from each other brought us infinitely closer together on Riddelle's return from the hospital. We bought an enormous Jamaican four-poster bed. The house and garden started to look settled and lovely. This was enhanced when Tammy went on heat and tried to satisfy every dog in the neighbourhood. Sometimes she and a mate 'got knotted' and Tristan would say 'I'm fed up. Tammy is bottom to bottom again.' In no time she produced her litter. One of the puppies called Satchmo died early on and the children cried. They told all their friends that Satchmo died, and everything was very sad. We found good homes for the others and kept a yellow and a black one, called Engelbert and Humperdink. Everything got better.

The friendships I had started almost on arrival were maturing and meaningful. The politicians were mostly in the opposition party, the journalists and writers of every point of view. My relationships with all of them had started with a bang at Edna Manley's house. A big man and his big wife, Douglas and Sheila Graham, were trying to work out my family background. I took the time solemnly to explain the grandparents, step-grandparents, half-grandparents, the many and varied parents, and even more lugubriously the generation further down the line of half-brothers and sisters, my stepsister, and summarised by saying my father had really fucked up the family tree. They burst out laughing. After that I was one of them.

An increasing concern in Kingston was the burgeoning crime, especially in the slums of Western Kingston. The gangs had strong political allegiances. If you, a municipal worker, were a supporter of the People's National Movement, the PNM, and the Jamaica Labour Party, the JLP, won the election you were out of a job. This division was sealed in blood. Elections were fought with machetes and terror. There seemed no way towards harmony.

I had an idea. The rich industrialists, financiers and propertied families had marked civic consciousness and charitable dispositions. The main companies were conglomerates, making everything required for building anything. There was a shortage of simple wooden schoolrooms and hospital wards, while in Western Kingston and elsewhere there were men with craft skills such as plumbers, electricians, carpenters and cement layers, unemployed. You could put these together with the right materials. In return for an excellent lunch you could attract the labour to do the work.

We had Michael Manley and his girlfriend Bev to dinner, together with the Grahams. Halfway through the meal I described my idea. If he liked it, as Leader of the Opposition, he could promote it. Everybody expected him to win the next election and this would help. He leapt to his feet, smacked the wall and said it was the best politics he had ever heard. I was delighted with his reaction but said that we had to find a word to identify the idea, a phrase, preferably a Jamaican one in dialect, for the concept to be made attractive for everyone involved, including the providers. He agreed.

I took the family halfway up Blue Mountain to a house built during the reign of Charles II, which belonged to a lovely old pantomime actress Louise Bennett, 'Miss Lou', and her actor husband Eric Coverley. They had a Bechstein grand piano which I played and so did Isis, sort of. I told them my idea. Miss Lou understood it very well and liked it; but I said that to get it accepted there had to be a by-line to sell it. I told her: 'Me want me word.'

I telephoned a week later and she had thought of it.

'Brawta,' she said.

'What di hell is that, Miss Lou?'

'Man, ye go to di market and buy some tings. You then say "gimme brawta" and him give you two more.' So that was it. 'Gimme brawta.'

Michael's advisers told him to wait until he had actually won the election. Then the providers would be happy to support a party which was in power. After I had left Jamaica and after he had won the election, he put the idea into practice. A couple of dozen wooden schoolrooms and small hospital wards were put together over a few weeks in a surge of political support for him, from PNM craftsmen as well as JLP, all for the sake of the excellent lunch provided by the Matalons, the Ashenheims and others. He had been nicknamed 'Joshua' as the one who would lead them out of the wilderness. The idea matched the mood. Years later, when Douglas Graham, as a minister, had to go to England he came specially to Norfolk where Riddelle and I were having our family holiday, to convey Michael Manley's thanks. I have to say that is the only thing I started which was of creative help to Jamaica, modest though it was. Unfortunately Michael and his top followers fell in love with Castroism and their first government ended in catastrophe.

Almost everyone we knew came to the opening of Riddelle's exhibition at the John Peartree Gallery. We had to invite Gordon and Joan. It was obvious that they knew hardly any of them, not even the Bank of England representative. No wonder they had no feel for Jamaica.

When eventually he gave me my marching orders he was compassionate, using well-worn phrases such as 'I think that with us you are wasting your time'. He was supportive when the General Manager of the Sheraton Kingston recommended me to his hotel's Group Treasurer whom I went to meet in Boston, Massachusetts on 14 November. I was excited because I had enjoyed my involvement with CDC's hotels. The whole of life happened in them, a people business. I had written to Hallway but they were retrenching although they said that normally they would have liked to have me. Sheraton, a subsidiary of the mighty ITT, had just committed $750 million to hotel development. A meeting was arranged for me with the President of Sheraton International, Claude Fenninger. We discussed Cyprus and he was interested that I had recommended against CDC involvement there. He wanted me to work for him in Brussels starting next February, 1971, to represent them all over Europe, negotiating franchises, leases, management agreements, eventually even internationally, all towards their objective of becoming the world's best. Back in Jamaica Riddelle was sceptical. Wisely, because everything fell through. Sheraton also had decided to retrench.

During our year in Jamaica we had made wonderful Jamaican

friends, This made the disruption of being sacked much worse. We found a good home for Tammy, and one for her two puppies to be taken together. We advertised an end-of-term sale of house furnishings and sold everything, even the chairs and sofa I had made. Everything except the pouffe. Perhaps I should have called it something else.

Thirteen

Luckily the tenants of 31 Queensdale Road were keen to terminate their lease and we could move in, home, on our arrival. Both children went to Basset House School nearby. I began job-seeking, humiliated by the dole but grateful for it. Gordon had suggested I go for something related to the arts, antiques perhaps, or a particular era of painting or sculpture, become an expert and so forth. That all struck me as a zero sum game; I wanted to contribute to wealth in the Third World. Many were the meetings I had with the great and the good.

For occupation between times I converted our dining room into a playroom. The hefty table was sold. Using the pinewood from our packing cases from Jamaica I made an ottoman for toys, a carpenter's bench with shelves on one side, and a folding dining table which could seat eight when unfolded. The floor I laid with black and white temple tiles.

At the Garrick Club the founder of the Edinburgh Festival, Sir Ian Hunter, said the next big thing in people's homes would be video tapes and recording machines, so they could record television programmes and buy or rent tapes of any films they wanted to watch. A company had already been set up called Crown Cassettes. While networking I found that Alun Chalfont was looking for someone to lead a similar company which he was putting together with the publisher George Weidenfeld as chairman. We had a series of discussions and they very much liked my idea of using this means to create video tapes on education for developing countries, using local teachers, the best ones, to help make up for their scarcity. Education was the key to practically everything.

This took flight. It suited my idealism, was practical and carried with it a salary which was substantial enough to cope with that worry, far off but still looming: public school fees and the interim premiums for assurance policies to help pay for them. They said they would prepare a contract for me, meanwhile they had rented offices in Wimpole Street and were drawing their directors' fees. I was called upon to pay a visit to the labour exchange. For six months they had been paying the dole and wanted to know of my progress. The interviewer was alert and supportive. He said that what I had found was perfect for me and wished me the very best.

A couple of days later I was telephoned by a senior partner in a City law firm. He knew all about my progress but had bad news. That morning, he said, the financier behind my company had broken his word in the City and so 'My dear fellow, I thought I should let you know: the whole thing is fucked. Including your job.'

So that was that. I could not go on living in Queensdale Road and still send the two kids to school on dole money. I rented the house out and took a cheap and gloomy basement flat, 3 Holland Park, next to the Greek Embassy Residence. It was a good address and was next to Holland Park, but we hated it. I was elderly – all of thirty-four – and difficult to employ. Riddelle and the children were miserable there, but needs must. 'This grotty flat' we called it. I had no idea how long it would take to get a proper job with career prospects and I was damned if I would sell our house.

The basement flat was in a large house owned by the dreariest of men. The top two floors were occupied by a former diplomat, Mr Moumin, who had been Pakistan's Ambassador in the Argentine. The unity of Pakistan, East and West, separated by thirteen hundred miles of India, had been led to Independence in 1947 under Mohammed Jinnah. Now it was tearing itself to pieces. With the bloody civil war between them Mr Moumin, a Bengali, eventually resigned his position and declared his support for East Pakistan, newly named Bangladesh. He had been granted asylum in Britain and was awaiting events. The leader of his people, Sheikh Mujibur Rahman, was in a West Pakistan prison, allegedly having had to dig a grave for himself in the earth floor next to his bed. He came to be called 'Father of the Nation'.

We took the children to spend a weekend with Larry and Joan in Brighton. Richard was aged around nine, Tamsin seven and Julie-Kate four, and a nanny looked after them. Tristan was five and Isis three and a half, so the families of father and son overlapped. Larry's previous enchantment had been outstripped by the children's interruptions and demands which could not be contained even by the most experienced nanny. The magic balm of Mother Nature was no longer the preserver of his love life with Joan. He also felt put upon by the stresses of the National Theatre. His magnificent Rolls had been replaced by a hearse-like ten-seat Volvo. I asked what had happened. He snapped that he couldn't afford it and it would have been better if he *had* shot himself.

Larry and Joan had bought an acre of land half an hour away near Steyning, with an old cottage called The Malthouse. He found a wonderful old gardener called Reg and set about landscaping a series of spaces, each separate like a small stage set, the main feature being a curved 'where'er you walk' tunnel of trained lime trees, redolent of Notley. Herbaceous borders abounded. Beyond the pond was a small swimming pool and then a tennis court and a fine view of the South Downs. The house itself was cosy and they hung vibrant Spanish curtains. There were large fireplaces in the tiny drawing room and dining room where they hung French Impressionist paintings and a portrait of David Garrick.

During those summer months any interest in recruiting me for an executive job had ceased. Riddelle and I decided to have a holiday in Glen Tilt, staying in a Scottish friend's cottage. At the same time David Mitchell-Innes asked if I would like a cruise of a few days to Honfleur, the harbour which William the Conqueror had used to mount the Norman invasion of 1066. Riddelle, ever the free spirit, said that was fine. She would drive up to Scotland on her own with the cat and the children, stopping to see friends on the way, and be ready for my train when it stopped at Blair Atholl.

On the most enjoyable cruise with David and his wife Christine and another couple we discussed school fees. Over our wine we decided that it was almost certain that we would have to plump for state schools after all. That meant that we could have more children. I knew this would please Riddelle and might help her settle down, at least for a while. She had been very good about our reduced circumstances, the limitations of the dole, and I did so want to please her.

The London-Scottish Express halted at tiny Blair Atholl station at five in the morning. There was Riddelle, and in the back of the car the children asleep with the cat. It was half an hour's drive to the glen and I told her of my decision that we could have another child if she wished. She wanted to stop the car, rush off into a field and make love immediately. I persuaded her to wait until we were inside the cottage.

We did have a wonderful holiday. For some reason the estate factor kept leaving us freshly shot grouse. They were delicious but I had to pluck the little beasts, shirtless in the sunshine, feathers sticking to my chest in the breeze. On our next shopping trip I bought bamboo staves, a ball of string and then made a big kite with one of our sheets, modelled on the ones the RAF used, seven feet by four and with a long tail. It rose up high into the sky to the end of the hundred yards of string. The children hung on to it together. I made some handkerchief-sized parachutes and spiralled wire runners to slide up to the kite and then break away and float down. The children chased after them, rushing back and saying 'Daddy, do it again.' While the cat played with butterflies.

That autumn I went to see a headhunter called Ella Heath. I had sent her my curriculum vitae. She called me into her little office in St James's Place, off St James's Street. She was a Polish lady with a great length of red hair wound round her head, over and over, and a conspiratorial voice. I felt that spiritually she had never left the Polish Secret Service. She bade me have a seat.

'Der Ler Roo,' she said.

Next time I understood better. 'De La Rue. The banknote printers.'

This sounded excellent, and involved developing countries: what more could be done for their good than assure the integrity of their currency? Economic plasma, while I had the prospect of an overseas posting and the company paying two-thirds of the school fees. The company was based in Basingstoke which was a bore, but then I could always sleep or read on the train. The point was that it was a job with career prospects and a fine reputation. I was dying for it. Ella assured me they would like my c.v.

I took the train to Basingstoke and walked over to their new two-storey building, flat and undistinguished. My meeting was with the Field Sales Manager, Pat Turner. He had been a non-commissioned officer in the RAF for his National Service. All I saw now was that he had a well-cut suit, black hair like an overgrown pot brush, a turned-up nose and a brusque manner. Like a sergeant major.

'I liked your book,' he said as soon as I had sat down. He seemed the sort to appreciate a challenge so I asked whether he had bought a copy or got it from the public library. 'The latter, actually.' South-East Asia was a part of the world he was extremely fond of. He asked about Livingstone, CDC and home life. He introduced me to the General Sales Manager, David Rowe-Beddoe. Now *he*, in rolled up shirt sleeves, with domed head and rounded features, was a most impressive man, a booming extrovert comfort figure with a twinkle. He was pulsating with energy. He was more like an actor in the role of Brigadier Gerard. All I remember him saying was what fun it was flying round the world flogging banknotes.

I had lunch with the Banknote Sales Manager, Don Ring, who had been a policeman in East Africa and spoke Swahili, so we had plenty to gossip about. He asked if I had any questions about the company. I said I had done my homework and looked forward to getting a detailed understanding of the business. He wanted to know if I intended to continue writing. I assured him that I would never write anything that would compromise the company and in any event would always submit anything for approval.

My job started in mid-November 1971, with a note on my company desk from Pat Turner saying 'Welcome to De La Rue, hoping this would be the start of a long and fulfilling career.' This set me up. Never anything like that from CDC. The letter set out a programme for the next six weeks. I would have to learn about banknote designing with their Preliminaries Department, followed by a month in the main banknote factory up in Gateshead, and then the Security Print Factory in Dunstable, for passports, bonds, stamps and cheques. He took me round and introduced me to everyone in Basingstoke. My overwhelming impression was that they were free men, unlike CDC. They had no constraints. My kind of people.

I wished the tenants would move out of our house but for a further six months we were stuck in the grotty flat where the north-facing semi-basement drawing room was also our dining room, playroom, and store for whatever we could not fit anywhere else. It was full to bursting. Arthur Lewis and Maud came to dinner. I asked him to behold what we had been reduced to. He lightened the moment by saying we seemed to have everything. Larry was more direct but in his own way just as funny. 'Yes,' he said, 'it is a bit shitty.' He bought us a share in the Wine Society and had a carefully selected case delivered to us in our time of need. Our own good news, which we kept to ourselves for a bit, was that Riddelle had conceived. She was radiantly happy.

In Basingstoke I was getting to know my colleagues in the sales force and it seemed they were made for friendship. Considering the top level people overseas whom regional managers had to deal with the pay was paltry, but survivable. Someone said that to work for De La Rue you needed a private income and a sense of humour. The atmosphere made everything worthwhile, the product of the best schools, the best universities, and wonderful management. It was more like a club than a company.

In December 1971 I overheard David Rowe-Beddoe's booming voice complaining that Bangladesh had burst upon the world as a country, declaring its independence. It needed a national currency and we did not know anyone. We had a regional manager there who was making no headway. I went into his office and said that I knew the newly appointed Foreign Minister, Mr Moumin. Immediately I was drawn in to the situation which confronted Bangladesh as well as West Pakistan. Both enemy states used the same currency, with Mohammed Jinnah's portrait on the banknotes. This was hair-raising. Either country could have destroyed the other's economy by flooding it with planeloads of its own banknotes, destroying the medium of exchange. Mass starvation would soon follow. Hitler had wanted to use this as a method of warfare against England. Nazi Germany printed millions of counterfeit five pound notes. Before sufficient were accumulated they were identified as false when they used them to pay their spies in England. The quality of their paper was superior to ours. As an insurance we counterfeited the Reichsmark, and let that be known to the Germans. Stalemate was a welcome consequence.

Both new countries desperately required their own banknotes. Pakistan printed their own in Karachi, enough to keep going when times were normal, but nothing like enough capacity to meet a total replacement at speed. For that they would need the De La Rue capacity of Gateshead, as did Bangladesh for its total needs.

I was bundled off with two of our design artists and a lettering artist on a flight to Calcutta, to await any flight to Dhaka. The drive from Dum Dum Airport through the fetid streets of Calcutta was the most sickening I have ever known: fly-blown piles of excrement lodged here and there. The filth of the poor Bengali Hindus was horrifying, they defecated everywhere, yet were busy making things, bargaining, shouting and pointing. My artists were almost retching with disgust. The Oberoi Grand Hotel was behind an overcrowded arcade which hid the entrance. A couple of magnificent moustachioed doorkeepers pushed through the scrimmage and opened our taxi doors.

What had happened to the Paris of the East? Shortly after Independence in 1947 the municipality was dominated by Communists. Nothing was done to prevent the influx of tens of thousands of ever-self-reproducing peasants made landless by overcrowding. They were strangers to urban life, hence the squalor. The city is now much improved.

Once inside the hotel we were uplifted by the classic colonial decoration, the spaciousness and service. My artists liked the little mogul pictures in their rooms and after dinner we went to see a performance of Indian dancers. Next day by the pool they admired the elegance even of the women labourers in saris, climbing ladders, one hand steadying a hod on their heads, heavily loaded with tiles, straight-backed, hips swinging, slim and energetic.

We took the afternoon flight to Dhaka in a Hawker-Siddeley turbo-prop; very different from the glorious VC10, but at least it was new. From the plane the city of Calcutta presented a view which showed how handsome the buildings were, Victorian and stylish, the streets well laid out, and a green park surrounded the Victoria Monument which looked like a version of St Paul's. Had it been clean the place would have been spectacular.

Dhaka, being Muslim, was clean, but just as crowded with Bengalis. The airport was jam-packed, hectic with nervous energy, slow queues because of frantic incompetence and the mass of thin brown hands and arms, and sad tired eyes. The drive between the flat rice fields showed village after flattened village, the aftermath of the civil war. Seldom has any country faced its hard-won independence with such huge losses of soldiers, civilians, the very fabric of its institutions. More than a million killed. Our two taxis had almost to force a way through the crowd outside the modern Hilton Hotel. The stress was enervated by a man scraping a single-stringed viol, much amplified, the same two bars over and over again. As in Calcutta, the doormen did a good job keeping the crowds out.

Once we had signed in we took the lift. There was an elderly Danish banker almost crying between gritted teeth, because the wretched viol's screeching notes could still pierce his ears, even inside the hotel, and he felt he was going mad. We met our banknote sales manager Don Ring at the bar for a well-deserved drink. Even there everyone seemed at the end of their tether: aid organisations of every kind and country, Russian and American helicopter pilots, young uniformed nurses shouting at each other, trying to make the horrors they were facing sound as bad as they could: the injuries, the diseases, lack of equipment, electricity or proper hygiene. Compassion featured less in their conversation than morbid point scoring. An old American irrigation expert, in his cups, said: 'As far as I am concerned, this is a permanent international disaster area, and the people are just fuckin' themselves into the grave.' The vigour and the hopelessness.

The State Bank was an imposing 1930s building at the end of the city's main avenue. The Governor, Mr Hamidulla, was a soft-spoken clerical man. His wife and son had been killed in the civil war. The Executive Director most in touch was the excitable Khalid Khan. He gave us the use of a large office so that our artists could spread themselves out and we could all feel at home there. Our search started for local design material, assisted by a moustachioed local artist none of us could stand.

The watermark agreed was the Royal Bengal Tiger. Our leading designer Ron Turrell set to work creating a miniature portrait of Mujib, the Father of the Nation, now being treated in the London Clinic after his ordeal as a prisoner in West Pakistan. The Bank had given us an excellent photograph of him. We leafed through illustrated books for suitable vignette scenes. The Bank in its ignorance asked us to quote for many times the quantity of banknotes required and here we felt honour bound to advise them. Our banknote product manager flew out to make a study of their needs, accompanied by David Rowe-Beddoe. We were also joined by the regional manager responsible for Bangladesh, Julian Wethered, who was based in Manila. So there were now eight of us. Julian had been there before, but had had to withdraw in order to fight an enormous tender in the Philippines, which we won. His was the voice of calm. The others were inclined to respond to the Bengalis' excitability in kind. Everything was complicated by the presence in the Bank and in the hotel of our competitor Bradbury Wilkinson, an English subsidiary of the American Banknote Company.

The presence of so many of our executives added fuel to the Bengali tendency to emotion. The creaking international telephone system made contact with Basingstoke a tremendous strain. Even David, with his stentorian voice on the phone, could not make himself understood. We had to rely on telexes. This did quieten things a bit. It meant that the originator had to think clearly before sending any message, and reduced the number of shouted contradictions.

When it came to their quantity requirements it was difficult to convince them of the fruits of our researches. Our report had been beautifully typed by the Bank's secretaries, but when it came to making photocopies there was a problem. The Bank had no photocopying paper. I managed to find a stationery shop with thirty remaining sheets. So we made two copies and had to ask the typists to type out more. When this was done David presented the case to the Governor. Our volumes were agreed and Basingstoke started to prepare our offer on beautifully watermarked Thomas De La Rue all-rag paper, the sort used in banknotes.

Our superiors then left. Julian was in charge with me as his side-kick, and our design artists. I thought they should get a glimpse of the countryside so I took them in a couple of taxis and drove north. The land was flat. It was a dry day, the sky blue and the rice-fields emerald. Wherever there was a little plateau, three or four feet high, it was occupied by village huts, above the flood levels as far as possible. Many of them were still in ruins. We drove along the mighty Brahmaputra River, the source, along with the Ganges, of all the delta mud which had created Bangladesh. It was bedecked with fishing boats, their full sails billowing.

After an hour I stopped the taxis and we all got out. We walked beside a pond the size of a tennis court, man-made, with a loo platform at one end, little boys splashing around and an old man with a fishing rod. It was overhung with blossoming jacaranda trees. Beyond the fields of young rice, behind plumes of bamboo, was the first village,

I led the way. The path between the paddy fields had sharp corners, each reflecting disputes as to who owned what piece of land. The rice was newly planted, the shoots six inches high, but with scars, abscesses and varied dots indicating a whole variety of diseases. As we approached the village dozens of bare-footed children in shorts and shirts and little dresses came out and followed us. The villagers stood still, only their eyes moving as they watched us pass. I said good-day in Bengali and they reciprocated with the *wai* gesture, pressing the palms of their hands together, wondering what we were doing. The children followed us along the much-cornered path to the next village, a quarter of a mile away. As we got nearer one of them put his hot little hand into mine. When we got there he told everyone where we had been. As we left, Julian took the lead. Afterwards he said how much the walk had meant to him, and how his view of the people had become so much friendlier, seeing how they worked, and how vulnerable they were to monsoons and floods, how desperately over-populated and under-nourished.

On our way back to Dhaka we saw people with piles of bricks which they hammered into pieces. That was because the delta mud had no gravel, no stones of any kind. For their roads they had to bake bricks and smash them up as a substitute.

Thomas De La Rue's leather-bound offer came by Fedex and we presented it to the Governor. He was accompanied at the end of his desk by a most excitable man of indeterminate status whom I shall call Mr A. This persistent, interfering and loud-mouthed man thought he would gain promotion by insulting us. As Julian explained a technicality, Mr A shouted: 'He's lying, Governor. He's lying.' It was good that Julian and I had so much in common. Nothing would divide us. He became my closest friend in the years which followed.

The hand-drawn design of the ten taka banknote was approved by the Governor. I took it myself back to Basingstoke by plane to save a day's time.

The children were fine and so was Riddelle, the morning sickness long gone. Her pregnancy was starting to show and her features were becoming more robust. Her dislike of the flat was made worse by the cold weather which drove lots of mice inside for warmth. They scurried everywhere. They thrived on the poison put down by the Council. I have always liked mice and so did Riddelle, but her mother was pathologically terrified of them. Once at dinner, when she was facing us with her back very close to the mantelpiece, a mouse trotted along it and stopped in the middle, inches from her ear. We saw and managed to keep the conversation going. The mouse proceeded on its way and tiptoed down to the floor. At night they sometimes ran over our bed. Riddelle said she admired their spirit.

I returned to Dhaka and the stress induced by Mr A. Brickbats were coming from other quarters, including Executive Directors. I gave KK a copy of *Eye of the Day* and inscribed it to him. Julian phrased our next telex: the brickbats ceased. Then he was handed a letter from the Governor ordering the ten taka banknotes we had quoted for. Unfortunately the letter added that the price might have to be renegotiated as Bradbury had submitted a cheaper offer, even though they could get nowhere near our speed of delivery, not by months. So his letter was not contractual and we had to reject it with unctuous courtesy.

We inquired what Brads' price might be in case we could match it. The Governor told us, which was unethical. He even showed us Brads' letter. We telexed Basingstoke and could practically hear the consequent rumpus. We wanted that business. Julian was beside himself with fury. How could Brads be so hysterical? They could not even cover production costs at their price. The Bank was entirely within its rights to play one competitor off against the other, saving itself many millions of pounds. We lowered our price, not the full way, relying on the Bank's desperation for its new supply. The ten taka was the workhorse denomination for their medium of exchange and would save the economy. They placed a proper order. Our engravers set to work: the engravings on steel by the portraitist, the vignette specialists and the lettering engraver, all to be merged by transfer engraving to the single plate for intaglio printing, to follow on top of the lithographic tints and vignettes.

Normally it takes many months to produce a proof, pulled from the hand-engraved steel. We did it in weeks. I took the proof and flew out to Dhaka. There I had to clear it through customs. Their regulations had no category for such an object: a banknote proof, uncirculated, unauthorised. I was ushered into their dreary main office with accounting clerks bent over large tables. They were writing everything by hand, from one large leather bound ledger on one table then over to the other. Nothing had changed for generations: pure double entry in the Bengali equivalent of copperplate.

The Chief of Customs deferentially looked at the banknote proof and refrained from touching it. What a delicate object, he said, very beautiful. He waggled his head from side to side, Bengali fashion, and said that their searches for a customs coding were in vain. Hourly hourly could they be seeking and weekly weekly not finding. I made a joke of the situation and they were relieved, the whole room, to be reminded that there was a world outside. When I had signed yet another ledger I asked them, in the nicest possible way, what all these procedures were for. I said the ten taka may have cost tens of thousands of pounds to produce, but until it was issued by the State Bank it had no worth. A dear old man explained: 'Sir, we pass on. The record stays behind.' There really was something irresistible about them, excited as they were by the sight of a national emblem as strong as their new currency, depicting the Father of the Nation, their artefacts and scenery, being in the administration of *their* country, now in peace.

During the sales conference David Rowe-Beddoe had the sales force and our wives for dinner at his country house west of Basingstoke. It had wooden beams, some lovely paintings including primitives from Haiti, and a roaring fire. Riddelle, now great with child and radiant, sat next to Julian. He asked what sort of a person she was. She blurted out the truth: 'I'm a rebel,' she said.

'Then why', he asked, 'are you sitting down?' They got on splendidly.

I planned to go to Bangladesh to meet the arrival of De La Rue's first massive delivery of the new currency, two hundred and seventy-five cases, each with fifty thousand banknotes. Unfortunately a mighty typhoon prevented the Boeing 707 from landing in Dhaka. The second airport at Chittagong did not have a sufficiently high load classification number to receive such a big plane so it had to land in Calcutta's Dum Dum Airport.

The cases were being stacked in the airport's Customs Hall, the other side of a glass partition and in full view of the airport public. This was unnerving. The total face value was in the range of one hundred million pounds. The De La Rue security officer was organising everything well, but the only local security was in the form of two dozen khaki-clad askaris armed with bamboo staves. They watched the porters in dhotis laboriously bringing in the tons of cases from the plane and stacking them, one above the other, four high in a huge rectangle.

In the main office, telephone and telex messages about the typhoon flew in every direction. It had caused huge damage and poor Bangladesh had to seek yet more international aid. I obtained the use of two airplanes to transfer the banknote cases to Chittagong. One was an old DC4, with a payload of ten tons, the other a Fokker Friendship with a payload of two. I thanked everyone for their help and went back to the Customs Hall. Our De La Rue security guard was suffering from jet lag and was almost asleep on his feet, so I said he should go to the Oberoi Grand Hotel in Calcutta and be back on parade at ten in the morning. I checked out the local security askaris with their sergeant. They seemed alert and keen, but I had little confidence in the arrangements. I decided to sleep on top of the pile of crates to keep an eye on things. I had all the lights left full on, all night, clambered up and lay down exhausted.

I fell into a sound sleep. It was fearfully hot, the mosquitoes were in full cry with an insatiable appetite but nothing made any difference. I can sleep anywhere. Perchance to dream, and I did so vividly: about the Queen. She was wearing a summer frock and one of her hats in an English village. She was congratulating a couple on their practice of birth control. She was her usual natural self, thoughtful, with wisdom and gaiety. The subject being discussed was so incongruous that it awoke my troubled mind. I sat up.

I looked around. What I saw was extraordinary. From my vantage point on top of all the banknote cases I saw all over the floor the dark hairy legs of Indian men, their dhotis pulled up over their heads to keep the mosquitoes out of their ears. I thought that *that* was a dream. I pulled myself together. The askaris were wandering round with their bamboo poles. The sleeping men should not have been there but they seemed harmless. So this was reality.

Next day I was awakened by the sergeant offering me a cup of coffee and sandwiches, kind-eyed, enjoying the absurdity. Our security man arrived, well rested, and he supervised the transfer of all the cases to a lock-up alongside the runway. He wrote down the identifying number of each of them in his notebook. When the job was done he said he was one case short. I asked to see his list and was able to put it right. The DC4 arrived that evening. We had the porters stuff ten tons of cases in the hold, between the seats and down the aisle.

As night had fallen and we did not know Chittagong we decided to hold our horses until the next day. I asked the sergeant whether he had sealed the aeroplane. He did not understand. I had him accompany me for an inspection and we wandered round it. On the other side there was a passenger door hanging wide open leaving the contents totally unsafe, like a man with his fly unzipped. Ladders were brought, wires were inserted in the corresponding holes between all the doors and fuselage, and lead seals squeezed to fasten the ends. The remaining bulk of the crates were securely locked in their store and our man had the key, so we both went back to the hotel.

It was to be a long day so we agreed to start up at Dum Dum Airport at eight o'clock in the morning, suitcases in hand for an overnight stay in Chittagong. We worked out that we would need three journeys of the DC4 and four of the Fokker Friendship. I went outside and saw that the DC4 had gone. It was at the far end of the enormous runway, propellers reflecting the hot sun, engines roaring. I dropped my suitcase and ran across the hard surface as fast as I could until I reached the centre of the take-off path. The engines roared up and up as the plane gained speed heading straight at me for take-off. It was very large, the wheels were my height, its tail fin far off behind it, the engines deafening, the wing span majestic. I stood, feet slightly apart, and held up my right hand in a stop sign. It bounded towards me but at least it was not accelerating. I could see the pilot through the cockpit window. He waved in acknowledgement. The plane came to a halt twenty yards from me. I wagged my forefinger as if to a naughty child and he laughed.

Just then I saw my suitcase had acquired a pair of legs and was running away towards the car park. Luckily it was heavy. I caught up and told the man to take it to the DC4. He was cowed and ashamed, willing to please and be forgiven. I told our security guard to load up the Fokker when it came and await my return, while I accompanied the DC4 to Chittagong to unload the cargo, hand it to the Central Bank's officials and obtain a receipt. And so the exercise went on. As soon as the plane's emergency ladder was down I and my suitcase were up and inside. The things we did for De La Rue.

The ten taka banknotes were issued by the Central Bank in their hundreds of millions all over the country. The portrait of the Sheikh, the lithographic scenes of their countryside, and the local artefacts delighted everyone. The issue was a great success, despite having English serial numbers. At the Bank itself there was deep embarrassment at not having Bengali numbers. A series of outbursts from Mr A. made me wonder if Bradbury had put him up to it. They had obtained about a quarter of the total order and when he visited England they had put a Rolls-Royce at his disposal. We had only managed a Jaguar.

The lowest banknote denomination, the one taka, came within the portfolio of the Minister of Finance, who was still Acting Prime Minister. There were two separate designs, the first by us, the second by Brads. I went to see him. His office was in one of the large Secretariat buildings, three or four storeys high, about eighty yards long with central corridors filled to bursting with clerks, couriers, messengers all shouting at once, gesticulating, recalcitrating volubly, and the occasional suited executive picking his way with distaste through the tumult.

In quietness, the other side of the wide ministerial desk, the Minister beamed the pleasure of power. We had a perfectly satisfactory discussion and the phone rang. He accepted the call as it was from the Father of the Nation himself, Sheikh Mujibur Rahman, calling from his hospital bed in the London Clinic. There had been concerned reports about his state of health. The Minister put on his serious expression and had five minutes of intense conversation. He lowered the receiver into its cradle as if it had brought most precious news, his eyes wreathed with smiles.

'How is the Prime Minister?' I asked in a worried tone.

'He is very ill,' he said, with deep satisfaction for he was next in line for the premiership.

'What is he suffering from?'

He put his finger-tips together in a series of taps, admiring his hands, feeling very alive. 'He's suffering from loss of blood.'

Horrible man.

Mujib recovered. About fifty thousand Bengalis and the world's press went to Dhaka airport to greet him. As he stepped out of the plane he stood at the top of the stairs, wearing homespun beige trousers and long coat, and a similar cloth round his neck like a priestly stole. The cheers were an uplifting acclamation of his leadership in the struggle for independence, and the horrors that he too had suffered at the hands of Pakistan. He was now back in power over fifty-five million Bengalis, the symbol of rebirth, innocence and incorruptibility, the clear way to the future.

Fourteen

Riddelle was nearing her time. It seemed she had been pregnant for ever. The summer was hot and she had been suffering in the grotty flat. Larry and Joan took us to dinner at Overton's Victoria, after drinks in the modern apartment he had bought in Roebuck House. It was under the penthouse which was occupied by Arabs. His drawing room was high enough for his favourite view across the rooftops, to the site of the National Theatre at last being built.

Over dinner Joan was considerate towards Riddelle, stiff towards me, and miffed with Larry for being at his most effusive. We discussed names. For a girl's name the only one he could think of was one which Joan had not let him add to the names for their second daughter Julie-Kate. He suggested 'Clavelle'. We loved it, like a fine keyboard instrument.

Bangladesh beckoned for attention but I pleaded with Pat Turner and he agreed to go on my behalf so that I could be present at the birth. We went to Queen Charlotte's Hospital. A girl it was. In Tanzania both gynaecologists had been European but this was London. The gynaecologist was a Guyanese woman and the midwife from Sierra Leone, both skilled and charming. Riddelle bore her pain soundlessly, twiddling a button on my shirt.

In Bangladesh our designs for the other values were approved and I had some spare time. That summer at the 1972 IMF meetings in Washington David Rowe-Beddoe reported that 'for some extraordinary reason' it had been attended by representatives from the three High Commission Territories of Southern Africa: Swaziland, Lesotho and Botswana, now independent, but still using the South African rand for their medium of exchange.

The Swazi High Commissioner in London arranged for me to meet their Minister of Justice at the Dorchester. He came down from his room, a teddy bear of a man, his mind miles away. I offered him tea. He said in a bass gurgle: 'That would be lovely.' He sat back in his armchair, undid his top trouser buttons to relieve his belly and looked almost cuddly. I asked whether the Swazi Cabinet had considered breaking away from the rand and having its own currency and issuing authority. He said no, but gave me the name and contact numbers of the Finance Secretary. A week later he wrote to confirm that his government was not interested in having its own currency. So I went to see for myself.

In the British Airways 747 to Johannesburg there were half a dozen people I knew in first class. What I was up to was most secret so I told them I was on holiday. Jan Smuts Airport was grand and spacious, the motorways new and the city the acme of high-rise modernity. In the fourteen years since I had been there the main change was in the faces of the Africans. They were alert, no longer cowed, for under apartheid they had received the best education in Africa. Yet it was outrageous to see how many of them looked more intelligent than their white masters, and irritating to see the buses still segregated into 'net blankes' and 'nie blankes'. I again forgot which was which and got on to an all-black bus. They gently asked me to get off. That night a telex from Basingstoke asked me to go to Cape Town where the Trust Bank wanted us to design new traveller's cheques.

There I stayed at the Mount Nelson Hotel, a lovely building with Georgian windows, a large garden with a pool and palm trees. Larry and Vivien and the cast of the Old Vic Company had spent a weekend there en route for their tour of Australia and New Zealand in 1948. After my meeting at the bank I decided to climb up to Lion's Rock and across, further up, to Table Mountain. From there I was rewarded by a view over the whole city, the harbour beyond and Robben Island in the distance.

Swaziland was described in Kipling's *Just So Stories*, with its high, middle and low veldt. The capital Mbabane was atop the High Veldt, a small town for bureaucrats and politicians and students, with suburban houses and gardens all nicely done. The view over a valley led to twin peaks which had inspired Rider Haggard's landscape descriptions in *King Solomon's Mines*, where he exaggerated their size and compared them to the Queen of Sheba's breasts, with snow tips for nipples; breathless reading for prep school boys. On a lower slope was a Swazi village of straw houses like tea cosies, surrounded by poor grassland, communally owned, therefore untended and overgrazed. There was a glistening hotel with a casino. I stayed at a country hotel which was more anonymous.

Mr Stephens the Finance Secretary was an English-speaking South African, now a Swazi citizen. He was calm, clerical and informative. He remembered David Rowe-Beddoe at the IMF and the De La Rue cocktail reception. He confirmed that Botswana and Lesotho had been discussing having their own national currencies. He noticed that I was wearing a Christ Church tie with cardinals' hats, and told me that his opposite number in Lesotho wore one. He would be the man for me there, while in Botswana there was an English adviser called Jack Lyle, a very good man and yes, he had worked in Tanzania. I recalled having known him well. Together we had signed that country's Permanent Housing Finance Corporation into existence..

All this was promising. To help them break away from South Africa would be a splendid blow against apartheid. It would also strengthen their sovereignty and be an economic benefit straight away. I gave him a simplistic view of the numbers. A pound note costs, say, a penny to produce: one percent of its face value. A customer takes one from the bank and is charged a several percent rate of interest: pure profit for as long as the banknote remains in circulation. If you use another country's banknotes, they get that profit. Mr Stephens had not realised this. The conversation warmed up.

I already knew a certain amount about Swaziland because it had more CDC projects per head than any other country. As Secretary of the Estimates Committee I had analysed every one of them. Our General Manager had fallen in love with the place. King Sobhuza II was Africa's last traditional king. His face was heavily lined and he looked wise, with dark skin, moderately wide nose and lips, and two short feathers in his cropped hair. Swazis ascribed mystical qualities to him: the ability to disappear and become a rabbit. He had many wives and children, the First Wife being called the Great She Elephant. His word was law. Since Independence he seems to have spent time breaking undertakings he had given the British colonial power.

Our High Commissioner asked me to stay for lunch. His Residency had a fine view of Sheba's breasts. He was a Channel Islander, Mr le Toq. There was not much in the country that interested him so we discussed books. I said my only business there was to secure a further order for Swazi passports before they ran out; no mention of currency.

I took hundreds of pictures of the museum's spears, ceramics and beads, and in the market even more beads with intriguing patterns. The official portrait of the king was a gift for the portrait engraver and the watermark. I went from village to village. All the Swazis were welcoming and called after me when I left. The vivid cloud formations were made for landscape photography. The bookshops had calendars and books full of pictures.

Mr Stephens was excited by my concept for banknote designs. His worry was over coinage, and how it could be differentiated from the coins of South Africa. I suggested a wild idea. The Swazi coins should be every other shape but round: twelve-sided, square, scalloped, and ten-sided. They would be more expensive than round ones but very attractive to numismatists. He liked the idea but wanted to see the differences in costs before commitment.

There remained the question of naming the currency. We went to consult the Minister of Finance, a burly, soft-spoken Swazi, but with little knowledge of the language. He said we should use the name 'Emalangeni', but was unsure what the plural would be for the higher denominations. He would advise through the High Commission in London after consulting His Majesty.

I took the short flight to Maseru, capital of mountainous Lesotho, previously named Basotuland. That October springtime gave it more flowers along the roadside and up the wild slopes than I had ever seen; high-standing daisies of every colour, meadows filled with them, and the foothills crowded with red-hot pokers like guardsmen in scarlet tunics. There was a Holiday Inn staffed by young South Africans. The Finance Secretary Ted Waddington was in his office, both of us wearing our Christ Church ties. The only CDC project I remembered was an agricultural college, with pupils from all over east and southern Africa. The mountainous land did not lend itself to plantations and the Basutos were not adept at wealth-creating skills. So there, just as everywhere, education was the paramount need.

Ted said the last thing the country needed was its own currency. The Ministers might well fall over me with enthusiasm, seeing the opportunity for corruption. I could see what he meant. The Prime Minister, Leabua Jonathan, was the caricature of a jumbo buffoon. There was an illustrated book to his glory. The most notable photographs were of him being received in Singapore in front of a line of Chinese stewardesses. Their expressions of disbelief at beholding such a smiling cretin were priceless. The other photograph was of him, chin in hand, gazing at the rump of a departing elephant. The caption was: 'The Prime Minister contemplating the future of his nation'. With leaders like that ...

I told Ted my background and he understood that the last thing I wanted was to do harm. He also understood that 'the readiness is all' and said he had no objection to my assembling artistic reference material. So off I went with a rented car and my camera, trusting the map and braving the axle-threatening potholes.

The principal historical feature was a plateau called Thaba Bosiu above vertical cliffs. It was a mile and a half long, half as wide, with a slight slope and a freshwater spring. It became the refuge of the Basuto people when they were besieged by the Boers. Under the leadership of their king Moshoeshoe in the 1850s they made deadly sorties with their shields and spears against the invaders' rifles and eventually convinced them that their quest was not worth the cost. The Basuto people became a single polity. Under the king's leadership they made their capital in Maseru. After further skirmishes with the Boers he appealed to Queen Victoria and was granted protectorate status within the British Empire. Independence was granted in 1966.

I stopped and asked a Basuto how to get to Thaba Bosiu. He was traditionally dressed, with a thick brightly patterned blanket over his shorts and T-shirt, and a conical straw hat with twin loops on top. This features in the national flag. He led me into a cave at the foot of Thaba Bosiu. Inside he introduced me to a middle-aged Lesotho lady in a cotton dress, with a red wig on the table beside her. She sat me down for a cup of tea. She said she was fighting for the World Bank to invest in a hydro-electric dam project which would be the source of electricity and irrigation. This sounded like a project for CDC but she was not sure. They were bureaucratic.

Here in the middle of nowhere was this semi-educated woman, full of good will, the only real power in the valley. I said I was a tourist and had come to take pictures. She insisted I take one of her, put on her wig, took up a fountain pen and poised it over some papers. She wrote out her name and address and wished me luck.

A couple of miles away was a pyramid-sized mountain, topped with a massive cube as wide as its thick base: the remaining core of a volcano. Further on there was a hinterland with almost unusable roads going west into a great valley with the Drakensburg Mountains far beyond.

I flew to Gaberones, capital of Botswana, one time Bechuanaland, a low-lying and much hotter country mainly of bushmen and the Kalahari desert. The town was still under construction. Someone complained that we were giving independence to a building site. Again the hotel was a Holiday Inn, one of the few finished buildings. The main tourist attraction was the big game reserve near Francistown in the north. Recently discovered copper was being extracted from the Selebi Kitwe mine, and fairly soon Botswana would out-produce South Africa in diamonds. The most important resource at the time was its people, not all of them bushmen by any means, but an enlightened body of men with the discipline and fair-mindedness to make it the first country in Africa to develop a fully-functioning democracy – which is still the case.

The Finance Secretary was an Afrikaner called Quill Hermans. The Chief Adviser to the Treasury was my old friend and associate Jack Lyle. He told me the Reserve Bank of South Africa had set out proposals a long time before, covering any High Commission territory's decision to break away and set up their own issuing authorities and monetary regimes. Botswana, guided by Jack Lyle whose idea it was, would have been treated by the Reserve Bank of South Africa as generously as Swaziland. Likewise Lesotho. All good news. After buying such picture books as there were I was keen to go home to Riddelle and the children after an absence of two weeks.

For the first time in my life I was doing something I really wanted to do, which would benefit Third World countries, and I knew I could *do* it. At the same time the tenants of 31 Queensdale Road, the American philosopher Ted Roszak and his wife, were due to move out. With my legs under the table of the Bangladesh Central Bank, and the opportunities in Southern Africa, I felt confident enough to increase the mortgage and build on serious additions to the house.

We went to Brighton to see Larry and Joan. His health had really deteriorated. He had had a diseased kidney removed, had prostate problems, and thrombosis blew up his right leg to elephantine proportions. He should have grown replacement veins but after such a lifetime as his, the extraordinary outpourings of every kind of energy, his recuperative powers were poor.

He and Joan came to see our house and he was impressed. The newly plastered walls had dried and I had started painting them. Above the new garden drawing room the patio was sunlit with an ornamental fence, a table and chairs set ready for drinks. On cue our cat, Oedipus, crept out to join us.

When Riddelle and I had put the children to bed and read to them, it was time for our own bath. The cat would join us. He contributed to our togetherness. As we lay facing each other in the water, knees protruding, he would tread fastidiously from one knee to the other, stepping stones, then having checked us over he would sit on the edge of the bath and purr, in perfect control.

My mother let me take the grand piano. She still had my Balinese painting. She had made me promise to let her keep it. Now our new drawing room was crying out for it. I consulted my godparents. I had made a promise, after all. Sybil Thorndike said I should just give it time, and maybe drop a hint when my mother came to see us. Mercia Relph had no ideas. I asked Larry and he said: 'What you do is this. You say: "Remember I promised you could keep the Balinese painting? You do? Well, I'm taking it."' Which is exactly what I did, saying it was his advice, impersonating his voice. She was gracious and compliant.

After a milk run kind of visit to Bangladesh I dropped in to Swaziland. Until our designs there were finished and approved we were vulnerable to our competitors. I went via Calcutta, Bombay and Lourenço Marques, now Maputo, where I telephoned Mhlume Sugar Company in Swaziland, a major Commonwealth Development Corporation project, now managed by my old boss at Kilombero, Mr Wevers. It was a grand reunion with him and his wife. Being a Sunday there was a staff party at the estate club. Wevers introduced me to everyone with almost fatherly pride. He showed me round the factory and estate, four times the size of Kilombero, and they had me to stay the night.

The Swazi Minister of Finance came to Basingstoke with two delegates. Ron Turrell and his fellow artists had finished their most beautiful set of banknote designs. First I showed the Swazis our prelims, round the couple of dozen artists, then the portrait engraving, vignette etching, numbering, and machine engravers, followed by the computer graphics department. There was one distinguished senior portrait engraver there who assured them that it really did take fifteen years to train a portrait engraver. If there were a quicker way we would have applied it. After being bedazzled by the immense camera equipment in the photographic department they followed me into the prelims manager's office and we showed them their own hand-drawn designs. Ron Turrell was there.

They could not get over the splendour of his portrait of their king. The powerful eyes had seen countless vicissitudes of life. The lettering had been composed of spears. They loved the Swazi beads in the litho background tints. Across the centre of each denomination's front were two opposed spears, hung with a machine-engraved doily. They asked that those be replaced with traditional tassels. Ron said he could do that while we had lunch. That was a meal charged with good will, nurtured by David Rowe-Beddoe and a few others. Afterwards I showed them the designs with the spear tassels in place and the minister signed his approval. We could now submit our prices and, once accepted, the long process of engraving and origination could start.

Our lunches were always popular. Only one veered near to catastrophe. When Idi Amin was deporting the Asians from Uganda we had his High Commissioner down to Basingstoke. He was important to us because of his country's appetite for banknotes. Don Ring, as Banknote Sales Manager, was in the chair, careful not to reveal his fluent Swahili and background as a colonial police officer in Kenya. Also present were Dennis Paravicini, General Manager of Minting and Metals, Edwin Eggins, a tall sleek grey-haired ex-ambassador, and me.

As we sat at table, Don Ring tried to make conversation. He drew the High Commissioner's attention to our place mats. They showed the Bayeux Tapestry's depiction of the Battle of Hastings. By way of explanation he said that was the last time we had been invaded. Dennis, who was also chairman of the Basingstoke Conservative Association, added a rejoinder: 'Oh I don't know. What about the Ugandan Asians?'

The High Commissioner did not understand.

Edwin cut in immediately: 'Well, it was the last *armed* invasion.'

Luckily the High Commissioner was so dreary this flew past him. In retrospect, of course, the arrival in the United Kingdom of the Ugandan Asians transformed our country for the better, keeping shops open at times when working people could actually buy things, outside the traditional British hours of nine to five.

To avoid seeing people I knew on British Airways flights I took to South African Airways. They had four 747s and because of apartheid were forbidden from flying over black Africa. They went south-west round Mauritania, sometimes landing in the Cape Verde Islands, then over South-West Africa, a flight of fourteen hours to Johannesburg, perfect for an excellent cocktail, dinner, full night's sleep and a leisurely time to get up and have a proper breakfast.

They pronounced my name as if it were Dutch. 'Meinheer Ooliffyiear, what would you like to drink?' This was after the champagne before take-off, and once we were settled in the air. I asked for a vodka dry martini. They had never heard of it. Word obviously got around. On my return journey when I asked for one the steward exclaimed: 'You must be meinheer Ooliffyieer!' They had the right kind of vodka and the Noilly Prat. A superb airline.

One time at Jan Smuts Airport on my way home I read in the London *Times* that Larry had been smitten with dermatomyositis and was in Brighton Hospital. My neighbour on the plane was a consultant physician. I showed him the article and asked what it meant. He drew a deep breath and prepared me for the worst. It was a rare and horrendous illness; every cell of muscle and skin gets inflamed in a state of uproar. It could have been brought on by a lifetime of exhausting physical and mental demands denying the requirements for rest. It could induce periods of raving insanity. He said that to judge from the report it was likely to be fatal within six months.

In the hospital, Larry was exactly as the man had said, if not worse. He was scarlet-faced, features swollen almost beyond recognition, and raving. I met the lady consultant. We sat together in a shiny white room. I started by saying it might be easier if I told her what I had found out about dermatomyositis. She agreed. She heard me out, then said that he would probably live no longer than six weeks.

A fortnight later the SAA flight flew directly over Brighton. From that height I could see the hospital far below. I felt all the love in my heart surging down to the tile roof and into his room. Quite a catharsis.

Further UN sanctions against South Africa led to oil and fuel shortages. Internal flights became permanently filled to capacity, so I had to rent a car and drive everywhere, to Mbabane, to Maseru, than across to Gaberones. I loved it, even if the speed limit was only 40 m.p.h. I gave lifts, mainly to working-class Africans as the others had their own cars. Their knowledge of the status quo was detailed. They knew when it was safe to drive at 80 m.p.h., when the police at a particular *dorp* spent their time playing dominoes, and when I had to slow down, because the police always waited behind that poplar tree in their pursuit car. We never discussed politics. They were much more interested in the Springboks rugby football, especially when playing against the British Lions. This was true of all races. When I was strolling in Bloemfontein I was stopped by an elderly white woman. The Springboks had lost. She said it was 'Tirrible. That man Bennet. Virry virry strong. Our forward was in the air with the ball, going down over the British line and Bennet caught him. He held him mid air and turned him round. Virry virry strong.' I said I was English and thanked her for the news. She laughed and patted my shoulder. When international sport was later subjected to sanctions that really upset all of them.

It has to be said that the application of sanctions had the opposite political and economic effects to the ones desired. South Africa, under strong leadership and with an able workforce, set about becoming self-sufficient in manufacturing its needs. As for oil, they had converted mass tonnages of their own coal into a fuel they called 'sassol', which they stored in exhausted coalmines. They then refined it.

With Swazi and Botswana's banknotes being engraved after obtaining confirmation of their order, we were secure, but not yet in Lesotho. There I had had designs prepared. They were among the most beautiful, with the edges ablaze with flowering red-hot pokers. Ted Waddington sat on them while he looked for a suitable successor to himself. If their currency progressed he knew that he, like the other two permanent secretaries, would most likely become governor of the issuing authority. 'A pleasingly select club' was how he described that, but he had dire forebodings about his government's combination of incompetence and greed.

Larry was still alive. His body was a wreck, his skin covered with purple smears, but he was sitting up and his eyes did have a twinkle. I was amazed. All those close to him had insisted he would rise up and be well again. They had not heard the consultant's prognosis which I could not very well repeat to them. I had found their optimism jarring. But they were right. I asked him why he looked so happy.

'Because they have given Peter Hall that *fucking* National. All power to him. Being Artistic Director should suit him fine. I, of course, had to combine that with those huge roles I played, which I had to do for chrissake because I'm an actor. Oh the relief!'

His recovery against all expectation showed he really was tapped into some source.

At home our new drawing room was complete with piano, Balinese painting, cupboards and soft furnishing. For the bedroom I was putting together the big four-poster bed we had had in Jamaica. It was majestic but needed a canopy. I designed a softwood frame to carry the fabric. Tristan was seven years old and I showed him how to use an electric drill. Meanwhile Isis was becoming adept at drawing. Clavelle was being weaned and Riddelle was becoming restless, even though we both felt that my being home only half the time gave us both a break. She loved all the banknote and coin designs I showed her and she loved my homecomings.

Fifteen

Francophone Africa's fourteen countries were mainly our customers for passports and security print such as cheques and stamps. For years we had tried to prise away the banknote business, but the French Central Bank had tied their former African colonies except for Guinea-Conakry to themselves, creating the CFA franc. This was linked to the French franc to ensure stability. France had also established a Basic Law, which was a feather-light touch on the laws of the newly independent countries, all with representation in the French Senate. This was to avoid the obscene and inflationary dictatorship of Ghana's Kwame Nkrumah, the 'Redeemer'.

Abidjan, then the capital of the Ivory Coast, was well developed. Conversations with its civil servants and bankers were articulate and literate. They had attractive French accents and the intonation of African voices. The French genius for *maquillage* had created the most attractive women, disturbingly so some of them, with their high-arsed arrogant walk, lovely headdresses and satin black skin, much the best colour for diamonds. The Hôtel Ivoire had a slim skyscraper for all the bedrooms, centred round central lifts; enormous public areas, all alongside a swimming pool with islands in it, overhung with exotic trees and orchids. It also had an ice-skating rink. This *belle époque* put any Anglophone country in the shade.

French is a language which takes control of the speaker's body as well as the mind: the Gallic shrug, the particularity of accompanying gestures, the pursing of lips and different eye-language. I drifted back into all of these from my times in France, in particular with Jenny, and the years in Berne where I had been working in French. It seemed perfectly natural, until I returned home and my children were asking in astonishment: 'Daddy, what on earth is the matter?'

I replied in English, but still in my French mode: 'Nothing,' I said with a marked shrug, palms held upwards.

Thinking is also profoundly affected by the language. Pronunciation is a challenge for even the most fluent speakers, and the lashings of grammar produce a demand for precision beyond normal intent.

English vagueness resists distillation into French. Voltaire said: 'Tout ce qui n'est pas clair n'est pas français.' This is constricting. I liken the effect to the differences in our school notebooks. English ones have horizontal lines, all open-ended. Only for arithmetic do we have vertical lines to create squares for each figure. The French use square-ruled notebooks for everything, even for essays. That to my mind symbolises what I would call their comparative inflexibility: grid thinking. 'Il faut l'accepter. C'est comme ça.' It leads to point scoring, rather than an even-handed democratic exchange.

One of the years I was going there the whole of sub-Saharan Africa was afflicted with the worst drought ever. In Mali, Burkina Faso, Chad and Niger, all passport customers, the dried up countryside was a never-ending scene of horror, with the corpses of starved cattle, rivers a fraction their normal depth, easily fordable, as if in death throes of their own. More than a million people, families with children were dragging themselves over the parched land for hundreds of miles in search of food and water. I met one of the leaders of the American Peace Corps, hollow-eyed and frustrated by lack of response to his appeals and directions. He said that the most terrible irony was that people had portable radios and listened to the news, then reporting Nixon's problems with Watergate. That last name had been literally translated into Arabic, and they had the impression that water was round the corner, somehow to be flown in from America.

When in the Senegalese capital of Dakar I heard that neighbouring Mauritania was going through a phase of disenchantment with the French. I rented a Peugeot 404 and drove north. The start of the journey was tumbled over with thick green trees, vines splaying down, the people with negroid African features. The vegetation became sparser along the road side, the sun overhead no longer shaded. With the advent of palm trees human activity thinned out. Then there were the great baobabs, my favourite trees in all the world, standing apart like sentinels. They showed the end of what the poet President of Senegal, Leopold Senghor, called 'la négritude'. Then the last tree, the onset of thorn bushes, and finally the River Senegal: the border. On the coast overlooking the sea to the west was the small town of St Louis. Ahead, on the far side of the river was a ferry, a rusting hulk the size of a squash court. The only nearby human was a teenage boy fishing, his canoe pulled up on shore.

He spoke a little French. We agreed a fee for him to take me across and introduce me to the ferry driver who lived over there in a village of whitewashed houses. I locked my briefcase in the car boot. He paddled me over the slack river and made fast beside the ferry. He led me between corrugated iron gates and whitewashed walls, the soft sand making it heavy going. He pushed open a resistant gate and there, under a rattan awning, sitting on a rattan mat in a dazzling white robe and turban, was the ferry driver with his family.

He looked so like Larry as Othello that my jaw dropped, the negroid lips, trimmed beard and moustache, the fine well-bred nose and daunting eyes. They had an air of unspoken menace, for the belittlement of lesser men. The pale outstretched palm was to show how harmless he was, welcoming. He was a *Maure*, a Moor, a different species from *Nègre*. I wondered how Larry, who had never been anywhere in black Africa, could have so perfectly recreated the appearance and character of such a man. The voice had the same bass resonance. The Arabic he spoke to the boy who had guided me was euphonious and deep.

I had to stop standing and staring. He sensed that there was something about him that I recognised. I sat down. One of his brightly robed wives, a woman of understated beauty, held a tiny cup in one hand, the coffee pot two feet above it, and poured the thinnest and most accurate of streams. She handed me the cup and saucer. He did speak French, was intrigued when I said I had an appointment with the Governor of the Central Bank and he wondered why. I said, as a cover, that I was a financier. In those days that term attracted respect.

I followed him along the path. His white sandals covered only the front of his feet. His walk was not like that of a man, plodding laboriously like me in the soft sand. He moved with the grace of a stallion. We reached the ferry and climbed up the ladder to the driving platform. He took his denim overalls from a hook. Even when stuffing his robes into them he moved his hands with the self-love Larry had used as Othello, the Moor. He accepted my payment as if the sight of money were beneath him.

The engine started first time; we set off leaving the boy with his canoe. The other side I drove the car on to the ferry. On our return we were met by a few men wanting a lift the 120 miles to Nouakchott, the capital. I took my leave of the ferry driver, draped again in his resplendent robes. He raised his head and looked down at me with a compassionate look in his eyes and touched his heart. We never shook hands.

After a few miles we were stopped at the border post, not much bigger than a telephone booth, by an officious little Arab, typical of the country's civil servants. He asked a series of irrelevant questions, pretended that my visa was out of date and eventually my passengers, eager to continue, told him to stop being such an ass and let us all go. I think he was after a bribe. There were many times I was glad to be giving lifts to people.

The sun lowered. We proceeded down the well-kept, dead-straight road, and it was encroached upon by sausage-sized James Bond beetles, impossible to avoid. The thorn bushes grew further apart until we left behind the last one, and the last beetle. The purity of the desert. Minarets appeared on the horizon. Pretty soon I was in the restaurant of a little three-star hotel where everything was scattered with sand.

My negotiations were unmemorable, the creative process normal and the outcome successful after a number of visits. I enjoyed going to the telex building. The machines were operated by attractive young men and women, all Moors, full of banter and horseplay, and no overtones of sex. They were free and unaffected within established limits. The Mauritanian jewellery was distinctive, threads of silver, wound in arabesques and all kinds of shapes, pressed into necklaces and bracelets made from dark wood. Riddelle loved them.

Sometimes I went from Dakar to Nouakchott by plane, but the DC4 really was on its last legs. It had no air-conditioning. Instead, along the rack for hand luggage were rubber-bladed fans. When the engines outside were all started up and howling these tiny fans whizzed on and I felt they ought to be outside on the wings, helping.

On the coinage front the United States had started a major change. They wanted to reduce the intrinsic metal value of their coins so that it would be well below their face value. The difference is called seigniorage. Some decades earlier even the well-ordered Swiss had had a problem when their white metal coins were made of silver and the London Daily Price of silver shot up, causing negative seigniorage. The intrinsic value was worth more than anything the coins would buy, so the coins disappeared into melting pots to be sold off as silver. The Swiss solved the problem by replacing them with the white metal alloy cupro-nickel. The Americans had done that already. They wanted to go even further. For the copper one cent they created a sandwich coin with a zinc core, clad with the traditional copper alloy, top and bottom, the zinc showing at the sides. For the white metal coins they used a core of copper. The process required immense pressure and stunningly clean surfaces for the un-struck strips of metal to adhere. Texas Instruments agreed that we, on behalf of the Royal Mint, could offer this technology to our customers worldwide.

On my way to Bangladesh I went to Bombay to see the Deputy Governor of the Bank of India, a most respected man, Mr Sheshadri. He immediately saw the economic attractions of reducing the need for expensive copper and nickel, using a zinc core and saving millions of pounds. He said that responsibility for coinage lay with the Treasury, as in England. So I went to New Delhi and introduced myself to the agents of De La Rue Giori who had provided the country's banknote printing presses, just like our own, and indeed throughout the world with one single exception: France. He was a grand old man called Kohli, head of a dynasty of businesses. He was delighted I knew something of his country's people and their history, and that one of my great-uncles, Sydney Olivier, had been Secretary of State for India, reported to by the Viceroy.

We were chauffeur-driven in one of his many Ambassador cars: Indian-made Morris Oxfords. We went along the main thoroughfare between the Lutyens-designed Senate, the House of Representatives, and to the top of the hill crowned on one side by the Treasury. The Deputy Permanent Secretary and his assistant were head-waggling, wrist-bending and articulate, with all-knowing interjections and delicate waving of slim hands. I felt like a supine orchestra which they were conducting. This was not a meeting at all but a prelude to prolonged background deals done out of each other's sight. They were very well disposed to De La Rue because we had originated and engraved their present issue of banknotes. I gained the impression that they were 'untouchable', but in safety at the top. In fact the problem was that Texas Instruments would only supply blanks ready for striking, and not rolled strip for blanking, and this would have put hundreds of Indians out of work.

Even where the countries did not have their own mints, which meant most of them, the sight round the edges of a different-coloured metal put people off, despite the example of the US. The Royal Mint pooh-poohed the idea for the coinage of the United Kingdom.

In Dhaka the main excitement was a visit by Senator Edward Kennedy. I went with tens of thousands of Bengalis to see his plane land. Such was his glamour that, despite the downfall of his reputation over the death of Mary Jo Kopechne, his reception almost equalled that of their national hero, the Father of the Nation, Mujibir Rahman, their President.

[187]

I started writing a novel, based on Kilombero and Mr Wevers, whom I changed into a heroic American called Wurzley. Every evening I wrote in my room, and between meetings in the daytime I would lie in the garden and write in my swimming trunks. The manuscript smelt of sun lotion. I was pleased with the opening lines, spoken by the African Minister of Industries to the English chairman of the sugar company, about the newly appointed general manager: 'So, he's never been to Africa before, this American?' Every journey I finished a chapter and Riddelle would read it. When I got back from the office and we were having our evening bath, supervised by the cat, she would tell me what she thought. She was an intelligent critic and this engendered lively discussions and reminiscences of our days in Tanzania.

The proofs of the Swazi banknotes were ready. As a courtesy to our High Commissioner in Mbabane I went to show them to him. He was most surprised. No one had reported seeing me. He appreciated my visit so that he could advise the Foreign and Commonwealth Office on the new currency before the story was in the newspapers. At lunch, apart from a kitten under his arm, there was a large nondescript Englishman whom I remembered as an officer cadet from Eaton Hall, a hackle in his beret. He was now in the Secret Service. I asked how many other secret agents there were in Africa. He said only two, just then, for the whole continent. All the rest were focused on the industrial unrest Arthur Scargill was engendering in Britain.

The Finance Secretary had been asked by the South African Reserve Bank to estimate the amount of rand currency circulating in Swaziland, due for replacement by the emalangeni. After consulting with local banks he had came up with a figure of nine million rands. To help them, the South Africans had offered to pay one year's interest on that volume. I put it to him that he should pressure the banks into justifying as high a volume in circulation as possible, to increase the payment of interest offered. Not only that, he should convince the Reserve Bank that after all those years they had been profiting from the interest Swaziland had paid for the use of *their* currency, they should pay at least five years of interest back.

My next visit was after we had air-freighted their banknotes and they had been released across the nation. The Finance Secretary was triumphant. The Reserve Bank had agreed to pay three years' interest on fifteen million rand. This yielded the equivalent of five pounds for every Swazi man, woman and child, giving the national accounts an unexpected budget surplus. My banknotes and coins were in every market stall, every distant tea-cosy hut, spreading into the distance to the borders of Mozambique, with their wonderful portrait of King Sobhuza II, and the uniquely shaped coins. This had done good to millions of people and enhanced pride in their sovereignty, apart from the cash bonus for the nation.

The two-day drive across Southern Africa was as pleasurable as ever. Quill Hermans and his Botswana colleagues were excited when I showed them the proofs of their pula banknotes and thebe coins. 'Pula' was on their national crest meaning 'Let there be rain'. 'Thebe' meant 'shield'. This was just after the success the new currency had had in Swaziland. I was able to explain the strategy I had suggested there and the most generous response of the Reserve Bank of South Africa. They could look forward to the same advantages.

It was time for President Sir Seretse Khama to approve the proofs. He had of course approved the designs at Cabinet. Quill took me in a small plane to the middle of nowhere, dry and barren, halfway to Francistown and the fertile game reserves in the north. We landed and plodded up a little hill with corrugated iron housing. At the top Quill left me on the terrace and took the proofs inside. Seretse Khama came out, the strong interesting face we had engraved. He shook me by the hand, put an arm round my shoulder and said in a fatherly way: 'So you have found another way of making money.'

He was due to leave for a conference in Salisbury on Rhodesian Independence, with our Prime Minister Jim Callaghan and leaders of the African Front Line States. Like everyone else he knew Rhodesia's economic success was mostly thanks to the white settlers and European-led government. There was nevertheless unlegislated social separation between the races which had somehow to end. That irreconcilability was the foundation for disaster. He said there was no compromise in sight anyone could believe in. Then he approved the proofs.

The tenth anniversary report of the Bank of Botswana, dated 1985, makes interesting reading:

PLANNING BOTSWANA'S NEW CURRENCY
Some difficult decisions had to be made concerning the denominations, design, name, metallic content and the quantities of the initial orders of Botswana's new notes and coins. Foresight and intelligent guesswork played their part in the process. For example, a representative of the British banknote printing firm of Thomas De La Rue happened to have a longstanding appointment

with the Ministry of Finance and Development Planning officials on the same day that Cabinet resolved to leave the [South African] Rand Monetary Area. By amazing coincidence – or brilliant planning – he had brought with him some sample Botswana banknotes, created by his firm's art department, to illustrate what local currency notes might look like if Botswana ever decided to issue its own currency. Not only was the timing of his visit remarkable, but De La Rue correctly anticipated the name 'Pula', which was subsequently suggested by a majority of Botswana by means of a nation-wide poll, as well as the denominations, sizes, colours, watermark and many other features of Botswana's notes. Not surprisingly De La Rue won the order to print the first batch of Pula notes and has retained the business of printing Botswana's banknotes ever since.

Off the east coast of Africa lay the thousand-mile-long island of Madagascar. *Le Monde* newspaper indicated that its relationship with the Banque de France was becoming sour. The doyen of our sales force, Alex Napier, accompanied me to Antananarivo. We became good friends on that trip. He had served in the Coldstream during the war, the Guards Armoured Division. We went first to the British Ambassador. He was, like everyone else, absorbed when turning over the pages of our hefty album of specimen banknotes. He made an appointment for us with the Governor of the Bank of Madagascar, Leon Rajaobelina.

On our way we caught a glimpse of the new Head of State who had led some kind of coup. He was in a general's uniform, an insignificant little man in a big peaked hat. The Governor was alert and decisive. He had formed an excellent impression of De La Rue after visiting us a few years before. He gave us a clear go-ahead. Alexis agreed that I had read the situation correctly and gave me the amiable task of gathering design material.

This had an added pleasure for me. Not only did the country have baobabs, it had lemurs. None of these lovely creatures survived in Africa because monkeys had killed them off. Madagascar had no monkeys. When my mother had lost a baby, Larry had given her a ring-tailed lemur to help fill the emptiness she felt. Tony was just over a foot tall, had a yard-long ringed tail, a black pointed face, big all-seeing eyes, and the most delicate black hands. At dinner he would sit on people's shoulders, lean forward, hands on the table, and sip from a wineglass. Then he would jump to another shoulder and do the same again. After a bit of this he used to miss his jumps. When the sun shone outside he would face it, hands spread wide and give a little purr. They both grew to adore him. Unfortunately he was irreconcilably jealous when I was born. He attacked my mother and was a threat to me in my cot. They gave him to the London Zoo where there was a lady lemur, but they never got on and he died of a broken heart.

Antananarivo was on high ground, crowned with a great wooden palace with a square spiral staircase and imposing rooms all around. The atmosphere was redolent of Java. Extraordinary. The prominent tribe, the Merina, could still be taken for Indonesians, who had colonised the place nearly a thousand years before. The palace overlooked a green lake surrounded by jacaranda trees bursting with mauve blossom. Nature was at its most profuse with the jungles, vanilla vines, and lemurs. There was a mass of reference material for our design artists.

A serious problem had arisen in Tunisia over our quality control. Some of our banknotes had tiny black dots over the watermark. The usual regional manager, Edwin Eggins, was struggling elsewhere, Burundi, so I took his place in Tunis with three lady banknote examiners from our Gateshead factory. In charge was Betty, their elderly supervisor, a good-hearted constant figure, married to one of the porters and earning more than he. Dorothy was married also, in her early thirties. Hilary was in her early twenties with a boyfriend called Trev. We stayed on the outskirts of the capital by the sea, near the remains of Carthage. Within hours of our arrival the attractiveness of the two young Geordie girls had spread round Arab males.

In the Central Bank they taught the local girls the techniques for examining banknotes, flicking through piles one hundred thick from various angles, so that any deviation would leap up, as movement, from the persistence of perfection, be visible at once, and culled. The French-trained currency officer was a M. Damaque. With him there was never any possibility of compromise. Should there be 'le moindre défaut' he read from his guide to currency examination, even a tiny dot, then the banknote was to be rejected. That was his *raison d'être*. He was grid thinking personified. *Il faut l'accepter.*

I kept my little team company at meals, and over the weekend took the two girls sailing in a dinghy, while Betty stayed in the lounge with her knitting. After dinner they were taken out by local Arabs who treated them like goddesses, they said. I could hardly prevent that. Yet, out of concern for them, I had the receptionist telephone my room to tell me of their safe return, usually around midnight. Dorothy kept wondering if her husband was up to anything during her absence and if so why shouldn't she. Hilary was the most fun. 'Eee,' she said with her Geordie accent, 'when I was yung with my thick lips no boys would dunce with me, so I ended up with some grot with a runny nose. But now, with Mick Jagger's squashy lips, they think I'm sexy.' Which she was. Couldn't help it. The slightest breeze would lift up her mini-skirt and show her flowery panties.

Our only competitor active in Tunisia was Finland, which printed the top value, using the same image of President Habib Bourguiba. They had seized the opportunity which our quality problems had offered them. They bid to print our values at a much reduced price. I immediately said to M. Damaque that their prices were obviously political. (Whatever that could mean.) This worried him. I am sure that he was scrupulously honest, but he seemed to fear the compromising character of the word 'political'. Meanwhile our Geordie girls' continuing presence, training *his* girls, made him feel his authority over them was reduced the more they learned. He felt his bank was occupied. It became a psychological pitch between us. I filled in time writing my novel.

De La Rue had a Tunisian agent, a handsome Arab. The two girls were fascinated watching the two of us speaking French to each other. They gossiped about how sexy *he* was. I had him make an appointment with the Governor, who agreed that it would be reprehensible to accept the Finns' offer. Yes, he would stay with our company in view of the immense goodwill he felt towards us for correcting our errors. This was not surprising because a change of a long-standing banknote printer would require justification to the President, who might well consider it suspect. He also said he would prevail upon Damaque to overlook any really tiny dots.

All was well. I paid the hotel bill. Before I left, the manager asked to see me in his office. He said it was highly personal. Please proceed, I said. He said he had been advised that every night, without exception, his receptionist had to tell me as soon as my two young girls returned. So every night, *every* night it would seem that I had had both of them. This was beyond his understanding of the English character. I said my behaviour was beyond reproach, and left him wondering how I could be such a ram.

I had to go to Guinea-Conakry. Through us, the Royal Mint had won a tender to purchase the country's withdrawn coinage for its metal content. Unfortunately quite a tonnage had been lost on the way to England, was still missing, and nobody knew what to do, least of all the insurers. They wanted evidence, from Conakry. The only place to get a visa for that seldom-visited country was Rome, so while waiting for the consulate to process my visa application I went to St Peter's and lay on my back, gazing at the Sistine Chapel ceiling.

In 1958 France had formulated the neo-colonial system for its previous colonies of West Africa and Madagascar. One country had refused to comply: Guinea-Conakry. Their dictator Sékou Touré said a resounding 'Non!' They had the most vibrant and artistic culture in Africa, plenteous natural resources: a quarter of the world's bauxite, plus gold, diamonds and iron ore, with a huge potential for hydro-electric power. They preferred total independence from France, in banking, economics, politics, jurisdiction, culture, everything.

In revenge the French, under President de Gaulle, behaved almost as unforgivably as they had in the early 1800s under Emperor Napoleon, when independence was won from them by Haiti. They left Port au Prince only after inflicting massive destruction on the sugar factories, and murder. In Guinea it was also pretty bad. They tore out all the telephones and equipment, gathered together all the government files, tax records, future plans and burned them. They destroyed the country's memory, leaving it nothing. This reduced the former potential wealth to penury, under a barely trained civil service, no *conseillers techniques* left behind to help. In the mounting chaos and resurgent tribalism Ahmed Sékou Touré became more and more autocratic and vicious. Stupidity and ignorance came to personify the regime. They had their banknotes printed by East Germany. A container fell off the ship delivering them and millions floated down the coast. More Guinean banknotes were collected on the shores of Liberia and Sierra Leone than the Central Bank had actually ordered. They were stuck.

From the airport to the capital was an hour's drive through magnificent jungle. The taxi driver was garrulous, delighted to meet an Englishman, highly but confidentially critical of the government. He pointed out a tree from which, only the previous month, half a dozen men had been left hanging. Not a good impression for visitors, he said. As a town, Conakry reminded me of the most run-down places in Java after the Dutch had been expelled. The whitewashed buildings had three feet of splashed mud stains all round them, eaten away with mould, the windows grimy, the streets soggy and pot-holed; but the people, no matter how poorly dressed, held themselves erect, especially the women in their exuberantly piled headdresses.

The one hotel barely deserved a single star. It was filthy, every item of fabric grubby, the food atrocious, and even the china plates were stained. In the dining room was an English ship's captain, drunk in front of a nearly empty bottle of champagne. There was a flash of recognition between us as coming from the same tribe but he was too far gone to talk to. I hoped he would sober up before putting to sea. He seemed to reflect the hopelessness of the hotel, its staff, everything.

At the Central Bank the chief cashier was solicitous and companionable. He said there had been a series of terrible mistakes. He knew that much of the withdrawn coinage had disappeared but there was no evidence to establish liability. We agreed that the Royal Mint should only pay for what it had received. By way of compensation he placed an order for twenty-eight million high-specification cheques. In the evenings he took me to see the national ballet. Never have I seen such dancing. They moved in African ways I could never have imagined, alluring grace interspersed with astonishing speed, arms and legs seeming to bend in impossible directions, to thrilling Guinean music, with stories about mystical birds and sacred forests. Each performance was preceded by a badly made propaganda film featuring their dictator. In his African robes Sékou Touré looked wild and wonderful, but in ill-fitting western jacket and trousers he could have been a stowaway. He was all-powerful and everyone suspected he had received a substantial bribe from the East German printers of their banknotes.

The next flight out was by Aeroflot in an Ilyushin turbo-prop. First class was at the back end, a single row of seats wedged under a ceiling sloping down behind them and a floor rising up underneath. The stewardesses were Soviet superwomen, bloated and used to getting their own way with mere passengers. I engaged one of them with what remained of my never-tested Russian and this made her more considerate. She even brought me a glass of water.

When it came to lunch I decided to rebel. It was a plate of cold spam and beetroot. I told her categorically that as a first-class passenger I would never eat *that*. She was taken aback, vulnerable for so huge a bully. I asked if their airline were a member of the International Air Transport Association. Of course, she said. Then the three flight officers would, I said, have to have their own different sorts of food. Naturally, she said – regulations: to prevent multiple food-poisoning. What are they having? The flight engineer was having chicken, the co-pilot fish, and the pilot steak and chips. I said she should bring me the flight engineer's chicken and he could have this cold beetroot and spam, which I handed to her. There were no other first-class passengers. How could she refuse, she obviously wondered. It was easy to read the thoughts in her troubled face. She grabbed my plate. I got my way. Never has plastic chicken tasted better.

One of the countries I visited routinely was Cameroon. At its independence there had been a referendum which had decided that a chunk of Nigeria should be ceded to it. So there was a sizeable minority of Cameroonians who spoke English, including their ambassador in London. He was convinced they should break away from French influence. He even accompanied me to the French-speaking capital of Yaoundé and obtained permits for me to take photographs of government buildings, as well as an array of lovely brass sculptures created by the lost wax method, and their intriguingly carved beads and hardwood panels.

Once the designs were completed I went there to present them, again accompanied by the ambassador. I had to wait for days for the verdict of President Ahidjo, whose fine portrait was on each of them. Apart from waiting, and writing my novel to fill in time, I enjoyed the absurdity of seeing a John Wayne movie, dubbed into French. There he was at his crudest, shouting: 'Alors, je vais te casser la gueule!' But alas, my banknote efforts, despite the glorious designs and the ambassador's stalwart assistance, were unsuccessful. The *conseillers techniques* had won.

Togo and Benin made little impression on me. The other two territories were Liberia and Sierra Leone, both set up originally as homes for released Caribbean slaves who wished to return to Africa, hence the name Liberia and of the Sierra Leone capital, Freetown. The difference between them was marked. The freed Afro-Americans set about colonising the native Liberians as best they could on their own, with overtones of America's Deep South, and hardly any guidance. The Executive Mansion was a sort of awkward Victorian US pile, the interior common parts hung with portraits of Liberian presidents, some of them dressed as admirals complete with brass telescopes. The speech patterns were a degraded version of the black patois of Louisiana: far from distinct and impossible to reproduce in writing. They used the US dollar for banknotes.

Sierra Leone's ex-slaves had been colonised by the British which gave them a better start. Parts of Freetown were almost replicas of Trinidad, even the street names, and certainly the accents. They were about to celebrate the tenth anniversary of their Central Bank, to be attended by about thirty African central bankers and ourselves. They were launching a new high value we had printed to mark the occasion: the twenty leone.

For the celebrations I was joined by David Rowe-Beddoe, now my managing director, and other colleagues. We went to the Presidency and were ushered into his office. On each side of the desk a stuffed leopard sat on its haunches. Pharaonic memorabilia filled the room. Siaka Stevens entered and sat, looking at us quizzically, a rubbery black face and a long neck bulging between a series of deep concentric creases. He burbled that this was a proud occasion for his country and the people, and expressed appreciation for all we had done.

After a couple of days' conference on banking matters, a couple of Trilander light aircraft flew us all in relays to a new branch of the Central Bank at Kenema, the centre of the diamond trade. The Star of Sierra Leone, at almost one thousand carats, remains one of the largest ever mined. The De Beers organisation was working an immense dragline in a grey sludge field of kimberlite the size of a football pitch. Its bucket was as big as a garage. The skilled African driver swung it far out, then gingerly retrieved it, scraping the surface and dumping the goo into a massive truck. The kimberlite was fed into a separation process in a factory. The sludge was culled and in the far end appeared the diamonds, almost all of them tiny grains, fit only for industrial applications.

Nearby, all round this major activity, were illicit diamond miners, digging in hope, knee deep in soggy holes. Gem quality was extremely rare. When they struck lucky they took the stones to De Beers for appraisal and immediate payment in orange two leone banknotes. When the civil war came it was financed by blood diamonds which they had found and not submitted for cash, evading official appraisal.

During the conference and the expedition to Kenema the differences between the Africans were highlighted, even though most of them had met before at similar bankers' meetings. The Ghanaians and Nigerians looked down on their hosts as descendants of slaves. The Liberians were even more frowned upon for their self-importance and excruciating articulation, and their continuing use of US dollars bills for their national currency. History was far from being a neutral topic of conversation. They resented their colonial past to varying extents, some appreciative of much that was achieved, the law and order, start of education and infrastructure, but almost all of them embarrassed by the strains of their early years of independence, the human failings in untested institutions.

In England that summer we rented a windmill. It was a five-storey high tower windmill on the north coast of Norfolk, Cley next the Sea.

We went for a weekend with Larry and Joan. They too were increasingly strained. I remembered when their children were infants how rapturously happy they had been together. I think those years, given to him by Joan, were the happiest in his life, the family fulfilment of a man, nearly sixty, who at last had a loving wife and family and nothing to feel any guilt about, at the peak of his powers as an actor, the summit of his life as Director of the National. That was now past, and his health destroyed.

He and I discussed how, once babydom is past, husbands and wives so often grow cold on each other. It had happened to him and was now beginning to happen again to me. At that stage we did not discuss his rumoured affairs with actresses. The effect of that on Joan was devastating, as she later wrote in her memoir *And That's Not All*. She gathered their children round her and they ganged up against him: their loss as well as his. They looked at him with hard expressions. The atmosphere was so changed that many of his friends, close enough to me, said they could not for the life of them understand what had drawn him to her in the first place. She was the wrong tribe. I said that it was Mother Earth, obviously, but in his case something even more powerful. He had needed a change of direction in his career, to move beyond drawing room comedy and the classics, and embrace the chancy and untested growth of present-day playwrights, almost symbolised by Joan's wonderful performances in some of them, and later his own. That no one can deny.

Sixteen

The news from De La Rue was excellent. I was to take over from Charles Cardiff as regional manager for South-East and South Asia, with a house in Singapore. Julian Wethered would soldier on in the Philippines, with Malaysia, Hong Kong, South Korea, the Pacific and Australasia. This had been my greatest hope, with Indonesia still my favourite foreign country in all the world. The pennies at home had become tight and this overseas posting ended my money worries. Renting our house would more than pay for the mortgage and its other costs, in Singapore I would live in a house with a garden rent free, with Tristan's prep school fees at Cottesmore two-thirds paid for by the company. Riddelle was excited at the prospect of life in the tropics again, overseas allowances, a servant or two, and simpler conversation.

I flew out to Singapore. Fifteen years had overwhelmed much that was historic. Even the Raffles Hotel was under threat, though there was a campaign, eventually successful, to preserve it. The new skyscrapers were majestic and the city gleamed with prosperity. Charles and his wife Angela had a mean little flat, not much to De La Rue's credit, so I stayed at the Goodwood Hotel, old-fashioned and family-oriented.

We took a taxi downtown and Charles introduced me to the Currency Board, one officer a Eurasian the other Chinese, both rather bland, and their impressive Chinese boss who was quite a banking authority in the island.

Then to Djakarta on a Garuda Airlines 707. In 1959 I had been the only one to get off the plane, a Qantas DC4 en route to Sydney. This was different. The first class air hostesses were elegant Javanese in their *kain* and *kebaya*, beauties with high cheekbones, languid brown eyes and lovely smiles. The men too were handsome. On the ground the capital, once so soggy with indecision, was energy-charged, a mass of new highways and hideous nationalistic monuments bequeathed by Sukarno. The most memorable symbolised freedom from colonisation: a monstrous statue of a man breaking the chains of servitude from his upraised wrists in a bionic outward thrust. The usual international hotels had sprouted on all sides, department stores, traffic lights everywhere, buses and taxis galore, the rickshaws now motorised. These bursts of activity from developments were led by the oil giant Pertamina, and the takeover by President Suharto. We stayed in the huge Borobudur Hotel, a splendid place with views beyond the Punchak of the volcanoes and surroundings of Bandung. Here we were in the southern hemisphere and the sun went from right to left, giving a completely new feeling to each day.

We drove through the smart suburb of Kebayoran, with its solid houses and pretty gardens, to the State Printing Works. The Chief Executive was General Hayono, in uniform, accompanied by several directors, all charming and fluent in English. I told them about my book and how much I loved Indonesia. In it I had not been entirely deferential towards President Sukarno, which won their smiles of approval, and every copy I had sent to my friends in Indonesia had been burnt. This had been done under the orders of Ganis Harsono, my friend, head of the Ministry of Foreign Affairs' Cultural Department. He had written me a letter. He did not mention the book's destruction, but did say how much it had moved him. This surprised him because he had always supposed the English to be unemotional. General Hayono sensed my joy at returning to their country. The head of production showed us round the banknote factory, equipped throughout with De La Rue Giori printing presses, just like Gateshead, except that it was built round a large courtyard, with flowerbeds and traveller's trees.

Travelling with Charles was a great pleasure. Introductions in Vietnam and Laos were brief, little more than a handshake, with problems to follow in a few weeks. Thailand was also a brief visit and I was dying to look up so many friends there. Charles was clearly in love with Nepal. It meant as much to him and Angela as Indonesia did to me. The refreshing thing about all these places was that they were sufficiently close to Singapore for me to be home every weekend.

Back in London I put our house on the market for rent. Almost immediately a French couple made the offer we wanted, but they needed to move in at once. Luckily our close friends Robin and Jane Mills lent us their house two doors down while they stayed in Gloucestershire.

I left Riddelle and the children in the Mills's house while I went to find a place in Singapore. Charles had heard of a large modern house with two kitchens, one for the servants, and a garden large enough to set up a cricket net for Tristan. It was part furnished. I obtained De La Rue's and the owner's agreement on terms and bought a beautiful teak dining table and dining chairs. Before I moved in the owner repainted the outside, so I stayed on at the Goodwood Hotel. Charles and Angela left me in charge of my new region and he went on to manage De La Rue's small banknote factory in Dublin.

Riddelle and the children came flying out to me and our new lives. They arrived very jet-lagged after the long flight. She looked ill. The journey was made worse by the plane bursting with noisy kids returning to their parents at the end of school term. We took a day off at the Goodwood Hotel, lolling by the pool, dozing in the shade with ice creams. Next day we went to a garage and the children helped choose our car, a silver Ford Cortina. Then we drove all round Singapore and they were amazed at the skyscrapers, wonderful parks and gardens. We took the lift to the top of the Mandarin Hotel and they gasped at the view between skyscrapers to the sea.

I showed them round the house, the master bedroom with bathroom en suite, a family bedroom which was huge and could be partitioned so that each of the children could have their own bedroom/study, and the two drawing rooms. The man next door would love us to use his swimming pool. The children all thought it was wonderful. It was ideal for our family in every way. All of them, that is, except for Riddelle.

That night she said she did not love me any more, that she was not prepared to live in Singapore, that she wanted another baby, but not with me as the father. No, she had not met anyone she was interested in. There was nobody else.

I explained that I, more than anyone, knew the importance to children of having a father *in situ*. I had never really had a father like that, and for me nothing equalled the importance of actually *being* one. That was the problem. She wanted them all to herself, and to have another baby, entirely hers. There was nothing I could do or say to change her mind. She looked forward to becoming a free spirit, she said. I did not telephone her parents because she had little respect for either of them, so we had a few days staying in the hotel for the sake of calm.

Then Riddelle upped and went, taking our children away with her. I then telephoned her parents. They said she must be mad. They knew how much I adored them all. They put a call through to well-ordered Changi Airport and got through to her. It made no difference. That was 31 March 1975.

I wrote to Pat Turner, the field sales manager, who had recruited me, to tell him what had happened, but chiefly to emphasise my determination to continue where I was as regional manager, so that I could fulfil my responsibilities to the company and to my family for schooling.

I handed the bunch of house keys back to the owner. He was kind enough simply to take them and shake me by the hand in sympathy. Then I spent a few days finding a suitable apartment: Cavanagh House, a high-rise block with a swimming pool. I went to see our High Commissioner, Peter Tripp. I intended it to be just a courtesy visit as a new British resident representing De La Rue, printers of the local currency and security print. I could sense his divining my emotional turmoil, so I told him. He asked me to have lunch on Saturday at his residency, Eden Hall, with his wife Rosemary. He and she became my link to any kind of emotional sanity.

It is hopeless and self-pitying to describe or share the acute and deepest sorrow I have ever known. The full horror of my loss hit me most the first time I went, on my own, to a supermarket to buy everything for self-catering. I had plenty of friends in Singapore from my previous experiences there in 1960, but now I wished to see no one I knew. I couldn't have faced them.

For musical catharsis I went to the Soviet shop. When my mother was going through her equivalent terrible time after Larry had left her for Vivien, she had found comfort only in the harsh music of Stravinsky. I started to put myself together with Scriabin's music: I needed its carnal spirituality, and with those records I worked slowly through Faubion Bowers's masterful biography of the man and his works.

Luckily my job provided plenty of challenges. Vietnam needed immediate attention. We had to redesign their banknotes every six months because that was the length of time it took People's China to counterfeit them. Our constant replacement of Vietnam's banknotes prevented China from causing it total economic paralysis, with mass forgeries of their circulating banknotes. It also meant that Vietnam accounted for a significant percentage of our turnover.

The war in Vietnam had gone from bad to worse ever since the French rout at Dien Bien Phu in 1958. By 1975, after Nixon had been elected President by forty-nine of the fifty US states, two million Vietcong had been killed, and 58,000 Americans. The bombing, before Nixon's resignation in 1974, had amounted to 200,000 tons a week, equivalent to one Hiroshima atomic bomb. When Gerald Ford took over he scaled it right back, and the crucial US air cover was withdrawn. The effect on every Allied soldier, American, Vietnamese or the many other participants, was hugely demoralising.

In Saigon I checked into the Continental Hotel, a French colonial relic where Graham Greene had stayed. It featured in *The Quiet American*. On the terrace downstairs at breakfast time there was a fat American colonel, rows of medals on his uniform, with a local teenage tart. Spring was in the air and the birds were cheeping. Frangipani flowers were on every table, heavy with fragrance, and in the street the women all wore their national *oudzais,* with separate panels from their waists to their knees, hanging down front and back. Their pale silken trousers shimmered loosely round their legs, tight around the hips, gloriously elegant. The atmosphere was benign, with the buzz of flower sellers, the markets and moneychangers, anything for a dollar, and the sated relaxation among Europeans and Vietnamese, smoking outside the cafés. The sense of harmoniousness was unjustified. The street hustled with motor rickshaws; how many of them were being driven by enemy Vietcong, nobody knew. The absence of warplanes flying overhead gave the misplaced semblance of peace. A few days earlier the Ben Hoa ammunition warehouses had been blown up not so far away.

In the daytime American troops were not much in evidence. Once twilight fell the nightclubs were full of them, black and white, in uniform, well-built boys uneasy together. The spaces between them were laced with divinely feminine tarts. 'Let's go back to your hotel.' One of the girls said to me in French, 'We could play backgammon in the nude.'

I wondered what the soldiers were like and chatted with two of them over Johnny Walker Black Label whisky which they had not tried before. They liked it. A change from beer or rye. One of them described an altercation he had had with his lieutenant. The man's vocabulary carried a familiar choice of words but the loathing was something else. So what did I think of that? I said that I had only been a peacetime soldier, a platoon commander, who had never had to fight a war of any kind, least of all so deadly a one as 'Nam'. He said he had heard of the Guards so I proceeded. I said that if one of my men, no matter what the circumstances, had spoken to me the way he had to his platoon commander I would have had him put under arrest.

The American grunted. He said if that had happened in 'Nam' I would have woken up to a hand grenade killing me in bed. I accepted a return drink from him and he spelled out many experiences of the kind the world knew so well and had been horrified by. In the movies I think the best line ever written about these soldiers' despair was delivered by Sylvester Stallone. His muscle-puffed character had said, with studied slowness: 'All we want – is for our country – to love us – as much as we – love it.' The tragedy was: it didn't.

De La Rue had a remarkable Vietnamese agent. He had contacts everywhere, not to be pried into, which enabled him to distribute mass tonnages of rice harvested in the extreme south of the Mekhong Delta, despite its being occupied by enemy Vietcong. He invited me to his house for dinner with his wife. We spoke French. They served Puligny Montrachet. I said the wine reminded me of Larry, which pleased them. Then we listened to the BBC World Service on the radio and the whole atmosphere changed. The gaiety of the day, the flowers and pretty girls, all were shrouded by the accelerating news of South Vietnam's losses, deaths and shrivelling hopes.

In despair he showed me his priceless collection of jade, beyond the beauty of any I had ever seen. One piece draped with fine chains combined with a foot-high goblet was all carved from the same stone. He wanted me to do him the most immense favour and take it out of the country. He could see the impossibility from the expression on my face. I remembered how thoroughly my suitcase had been scoured at Tan Son Niut Airport when Charles Cardiff and I had left.

Over dinner he raised the subject of my failed marriage. Had I ever been unfaithful to my wife. I assured him I had not. 'Then,' he said, 'it is time you were.' The sooner I started the better, before I froze into morbid self-doubt. That could end whatever joy of life remained for me. 'So, lunch tomorrow and I'll make an introduction, a well-educated girl.'

The classic French-built Central Bank had high ceilings lit by strip lights. Air-conditioning made everything tacky and damp. The currency officer welcomed me back to Saigon, asked after Charles Cardiff and other colleagues of mine in De La Rue, all very affable. I then had to tell him of my company's concerns, as gently as I could, and our need to change payment terms. I had to advise him that because of the worsening military situation we would need a one hundred percent payment in advance for any future work, even for designs.

He was speechless. He picked up the telephone and called for the bank's design artist. He then produced our four new design folders, opened them and laid them before me. They were magnificent, one of the first examples of using multi-colour in the engraved intaglio printing process. The high value depicted a tiger's head with open mouth in blood-curdling pink, its fur splendidly tawny and tactile.

Their design artist was a half-starved old man in moth-eaten T-shirt and shorts. He pulled his bare feet up to the seat of his chair, hugging his legs for warmth. He looked at me with contempt, and unrolled a tracing paper which he gave me. It was an outline of one of the vignettes on the back of our design. He stood, took it from me and laid it down on the desk next to our design. It showed how the perspective could be altered, with much improved effect. I expressed admiration, trying to introduce an element of esteem in the frozen atmosphere. He understood no French. His eyes seemed like those of a man studying a victim who had just swallowed a poison pill. The currency officer interrupted by telling me to come for tea with the Governor the following morning. That was the end of the meeting.

The Governor was viperous with fury. His long silences and eyes like lasers made it worse. I leant well back in the chair opposite his desk, graciously accepted the cup of tea and resisted the proffered cigarette. He eventually brought himself to say he felt stabbed in the back by De La Rue. He repeated the French word 'scrupules' with the pursed lips of a wet kiss. He spoke about the prestige of the Central Bank, its effectiveness under unprecedented difficulties. In support of all this he said they had ample balances in a number of countries.

Here I saw a chance to redeem things. I said that if the bank transferred the requisite sums for De La Rue to hold on deposit, in the bank's name, then it would make no difference to the bank because the conditions of a deposit holding would apply, while De La Rue would not be exposed to the risks of the war. I did not mention the implied payment by De La Rue of deposit interest to the bank. He got that point in an icy flash. His pride was importuned by such a supposedly generous compromise from a mere supplier. He told me to come at the end of the week to receive the bank's letter authorising immediate transfers to De La Rue in full. My unauthorised offer had stung him into concurrence. That was everything I could have wished. I put on the most solemn expression, bowed and took my leave. No hands were extended, none shaken. As an afterthought I asked about their design artist's suggested amendments.

'You must ignore that,' he said, satisfied that there was something he could tell *me* to do. I collected our designs from the currency officer and put them into my briefcase.

Our agent sent his Mercedes to collect me for lunch. I was driven to a pretty harbour with fishing boats and tall reeds. The restaurant was under an awning where he sat with a beautiful girl in an *oudzhai*. Her name was Annie, her French perfect and her nature simple and trusting. Her husband had been killed in the war and she was bringing up their eight-year-old son on her own. She worked in a coffee shop. We had a happy lunch. Our agent was delighted because my deal with the bank meant his commission was secured and would be paid weeks earlier than usual, though we never mentioned that. We telexed De La Rue with our excellent news. This started the long-lasting perfect end to the day.

Next morning in the British Embassy our Ambassador was unable to see me so I went to the Head of Chancery. There was the smell of burnt paper. They were shredding and burning their files. The corridors were stacked with them. I was hurriedly led into his office and even as I sat down the diplomat rose and practically shouted at me to get the hell out of the country now, immediately, don't even bother packing. I protested that in three days I was to collect payment instructions worth millions …

There was a knock on the door and it was a well-known British TV journalist and news reader.

The diplomat looked up peevishly as if to a tiresome cousin. 'What is it now?'

The journalist smirked: 'As you seem to be wrapping up I wondered if there were any cases of whisky …'

I had seen a bevy of western journalists the night before at the Caravelle Hotel, smoking and drinking themselves into a stupor. No wonder their stories, all shared over whisky, were similar and frequently wrong.

'You old vulture,' the Head of Chancery smirked. He pressed the bell for his secretary and told her to give the journalist whatever he wanted.

He turned back to me: 'Get on a plane. There are still seats but soon there won't be. You should go *now*.'

So I did, that very day, with suitcase and designs but no letter. The exit visa remains in my passport: the date was 25 April, a few days before Saigon was murderously overrun, with images from the American Embassy roof of people fighting to get into the escaping helicopter, the pilot hitting them in the face, the final ghastly humiliation.

I was back now in Singapore. Riddelle and my family had returned to Robin Mills's house in Queensdale Road. Thank God for such a stand-by. Our friends were horrified at what she had done. Her mother said on the phone to me, in tears, that if she ever heard the phrase 'free spirit' again she would scream. She and Pat Gibson solved the housing problem by giving her their own little house in Whitchurch village, just beyond Pangbourne on the River Thames.

Meanwhile the symptoms of what I was going through afflicted my eyes. I awoke with them in pain. Whenever I opened and shut them it felt as if the inside of the eyelids were being scraped. The eyeballs, according to the ophthalmologist, had grown rough dots. I put my feet on the ground and was convulsed with stabs of arthritis. I was diagnosed with Reiter's Syndrome. When walking I could conceal the pain, which then spread to my neck so that I could not move my head much. My hands swelled up and it became difficult to write, or type, or carry a suitcase. This made me bloody-minded and defiant. There was the sales conference in Basingstoke in a week or two and I was damned if anything was going to have me invalided out of my job. It was all I had, except for visiting my children.

To snap out of it I went to Chinatown to see if Fourth Brother was still at 40b Temple Street. Nearby the shop-houses had been replaced by high-rise apartments. It was as if Sago Lane, the death houses and all the market stalls had never existed. I went into the arcaded pavement, and down the dark passage into his building. The reinforced teak door was still there, so was the string for the light switch and I pulled it. I looked up and saw the lino flooring on the upper floor pulled up and a girl's eye appear.

'Ah, Takwan!' she cried. It was Third Sister. The bolt shot back and the heavy door swung open.

I took off my shoes. We shook hands. There was no sign of the black and white amahs nurturing opium smokers. That room was now rented to a young couple. In the main room the old man's big wooden bed, with his porcelain pillow the shape of a book, was replaced by a modern sprung bed. Things wooden had been replaced by things plastic. Fourth Brother's wife had heard my name and greeted me. She picked up a phone and telephoned him, saying he now called himself 'Lawrence'. Coincidence, no doubt. A small baby nestled in her arms. She was expecting another.

He was glad to hear my voice. He had qualified as an accountant and kept his promise to close down the opium den. I congratulated him and he, being Chinese with all the frankness they treasure, said he was not happy. He did not like his job. He wanted to earn more. He did not like his workmates. He was unhappy with his wife and did not want any more children. He hoped to move out of Chinatown and was on a list for a new apartment on the outskirts near the sea.

I renewed my congratulations to him. I said I was just passing through Singapore, not wanting to say that I was negotiating a contract to print their newly designed currency. That would have had him waiting outside my flat by the hour, never believing that I could not peel away a few thousand for myself and friends. It was relieving to hear what was, *au fond*, his extremely good news.

Before the sales conference the specialist in London prescribed drops for my eyes and for the arthritis some pills called Indo-Methycin, which did reduce the pain and the swelling of my feet, which he called 'planters', but my neck remained stiff and my hands so puffy you couldn't see the knuckles even with clenched fists. I caught a glimpse of Riddelle. The children cried out 'Daddy's here, Daddy's here!' and took me for a walk. Isis held my hand.

Indonesia beckoned. After pleasant meetings in Djakarta with the directors of the State Printing Works I flew to Bali to see Oka. Fifteen years had passed so I expected her to be married and with children. I took a taxi from Den Pasar to Ubud and stopped outside her compound. There was a new art gallery with a high roof and a pretty tourist shop. She saw my taxi and came out to welcome me as a customer; no recognition yet. She was as lovely as ever in traditional *kain* and *kebaya*, her long hair as before, folded into two loops behind her neck. I stood as she approached and suddenly she saw who it was, buried her face in her hands and said: 'You!' in a shaky voice. Before our emotions attracted attention she said 'Let's have tea', and led me round the gallery into her compound.

The soft bricks and stones of the small thatched buildings had more carvings than before. Statues stood, each with a hibiscus behind one ear. surrounded by flowering shrubs. We sat at a table in a veranda and she placed her dancer's hands on mine.

'You look so sad,' she said.

I told her what had happened. She said she could not understand how a family, *any* family, could be broken up like that. Not the Asian way. She had married and had children who were the love of her life. Her elder daughter, aged twelve, was a dancer, as she had once been.

I told her about the book I had written, and the chapter where I had described that happiest of months she and I had had together. I reminded her how we had bicycled for hours on end, searching for a place to be alone, even in the darkest of forests, but as soon as we had sat down anywhere we saw children's faces, grinning from behind every tree. We laughed at our memories. She said she could think of no other time that had meant so much to her. I explained that in my book I had given her another name, so that she would not be recognised. I had chosen a name that was not even Balinese, quite deliberately, so there would be no clue who she really was.

'What name did you use?'

'It's a Javanese name. The Goddess of the Rice Field: Sri.'

This overwhelmed her. Eventually she asked when exactly I had written the chapter about our love, which month.

I told her.

She was deeply moved. She said: 'That was the month my daughter was born.' She hesitated. 'And I called her "Sri".'

Hindu-Buddhism nourishes belief in the transmigration of souls. This was not that, but a powerful transmigration of emotion, all the way from Bern to Ubud.

She and her husband Rai had me to stay in their lodging. That evening she took me to see her daughter Sri dancing in the Tebesaje troupe. She was as lovely as her mother, too mature to do the classic *Legong*, so she and her girlfriends performed something slower and more serene, suggesting a passion which they were still too young to have experienced.

Next day I went to the Puri to see the prince, Chokorda Agung Gde Agung Sukawati (Happy Heart), whom I had met on a previous visit, on introduction from Faubion Bowers. He remembered me well, even the nickname he had given me: 'Talkwind', because I talked like the wind. It sounds as if I had been full of hot air, but I had made him laugh. I gave him news of Faubion. I also gave him my own sad news and he said there was a saying in Dutch: 'Every family has its cross.'

He proudly showed me a letter he had received from the American Ambassador, thanking him for all the wonderful things he had written about President Nixon's visit to Chairman Mao Tse Tung. Chokorda's reaction was a wry comment on world leaders: 'Like shadow puppets, creating a night long drama, and when the dawn comes, they are all laid together in the same box.'

A combination of serial numbering errors on the banknotes we had delivered and Nepalese vagueness called for several visits to Kathmandu. The currency officer was a dreamy man, referred to as the Guru. With his Nepalese cap he was the image of Hindu-Buddhist calm. Next to him side by side on a bench, also in Nepalese caps, sat two young men, like pawns to a bishop. They smiled in unison when things were going well, but if there were any cause for concern they frowned their unlined brows, on cue. Even after a couple of visits the Guru had not responded to our plea that they would run out of banknotes if they did not order immediately, in time for printing and delivery before winter made the Himalayan roads and trails impassable, even for porters on foot with banknote boxes slung on their backs. I pleaded with him but without effect before I had to leave.

I went again the following month from Bangkok, flying over Rangoon, and seeing the golden Schwe Dagon Pagoda gleaming in the Burmese sunshine. When I entered the Guru's office the pawns' frowns assumed waxwork stillness, held throughout my renewed pleading. The Guru then spoke of his wife. I had to hold my peace out of respect. He said she had borne him fourteen children. Many of them had lived but, irreplaceably, she had died. His place was no longer in the world. She had been his soul and she was gone. The Shah Hazan had built the Taj Mahal to memorialise the love of his wife after her death, but he, the Guru, was a poor man and could do no such grand thing. All he could do was build a temple to her in his mind.

This made any currency crisis seem far away, even though in similar circumstances he had told Charles Cardiff exactly the same story.

I asked him to show me the bank's vaults. He led me down the broad wooden spiral stairs to the ground floor of that particular Rana Palace, past the bicycles leaning against the wall and into a courtyard. It was surrounded by tall inch-thick iron doors in pairs, linked together with drooping chains secured with big padlocks. He pushed one of a pair of doors and between them I could just see a dozen banknote boxes. Yet these were the vaults for the entire nation. What about security? As if in answer to my unasked question the Guru indicated the face painted on each of the iron doors: the Lord Buddha. Security enough.

I reported the practicalities of our conversation to De La Rue and although no order had been placed they printed enough banknotes for a last-minute delivery to tide the Nepalese over winter.

In Bangkok some of the Thais I had known in their late twenties had become heads of department, one of them about to take over as Permanent Secretary to the Treasury. The Thai prince I had written about was their UN Representative. The other delight was the location of the currency officer. His office was inside the entrance of the Grand Palace with its glorious golden courtyards and mighty variegated pagodas.

With my little dark suit and black briefcase I felt like a chiropodist going to see Anna and the King of Siam.

Laos had two semi-governments, one capitalist and the other Communist, represented either side of the main road with soldiers mildly facing each other from trenches. The Laotians were ideal De La Rue customers because they had no coins, only banknotes. The Central Bank Governor was capitalist, the Minister of Finance Communist. It worked, somehow. With their literary French and immersion on the teachings of Rousseau and the Buddha, plus their fondness for good wine, conversation was stimulating.

The fifth of September was the date for their annual boat races in the royal capital, Luang Prabang. The entire Diplomatic Corps went. Our Ambassador, who had written a famous book on Laotian fish dishes, took me there in a private plane. The races, two boats at a time, like Henley Royal Regatta, took place on a small tributary of the River Mekhong. They started off with an awkward curve then went straight downstream to the end a mile away. The boats were thirty yards long, hewn from a single hardwood tree-trunk, hollowed out and weighing several tons. They were crossed with benches for the rowers who had spear-shaped paddles, twenty sitting in pairs in the front, twenty at the back with a platform in the middle for a loud brass band. At the stern were three old men with long steering paddles. When the rowers accelerated the band struck up and all the men shouted in bass unison with every stroke. On the bow were four hefty men doing simultaneous press-ups to make the hull bend up and down like a serpent, to raise it higher in the water.

Each crew represented a guild and I was allotted to the flower growers. Lunch was made largely of flowers in a salad, plus river fish. Their crew's costumes were scarlet tunics and sarongs, with pale blue conical hats. They won their first race and lost the second. Late in the afternoon the final produced a dead heat. The crews were given an hour to rest for a re-row. At the start everything was tense. Both crews rounded the curve under perfect control. As they drew away they matched each other stroke for rapid stroke, the drums and cymbals clattering and banging, the men's voices hoarse and at the end of their energy. The result was another dead heat, watched at the finishing line by the King himself. It was all too much. Everyone knew the Communist takeover was only weeks away and that this would be the last boat race. The crews leapt into the water. They went for each other, fists flying, despite the presence of the monks, the Lord Abbot and their sovereign. It was too awful an end to kingship in the land of a thousand elephants.

The tiny Sultanate of Brunei is an oil-rich country at peace with itself and its neighbours. Oil was not the curse it so often is. I had met the retired sultan in Nairobi when staying with Malcolm MacDonald. He had handed over as head of state to his elder son. The royal family endlessly spoilt its lackadaisical population. They were all subsidised with free television sets, even the ones who lived in the *atap* village houses on stilts in the middle of the river. Every year the government spent a million pounds at Spinks in St James's, London, on orders, medals and decorations, to be solemnly pinned by the young Sultan in golden regalia on the breasts of dozens and dozens of men, seemingly just for being good subjects.

I looked forward to seeing the High Commissioner, Jim Davidson. Julian and I had known him when he was Deputy High Commissioner in Bangladesh. He had bristling eyebrows, suitable for an actor playing the role of an admiral. He had won the young Sultan's admiration for presenting his credentials not in a tropical suit, but in the full fig of Royal Ascot, handing in his top hat and rolled umbrella to a flunky on entry.

He beetled his brows in friendly welcome as I entered his office. I told him that De La Rue had the passport and airline ticket business, but were after the banknote business supplied by Bradbury. He did not take sides. He said the best man to meet was the Pehin Issa, who ran just about everything.

He had a call put through.

He sat back with the phone to his ear: 'Issa,' he said familiarly. A slight pause, then an all-embracing smile and a resonant 'Jim!'

There was a pause. His brows knotted and he leant forward adroitly. 'Jim *Davidson*!'

Oh the humiliation, and how easy for Pehin Issa to score points against such a benign man.

A few years later we did secure the banknote business.

Meanwhile De La Rue received a strong letter from the new Communist government of unified Vietnam, repudiating all contact with us. One came from Cambodia too. With the loss of two such significant customers, and Julian Wethered's main customer the Philippines now scheduled for us to construct their own state printing works, it was felt that I could combine the rest of his region with mine.

I went to Singapore for a couple of days to meet our Chairman, Sir Arthur Norman, DFC and bar. Gerry to his colleagues and friends. He was a wonderful man, with De La Rue from the start, and recently head of the Confederation of British Industries. He was of solid stature, and when his green eyes were at their most focused one almost felt sorry for the Luftwaffe. I introduced him to the Currency Board, the Chairman of the Central Bank, and Singapore National Printers (SNP) who were interested in forming some sort of association with us. After lunch he wanted to see my flat and have a lie down. There I gave him a copy of my book. We dined with the directors of SNP.

Next day there were more bankers and lunch with the local head of HSBC. That afternoon I had made an appointment for him to meet Prime Minister Lee Kuan Yew from 2.30 to 4 o'clock. He took my book with him which he was enjoying and wanted to show the President when he introduced me. On the way he wondered whether I could write about De La Rue. I felt that a book of that description should be by an author who was a master of the flat style called for, while I could not help but be flamboyant.

Our limousine drove us through the gates and security checks up the green grassy slope and flowerbeds to the white Istana, the President's official residence. There our licence number was checked and our passports, and we were invited to sit in the waiting room. Our turn came and we both stood. At the office door I was turned away and Gerry went in alone, still with my book. Their discussions centred round Singapore's desire to enhance its reputation as a financial centre by having its own State Printing Works.

That night we flew to Sydney to meet Julian Wethered for the start of his handing his region over to me. Gerry spent the day there to be with his daughter while Julian took me round the Australian commercial banks, trying to interest them in having us print their traveller's cheques, a worthwhile business before the advent of credit cards.

Julian's Aussie friends Mike and Di Nicholas invited the two of us to dinner. They were of the mega-rich Nicholas family which had developed Aspro tablets. Their drawing room had a couple of Italian marble tables, Georgian furniture and a Steinway grand piano. The house was on a slope with terraced flowerbeds leading down to the upper reaches of Sydney harbour, with clear water, a few yachts moored and on the far side a cricket pitch with players in whites. Perfection. The guest of honour was the Chinese pianist Fu Tsong, who had escaped the terrible Cultural Revolution which had killed his parents. The night before he had performed at Sydney Opera House. His wife Hepsibah was the daughter of my old friend the violinist Yehudi Menuhin. There were one or two other men and three attractive single girls in their thirties, one of them Joan Stanbury, a recent Miss Australia, now getting over a vicious divorce. She was lovely. Her long straight scarlet dress was chic and discreet. After dinner, when Fu Tsong had finished playing a Schubert Sonata, she gazed at me and asked: 'Tarquin, what's it like being an Englishman, in an Australian house, listening to German music, played by a Chinese?' I was to see more of her.

Julian and I flew on to Auckland with Gerry, staying overnight in a modest hotel. The marina was filled with yachts, more per head than anywhere else in the world. Many of the younger men dressed like colonials, in shorts, long socks and sandals; the girls looked much more fun. After dinner Gerry called us up for a drink to have a nightcap. So we sat in our dressing gowns with our Black Label, he with bare feet like the roots of an apple tree, loving being with his front-line troops.

Windy Wellington, the capital, had no vitality, no obvious wealth creation: mainly bureaucrats, politicians, diplomats and students. Four kinds of parasites. The Prime Minister was the oppressive Mr Muldoon. The one good hotel was the James Cook. It was very tall and earthquake-proof, as were a few other buildings, but most were built deliberately squat to be more resistant. The waitresses wore full-length skirts like under-carpet and everything they said sounded comforting. There was a new book by a New Zealander entitled *The Passionless People*. It said their women aged rather well because they had so few moving parts. Noël Coward had commented: 'New Zealand? Sixty million sheep can't all be wrong. The people? Well balanced – chips on both shoulders. The place? Well, quite frankly, it was closed.'

We met the Governor of the Reserve Bank, the chief executives of the National Bank of New Zealand, whose traveller's cheques we printed, and of the Bank of New Zealand, a government-owned commercial bank of which Gerry was a director to keep an eye on things. Everything was so smooth and rounded and repressive I felt ill at ease. I sensed there was a carbuncle of treachery waiting to burst. I said nothing, lest it make my masters think I was unsuited to look after this prestigious customer, ours since 1934. I decided that the best approach would be for me to visit every three months on the dot, to become part of the woodwork, and cast my net as wide as their tasteless brown ale would allow. It was as if the Kiwis were descended from Edinburgh's genteel suburbs. I much preferred the rough cockney, the classless vitality and badinage of Australia. So, on the way to New Zealand or on the way back, I would stay in Sydney for a weekend with Joan.

I did, over the years, spend one weekend in Wellington. On Saturday morning I realised I had not packed my hairbrush so I asked where I could buy one. The receptionist said I could take a train to Parapara-mou, then a bus to Pykakareeky (or vice versa, and I am spelling onomatopoeically) where the resort shops were open. As I had nothing planned I went. I even chose a hairbrush, but hadn't enough money to pay for it. There was a branch bank open but they refused my Ameri-can Express traveller's cheques because the Reserve Bank was closed and they did not know the day's rate of exchange. I suggested they pay me 95% of yesterday's rate, but they refused. Very calm they were. I could have hit them, but put my hands in my pockets and gently wished them all the best.

On the way back I was impressed by the country's vigour when it came to sport. There were many runners, swimmers in the sea, and dozens of hang-gliders expertly catching the thermals overhead. Next day I was invited water-skiing on a beautiful placid river in the same part of North Island. They let me go first and I slalomed as best I could, at least to my own satisfaction. Then they showed me. The girl jumped in, no ski, and clung on to the bar of the eighteen-metre rope. The boat accelerated to forty miles per hour and she swung increasingly wildly, like a pendulum, from side to side on her stomach. She gave a lurch, turned all the way round and sat on the rushing water, feet in front of her. She gathered her strength and stood. She bare-footed across to the wake and back again. The muscular young man did the same later, and then turned round and bare-footed backwards. Now that was terrific.

Our final destination with Gerry was Hong Kong, where Julian had settled from Manila about a year earlier, with his second wife Antonia and their two tiny boys. We had an appointment to meet the Chairman of the Hong Kong and Shanghai Banking Corporation, Michael Sand-berg. That was by far the most important Bradbury Wilkinson customer and of course we were after it.

Julian was the Old Etonian son of an admiral, brought up in a classic house called Remnants, in Marlow, only a few miles from my grand-mother Eva's house Apple Porch and with a similar atmosphere. He was a fine strategist. He had noticed that the HSBC branch in Manila was approaching its centenary. He persuaded it and the Philippine Post Office to let us print a commemorative stamp to mark the occasion:

1875–1975. It depicted a top-hatted gentleman and long-skirted lady shaking hands, their luggage beside them on a quayside, a tea clipper beyond and some Chinese junks. President Marcos had accepted the invitation for the occasion from HSBC's Chairman, to be joined in Manila by Sir Arthur Norman and the Earl of Lichfield.

A month before that Julian and I were in Dhaka, in his room, imbibing. We received a telex from our Security Print Division, never our favourite, which was in charge of postage stamps. They reported that the colour of the commemorative stamp was unsatisfactory, the perforation wavy, and they wondered whether this was all right. What the hell else could be wrong: cyanide on the back? Julian telexed the Banknote Division to knock everything into shape. The printing was whipped away from our factory in Bogotá, given to Dunstable and all was well.

I went to Singapore to pack everything for my move to Hong Kong. Julian booked me into a suite next to Gerry's at the Mandarin Hotel. His wife and two little boys had left for England. I went with him and Gerry to meet Michael Sandberg next morning in his grand old office, a few years before the bank's new building replaced everything with the cantilevers of modernity. There were classic paintings of Hong Kong by the English painter Chinnery.

Michael Sandberg said how impressed he had been in Manila. He then explained HSBC's embargo against De La Rue. During the riots which had burst upon Hong Kong a number of years earlier there had been a run on banknotes. Bradbury had leapt to the rescue and devoted the whole of their capacity to printing his bank's notes.

'Therefore,' Michael turned to me, 'we are loyal to Bradbury. While Tarquin may discuss other DLR products and services within the bank, currency is taboo.'

Gerry suggested that maybe one day, like the Philippines, they might opt for local production at their own factory. Michael acknowledged the possibility, almost certainly with Brads at the back of his mind.

He invited us racing at Happy Valley racecourse. I had never been a gambling man, except for poker in the Army, but that day I studied the form in the *South China Morning Post*. I saw that one jockey, Tse by name, was riding a favourite in one race but a fifty to one outsider in another, so I bet fifty dollars on the outsider.

We sat in the Chairman's box enjoying Krug champagne (only £6 a bottle in that civilised island). My horse romped home. A messenger came to me with a brown envelope stuffed with two and a half thousand dollars. I was expected to be modest and unassuming, so decided to carry on betting randomly so as to lose most of my winnings. Sometimes I told the messenger the number of a horse I had not even identified by name. Several won. The whole thing became hilarious. At least it more than paid for the expensive suite Julian had put me in, saying it would do me no harm to be next to Gerry in the Mandarin.

Next day Gerry and I went to Julian's apartment, Riviera Apartments on South Bay Road. He had risen at six in the morning to grind all the spices in preparation for the curry lunch he had prepared. 'What a lovely home,' Gerry said, 'and what a love of life to make such a curry.'

Gerry flew back to England after we visited the Chartered Bank and the Mercantile Bank whose notes we did print. Julian and I went on to Manila for a whole week because of the range and number of his contacts. Governor Licarros received us in his office, sitting between Senior Deputy Governor Briñas and the Director Benito Legarda. The two of us looked very different from each other: Julian, with his pale red hair, never suntanned. I, supposedly with *some* Latin blood, had gone the colour of toast. Julian gave a generous introduction, speaking of my previous associations with the East and how happy I was to return to the Philippines.

'Like MacArthur?' One of them asked.

We laughed. Licarros looked at my hands, darker than his own.

'Are you Indian?'

I waggled my head from side to side like a Bengali, and in their accent said: 'Nert ixectly.'

They laughed. I asked Ben Legarda if he was related to the Legarda who had recently died. He said it had been his father, who had had me to dinner in 1959 and I recalled playing the piano to him. The other guest had been General Basilio Valdes. That was Ben's uncle. They all had great respect for Julian in that institution with its endless corridors. A number of new appointments had been made in the bank in view of our forthcoming construction of their state printing works and security print factory, with Johnson Matthey equipping the mint and gold refinery. We met them all, and then went elsewhere to see our customers for passports and security print.

Julian returned to Hong Kong to pack and I looked up my own old friends in Manila, the Liboros and Benitezes. After going to a party with them in Andy Liboro's garden it was as if I had never left.

I mentioned to them the name of the De La Rue Giori agent, an

Italian banker called Mario D'Urso. They said I should immediately make contact with him because he was influential with Imelda Marcos, whose purlieu included the Central Bank, plus a huge portfolio called 'Human Settlements', and much else. There seemed to have been some slur against Mario's initial approach to us in Basingstoke. Naturally there was a difference of interests worldwide between ourselves as printers and Giori's machines taking our customers away, but we did have a one-third share in Giori's company, and now that the joint deal was signed with the Philippines it made sense for me to have Mario as a colleague.

I initiated a number of quiet meetings in the Philippines equivalent of the House of Lords. This was the elite lounge of Wak Wak Golf Club. Yes. It is a country sometimes difficult to take seriously. There I was introduced by Andy Liboro to a series of soft-spoken Filipinos over pre-lunch drinks. I was contrite and apologetic, for quite what I did not know. They expected Mario back the following month. He worked ostensibly for Lehman Brothers Köhn Loeb in New York. His main activity in Manila was to secure a contract for Fiat to provide a fleet of buses, nationwide. I felt that our plant and equipment activities were vulnerable to corrupt outside interference. It was to prevent this that I needed Mario's close relationship with Imelda. They understood.

Seventeen

I settled into Julian's glorious flat overlooking Repulse Bay, its islands and the occasional Chinese junk passing by. He and Antonia had a genius for comfort: a large drawing room, sofa and armchairs, honey-coloured carpet and a fireplace, My long teak dining table and chairs from Singapore were perfect. I had to buy a couple of bedside reading lights and bought exactly the same as Julian's. I found that thoughts of him and his new family were reassuring.

Being alone again after a couple of weeks of company made me more aware of the increasing pain of arthritis. It helped to lie on the floor when putting on my trousers. My grip was so feeble I had to hold the toothbrush with both hands. It was difficult to open my mouth wide enough to get the thing between upper and lower teeth.

After breakfast I was sitting on the floor putting on my shoes when in came the housekeeper Ada, whom Julian had discovered. She was sixty-four, mainly Chinese, with fractions of English, Portuguese and Jewish, and a range of recipes to match. We chatted about the Wethereds and their boys whom she loved. I said that I too had children but my wife had left, as had Mr Wethered's first wife. I hoped to marry again, but not quite yet.

I said: 'In the meantime I do not mean to live like a celibate monk. I mean, for goodness sake, Ada, you're a woman of the world. You know exactly what I mean.'

'Ooh sir,' she said. 'I don't mind if you have an awgy.'

I had never had an orgy, but let it pass.

'But sir,' she added, 'I won't let you have any Chinese.'

I had rather looked forward to that. After all ...

'Why not?'

'They're terrible, sir.'

She went through some of the names in the Legislative Assembly, list-ing the men who had been compromised and blackmailed by Cantonese girls having affairs with them, pretending to get pregnant, or actually giving birth.

'No sir. If you have a Chinese I shall leave.'

She was in charge. I had almost double the work load normal for a regional manager, which I was extremely happy about because it was therapeutic. With the Pacific Islands still for me to visit, the distances were immense, from Pakistan to Tonga, South Korea to New Zealand. Hong Kong was the most ideal home in space, but I also needed a home in time. I decided that whatever happened, the first week of every month would find me there. My Hong Kong friends coped with this. We all loved last-minute arrangements. I could give a dinner party at a day's notice for twelve, after only asking eighteen if they could come. And as they knew when I would be home their invitations awaited my return. Without Ada things would not have been the same. She managed me, the apartment, and all the entertaining I did.

I hurried to Kuala Lumpur where the Governor, Tan Sri Ismail, had complained fiercely of serial numbering errors on our banknotes. Why that always happened with the Bank Negara Malaysia was a mystery. My predecessor at Kilombero Sugar, Richard Beacham, was in CDC's Regional Office for Asia and the Pacific. I asked his opinion of our agent, John Annersley, the local director of Harrison and Crosfield, a classic plantation company. He said that while Annersley was scrupulously honest, as an agent for us he could not be more inappropriate.

I was met by an H & C Malay trainee for a meeting with the Deputy Governor, who was an ebullient Malay in a white suit and colourful shirt. When he bent over you could see the garish patterns on his boxer shorts. A twit. So was the agent's trainee. The currency officer was Chinese, so was the Bank's Director of Finance, both adroit and informed.

John Annersley and I lunched together with the Malay trainee and their Chinese executive who did all the real agency work. Annersley was a bull of a planter type, fluent in Malay but with no local sensitivity. I spoke to him of the people I knew in KL, starting with the Commissioner of Police, Claude Fenner, many still in government, in businesses and the arts. Annersley was not on friendly terms with Claude nor any of the others I mentioned. Richard Beacham was right. As always in every country of my region I introduced myself to the local HSBC manager.

In England, before the sales conference, Riddelle wanted me to meet her lawyer. I went straight from Heathrow to her parents' little house in Whitchurch where she and the children were ensconced. It had been an all day flight from KL and I asked her if I could have a bath. She rushed upstairs to draw the water; something she had never done when we were together. The children were all over me in a restrained rather pained sort of way, which was easy to understand. She shouted down that the bath was ready. It certainly was: about a foot deep in luxurious suds.

I felt much better after the bath and lay down on the floor beside Riddelle, in front of the log fire. The doorbell rang and Tristan opened it to the solicitor, a pleasant man called Alan Edwards. As he came into the room he stopped in amazement.

Eventually he said: 'What nonsense is this about you two getting a divorce? I have seldom if ever seen such a happy couple.'

We discussed what we had to in a friendly way, and he left.

Then Riddelle came up with her suggested compromise. Supposing we shared a house in England, fairly large, with me at one end and she at the other, so that the children would be with both of us, and I could develop the whole place with my carpentry and decorating. She wanted to have more babies. I said I did not want further children; three was quite enough. She said she wanted to have a baby by another man, not me. Anyone in mind? No she had not met him yet. I said that I could never live like that. A couple of years later she did give birth to a baby, now a chartered accountant in her late twenties. A nice intelligent girl and very pretty.

I went to Manila for a further meeting in Wak-Wak Golf Club. Andy Liboro introduced me to one of President Marcos's principal movers and shakers, a rather sinister man. He said that his associates had been impressed by the genuineness of my apology. In view of the importance of our factory project he had decided to further our cause. I was to have breakfast with Mario D'Urso at 9.30 that Saturday, 6 December 1975, at the Hyatt Hotel. I was invited to a State Dinner in Malacañan Palace in honour of President Ford and the following day to accompany them on the Presidential yacht, *Ng Pangulo,* for a journey to Corregidor Island to commemorate General MacArthur and the Second World War.

Mario was one of the best-looking men. Tall, slim, broad shoulders, pointed Italian features and amazing green eyes. Everyone knew of his closeness to Imelda, the First Lady, and sometimes referred to him as the Second Lady, but I don't think they were more than good friends. He was in the Hyatt penthouse. We had actually both had our breakfasts. He was still in his dressing gown awaiting a telephone call at ten.

He had an arrangement with the operator in Rome to call him at fixed times. This enabled him to make calls to wherever he liked, and put anyone in direct contact with whomever they wanted, anywhere in the world no matter how incompetent the local exchange. This was long before reliance on telephone operators was replaced by our own personal cell phones. I explained the informal approach I would like him to adopt as a contact man for me, and said that if this worked then an arrangement would be made with Basingstoke. He was happy with this. He put on his swimming trunks, towel robe and we went down to the pool. I took my leave and he dived in.

That afternoon Air Force One landed at Manila Airport. Thousands and thousands of children filled the streets in gay new shirts and dresses and lined them as the motorcade proceeded. The Philippines welcome, masterminded by Imelda, must have been the most decorative and ebullient, the most spontaneously joyful that President and Betty Ford ever received.

I wore a Filipino *barong tagalog*. Mario wore one too. His chauffeur drove us to Malacañang. The car had flashing lights on the front, as if for a minister, and we were waved through the gates of the Spanish-built wooden palace. It had small windows to keep out the sunshine, and air-conditioning against the vapours of the squalid River Pasig. An impressive staircase lead up to the State Dining Room. The distinguished visitors, mostly men, were in black ties. The Filipina ladies were exquisitely dressed, especially Imelda's closest companions, her 'Blue Ladies'. The younger ones, the most beautiful in the world, exceeded even their own supreme standards in jewellery, fabrics and shapeliness.

Speeches came with the coffee. President Marcos referred to the Philippines' identification with a large number of American causes, his words fluent and with an attractive accent. His speech was the first time I had heard any leader say the much repeated line, that while the United States could not be called upon to solve the world's problems on its own, none of the world's problems could be solved without it. President Ford said, among much else that was poorly articulated, how totally overwhelmed he and his wife had been by their welcome. At the end we all lined up to shake hands with both Presidents on our way out. Gerald Ford looked impaled with fatigue. Marcos and Imelda remembered the names of every single guest.

Our driver dropped Mario at the Hyatt and took me on to Andy Liboro's in North Forbes Park, lights flashing all the way. Next morning he returned and we collected Mario. In the harbour was the Presidential yacht: the liner *Ng Pangulo,* Filipino-designed and built by the Japanese as part of token reparations. It was the Philippine Navy's flagship.

The top brass were waiting in the stern, including Secretary of State Henry Kissinger and Undersecretary Habib. The two Presidents and First Ladies were piped on board. The engines thrummed and we put to sea amid a flotilla of patrol boats. Jet planes flew high in the sky above a few clouds. There were plenty of chairs and tables for the thirty of us so we settled down, changed places or wandered around during the two-hour voyage. The breeze helped reduce the intense damp heat. Even Imelda stood laughing sadly as she mopped her temples with tissues. Light refreshments were served.

A long table was set for lunch and we sat down. In the next room was a sofa-sized black container with the thermonuclear triggering devices within easy reach of President Ford, the Commander-in-Chief. It was tended by three or four signals experts who murmured to each other urgently but inaudibly. Just in case. Always in contact with America's immense defence network worldwide.

After lunch President Ford read a speech about the Philippine people's heroic resistance during the Japanese occupation; how they had suffered so terribly, and yet protected American soldiers against capture at great risk to themselves. He dwelt on the symbolism of Bata'an and Corregidor, how they had held out for weeks in early 1942 even after General MacArthur had been ordered home by President Roosevelt, and left with the memorable words 'I shall return'. Marcos gave a better speech in reply, with no notes.

Throughout the day, like a visual magnet, whether standing or sitting, was Henry Kissinger. Even the bulging back of his neck exuded vigour. Those eyes behind thick pebble spectacles, that self-conscious accent and bassest of voices, all struck me as phoney. When he spoke he looked entirely absorbed by his own self-hypnosis, as if nothing anyone else said could ever disturb his chain of thought.

The tunnel running through Corregidor Island was the only iconic testament to that terrible time. Here the two Presidents stood in silence, as did all of us, heads bowed. The temptation was to linger. President Ford leant over a car which was parked between him and Marcos and said, 'Mr President, unfortunately we have to adhere to our timetable.'

From his tone I deduced that he had been well briefed on the

Marcoses' shameful aspects, their insatiable greed, martial law as they practised it, the use of torture.

For the return journey I had a chat with Undersecretary Habib about the tribulations of People's China, and what a superb and unforeseen breakthrough Nixon's visit had been in February 1972. Habib told me an unforgettable story. After the two leaders, assisted by their interpreters, had established a rapport, Nixon asked what Mao thought would have happened had it not been President Kennedy who was assassinated, but the Soviet leader Khrushchev. Chairman Mao was intrigued by the question. After some reflection he said he didn't think that Onassis would have married Mrs Khrushchev.

For the holidays that winter Tristan and Isis came to me in Hong Kong. Clavelle was too young. Away from the teeming arrivals hall I had the use of my travel agent's driver with a black London taxi. The children loved it. Their voices yelped with excitement as they described landing at Kai Tak Airport, with the plane only a mile from the runway doing a sudden turn and banking sharply, so that you could see into people's rooms. They were bursting with news of Riddelle and Clavelle and the cat and school; and constantly interrupting each other.

They shared my enthusiasm for flying kites so we bought a couple, shaped like falcons, and climbed to the top of Mount Stanley. They were excited by the strong wind and aimed each other's kites at each other to attack, high in the sky until it was time to go home. There I poured myself a whisky and became the soul of contentment, hearing the odd thump from their bedroom of a pillow fight. Then there was a bang and a pained scream.

Isis came running out with blood pouring from a big cut in her forehead. She had hit the corner of something. It was serious. I wound a bandage round her head and drove the three of us to hospital. She needed five stitches. In a dazed state she lay back and clasped my hand as the doctor swabbed her forehead and reduced the blood flow. He was worried she might be concussed. While he worked on her she squeezed my hand harder and kept repeating endearments. The words almost broke me. I could barely speak. Once finished he said she must lie still for half an hour. Tristan gazed calmly into space.

Back in my flat they had their baths, separately now that he was a prep school boy, and their dinner in dressing gowns. I tucked them up in bed, which amused them because they were rather old for that, and went back to my patiently waiting whisky. I meditated. I became aware of a disturbance, a series of disturbances in their room. I went in and saw the full pelt of another pillow-fight, Isis's bandage knocked to the back of her head. Angrily I made them stop. They climbed back into their beds, meek and rebuked, and burst into laughter.

In Manila we stayed with Andy and Teresita Liboro, in North Forbes Park. The house was a modern Spanish mansion with a pool, a pelota court and a garden. They were a childless couple, to their regret, and immediately took to Tristan and Isis. The three of us they installed in one enormous bed in Andy's sound-proofed and holiest of holy dens, with stereo, colour TV, a bar and no windows.

Dinner was served and the table heaped with tiny delicacies. I had explained that Filipinos were proud of their food, a series of strange concoctions reflecting their culture. Isis said she got the message, Tristan said he would try to remember. They piled their plates in an act of faith. Isis tasted three grains of boiled rice and said it was delicious. Cries of approval from Teresita, who translated the words into Tagalog for the servants in attendance. They said that in no time my children would be true Filipinos.

Tristan said, with his mouth full, 'This food is odd.'

All eyes were on him.

He swallowed. 'I've never tasted anything like this before.'

A fair statement.

He edged his fork into a piece of chicken *adobo,* swallowed hurriedly and said, 'Daddy, all this is absolutely extraordinary!'

'*Very* good,' said Andy.

I took them to the rapids of Pagsanjan. There we climbed into a canoe, Isis between my knees, Tristan between hers, and the boatmen fore and aft paddled us up the magnificent gorge – ferns, lianas, flowers and tiny rivulets from high up on either side. The men strained to push us up each series of rapids, a dozen or so, and at the very top was a majestic waterfall tumbling down, the sun making rainbows in the spray. The boatmen turned the canoe round and we shot the rapids. The cries of joy added to the excitement. In the calm water between rapids we sang 'Greensleeves'.

On the way home, a couple of hours away from Manila, I parked the car and took them for a walk. We picked our way along the bunds between fields of young rice, and watched the people planting, and looked at the tadpoles and frogs. There was a village hidden under coconuts and fruit trees. The people stared suspiciously from their *atap* huts. Two scrofulous dogs barked and wagged their tails.

Once through the village the bunds between fields became narrower and we fell in several times. We turned back. The villagers' curiosity got the better of them and a family of children asked us to sit down by their poor hut. Two very pretty girls, aged about twelve, took care of Tristan and Isis. They started to comb their fair hair. This gave Tristan unaccustomed pleasure. The girl gazed into his face admiringly, her dark eyes shining keen. She combed and combed round his head. She stroked his face with her cool brown hands. He looked up at her and breathed in.

'Daddy, this has never happened to me before,' he said.

On our return to North Forbes Park, Andy asked how they liked the Philippines.

'Number one,' they said.

'*Very* good,' said Andy.

We all went to a big party in his sister Nena Benitez's garden. We joined in the craze of the day, a dance in unison called 'The Hollywood Walk'. At sunset over Manila Bay the generous cumulous shapes of the entire sky, all the way from the west overhead to the east, were daubed from palest pink to scarlet and solferino. As it darkened there was the crackle and pungent smell of suckling pig roasting over the flames. Lovely girls with manicured hands stuck their nails like talons into the crisp skin, and pulled out gobbets of hot meat; the best way. When we got home Isis said, 'Let's have a swim', so we did, the three of us at midnight, and the moon was new, and the cockerel kept crowing and I went to sleep with my children, one in each arm.

The next day I took Isis to see Andy's brother Oscar who was a doctor. He took out her stitches. We then had lunch at the Intercontinental Hotel, the first time they had seen such a place.

While in Manila I had to leave them several times to fight on behalf of the Royal Mint for a $5 million contract. They bathed and played pelota. With Mario on side my lobbying in the Presidency was established, and in the Central Bank enhanced. I also had to put the finishing touches to a $2 million contract for a repeat banknote contract. That at least was safe. I joined Mario to dine with President and Mrs Marcos to try out a newly opened restaurant, something they often did. The President had me sit next to him. He wanted to know all about the manufacture of banknotes, coins and passports. He was attentive and pleasant. Opposite us was a beauty who was runner up in Miss

Philippines. Marcos said that that morning he had signed a Protocol authorising the Central Bank to place a $2 million order for banknotes with us. I said I knew. This intrigued him. 'Already?'

To ease the conversation I told him of Undersecretary Habib's story of Chairman Mao and Nixon and he laughed out loud, turning a number of heads.

After dinner there was dancing and I asked Imelda. Andy had advised me never to forget that she was all woman. In high heels she was a bit taller than I, but easy to dance with. She said she was going to London soon. I said that in an English winter nothing would cheer Londoners more than a visit from her. She glowed with pleasure.

I had a cable to say that Malaysia wanted to order £700,000 worth of banknotes. Away we three flew to Kuala Lumpur for my meeting in the Bank Negara. That too seemed safe. The Deputy Governor was his bumbling self though this time he wore a dull grey suit, perhaps as ordered by the austere and punctilious Governor Tan Sri Ismael. He gaily said he had bought a sheaf of lottery tickets and half of them were mis-numbered, so why couldn't the Governor be more forgiving about our banknotes? He misread Tan Sri's character. Comparing lottery tickets to national currency.

We had lunch with Claude Fenner's wife Joan. Then I took the children to see the film *The World of Suzie Wong*, with William Holden, Larry Naismith, others I had known and the delectable Hong Kong actress Nancy Kwan. The story complemented the children's understanding of Hong Kong. I told them that in the London theatre my girl-friend Yu Ling had played the role of Suzie Wong's best friend. A Chinese? That surprised them. I explained now fond I had been of her and how much she had impressed Larry at the wedding party.

When I put them on the plane home they both said 'Please, don't say goodbye.'

At the end of January David Rowe-Beddoe joined me in Manila. We had time to talk over mutual friends, Emlyn Williams, Richard Burton, actors all. Then we heard that the Royal Mint had lost the $5 million Philippines tender. I thought I had not left a cutlet uncooked to secure that piece of business, but even then, despite reducing our De La Rue commission to a fraction of what we deserved, the competition won. Quite rightly because the price difference was unbridgeable no matter how influential we were. The Royal Mint needed to pull up its socks. But David was pleased about the banknote order and my new top level of contacts.

I introduced him to Mario who invited us to join him on a bus owned by the Head of the Chamber of Commerce. It was a single-decker, its roof raised and windows replaced with larger oval ones. There were two double beds at the back, and behind the sofa were shelves with glasses and various taps. Imelda joined us and I introduced David.

Then we drove through a poverty-stricken area which Imelda examined through the one-way windows. She dictated to her Human Settlements Secretary. There had been too little progress there and she wanted it speeded up. We eventually stopped in the middle of a slum, at a grisly nightclub. There was dancing inside, nearly in darkness, wonderful rhythmic music, and some seriously worn out ladies of the night. We danced and everyone became cheerful. Filipinos have the gift of living for the now, putting their troubles behind them, and being happy, especially the very poor and the very rich. Like everywhere else the middle classes are more stick-in-the-mud. The telephone rang. The music stopped. There was silence. I'm not making this up. It was midnight exactly. The call was for Mario, even in such a place as that. What organisation. David was bowled over by the man.

Our factory manager Gordon Martin took David and me over the State Printing Works being built. Everything under control. No interfering busy corrupt little local bees. My closeness to Imelda seemed effective. No one had dared even approach the place.

David and I went to Hong Kong for a meeting with the Commissioner of Banking. He had been Governor of the Bank of Sierra Leone and was well known to us. David told me later he was thinking of offering him a job, in charge of 'Integrated Money Systems'. We flew to Djakarta. There we spent the morning in Indonesia's SPW, gave them a delicious lunch, and spent the afternoon at the Borobudur Hotel, dozing in the sun. We then enjoyed them giving dinner for us. Relations could not have been better.

In Karachi we were joined by the De La Rue Head of Security for meetings with their State Printing Works directors, civilians all of them. They were the height of dignity, so unlike the Bengalis whom they despised.

'Bloody little Bengalis,' one of them said, 'put just one of them in a room and in an hour there are twelve.' How the two countries remained united at all is difficult to imagine. My own rather peripheral affection for Bangladesh had died when I read the year before, 1975, that on 15 August Sheikh Mujibur Rahman, the country's national hero and founding President who had led them into Independence in 1971, had been assassinated at home in a coup, with his wife and three sons, and others in his household.

In Dhaka I had expressed my horror. The man may have been corrupt but why assassinate him? Why his family and household? My Bangladeshi friends said it had all been entirely necessary, to rid the country of all association with him, forever. I then lost any desire to get closer to them. Thirty-five years later the five perpetrators were found and hanged, ending a decades-long fight by Sheikh Hasina, Mujibur's daughter, who had since become Prime Minister. This seemed like the Balinese Chokorda's simile about shadow puppets, except that here the boxes were coffins.

On my way home to Hong Kong I had to go to Singapore. They wanted some changes to a banknote proof. Then on to Djakarta where my old friend, the beautiful Didiet, had arranged an appointment for me with the general in charge of security at Pertamina, the giant oil conglomerate and leading star of the reviving economy under General Suharto. He wanted an outside organisation to audit their security. Our meeting went well, with major opportunities to follow. The man I recommended was an old friend, very senior in Britain's Secret Service and a De La Rue consultant. Years before he had introduced me to Claude Fenner, Malaysia's Commissioner of Police.

Ada was awaiting my first week of the month, together with the usual heaps of mail. She said I had lost a lot of weight. I could see that when I looked in the mirror. After giving liquid and solid specimens to the doctor, he said I was not assimilating my food and he prescribed something for it. I was more aware of loneliness in those less hectic days at home. The arthritis too was swelling up and my eyes were getting worse again. It was harder to get the toothbrush into my mouth.

To make up for my irregular life as a traveller I took up water-skiing every morning at nine o'clock. Round the corner in Deep Water Bay were a couple of Chinese with a speedboat for hire. I could just keep my grip of the bar and the surge of adrenaline reduced the pain I was in. They took me all round Deep Water Bay, Repulse Bay and the islands, then back. About twenty minutes, nothing amazing, just *virages* in big curves from side to side, feeling the wonderful windy waterborne *joie de vivre*. Once I broke the rope and came to rest between four crate-sized jellyfish, translucent umbrellas, their near-lethal tentacles trailing beneath them. The boat zoomed back and the men pulled me out.

I gave a dinner party for ten people, at two days' notice, and it was a success. Ada did everything beautifully after we had conferred about the food. All I had to do was order the Krug and other drinks. Afterwards we all went to Central Hong Kong to celebrate Chinese New Year in the flower market. I bought a couple of dozen helium-filled balloons and gave them away one by one to solemn sleepy Chinese babies, my other arm being pulled upwards out of its socket. I lost my grip and the remaining balloons flew up to the moon to boos all round. Charles Hoare and his wife Felicity took me on their junk with a group of friends. He was unlike most men in Hong Kong, widely read, a wonderful conversationalist and wit, the nature of an actor. He became a lifelong friend. Many of the others preferred discussing money, drinking and sex; the usual expatriate staples.

I flew away to another month or more of the same, a never-ending pleasure, the rediscovery of old friends. That, like the continuing love of parents and family, is a good way of giving a shape to life. It was also a shield against the continuing sad dreams that would not go away about the loss of what I had most to live for.

Towards the end of March I had to go to Manila to meet Rino Giori, the multi-millionaire genius behind our banknote printing machines worldwide. I was nervous because of his reputation for aggressive mood swings. Senior Deputy Governor Briñas had us to lunch. When I introduced Rino to him the sly old mandarin set the scene as if for the Field of the Cloth of Gold.

He said: 'So, we are in the presence of greatness.'

Rino bathed in glory as I led him through half a dozen meetings, starting with Governor Licarros. Rino was excited by the architect's model of the factory now well advanced in construction.

When I drove him to the airport he said he had been worried during his week in Peking. He had ditched his girlfriend in Hong Kong's Peninsular Hotel. Then he corrected himself. No, she had ditched *him*. This from a man who was said to have had an affair with Sophia Loren. An idea occurred to him. He turned to me, pulled out his visiting card, wrote down her name and room number.

'She is too strong,' he said. 'I give you my best wishes. I pay you a *royalty*!'

And off he went into the terminal, bound for Switzerland.

I went to Kuala Lumpur to ensure that the Bank had received our £750,000 offer for more of the same, then to Kathmandu. After the usual few days' rounds (everything took longer there), I was sitting in the hotel garden having tea; trim lawn, birdsong, cucumber sandwiches and spode china. An American lady on a chair a few feet away exclaimed to me: 'Oh my Gahd, your fingers!'

I looked at her, then at them.

'I meant to say fingernails.' As if expecting me to say 'That's all right then'.

She came and sat next to me. 'May I see?'

Diffidently I placed the palms of my hand on the table. She went into raptures, making me very self-conscious. We were not alone. As a special favour she asked would I turn them over. This felt as if she wanted me to unbutton. More raptures about the categories of my fingerprints. Then she said: 'I can see you are going through a tragic crisis.'

I asked how she could tell.

'Here,' she said, pointing at the centre of each of my palms. 'A row of crosses, like a graveyard.'

I peered and it was true; there they were. They have since disappeared. She said that as a face can show the experiences of life, so can hands. Like me she had no time for palmistry to foretell the future. She had a book illustrated with palm prints, including the Victorian Prime Minister William Gladstone's. She showed how his lines indicated what an orator he was.

Nepal was looking its best after the monsoon, clear as a bell. I went for a two-hour drive to get a closer look at Mount Everest. I stopped and climbed a grassy hill. At the top I turned and saw the astounding white sheath of Annapurna. Just then a tiny waif of a girl trotted up and pushed a flower into my hand. 'Rhododendron,' she said. She asked for a rupee. Her expression changed with a shy smile as she thanked me.

In Singapore I introduced De La Rue's computer expert to explain automated cheque clearing, direct debiting and various related technologies. He made such unfamiliar concepts simple. After Australia and New Zealand I was back for my week in Hong Kong.

On 4 April 1976 I had occasion to nurture my almost proscribed relationship with HSBC. My priceless old friend the actor Robert Morley came to lunch. I also invited the HSBC Chief Cashier, David Turner, and his wife Priscilla. For Robert I bought a high-backed emperor's throne made of basketwork and placed it at the end of the long dining table. The Turners were excited to see that the table was laid only for four. After we sat down, unfolded our napkins and settled over the hors d'oeuvres, she asked in her punctilious Scottish accent: 'Muster Morleh, what is your opinion of Chinese food.'

They both expected him to breathe warm streams of praise.

'Well,' he said, patting his mouth with a napkin. 'I mean you have to admire these poor countries. They certainly do the best with what they have. With such imagination too.' Who other than the Chinese would shin up bamboo poles inside grubby caves and scrape off birds' nests from the ceiling, and make them into soup? What they did to sharks to get their fins amounted to the wickedest and most painful murder, all in the name of soup. It was delicious, he had to say. And when it came to preparing sea food they spend hours hitting it with a hammer to make it edible ...

There was much more and the Turners' faces fell. Then *she* realised they would be able to dine out on this. She prodded David under the table with her foot. They started to enjoy themselves. It was an excellent lunch.

The actor and producer Derek Nimmo organised tours for English actors, many of them famous in drawing-room comedy. British Airways had spare seats, the hotels in the Middle East and Asia, sometimes Australia and New Zealand, had spare rooms, so he negotiated concessions all round for 'Dinner Theatre', at the Hong Kong Hilton and the equivalent elsewhere. This gave great pleasure to the locals, and the actors welcomed winter months away in the sun, and coming home with a few thousand pounds saved. Whenever they came I had the smallish cast home for a meal and invited my new associates at the Hong Kong Bank. The most fun was after a liquid lunch when some of us poured ourselves into the sea in our underwear, some still clutching brandy balloons. One fat man floated on his back and balanced the glass on his tummy.

HSBC had been put in a quandary by the behaviour of their beloved Bradbury Wilkinson. A whole range of banknotes had been delivered from Switzerland, and not from England. De La Rue had been tipped off by the shippers. I had the delight of advising David Turner that the actual printing had been done, without the bank's knowledge least of all its authorisation, by the Zurich firm Orell Fussli. He agreed this was most irregular, arrogant even. At the same time I showed him our design proofs for the new series which was about to be issued by their competitor the Chartered Bank. They were superb, the brainchild of Julian and a local artist, a whole series of Chinese mythological images, with the top HK$1,000 spread with a magnificent golden dragon, the image for good luck. It was to lead to a new figure of speech: 'I bet you a dragon!'

I asked for a meeting with the chairman, Michael Sandberg. There were now improving cross-currents between us in that small community. He granted my request. Just the two of us in his office at the top of the building. He said he had been told that my entertainment was different from the normal Hong Kong fare, and what fun the actors were. I said how much I valued the conversations I always had with the bank's head offices all over Asia and how much I had learned from them. He said this had been reported to him. I rejoined that there was one matter which I was sure had not been reported. This focused the conversation differently. I proceeded mysteriously to describe it as almost a kind of disloyalty. Not just one bank more than another, but a kind of consensus, a disenchantment, maybe not knowingly shared and I felt certainly not personal ...

During this run-up I watched him intently. Timing was of the essence. As he was on the point of throwing me out of his office, probably forever, I said: 'You see, Michael, they all think that I and De La Rue should be your printers ...'

He burst into laughter. He went on to say how much he had enjoyed going to the De La Rue dinner at the Dorchester, what an impressive evening Gerry Norman had given, with the entire Diplomatic Corps, and how much he looked forward to going to the next one.

I started being invited to the Bank's box at the races, and to a number of the chairman's dinners. By then I had long since risen before dawn unseen, to take photographs of the Bank's building. In the dining room I had seen the paintings by Chinnery and cited them for inclusion in prospective banknote designs.

Eighteen

My mother had lived in 31 Queen's Grove, St John's Wood, NW8 ever since her split up from Larry. It was much more than she could afford: high rent and a full repairing lease. For years I had been telling her that this was way beyond her means, such a large house and garden. In the nick of time she moved and bought a small house in Southfields. She and Joy had moved there and were settled in, with books, paintings, lamps and furniture, by the time of the sales conference. She was hard at work in the garden. I helped her set up the old-fashioned swing seat which had originally been at Apple Porch. I took the three children there for lunch over the Easter weekend.

The De La Rue chief executive Peter Orchard addressed the sales conference in Basingstoke, as ever under the watchful eye of our chairman Gerry Norman. We had long since guessed that Gerry had less than total confidence in him, because for years he had himself combined his role of chairman with that of chief executive officer, a practice frowned upon.

As usual for the second week our sales force retired to a country place, for our annual sessions of self-criticism and struggle, with David Rowe-Beddoe as our Great Helmsman. He was the best thing we had. We had begun to wonder whether he, being much favoured by Gerry, would take over as CEO while Gerry remained as chairman. Then on our last day Peter Orchard showed up again. He told us that David was leaving the company, and that our new MD would be Charlie Banks. This was a man we knew of but did not know. Years earlier he had built the banknote factory at Gateshead. He was now head of Security Express – armoured security trucks, delivery vans, that sort of thing. So Peter Orchard had won, we sighed. It was traumatic for us to lose David, with whom that evening was to be our last.

Julian and I sat him between us at the dinner table and Julian gave a moving speech of farewell. We all drank numerous healths. From that moment the company began to lose its stature. Orchard was a control freak, with little understanding, a double first in Classics at Cambridge perhaps but too clever by half. He doled out criticism far more frequently than support.

Later I was called to have a meeting with Charles Banks, a man of the people and one we came to respect for his fair-mindedness. He was heavy-boned with broad hands and wrists, and soft blue eyes with large irises, disconcerting but kindly. Being confronted by him at that hour I was not at my best. So much not so that next day Pat Turner asked me what on earth I had said that made Charles think I fell short of his expectations.

Nonetheless I had been selected that autumn to attend a three-month residential course at the London Business School. The previous DLR man there had gone on to be general manager of our security print factory at Dunstable where he was doing well. Meanwhile, before my course, I should take a trainee regional manager under my arm, show him the ropes for him to hold the fort while I was in London.

The London Executive Programme had forty of us, mainly men in early middle age being groomed. The sheer variety of businesses we analysed made me realise how much I had learned from the Commonwealth Development Corporation. Pat Turner came to the 'parents' lunch'. He was alarmed to see the summary of pay scales of the course members. My pay was in the bottom quartile, just ahead of the area manager for the Ulster Gas Board. No wonder De La Rue found difficulty in recruiting. The salary scales were improved by Charles Banks. At the end of the course I was elected to give the farewell speech.

I left for Hong Kong on 15 December after a couple of days with the children. I found Ada in a terrible state, sitting on the sofa crying. Her handkerchief was soaked and squashed in her little fist. The television was pulled into the middle of the room, the ironing board was up and there were snips of cotton on the carpet. I gave her a hug.

'Sir, you are too good to me,' she said.

'That doesn't sound so terrible.'

'While you are away I do work for other people. Sometimes your friends and they pay me.'

'So they should.'

'Sir, you pay me too much. You are only here for a week at a time.'

So we sat and talked it through. I agreed reluctantly to pay her less, so she agreed to stay on. I was able to make it up to her at Chinese New Year with the traditional goodwill bonus. Had she left I would have been lost. I was dependent on her and fondly so. When a couple of years later my tour was over and I returned to England she sent a Christmas card which said: 'Sir, I wish I was still serving you.'

The capital of the Solomon Islands is Honiara, on the main island of Guadalcanal. This was the scene of horrific but eventually victorious fighting by the Americans against the occupying Japanese: a turning point in the war in the Pacific, before the Battle of Midway. The main battlefields were steep slopes of grass and jungle. Walking ever upwards even in peacetime was demanding in that heat. In time of war, compounded by rainfall and enemy machine guns, it had been ghastly. On the surrounding plains were war memorials. Standing in front of each were disparate groups of Japanese and of American families, in remembrance, silent.

Pidgin English was the language there. It has engaging aspects. A helicopter is a 'mix-master belong Jesus Christ'. A problem is a 'bugger-up'. No problem, 'no bugger-up'. Foreigners have to learn it if they want to be taken seriously. I was invited to a formal dinner by the head of the Currency Board with his expat British friends. The conversation became riotous with good food, pleasant Australian and New Zealand wines, all served by their Solomon islander houseboy. Then, in the kitchen, when he was making our coffee he dropped the pot and the spout broke off.

He came in and told us. He confessed cheerfully, honestly in the manner taught by missionaries: 'Arse-end belong coffee pot me bugger up, one time, finish.'

The breathless silence of our self-control made him think he should clarify things.

He explained: 'No more piss like master. Piss like missy.'

Our host with great presence of mind said: 'What rotten luck. Never mind. We'll use the aluminium pot.'

The houseboy smiled nervously and left. We breathed again.

There was a problem in Fiji with some counterfeits. They had probably been printed locally on a commercial Heidelberg press. When looked at intelligently there were easy to identify. I had our counterfeit expert fly out and assure them that there was no reason to worry as probably no more than a few hundred had been printed. The Governor, seconded from the Bank of England, accepted this and placed a new order. He insisted on a particular delivery date even though they had banknotes in stock to last for months beyond that.

Then De La Rue told me that there had been some well-publicised revolutions and concomitant runs on currency in various parts of the world. These obviously had to take precedence. This was not a disaster, merely embarrassing. I had to present this information to the Governor. As the meeting was bound to be difficult I decided to get rid of all the adrenaline I could. After breakfast I water-skied over the mirror-flat sea all the way to the reef. The sun was so low behind me that each time I turned to accelerate and jump over the wake the shadows of the spray leapt across the water in front of me.

I had telexed for an appointment and the Governor must have guessed the reason. At our meeting I started by listing three of the crises, two in Africa and one in Central America, where death and destruction on all sides had led to every kind of chaos and a desperate need for supplementary currency. His reaction was to go for me with studied rage. What was the point of that, I wondered. I leant well back, soft-eyed, as he punched me verbally like a kind of tar baby. The water-skiing had sealed my mood of calm. He gave the impression of a man who had been passed over by his employer, lost his future, and wanted to make up for it through aggression.

I agreed to convey to De La Rue the full extent of his fury and Fiji's needs for updated designs, and flew on to Tonga. Nuku'alofa had few activities to amuse, except for a night on an enchanted palm tree island best suited to young couples, a bit of wind surfing, but not much else except for the friendships I made with the Crown Prince, his sister and her fiancé, with our delightful High Commissioner, and a number of government servants who liked playing vingt et un, using exactly the same language as an officers' mess. The country was still the Friendly Islands, as Captain Cook had called them in the eighteenth century.

A meeting was arranged for me to meet the King. I was led into the cabinet room of the old wooden palace. He was the largest man I had ever seen, proud and kind. He sat in a huge wooden throne a dozen feet away from the head of the Cabinet table. We talked about the Second World War. The room had a bust of Churchill and one of Bismarck. Tonga had treaties of friendship with Britain and Germany. I wondered whether the constant visits by Soviet Russia were of significance. He said they were because of Tonga's strategic value, but he saw no need for military bases. The Russian visitors gave him ukeleles. I didn't understand. Oh yes, he said, whenever they come.

I looked at his powerful hands. 'Do you play the ukelele, Your Majesty?'

'Oh yes. In fact all over the palace there are small mountains of ukeleles.'

At party time on Saturdays many Tongans came to the dances at the Dateline Hotel where I stayed. They were paler than Filipinos, with the straight hair of Polynesians, and with smooth features like Hawaiians but much larger. The women's rounded shoulders were bare and made shiny with coconut oil. After a dance the custom was to slap a banknote on your partner's shoulder and stick it there for her. This did make the lower denominations of our banknotes rather soiled. Of all the Pacific island countries I went to, Tonga was where I made the best local friends.

To the east, over the Date Line, was Western Samoa. Its little capital Apia has many wooden churches of different denominations. These are also enormous people, Polynesian, with villages of open *atap* houses along the road from the airport. By night, when lamp-lit, the villages look mysterious and inviting beneath the palm trees.

There were literary associations. Robert Louis Stevenson spent the last years of this life in a house he built there. He is buried high on a hill, where his farewell is written in verse on the lead casket.

> Under the wide and starry sky
> Dig the grave and let me lie.
> Glad did I live and gladly die,
> And I laid me down with a will.
> This be the verse you grave for me:
> 'Here he lies where he longed to be;
> Home is the sailor, home from sea,
> And the hunter home from the hill.'

In his memory the main hotel is called 'Tusitala', which means story-teller.

Somerset Maugham stayed in Apia and was held up for a month by monsoon rains. This inspired his story *Rain*. The same storm-lashed delay happened to me when I was waiting for an appointment with the Finance Secretary, a New Zealander married to a Samoan lady called Quinnie-Mary, and the Samoan Minister of Finance. The wait was made fun thanks to crews of Air New Zealand staying at the hotel for a few days each week.

From England a visit was made to the East by Peter Orchard and his wife Helen, and Charles and Peggy Banks. I met them in Sydney. Mike Nicholas organised a dinner for the five of us which was a disaster. He was patronising to Charles Banks and made clear that he would like to represent De La Rue in some agency capacity. When we had taken our leave of him Charles said emphatically that he wouldn't employ him if he were the last man in Australia. I took them to Melbourne to see the Australian State Printing Works, which I visited once a year just to keep tabs. This irritated them as well because the technical head talked as if he knew more about printing than they did.

Peter then started calling me by a nickname which I found unacceptable. I knew that if I let him use it then others would follow suit which would have been unbearable. It was difficult to dissuade him from using it. Time-consuming too because he insisted on having his way and liked to be surrounded by yes men. But I prevailed. It didn't do much good for our relationship.

We proceeded to Wellington's James Cook Hotel. There I organised a cocktail party for all the Reserve Bank seniors below the Governor and the civil servants in relevant government departments. Before they arrived, with their ladies, I explained to Peter and Charles that it was likely to be a piss up. It was. But eventually we cleared the decks and the Deputy Governor and his wife stayed on for dinner. Anyway it suggested to Peter and Charles that I was capable of generating a measure of goodwill. The vital impression that there were no secrets was reinforced next day when we had our meeting with the Governor. Everything seemed secure.

Our chairman Gerry Norman had taken charge of raising money for the new Battle of Britain Museum in Hendon, north London. He asked if I could help in Hong Kong. Of course he knew the head of Swire Pacific, whom I had appointed as agents in place of H & C. They owned Cathay Pacific Airlines, so that was the place to start. Their chairman pledged £3,000. Britain may have won a key battle in the Second World War in Europe, but our performance in Asia had on occasions been shameful. The fall of Singapore was well known, our guns only pointing out to sea, with no defence against the Japanese soldiers marching along the causeway from Malaya. Nor did we do much to prevent the fall of Hong Kong. So it was going to be difficult to arouse in the Hong Kong Chinese any feeling of gratitude for the Battle of Britain.

It did mean a lot to me. The Battle of Britain took place in August 1940 when I was in New York aged four. I recalled my mother, my governess and Jessica Tandy sitting tensely every evening to hear the

BBC World Service, the number of enemy kills, the number of ours and those of our Polish and Canadian allies. That battle meant even more to me after I had acted in *Eagle Squadron* with Robert Stack. My emotions were most affected, as were so many people's, by Larry's voice as Henry V crying out the Crispin's Day speech 'We few, we happy few, we band of brothers.' So even though I embarked on a bit of role-playing, the sincerity of my personal appeal was strong.

I began by going to the British Navy. 'Why?' asked the Admiral. I said that it was because my father had served in the Navy, in the Fleet Air Arm. This he did not know and he took it seriously. He remembered *Henry V*. My next observation was risky. I said it seemed right for me to start the appeal with the Senior Service. That sounds phoney but it really pleased him. He listed all sorts of things which could be done by the Royal Navy in Hong Kong. Participating in such shows was all too rare and good for morale. People knew all about the Army there but had little idea of the Navy's strength. He said he would write to Sir Arthur personally describing the support the Navy would give, so as to attract as many fee-paying locals as possible to a show presented by all three armed forces.

Next I introduced myself to General Redgrave, related to my old friend the actor Michael Redgrave. He observed my Brigade tie. He was wearing one as well. A Grenadier. Yes, I was a Coldstreamer. It was clear he had been contacted by the Admiral. He immediately volunteered that he would have his troops put on a proper tattoo, as done at Edinburgh. It would be wonderful for the men, a change from the exercises they did from time to time in the field. This would be something they could really put their hearts into.

By the time I saw the Air Vice-Marshal word had got round to him. 'Battle of Britain? We'll show the other services.' I told him that my father's film *Henry V* had been dedicated to the Battle of Britain pilots. 'This is *us*,' he exclaimed. 'We will fly out an RAF band, some Vulcan bombers for a fly past,' and on and on he went. I wondered whether it would be better for fund-raising if he just did nothing and sent a cheque for the money saved. Well, the upshot was that all three arms prepared for everything they had promised.

I contacted the government information officer, John Slimming. He was an old friend I had stayed with in Mandalay in 1960, just after his book, *Temiar Jungle* was published, describing his own experiences against the Communists during the Malayan Emergency. He filled all the Cantonese and English newspapers with every shred of information on the programme, where parking tickets could be bought, who would be there, from the Governor downwards. On the actual day I had to be elsewhere so I missed it, but it did raise £100,000 for Gerry's Battle of Britain Museum.

Nineteen

In 1977 Larry was in Hollywood filming. The script was taken from a Harold Robbins novel called *The Betsy*. Sort of a B movie. He was bored to death and implored me to go there and be with him. He had stayed with me in Hong Kong which had made him feel infinitely more paternal. Years before he had mocked his relationship with me as 'wicked avuncular'. Now it was changed. He had unburdened himself to me about the unhappy state of his marriage to Joan Plowright and his relationship with their children, ganging up against him.

At Los Angeles Airport he met me with his driver. There he was in a different state: free and happy. We went off to dine at Le Restaurant with his closest Hollywood friends Robert Wagner – RJ – and his wife Natalie Wood, plus Juliet Mills, an old friend of mine and a beautiful actress, sister of Hayley, daughter of John and Mary Mills, and her husband who was in real estate: Michael Micklanda. After the interminable flight across the Pacific I was overexcited, but as this was Tinsel Town so was everyone else. Larry and both the Wagners had played together in a television production of *Cat on a Hot Tin Roof*, with him in the role of Big Daddy and them as Brick and Maggie. This had cemented their friendship. Natalie had the same femininity as Vivien.

Larry was staying in Malibu Colony on the Pacific Coast, in Anne Bancroft's wooden bungalow, one of the few humble buildings remaining. The grandees' houses stretched up and down the beach, secure in the gated community. Before going to bed I heard him his lines for his next day's scenes. He was word perfect, as always. In the morning before dawn I awoke him and prepared a full English breakfast. The car came for him at six and he was driven away to downtown LA. The studio had taken one floor of an early twentieth-century building as the location for a few office scenes.

As I was staying with Larry I was an honorary, but temporary, 'Class A', on a par with the stars. The Wagners were 'A'. I was lionised. When Larry had to leave me for a week's shooting in Detroit my evenings were organised by the studio. The first party was given by Joan Collins, then Mrs Kass. Before going there I went to see Jean-Pierre Aumont and his wife Marisa Pavan, twin sister of Pier Angeli. The two of them had stayed with us at Notley. He and Marisa lived on the Pacific Coast Highway in a wooden house on stilts, lapped by the sea in a line of many similar ones. After a cocktail we drove up to the heights of Santa Monica. The houses became fewer and further between, the yuccas standing separately, awaiting their turns to flower and wither away. The view spread over the whole of Hollywood, from the ocean all the way round to the Rockies. On the eastern horizon through a telescope you could see oil pumps levering up and down, as if talking to each other.

Joan had bangle earrings and necklace, plunging décolletage, the narrowness of her waist and fineness of her ankles enhanced by a glorious full skirt, and on her feet were four-inch heels, sometimes called 'fuck me shoes'. She hugged me, called me 'Darling' and introduced me to all the film stars and starlets. I remember Lee Marvin, leaning back against the wall, drink in hand, pleased and looking at me with narrowed eyes as if challenging my recognition. Conversation with him was easy, with his leathery skin, deep voice and white teeth, 'Bor-orn under a wand'ren star'.

The cocktails were bracing, the talk faceted, brittle, point scoring and fun. These were the beautiful people. Joan took me by the hand and said she must show me the library ('lie-breh'). I felt dazzled and inexperienced. The large room was dimly lit, had a very long sofa under a wall hung with a dozen portrait photographs of her, all alluringly posed with her eyes saying everything. There were no books anywhere, no bookshelves. She looked up expectantly and I stupidly said something complimentary about the pictures and not about *her*.

Between times I lay in Anne Bancroft's fenced garden in the sun on a chaise longue, with the beach beyond and the ocean waves. I was very much enjoying John Cottrell's biography of Larry, just published. I have nothing but praise for his research, fair-mindedness and narrative skill. It carried nothing contentious or deliberately false. In time this became a quality almost unique among biographies. So many seem to pour through publishers, hell bent on dishonesty and dirt, all with a view to profit.

As people trudged by on the sand, all safe in the gated community, some dropped in to say hello. Among them were Merle Oberon and her young Dutch husband Rob Wolders. They invited me to dinner. Theirs was a sizeable two-storey house with a swimming pool tiled in dark blue for the sake of coolness. Her taste was as elegant as Vivien's, shelves full of books, Georgian furniture and wonderful paintings. One of her portraits made her look Indian, an appearance she had avoided as an actress. Her being half-Indian was often cited as a reason she did not have children, lest they should be dark-skinned. We remembered each other from the times she had stayed at Notley, between marriages. Rob was my age, but their age difference seemed natural as he showed her his love and every consideration. He was tall, quiet and good-looking.

On Saturday RJ and Natalie invited me to their poolside in Beverly Hills, together with Juliet Mills. That night we went to dinner given by one of Hollywood's topmost lawyers, Paul Ziffren, and his wife Mickey. They had the largest house in Malibu Colony. A dozen and a half tables were each laid for ten people. At the end of dinner Mr Tom Bradley, the black mayor of Los Angeles, gave a bullish political speech while we replenished each other's wine glasses.

I met Charlton Heston, looking ever more like Moses as he aged. I was dying to have a chat with him about the film *Gordon of Khartoum*, where he had played the lead and Larry had given his miraculous performance as the Islamic fundamentalist Mahdi. After only a minute's discussion with him I felt completely drained. On screen he had a most magnificent presence, two-dimensional perhaps, but focused and uplifting. Meeting him was different. He had the ambit of a man who does not exude energy, he absorbs it.

I rented a car and drove down San Vicente, past Brentwood Town and Country School, along Sunset Boulevard, past the polo fields, Gladys Cooper's old house and up to Pacific Palisades. I parked outside 1535 San Remo Drive, where my mother, grandmother Eva and I had lived during the war.

As I walked past the plumbago and poinsettias of my childhood I felt as if my feet were not touching the ground. Trance-like with memories, I went over to the trees the other side of the road, surrounding Thomas Mann's old house. Now this may sound fanciful, but it's worth the risk. That moment was so important. I felt those self-same trees remembered *me*. When studying Buddhism in Chiengmai I had been captivated by one of its most attractive precepts; the Oneness of Life. Now, embraced by the very air I was sharing with the trees, I sensed that Oneness as never before. It is wonderful to recall. That moment brought together so much: the childish years' continuum of gladness I had known in California, the house where my mother and I had lived, and now the unique first-time closeness I was enjoying with Larry. There is an ecstasy which combines such summits of life that cannot be exceeded, where the living moment makes memory, so many memories, more vivid than ever. That was the place and that was the moment I learned how to enter that balm, again and again.

I traced a friend from my childhood: Brooke Hayward. She was the daughter of the star actress Margaret Sullavan and the leading Hollywood agent Leland Hayward. They had built two houses side by side. The Barn was for us children, with the upstairs bedrooms round an atrium looking down on the play area. The Other House, where we never went, was for grown ups. I was six, not yet in love with Judy Garland, Brooke was five, dark, intense, could be wantonly destructive, yet was full of sunshine. Her younger sister Bridget was a platinum blonde, with pointed features, deeply quiet and didn't give a damn about me. Their young brother Bill had just learned to walk. Bridget was the one I was after. I was the one Brooke fell for. A love triangle so early in life.

A few years after the war Leland fell in love with the much-married Pamela Harriman. Maggie took her time to get over the shock. She stayed with us at Apple Porch to get away and talk everything over with my mother. Eventually she married a quiet English banker, Kenneth Wagg, who had three times won the doubles rackets championships in England and America. Everything went wrong. The marriage estranged Brooke from her mother. Bill suffered mental problems for a while. Bridget, after becoming a theatre actress and having an affair, died at the age of twenty-one. Finally Maggie, while rehearsing for a Broadway opening, suddenly died. Brooke wrote an astonishingly good book called *Haywire*. Leland's telegraphic address had been 'Haywire: ten percent'. Her memoir was a number one best seller and on *Time Magazine's* list for almost a year. It portrays Hollywood and Broadway in their halcyon days, and describes how she came to terms with what had happened to her family.

We had a dinner date. She was divorced, very attractive, with her mother's husky voice, and our shared past gave us a feeling of trust. She told me of the turbulent life she had led. She had married a drug-crazed alcoholic, Dennis Hopper. He made the low budget movie *Easy Rider*, which became a break-through cult movie celebrating licentiousness and abuse. A whole new breed of actors crowded in and marked a renaissance in Hollywood. She tried for the sake of their daughter Maria to stay loyal to him, even after he broke her nose. She had been through Tinsel Town in its hypocritical guise as heaven, and then its wild and pretentious version as hell.

Halfway through dinner her fifteen-year-old daughter burst into the restaurant wanting to meet her mother's big date. 'Everything okay?' She was very like Brooke to look at, except for her head and neck under frizzy hair, and the same careful low voice. Satisfied with her glimpse of me she was off some place.

Brooke wanted me to drive her to the house of the industrialist Norton Simon in Malibu. The security guard let us in and went back to sleep. The hall had two classical Greek statues. The swimming pool was dimly lit with a plate glass fence to protect it from the breeze, the Pacific Ocean fifty yards away, bumping and seething. We took off our clothes and for a long time lay separately on the still water. It was a slow start to a wonderful night.

I read *Haywire*. She inscribed it 'For Tarquin – An inscription – or toast – to the sweetest revenge of all: seeing one's first (and most important) love again after so many years and finding that those long ago primal instincts were unerringly perfect. Love, love (note pages 91–93) Brooke.' Those pages referred to were of delicious hyperbole: 'Tarquin was standing regally, taller and more handsome than he'd ever been before.'

The only time anyone has ever called me 'tall'.

She was wonderful company. Her book was an eye-opener on the human condition, revealing, as described by the blurb, the disparity between outer and inner circumstances. We had plenty to talk about.

RJ and Natalie asked me to join them for the weekend on their powerful twin-engined yacht called *Splendor*. It was the largest on the LA Marina. They were now married to each other for the second time. She had with her the four-year-old daughter whom she had had with her interim husband Richard Gregson, and his sixteen-year-old daughter from a previous marriage. RJ was a qualified sea mariner so there was no crew, just ourselves, fancy free for two days. For them this unwinding was an essential respite from the extreme disciplines of film actors, with their early wake-up calls. We cruised for a few hours out to sea and south to the island of Catalina. We anchored in Avalon Harbour and RJ made fast most expertly at his own mooring plug. Larry and my mother had been there in the Thirties and I still have her home movie of him catching a marlin.

After lunch on board we had a siesta. All except for Natalie's four-year-old daughter, who wandered around naked except for a life jacket. No danger of falling overboard. I was awakened by the sound of the anchor motor starting, and the chain clunking through the fairlead. I felt the boat pulled down by the tautness of the chain. I shot up to the wheel-house, pushed the little girl to one side and switched off the motor. I told her calmly, and so as not to disturb the others it really was calmly, that she could have sunk the boat. Her inimitable wailing response was: 'But I want the boat to siyink.'

To develop an appetite for dinner RJ and I water-skied behind his large Avon rubber dinghy. We dined on shore at a fish restaurant. We returned to *Splendor* to have a fun series of increasingly noisy night-caps, collapsing into bed in the not so early hours after a wonderful time of story-telling and gossip. We left Avalon very early while Natalie laid the table for breakfast.

With Larry's return to Malibu I resumed the routine of getting him up, making his breakfast and putting him into his limo. In the evenings I heard him his lines, cooked the dinner which the maid had prepared and then we enjoyed each other's company more and more. One Saturday for lunch we picnicked. The garden had teak furniture, everything silvery and the only colours were our glasses of pink gin.

In the evening Juliet and Michael took us to the Hollywood Bowl. The orchestra was conducted by the great Bangladeshi, Zubin Mehta. He strutted on stage, moving in a series of jerks, redolent of certain birds' pre-mating antics. The second half of the concert was Tchaikovsky's '1812'. Only Hollywood could get away with such exuberance. When the time came for Moscow to be set on fire a whole row of smoke dispensers popped into action, along the top of the huge shell-shaped roof above the orchestra. The smoke rose up. As it cooled it drifted down. On the mountainside the cannons were fired. Further billows of smoke combined and lowered. They wafted above the conductor's platform, and down his arms still beating time. He became completely enveloped but the orchestra visible beneath played on. The bells peeled, the *casa grande* thumped, the cymbals clashed as all the instrumentalists became hidden. The conductor's head and arms reappeared above the smoke, seen only by us, invisible to the players, sweeping his arms above the swirling cacophony milling around beneath him unseen. The audience, stretching high up the slope behind us, was convulsed with laughter. The air cleared as the players surged to the glorious ending and the whole orchestra became visible. There were shouts of applause.

For my birthday that Sunday, 21 August 1977, my forty-first, Larry took me, RJ and Natalie out to dinner. RJ had noticed the swollen arthritic state of my hands. He gave me a copper bracelet made by Sabona, of Bond Street, like the one he was wearing. It took him some time to fit it precisely round my wrist, so that it did not move out of place. That was the key. That night, around two o'clock, at a time in my life when I slept the whole night through, I was awakened by the pain leaving *both* hands. Within a few weeks the swelling disappeared and the knuckle bones became visible, back to normal. It no longer hurt to carry a briefcase, even a suitcase, and I could play the piano again. I have worn it ever since. The physical symptoms of a broken heart had been dissolved.

In England much blessed time was with the children, all three of them, in Brighton and Steyning, with Larry and Joan and their brood, and in Sutherland Grove with my mother and Joy. Clavelle was full of questions. She had heard that I had had difficulty getting a toothbrush into my mouth, having to hold the brush with both hands. 'Was the toothbrush too big?' she asked.

In Hong Kong I had a visit from Basingstoke from my old colleague Alexis Napier. The problem was that Charles Cardiff, my predecessor in South-East Asia, now sales director, wanted me to engage the services of a certain agent in Macau. I said that the man was corrupt, and that my monthly visits to Macau had secured sound relationships with the Finance Minister and the Governor of the Bank. Besides, it would soon become known in nearby Hong Kong if we retained a rogue for an agent. Alexis came out to adjudicate.

He enjoyed the 60 m.p.h. jet foil ferry across the Pearl River Estuary. We stepped ashore in Macau and we took a cycle rickshaw. He wished we'd had a camera to record it. At the bank he saw that we were well placed to challenge Bradbury as their current printer. Our new designs were under way. During our meeting we were joined by a director from the Bank of Portugal who practically embraced Alexis. As we left Alexis agreed with me not to appoint the agent.

That evening he went to bed early in my spare room. I decided to give a dinner party the following day and invited twenty people. Twelve came, including the Hong Kong actress Nancy Kwan who had played Suzie Wong in the movie. A friend in California had given me her phone number. She wanted to bring her German boyfriend so I said 'Of course.' While we did not end up bathing in the South China Sea it was one of the best parties. Charles and Felicity Hoare were there and other favourite friends. Alexis was overcome by the beauty of Nancy Kwan. After they had all gone and he was going off to bed he said: 'Really, you've got it made here.'

Next day he told me De La Rue wanted me to be based in Basingstoke, and look after the Middle East. After the loss of Indochina and the Philippines, the Middle East was the most important region for banknotes and coins. It would have been a natural progression from there to my becoming sales director, following Charles Cardiff. Cash-wise it would have cost me my 30% overseas allowance, two-thirds school fees (though their continuation was to be expected), the rent from Queensdale Road, and the divine Hong Kong income tax, which was 15% and only for those days I was actually there. Whenever I was away from home I was tax-free. In addition I loved my romantic and varied lifestyle in Asia and the Pacific where I had so many friends, from the top down. I knew no one in the Middle East, hated desert, and the proposal did not appeal. Mine was a gut reaction and I sometimes do wonder. But supposing everything had panned out; I could not possibly take on a big job like sales director and go on living in London, facing a forty-seven-mile car drive there and back every day. The thought of living as a single divorcé in Basingstoke was terrible. I was a Londoner.

The children arrived in Hong Kong on 22 December, all three of them, with Tristan very much in charge since becoming a junior monitor at Cottesmore School. We had Christmas Day lunch with my cousin Jasper and Virginia and their two little daughters. He had taken up residence in the next bay to mine, and was Hambros' local director. Next day we, as a family, gave a lunch for three couples and then flew off to Manila. Gordon Martin was going home for Christmas so he lent me his Ford Zephyr and we drove up to Baguio, capital of the Mountain Province. It was a perfect place for children with pools, playgrounds, pedal car races and a beautiful forest.

We stayed with Ben and Lita Legarda. While he was a Deputy Governor she was the bank's librarian. They had a nine-year-old daughter called Tweetie who fell deeply in love with Tristan. He was going through a handsome phase. She had her father's wide face and high cheek-bones, really rather exotic. She followed him everywhere. Whenever we took pictures she pointed to him and said: 'My love.' It became too much and Lita said that those words were not appropriate so soon after meeting him. So Tweetie changed her line. She still followed him around, and called him 'My like.' Their family house had twenty-year-olds and much younger cousins, but none as engaging as Clavelle.

We took our leave after a wonderful time and drove south, stopping in Manila for cheeseburgers at McDonald's. Everything was perfect. Then after lunch the car wouldn't start. It was the Friday before New Year's Eve. All any garage would sell was petrol. No service of any kind. We had a further three-hour drive to join the Liboros at Matabuncay. We sat in the car and wondered what to do. I remember looking wanly at the pebbles on the surface of the car park. Then as if by magic one of the pebbles seemed to grow and become a mechanic in white overalls, with a bag of tools and a Filipino smile. He diagnosed the engine as having a burnt out coil. Something I had never heard of. It just so happened that he had one in his bag, of the correct length and size. He fitted it. It worked. The car started at once. He charged $30. If I believed in miracles that would qualify. Away we went.

We drove between rice fields, through old Spanish villages, the houses with windows latticed with *capice*, like paper from mother of pearl, alongside sugar plantations, round and over palmy hills with sea views. The Liboros' compound was on the beach; six two-storey houses with *nipa* roofs. Grandma was there, her daughter Nena Benitez now widowed, various sons and daughters and a scattering of children.

On New Year's Day all the youngest village children came round in their smartest dresses, jeans and T-shirts and stood in line. All about Clavelle's age. She and the Liboro children dispensed packets with sweets, balloons and a large one peso coin. Clavelle was given a packet. When we returned to Hong Kong, after the best holiday we had ever had, Tristan and Isis wrote their thank-you letters. I said to Clavelle that I would write whatever she told me.

'Dear Nena,' she dictated. 'Thank you for the money.'

I waited. She had nothing further to say. I asked: 'Is that really all?'

'Yes, Daddy.'

'Don't you want to thank her for the holiday?'

'No. Only for the money.'

January was made remarkable by an invitation for me and Mario to join the Marcoses for a night and a day on board *Ng Pangulo*. Most of the people there I knew well: Ricks Cuanco, head of the telephone company, Jun Luz of the GSIS and chairman of Philippine Airlines and a number of hotels, Tony Floirendo the banana king, the ubiquitous Gaya Paravicini and Christina Ford, and the Elizaldes, he being Secretary for Minority Groups and very close to Imelda with her own portfolio of Human Settlements. The foreign guest was a Spanish count who wanted to build a marina in Manila Bay. Marcos had invited him to play golf on a brand new course laid out by Gary Player – yet to be played on – called Puerto Azul.

We arrived with our overnight cases in the blazing heat of late afternoon. Imelda greeted us on deck. We had '*merienda*': cakes and fruit, or 'fruits' as they say. We then went to our cabins to change into evening clothes, long dresses for the ladies, *barong tagalogs* for the men. As we prepared ourselves the President was piped on board.

We heard that Imelda had gone to take a rest. This was bad news. If she had a catnap lasting a couple of hours that would be all the sleep she would need for the night. We would have to sit up with her interminably. We went to the reception area for our champagne. The sun set in all its Manila glory, a fine crescendo from pink to scarlet which engulfed the entire sky, until at the end it seemed all the beauty of the earth was gathered up in a sad farewell as the sun slipped into the sea. And Imelda joined us. Long after dinner and the withdrawal of the President, all the rest of us had to remain, including a number of midwestern Americans keeping themselves awake with whisky. She withdrew out of kindness at about five, having finished giving dictation to her two secretaries.

We put on clean summer clothes for the golf course. It had only just been seeded. Hardly a sign of grass anywhere on the fairways. The thirty of us, but not Imelda, followed the President and the count, both excellent players with handicaps of six or seven. There was one incident which showed Marcos at his best. He hit an exceptionally long drive, the tiniest bit sliced, and the ball veered in mid flight. It hit a tree and shot upwards and forwards. It landed on a flat stone and bounced high, forward again, and came to rest six feet from the pin. We restrained our instincts to cheer.

Marcos murmured: 'There's always another way.'

We then surrounded the green as he sank the ball, two under par. Now *there* was a man in charge of himself.

Twenty

After a further visit to Western Samoa and a rainy fortnight I was at last able to collect the approved new designs and obtain the banknote order. This cleared Brads out of the Pacific. I telexed the excellent news.

That moment of radiance was hit on the head as soon as I pressed the send button. There was a message from Julian quoting from a press cutting. It announced that the New Zealand Prime Minister Muldoon had signed up for Bradbury to build a banknote factory there, in Whangerey, North Island, with the government's commercial bank, the Bank of New Zealand, as a shareholder. That bank had Gerry Norman on its board. They had not advised him but kept it secret, that board meeting he had not attended. The New Zealand treachery was compounded by the behaviour of the Reserve Bank. I had thought that the attentiveness and friendship shared with them, the Deputy Governor in particular, had meant something. He could have whispered a warning during one of our whisky-fuelled evenings. We had provided their banknotes without a break since the 1930s. This action of theirs was unforgivable. I could hardly bear the idea of ever seeing any of them again. I was glad when Julian came out to join me.

On my way to Wellington I dropped into Fiji which I knew would come under heavy pressure from Brads. Both they and we were preparing new designs. I paid a visit to the CDC man there, a former colleague. He read the newspaper report and sympathised, but said that sure as eggs is eggs the news confirmed a government commitment at the highest level. Nothing could be done to stop that.

Julian looked terrible on arrival after flying straight out, half way round the world, eastwards, against the sun. We took a day off and lolled beside a geyser, and sometimes in it. This was restful. We decided that we should first ask the advice of our friends at the National Bank of New Zealand, whose traveller's cheques we printed. They introduced us to John Marshall, one of their directors who had been Prime Minister, referred to as 'Gentleman Jack'. Julian briefed him. He was outraged at his compatriots' behaviour, both the BNZ and the Reserve Bank. Utterly reprehensible, he said. We retained his services as an adviser. When he went to London he met our directors and they trusted him straightaway.

Of course I felt I had failed. I received a long hand-written letter from Gerry Norman saying that in no way should I blame myself. I wondered whether it had been wrong of me not to have reported my hunch that the people I was dealing with were so bland and provincial that they could be treacherous. Had I done so my masters might have thought I was not the man to represent them in New Zealand. I had not wanted to risk that. Brads still needed a couple of years to build their factory and meanwhile the Reserve Bank remained our customer. We had to go on being nice to them, and blame Prime Minister Muldoon for swearing them to silence. Genuine hypocrisy.

We checked everything out with the Prime Ministry and the Treasury, and they confirmed that the secrecy had been ordered by Muldoon. Even then the bruised egos of De La Rue would not allow them to admit that Brads had beaten us. I had continually to go to London to be briefed for further meetings in New Zealand. This was ridiculous. Even Peter Orchard flew out on his own to scour the ground. Perhaps he intended to impress his fellow directors with his determination. The only new point in his report was that on the outward flight there had been fog in Dubai. For me the whole thing became a blur. I had to fly round the world three times in six weeks.

I always went with the sun, to the west, and took my time. When spending the night in New York I saw a play, then headed next day to Los Angeles. I had heard that Merle Oberon was unwell. I bought a beautiful pink cyclamen and left it with a note outside their front gate in Malibu. I then went to Topanga Canyon for what Americans call horseback riding. This set me up for the dinner and night flight across the almost never-ending Pacific to Auckland. There I rented a car and drove north to see the Brads factory in Whangerey and photograph it. On the way were the loveliest suburban gardens with herbaceous borders and trees. New Zealand at its best.

At Wellington the Reserve Bank was friendly. They showed me the Brads designs. Their portrait of the Queen made her look more intelligent than ours did. I consulted with Jack Marshall and he suggested I go to the Bank of New Zealand and give them hell. Basingstoke agreed.

I made an appointment with their chief executive. De La Rue were paying me to be beastly. Quite a change. Next to his bank's building, visible through his office window, was his new headquarters skyscraper under construction. Work on it had ceased because of bloody-minded builders' unions. I kicked off by inquiring sympathetically about that, which was sure to be an embarrassment for him. He spoke in a frank and friendly manner. Then I showed him a photograph of the massive SPW we were building in Manila, hardly to be compared with the three-bay factory being screwed together by Brads. I said we at De La Rue could not understand the factory's being located in New Zealand. With a population there of only three million Brads could perhaps justify a mini-factory for local needs, maybe for a Pacific island or two, but the distances to their main export customers would create serious problems.

He seemed sufficiently disarmed for me to show him the full horror of the balance sheets of Bradbury and their owner's, the American Banknote Company. To my surprise he, as a banker and fellow share-holder, had no idea how unattractive the numbers were. Brads was nearly bankrupt. He started shouting at me. Just what I wanted. He rose to his feet, put his face a couple of feet from mine, as if to hit me as I sat. Even better. He yelled that he had never been treated like this before. Was it normal De La Rue behaviour? So I started in on how he and his board had concealed their decisions from their own fellow director, our chairman, Sir Arthur Norman, and slowly described the reactions expressed by our friends, especially in the City of London, how they were mostly sarcastic, some even funny, belittling the bank he led and New Zealand itself. He sat down, elbows flumped on his knees. I replaced my documents in my briefcase, got to my feet, and left.

All this I described to Gentleman Jack who said I had done a worthy job of representation. My own point of view was that it was an unpleasant waste of time doing nobody any good. Two further rounds of briefing in London and Basingstoke, and twice more round the world. Never have I had such jet lag, despite breaking the journey for the sake of my health. Wellington time at two in the morning was far different from the time my body was trying to catch up with. In the middle of every night I became well versed in the tales of Dracula, Frankenstein and all the TV horror movies. When you are that jet-lagged, fatuous fancies become plausible. As for the Werewolf, the only possible death for that pitiable monster was to be shot with a silver bullet, fired by a beautiful virgin who loves him enough to 'understand' – that came to make tremendous sense.

My next time round I went to Malibu to see how Merle was and Rob Wolders was there to welcome me. Merle was upstairs in bed, back from open-heart surgery. He said the cyclamen I had previously left for her had wilted and seemed to symbolise her health. He had nurtured it and revived it and Merle started to recover. His love for her was palpable. It made me feel how empty my own life was.

Some months later I persuaded De La Rue to let me check out Tahiti. It was a 'Département', constitutionally a part of France. As I had prised Madagascar and Mauritania away from the Bank of France, Julian said I could spend four days in Tahiti to find out what I could. I went there from Western Samoa. On arrival in Papeete all passengers had to surrender their luggage to be fumigated. This was for protection against rhinoceros beetles which chewed up the palm trees in Samoa. Our suitcases were heaped into a vacuum chamber and the process lasted an hour.

Sitting on the floor in a corner of the grubby lounge were a dozen ill-dressed men with intelligent faces, all smoking: Tahitians, Eurasians and a few French. They had not been on the plane. This was an airport. They were having a meeting. I went over and introduced myself as a printer of banknotes and wondered if they were perhaps politicians? They were immediately interested. After a few minutes they stopped looking side to side at each other and then turned to me as I explained De La Rue to them. I gave them my business card. I asked whether they were disaffected with the colonial status accorded to their country by faraway Metropolitan France. They very much resented it and were working secretly to change it. They each gave me their names, addresses and telephone numbers and agreed the importance of keeping in touch. In that single hour the information I gained was excellent. I suggested, a trifle naughtily, that in gatherings such as theirs there was often a Swede, as there had been in Guinea Bissau where I had once traced the bush-occupying Revolutionary Council. They thought this a huge joke. They had had a Swedish colleague, quite mad, so they had dropped him. In my report to De La Rue I said they were not to be taken seriously. France would never let Tahiti go.

I collected my baggage, rented a car, checked into a hotel and drove off to see the Gauguin museum. It was worthless. No paintings, only postcards of them lined up, with France on first line showing that it had the most originals, then the Soviet Union, the US and so forth. Next day I took the plane to Bora Bora, a hundred and fifty miles away. On board were Rob Wolders and Merle, now fully recovered. They were staying at the Hotel Bora Bora, with Polynesian-style bungalows at the end of walkways over the sea.

I had the time of my life with young Americans at the Club Mediter-ranée. We went out in a large glass-bottomed boat. The canvas curtains were drawn and the only light came from the sea beneath us. We saw a giant manta ray. Beyond the reef there were big waves. The men threaded chunks of horseflesh along a chain which they lowered in an extended loop over the bows. We saw the blood oozing from the meat and in no time this was attacked by sharks, magnified to twice their size by the seawater. We could feel their strength as they pulled and sheered off with lumps in their mouths, tugs of war between them, a violent feeding frenzy only a few feet beneath our flip-flops. That afternoon we sailed in a ketch out to the reef and back. I dined with Merle and Rob, and returned to the Club Med for all that was best.

Early July I was in England again for further discussions in London with Gerry Norman and Peter Orchard. I had several glimpses of Isis and Clavelle in Whitchurch, with Riddelle. I put 31 Queensdale Road on the market, sold it for five times what I had paid for it and gave Riddelle a lump sum divorce settlement, while I continued paying school fees and maintenance of the children.

One evening Mario D'Urso invited me for a drinks party at his ground floor flat in Eaton Square, followed by dinner at Annabel's, for me to dance attendance on Princess Margaret and Imelda. I arrived on the dot of seven and HRH at five past. There were a couple of dozen others; the sort of people I categorise as the beautiful beastlies: rich men, often questionably so, and their trophy wifelets. Princess Margaret glanced at them despairingly and came over to join me. She remembered we had danced almost all night during a coming out ball. She asked how long ago that was. Rather than state the number of years – twenty-three – I said the party had been beside Regent's Park and the dance floor was on a scaffolding over the garden. The floor had moved gently up and down in time as we moved to the music. We had enjoyed that.

Unfortunately her mood remained bad. She was on a diet, sipping ginger ale, and had lost so much weight that her bodice was too big for her bosom. She made conversation difficult. I thought Imelda would never arrive. I asked Princess Margaret if she had heard the phrase 'Filipino Time'. She had.

Imelda arrived at half past eight. One had to admire Mario's style. Both his guests of honour had to be called 'Ma'am'. This was a further irritation for Princess Margaret because it put Imelda on the same level as herself. We left for Annabel's, Imelda in a Rolls and Princess

Margaret in a big Ford, both with chauffeurs. At a long table near the dance floor Mario placed me on Imelda's right. He sat opposite her and Princess Margaret on his left opposite me. The beautiful beastlies extended to each end of the table. I sensed that Princess Margaret would not relish sitting nearly opposite the other Ma'am. She was pleased when I asked her to dance but her pleasure had gone by the time we reached the dance floor.

She settled into sourness. I raised an eyebrow in the direction of our table but she definitely did not want to return there. She gave me a little thump. Not a pleasant little thump. Eventually we did sit down with the others and dined. Imelda's graciousness was ignored and so was Mario's. Mine had been written off completely.

At the end of a testing dinner, when it was tempting to look at our watches, an Argentinian banker leant towards Princess Margaret and asked if she knew that her birthday was on the same day as mine – 21 August. She gave me a hostile look and asked: 'How long have you known that?'

I was the soul of discretion and did not count the years. I said: 'Almost as long as I can remember, ma'am.'

There were approving smiles all round.

Her face hardened and she demanded, sarcastically: 'And have we anything in common?'

That was beyond even what I could tolerate. I am a man, not infinitely *mol* nor *mou*. 'Yes,' I said, metaphorically wiping the blade of a knife on my sleeve. 'Yes, ma'am, as a matter of fact we have.'

'And what', disdainfully, 'could that possibly be?'

I leant forward archly and carefully delivered the line; 'We're both, ma'am, just divorced.'

Hardly gallant. There were a few titters which she deserved.

Imelda asked what I was doing next day. I told her I was going to New Zealand. She said she was flying to New York and would I like to join her on the way.

I went to the Philippine Ambassador's Residence in Kensington Palace Gardens at nine. The two of us were driven to Heathrow, a special area where the Philippine equivalent of Air Force One was parked. A PAL Boeing 707. She was met by an English protocol chief, resplendent with moustache and three-piece suit. He had actually had an illustrious career, becoming head of London Underground and was David Mitchell-Innes's father-in-law. The chairman of the airline, Jun Luz, and one or two other men were there, the rest being 'Blue Ladies', her favoured friends, all looking their self-conscious best. They sat in the middle and rear seats. The front had a walled off bedroom down one side and a couple of seats facing each other on the other.

Five minutes after take-off Jun Luz came in deferentially and said there was a problem. One of the doors for the landing gear had failed to click shut. So many flights into Heathrow were stacked up, waiting to land, the best solution was to proceed to Holland and land at Schiphol, Amsterdam. Imelda agreed. That airport was famous for its enormous duty free centre. As soon as the airport stairs were in place and the aircraft door opened out, she and the Blue Ladies stormed down the steps and clacked their high heels into the airport bus. They spent more than an hour buying Jaeger, Rolexes, Leicas and jewellery. As our departure was announced I bought a large bunch of red roses. At the bottom of the aircraft steps I presented them to Imelda. She buried her high cheekbones into them and took a deep appreciative breath. Then she handed them back, making me feel an idiot.

She went into her room and slept for a couple of hours. She came out refreshed and wanted to discuss the problems boys can have if their fathers are world famous and lack 'quality' time with their children. Their son was doing well, had always had sensible friendships, and he seemed free of the horrors of teen age. So we had a long and confidential chat.

She looked at the watch on my wrist and asked how I got it. I said my mother had given it to me as an engagement present: an Omega Constellation, with a white face. When my wife left me I had changed it to a black face. Now that my divorce had gone through I had had it changed to gold. I intended to fend off the offer of a Rolex, just bought at Schiphol. She got the message, went into her room and came out with a tiny box. Inside was a pair of cufflinks; chrome and some diamante bits. A bit nouveau riche but appropriate. In the lid was her card: 'Imelda Romualdez Marcos. First Lady of the Philippines'.

She understood the use of power. For example she had had an intriguing altercation with President Gaddafi of Libya. He had been supporting the breakaway movement by the Muslims in the southern island of Mindanao. Diplomatic exchanges led to her being invited to make an official visit to Tripoli. The only people at the airport to meet her Presidential plane were her exceedingly nervous embassy staff. She told her Ambassador that if Gaddafi did not come by the time her plane had refuelled she would return to Manila, creating a diplomatic incident for the world to enjoy. This rattled Gaddafi into meeting her there and then. For two days he showed her his projects for economic development and irrigation in particular. She was impressed. She asked what he wanted her government to do for Mindanao. He said the people should be given a referendum on whether they wanted independence from Manila, with their own foreign policy, defence and other trappings. She made the condition that he would stop supplying weapons if there was a majority 'no' vote. He was pleased to agree. However, the people of Mindanao were too disjointed and scared to break away from Manila. They voted overwhelmingly against the referendum as she and her husband knew they would. Her initiative put an end to the Libyan arms supply for a number of years. She knew her people.

Fiji advised that at their next board meeting they would chose between us and Brads for their new banknote designs. On my way there I paid my usual visit to Wellington. Gentleman Jack advised me that Brads had been nobbling the Fijian Minister of Finance, who was ex-officio chairman of the Central Bank. He was a large white man in colonial shorts, the owner of the country's largest chain of department stores. Before seeing him I had to find out what the bank's preference was. Much to my relief they preferred our designs and prices, but said the minister could overrule them. Armed with this highly confidential knowledge, gathered from the bank's lower echelons, I went to see the minister, my fifth or sixth such visit, so the atmosphere was informal.

After we had settled down over coffee I explained that I had received some information about him in New Zealand which I felt he should know, even though I myself did not believe it for a minute. I had his undivided attention. He knew about Brads building a factory in Whangerey and agreed that for them to target Fiji was only to be expected. In the most tangential way possible I indicated the suspicion, held at a high level in New Zealand, that he had been seeing rather more of Brads than usual. His reaction was unexpected and rather charming. He said that the trouble for people in high places was that almost any interpretation could be put on what they did. When Prince Charles had visited Fiji he had gone for a walk along the beach with his daughter. The newspapers had picked up the story, embellished it and he, as her father, had to write a letter of apology to the Prince. Too embarrassing. Then he recalled that there had been some mention in the papers about my own divorce, the Olivier marriage had foundered, that sort of thing. He ended up by saying that whatever the Central Bank decided would be taken as final by him. He was as good as his word. I now think the

Wellington gossip was misplaced. We were given the order and I let the matter drop.

The Bradbury factory in Whangerey did cause them many headaches because of its being so far away. When De La Rue took Brads over a few years later we closed it down. Everything returned to normal, with us printing New Zealand banknotes in Gateshead, as if nothing had happened. A sweet revenge was HSBC's agreement to our building a banknote factory in Hong Kong, for us to replace Brads as their printers.

My own swansong as a regional manager in Asia and the Pacific was in Manila. There was a seminar: 'The Future of Asian Payments Systems'. It was chaired by my friend Ting Roxas, President of the Philippine Development Bank. A number of Central Bank governors and senior banks' directors were there. The two-day programme was led by an American technical expert in Electronic Funds Transfer Systems – EFTS. He was confident but insensitive to the seniority of the fifty or so Asians in front of him. His main thrust was that EFTS would replace handheld units of currency such as banknotes. He and his associates took us through what was then, more than thirty years ago, new territory.

Before the first lunch I introduced myself as the De La Rue man to those whom I had not met. Over the two days the EFTS expert spoke repeatedly about the ease of counterfeiting banknotes. That audience knew more about banknote security than he did. He had hardly travelled beyond the shores of America, served by the US dollar. His other major weakness was that he made no mention of the grave dangers of fraud misplacing huge sums of cash on line, far more serious than any threat from counterfeit handheld banknotes. He took questions from us, some of them tentative because the subject was so new. His answers tended towards the patronising.

After the final question, and to an uneasy audience, our chairman Ting Roxas gave a brief summary. Then to my surprise he said that there was in their midst a De La Rue man, known to many of them. He wanted to hear my comments. I rose and thanked him, rather nervously, and said that amidst such a gathering of central bankers, development and commercial bankers, I felt that from me, as a printer, a mere provider, a silence would be considered golden, and resumed my seat.

Ting Roxas repeated his introduction of me, calling me Tarquin, in tones of friendship and asked me again, as a favour, to give my views.

This changed the atmosphere. In return I called him Ting and said that De La Rue shared everyone's concern about counterfeiting of any kind. No country suffered from this anything like as much as the United States. The main reason was that it was the world's reserve currency, but it was insecure for modern times. How many, I wondered, had looked closely at the twenty dollar bill. They would see the Supreme Court building on the back, with some ancient cars in the street, the sort people remember in Charlie Chaplin films, the T model. This made it obvious that the United States, leader in so many fields of activity, was more than sixty years out of date with its banknotes. The front was black, the easiest of all shades to copy, and the back was green, also a single colour. No use of multicolour intaglio, no security thread, no watermark, no lithography. The currency was among the least difficult to forge. That aside we shared the views of Interpol that a national currency should be replaced with updated designs every ten years or so, with machine-readable security features, now in place on all the banknotes we printed. These could authenticate all banknotes mechanically.

The audience liked this. As we filed outside and said our farewells to each other I saw some men deferentially making way for someone who wanted to see me. Of all people it was Tan Sri Ismail, governor of the Malaysian Central Bank who had taken the business away from us. He seized both my hands. He said he was delighted I had had to be coaxed into saying something, so modest of me, and even more delighted that I had belittled the mighty US greenback. The real significance of this was that the next time the Bank Negara went to tender for banknotes De La Rue were awarded the lot.

The United States has since modified its banknotes a little, and among a few other new features they now have watermarks.

Coldstream Guards, dress uniform, 1955

Author on a Malay fishing boat, 1960

With Tristan in Africa, 1966

Riddelle, Tristan and Isis in Jamaica, 1969

Riddelle, 1973

Isis riding her horse Goldie, 1978

Clavelle snowboarding, 2009

Tristan climbing, Malta 1989

Engaged to Zelfa, 1988

Married to Zelfa, 1989. Left to right: Clavelle, Tristan, Zelfa, author,
Richard, author's half-brother, Isis

Author and Zelfa in Theatre Square for the unveiling of Larry's statue, 23 September 2007

The statue unveiled: the author with sculptress Angela Conner and Lord Attenborough

Twenty-one

The years in the East put me together again although the delights had only been fleeting. I returned to England hoping to find a lasting relationship. I bought a small apartment in Kensington. Its address appealed to me, as an Olivier, working for De La Rue: 4 de Vere Mews. Very prissy. It was in a converted stable block which had had stalls on the first floor as well. One or two builders' wheelbarrows remained and I was the first occupant to move in, to the accompaniment of workmen finishing the courtyard, fountain and flowerbeds. Tristan was at Westminster, after being head boy at Cottesmore, and Isis was slotted to go there in Sixth Form. Clavelle we kept at the state school near Whitchurch because her mother and I were relieved that she had settled down somewhere at last.

My new job was General Manager of Minting and Metals, starting early November 1979. This opportunity provided me with greater fulfilment than anything I had ever done. The Royal Mint was represented by De La Rue except where it dealt direct, as with the colony of Hong Kong. It shared out its business in a consortium with Imperial Metal Industries and the Birmingham Mint. Our market was worldwide. My predecessor was Dennis Paravicini. He introduced me to Dr Jeremy Gerhard, the Deputy Master of the Royal Mint. It was the tradition to refer to him as 'The Deputy Master' and to use his title when speaking to him. The title 'Master' belonged ex-officio to the Chancellor of the Exchequer. Dennis introduced me to the mints, and the manufacturers of their equipment. Seeing the mighty machine tools in operation at the Royal Mint's new factory in Llantrisant, South Wales, was an inspiration.

Its line of furnaces melted and blended the alloys at a heat of fifteen hundred degrees Celsius, and pushed them continuously through a sleeve into a strip about an inch thick and a foot wide. These were cut and stacked in lengths of about seven yards, then rolled repeatedly until reduced to the right thickness for the coins. These rolls were fed into blanking presses which struck out the required shapes, mainly round, sometimes scalloped or even square as in the case of Swaziland. Surface impurities were washed away from the blanks in revolving acid baths.

Then they were annealed and rimmed to give the high edge the Royal Mint prided itself on, and fed into the minting presses to be struck by the obverse and reverse dies.

The Royal Mint had recently moved there from its traditional site beside the Tower of London, where Bert Fichter had been in charge of production. He oversaw the new fifty pence coin. This was an ingenious shape: a curved equilateral heptagon, designed to behave as if round when pushed into a slot machine. He did not want to transfer to Wales and was pleased when Dennis offered him the job in Basingstoke of technical minting adviser to De La Rue. He was a stalwart hard worker whose family originated in Alsace. He had very strong hands, always cold, which was the hallmark of a man brought up in the craft of tool making.

Overseas, Dennis introduced me to the Swiss Mint, the two German mints near Düsseldorf, and the Colombia Mint in Bogotá. There, when we checked into the hotel, the receptionist mispronounced my name, calling me 'Señor Oliver'. I politely corrected him, and pointed out that Olivier had two 'i's'. Dennis followed up by saying he was 'Senor Paravicini, with three.'

On our way home we paid our respects to the main US mint in Philadelphia. This cathedral-sized place manufactured only US coinage, with the occasional exception of Panama. The cutting edge management was executed by a sharp-featured and vigorous little man while his boss was a giant Dutchman. The two of them, of such contrasting sizes, reminded me of John Steinbeck's *Of Mice and Men*. There the pace of striking appeared to be slow, but the majestic Bliss presses struck four coins at every stroke, producing more per minute than high-speed presses striking singles.

In addition to my being General Manager of Minting and Metals I was to be the first managing director of Royal Mint Services – RMS. This was an idea the Deputy Master had put to Peter Orchard, for a new venture to be sales-led by De La Rue, with the incomparable technical expertise of the Royal Mint in support. It was to offer expert advice and equipment to existing mints, and to construct mints in their entirety for countries which insisted on having one. The chairman of RMS was the Royal Mint's number two, Roy Gravenor, the other two directors being Dennis and Bert's successor in Wales, Ernie Howlett. We had only one employee to start with, Dave Rolf, a safe pair of hands, based in Llantrisant.

Dennis became the De La Rue Group's company secretary. We have been the best of friends ever since, seeing each other each year at a dinner with other old timers from De La Rue, and send Christmas cards to each other from 'two i's' to 'three i's'. He helped with the phraseology and design of a brochure Dave Rolf and I put together on RMS.

I spent Christmas in the pouring rain in Devonshire with Alan Dowling, the previous sales director of the Royal Mint. He had become our consultant and his advice was alarming. He said the Royal Mint had become so uncompetitive it would soon lose its overseas markets. This tied in with what Dennis and I had heard from the two German mints, that the Royal Mint had had it too easy for too long in its traditional African and Middle Eastern markets, and they were going to attack as never before. I asked Alan to get together with his successor, the new sales director of the Royal Mint, Alan Lotherington, and write a paper on Export Prospects. Their findings were: 'The Royal Mint still has more export customers than any other mint, though in terms of volume its market share has declined. ... The Royal Mint has a poor record in competitive tenders in recent years, winning only two orders outright since January 1977.'

Eventually this hard-hitting report percolated through both the Mint and the Treasury. They recognised the call for drastic action to reduce costs. Plans were announced for voluntary redundancies of the Royal Mint's workforce of 10% in 1981–2 and a further 7% in 1982–3. This was without precedent. I was not the most popular man but the policy did enable us as a team to win the next major tender, for more than one hundred million coins for the Philippines. We also won the largest coin tender in history, for 2,700,000,000 coins for the Argentine, to reformulate their entire currency by reducing the number of zeros caused by hyperinflation. Unfortunately the Falklands war made them cancel it.

Meanwhile RMS sent brochures to a few carefully selected countries. Almost immediately we received an inquiry from the Central Bank of Iraq. They had decided that with a population of more than ten million they should mint their own coinage. They wanted an offer for a striking mint, and the supply of blanks ready for them to strike, plus the technology for origination, the pantographs and tool-making equipment for the dies. Just the cold metal end. Two weeks later there was a request from Iran for the same, plus the hot metal end as well: the melting, rolling and blanking. This called for a contract worth three times as much.

Dave Rolf worked flat out with one of the first word processors and produced long and detailed offers for each, in time for RMS's first board meeting. My board approved and the two offers went out by special courier that day.

De La Rue was visited by the special adviser to the Central Bank of Iraq, Mr al Kassab. He was the terror of bank employees and also of our own regional manager. Our banknote division sent along three of our best whom I accompanied to meet him at the Sheraton Hyde Park Hotel. He presented himself as almost grotesque: fingertips thrust together, lips pouting. He dealt fast with his banknote problems and dismissed the others. I realised he was an actor, enjoying himself behind his terrible mask. He sat further back into his armchair, sipped more whisky, lit a cigarette and gazed back at me, quizzically. I had seen through him. 'Hey,' he said, 'don't look at me like that.' And burst out laughing. He offered me a whisky and we had dinner together.

The business called me to Baghdad. It was springtime and the Tigris was bursting its banks with floodwater. Entire trees were rolling down under the bridges, yet the air in the city was harsh and dry. I went to see Mr al Kassab. He was most welcoming over a cup of tea. I asked him about the hostility of the western press to Saddam Hussein and the Ba'ath Socialists. He said it was misplaced. The government had provided every single village with electricity, fresh water and primary education. Discipline had had to be harsh because the population was so disparate. In the North were the Kurds, non-Arabs, who shared the same language and blood as the Kurds in neighbouring Turkey and Iran. The Iraqi government was run by minority Sunni Moslems, like himself, in a predominantly Shi'ite population which was increasingly influenced by the Shi'ites in Iran. The interference of Iran had surged with the overthrow of the Shah and the arrival of the Ayatollahs. He felt it would not be long before Iraq invaded Iran with weapons supplied by America, and with the encouragement of an American Administration traumatised by the incarceration of its diplomats in Tehran. He therefore said that with regret he had decided not to sign up for RMS to build their mint. Next year his forecast war did break out.

Iran had similar fears. They advised our regional manager that they too would postpone building their mint. These were two huge setbacks. We had to do the rounds of all the suppliers included in our quotations, mostly in Birmingham, and bring them diplomatically into the picture for them to understand that the two big cancellations in no way reflected a failure by RMS. This gave me the time to learn from their engineers, all keen to share their knowledge.

The Mint Masters' Conference took place that year in Utrecht, in

May. Bert Fichter and his wife came with me and we stayed in Amsterdam. There I found an answer to my continuing desire to help Third World countries. The development of clad coins by the US had not gone well overseas. The edges looked messy. An alternative would be to electroplate blanks made of mild steel, with a thin layer of alloy all round. The coins would look exactly the same as solid ones of bronze, cupronickel or any other coinable alloy. Ninety percent of the coin would be a mild steel core, with each surface plated five percent with alloy. This would reduce the intrinsic value of the metal. No matter what the scourges of inflation on purchasing power, or any hikes in metal prices, the quantity of alloy would be so small that it would be worth no one's effort to recover it, whether copper, nickel or anything else.

Taking the world coinage as a whole, the millions of tons in weight had an intrinsic value worth billions, all subject to the London Daily Price for copper, nickel and other metals with fluctuations which were unpredictable and at times alarming. The target I wanted to aim at was to revolutionise the composition of coinage throughout the world, reducing the cost to national exchequers by millions of pounds.

There was a problem in presenting the case unarguably, showing at a glance the relationships between so many variables: metal prices, production cost, intrinsic value, face value, purchasing power and the time ravages of inflation. I had to find a way of presenting my case with the simplicity of Copernicus. Even so it's a bit technical for a memoir with its tables and graphs so I have summarised and simplified my presentation in the Appendix.

It was successful. The Deputy Master wrote to my CEO Peter Orchard:

Dear Peter,

I would like you to know how much we appreciated the contribution made by Tarquin Olivier in yesterday's seminar on materials for low value coins. On his own initiative he had prepared a paper which made a significant contribution to our discussions through the insight it gave into the importance of black market rates of exchange, and which he presented in a thoroughly straightforward manner. I have, of course, expressed our appreciation to Tarquin and I am most grateful to you for making him available for the session.

Yours,
Jeremy

There was more depth to my presentation than hinted at in his letter. The Royal Mint decided in January 1982, after the Treasury had approved, to invest £425,000 in a capital project to install an electroplating plant for the production of plated mild steel blanks for our 1p and 2p coins. So all our bronze coins are now magnetic. With metal prices prevailing that year the saving to our Exchequer was around one million pounds. In the ensuing years they started plating in brass as well for export and eventually nickel in 1990.

So, as in the best of all possible worlds, they had developed a healthy new overseas market on the rock-solid basis of a captive home market. My contribution at the very least had been to hasten the process. I think that is the most significant thing I have ever done for developing countries. It saves them millions of pounds, every year, while protecting the integrity of their coinage.

In Third World countries the need was especially acute. They needed extremely low denominational values for their coins, for the survival of their poorest people having a medium of exchange of any use to *them*. In India they had had to give up their low value aluminium coins because people melted them down to make kettles. Their need for electroplated coins was paramount.

The early steps of Royal Mint Services led to a revival of a mint building contract which Dennis had initiated years before in Morocco. It had to be renegotiated in Rabat, an unexciting capital. French-trained Moroccan civil servants abounded with their self-conscious grid-thinking French, every syllable, every comma. This involved a number of visits.

RMS also had a call for help from the Sudan. This was very different. Twenty-two years earlier I had stayed there on my way back from retracing Livingstone, the journey which had pointed my life towards the Third World. The only hotel in 1958 was the brick-built and imposing Grand. The Nile was a-sailing with large Arab dhows. Everything was orderly. The Sudanese Civil Service had been even more prestigious than the Indian Civil Service. Second to none in the British Empire. The Main Square's flower-beds had been laid out in stripes like the Union Flag, with a statue of General Gordon on his camel in the centre. After Independence the Sudanese had discreetly taken him down by night, enshrouded in a tent, and set him up in the museum.

Now, in 1980, there were no boats to be seen. There was a new hotel, the Hilton, with air-conditioning. The town was a mess, although the men were tall and distinguished, with their finely featured dark faces and gleaming white robes and headscarves. The atmosphere was listless, everywhere run down, dried up and weedy. Religion was creating its scars. The hotel was about to wall off a section of the swimming pool to divide men from women. Next would come segregation in the coffee shop. If the customs caught you entering with a bottle of whisky you went straight to prison.

The Sudanese Mint symbolised everything that had fallen apart since Independence. The Nile's black cotton soil at the end of the drought had dried out, with cracks several inches wide and several feet deep. When rained upon in the wet season it expanded with immense upward thrust. It had broken through the concrete floor of the mint building. Within a few years it pushed the levels into a series of concrete slopes; fatal for powerful machine tools. Worse than anything else was that water accumulated under the furnaces, with molten cupronickel above it at 1,500 degrees Celsius. Had molten metal dropped into the water the explosion would have obliterated that part of the building, and the roof. It was an unspeakable danger.

I took Dave Rolf there. We had a slow walk round, decided where the furnaces could be repositioned out of harm's way, what to do with the water cooling for the furnace coils, where a new blanking press should be set, and where a new foundation should be sunk for the minting presses, and much else. Our offer was £1.25 million. The Bank of Sudan honoured our brief contract both in letter and in spirit. This was very different from the French-trained Moroccans in Rabat, who wanted to renegotiate every phrase, so that the agreement would be all letter and no spirit. It was dozens of pages long, as if they wanted it to fail.

I returned to Khartoum several times for various odds and ends. I introduced the Royal Mint's engineer whom I had selected from the three short-listed to front up the project in Khartoum, supervise the suppliers' installation specialists and train the Sudanese operatives. Within a few months, when all the equipment orders were placed, the project was extremely profitable. The RMS Chairman was so impressed he applied for a British Industry Award For Exports.

RMS was set to make a profit of £150,000 half way through its third year of operation, having broken even at the end of the second year from various consultancies in Nepal, Mexico and Peru. In minting we were gaining market share through the Royal Mint's newly competitive pricing. The world's coinage really was going to be revolutionised by electroplated blanks, and client countries saved millions. I really felt I was doing what I had been born to do.

Before Christmas 1981 in Basingstoke my then managing director called me in. He was on the point of going away to the Pacific for a holiday with his wife and I had given him heaps of advice, much appreciated. He had news which for me was shattering. He said that I would be replaced in Minting. He had no idea why. He was simply passing on a message received, presumably from Peter Orchard, and at the behest of the Deputy Master. He then shamefacedly rushed off on holiday, leaving me in the dark. For the life of me. and I have discussed this with Dennis, my predecessor, the only reason I can think of was that the Deputy Master felt I had taken too many initiatives. I was dying to implement them, but that was prevented.

When I began writing this memoir I wrote to the Royal Mint for news. The Director of Circulating Coin said that the Mint still remembered me after thirty years. He wrote: 'The penetration of plated steel coinage has increased dramatically as a result of increasing metal prices and inflation leaving many low value denominations of homogenous alloys around the world in negative seigniorage. There are a number of significant suppliers of plated coins and ready-for-striking plated blanks worldwide, and we at the Royal Mint continue to work hard to maintain our capability at the head of this list.'

So, much as I would have loved to lead it, the revolution I had sought in coinage was well under way.

I became a bureaucrat tied to Basingstoke, charged with improving the relations between ourselves as banknote printers and De La Rue Systems in Portsmouth who made banknote handling and authenticating machines. Some of them were very ingenious. My title was dull: Used Note Sorting Co-ordinator. If the machines did not work they blamed our banknotes, and we blamed their stupid machines, just like that. Classic. All our sales force needed was a proper understanding of the machines' technology, which I was able to learn and teach. I co-ordinated our sales efforts worldwide with De La Rue Systems people, to keep the wires uncrossed and ensure that the focus of effort was where it was most effective.

Their major machines were the size of a car. They had specially developed detection devices to read the banknotes fed past them at speed. These recognised and rejected counterfeits and distressed notes, and culled authentic used banknotes which could be packaged for reissue. They could destroy authentic distressed notes on line, reducing them to sawdust. Systems like these enhanced the development of banknote security. Even in the early stages when installed by the Bank of England, they revealed precise information on the volume of counterfeits. Public visual recognition had culled them more successfully than anyone had estimated.

For Third World countries Systems invented much smaller desktop versions, slower and easier to operate. Our regional managers were more preoccupied with these. Many central bankers sent delegations to be introduced to this new technology, manufactured in Portsmouth. They were always excited by such high tech new departures. These developments followed the company's earlier years of pioneering in counting machines, and most importantly the delivery of through-the-wall cash dispensers of banknotes which revolutionised the public's banking habits worldwide.

With no more travel I could live normally. Throughout the late spring and summer on my way home I water-skied at Kirton's Farm, by Exit 11 of the M4 Motorway, to get physically tired enough to sleep well at night. Weekends I divided between going there, or to the Garrick Club for lunch.

Life in London blossomed. Almost every week I gave a dinner party for eight people. The housework, shopping and laying the table had to be done the day before. When on your own, cooking is difficult to combine with the hour of people arriving, being introduced and given their drinks. The main danger is a lady coming into the kitchen offering help, and you forget to turn something up or down, or even on. I evolved a system, starting with the main course: something that did not require my absence more than a couple of times nor for longer than a minute. Roast meats of every kind, game in season, fresh vegetables of every variety; not exactly original but certainly delicious, *à point* or *al dente* as the case may be. In the French way we finished the claret with cheese, and then had champagne with the dessert. If they left before midnight I considered the evening a failure. They seldom did. And I tidied everything away by 1.30 or 2 a.m. so that next day everything was in place.

Robin and Jane Mills invited me to a ball in their Gloucestershire house soon after my return from Hong Kong and that switched me back into England. There was a beautiful woman my age called Julie and we danced. Later I got her address, wrote to her and she came for dinner in London. She was the first real girlfriend I had had for so long. She met my family and children and I met her two sons, both in their twenties. One of them endearingly asked: 'When are you going to marry Mother?' She suggested I move into a larger flat.

De Vere Mews was sold almost at once. I consulted all the estate agents in Gloucester Road. It was one of the least expected, a rank outsider, who telephoned to say he had found the place. 40 Lexham Gardens, the second-floor flat. It had a large drawing room, big enough for my grand piano, and a dining/bedroom next to it, both facing south-west with spectacular views down the length of the square; balconies front and back, with the bedroom and kitchen facing east, so there was sunshine all day.

There was a curious occurrence of my being impersonated. At a Garrick lunch I was sitting next to an American literary friend, David Farrer. He immediately said how splendid I was looking. I thanked him, let it drop and asked what he was up to. After a few moments he said he could not get over how much better I was looking. I asked when was the last time we had met. He said it was the previous week at the Players Club in New York, one of our corresponding clubs. I told him I had not been there. I wrote to them, the letter countersigned by the Garrick secretary, and complained that an impostor was staying there pretending to be me, and borrowing money from members. I received no reply. A couple of weeks later I wrote robustly that I was now an accessory to the impostor's continuing crime of borrowing in my name, and regaling falsehoods about my family.

By return mail their club secretary wrote an 'Oh, Mr Olivier' letter. He said what an enchanting man my impostor had been, how popular, and he made it seem I should be proud of his performance as me. He ended by saying how much everyone wanted to meet the 'real Mr Olivier'. The impostor left and repaid his debts. He was an out of work actor who had put on his impersonation as a bet. He had arrived at the Players Club saying he was a Garrick member, but without the requisite letter of introduction. An old Garrick member saw him and mistakenly said he was me. They let him in. I was asked if I would like to know his name and I said not.

Derek Walker-Smith, Lord Broxbourne, told me that even though my father was only a life peer, as he was, I as the elder son was entitled to sit on the steps to the throne in the House of Lords. We agreed to meet in the Peers' Lobby. I waited while people of maturity and moment strolled and chatted. Eventually Derek arrived. The doorkeeper approached respectfully and asked: 'Can you tell me the name of your guest, milord?'

Derek cleared his throat and mumbled: 'Mr H'm H'm 'liviyer .'

The doorkeeper took a step back, aghast. He looked to his left. He looked to his right, gathered himself, leant forward as if in pain and asked in horror: 'From *Libya*, my lord?'

My parents had told me never, ever, attempt to act on stage, not even in a school play. In my mid-forties I discovered why. The Garrick Club asked me to take part in a one-night review at the Ambassador's Theatre, with a dozen other members contributing their talents. The entertainment was to mark the publication of *The Ace of Clubs* by Richard Hough, on Sunday 26 October 1986. I automatically declined, of course, but then the playwright Ronald Harwood who was producing the show inveigled me into doing a one-man piece on my feelings about the Club and its members. So I wrote it, about twenty lines, allowing for plenty of impersonation, over-acting and slightly patronising good cheer. I learnt the lines and acted them out to Larry one evening at Steyning. He tightened up some of my gestures and was encouraging.

Ronnie took us all through a dress rehearsal to an empty theatre. Six of the club's small dining room tables were set about with two or three chairs facing downstage: a touch of familiarity. Then came the time for the audience to arrive and for us to sit in our places. Hubert Gregg played the piano and sang a few much-loved songs: 'We'll gather lilacs', 'Keep the home fires burning', and Richard Pasco and his wife played a poignant piece from Shakespeare which they had both performed twenty-five years earlier. Sir Michael Hordern read a poem 'In Praise of the Garrick Club', specially written for the evening by Kingsley Amis, and eventually it was my turn.

I stood and walked down the unaccustomed slope of the theatre stage down towards the audience. With each tread I felt energy surge from the boards. It was empowering. When I stood and faced the audience I could sense them thinking: 'You, son of', with mocking expectation. I looked slowly from one side of the audience to the other, not archly but with a hypnotised confidence that I would show them, and their quiet reaction made me feel that they knew it, their presence energised me with the feeling of total control. My little act raised frequent laughter and at the end they cheered.

I was hooked. I realised this could be addictive. Just as well I had never tried it seriously. After all, only a few percent of all actors actually make a living. At that time the only successful sons of stars had been Douglas Fairbanks Junior and Kirk Douglas's son Michael. The inheritance of great talent is rare in any branch of the arts. With Larry as my father, even if I had been any good, the feelings against nepotism would have been marked in that most envious of professions. I understood why the parental advice to me had been so total.

The Central Bank of Vietnam asked for advice on building a state printing works and a full-blown mint, together with recommended specifications on all equipment, plus banknotes and coins. I went out to Hanoi in April 1983. I contacted the Vietnamese Embassy, round the corner from me in London, and our embassy in Hanoi. Our Ambassador Michael Pike asked me to stay with him at the Residency with his wife, a Malayan Chinese who had liked my book. The day before leaving I went to Harrods and bought a big Stilton cheese for them.

I flew to Bangkok and spent the night as usual at the Oriental Hotel, managed by my old friends Kurt Waschweitel and his Thai wife Penny.

Next day Hanoi. The airport was in the middle of fields overflowing with green rice, and surrounded by immense bomb craters, thirty yards across, water-filled. Not many people were on that flight. A bedraggled crowd waited outside. Michael Pike was in a suit and tie, chatting to a government official. We drove off, flag flying, in a diplomatically modest car.

I was expecting to find the Hanoi bombed to smithereens. In fact it had been avoided by the B52s. There had been one single accidental bomb which hit the wing of the main hospital. Next day when two of the Central Bank's English-speaking guides showed me round the city they pointed to the damage. The French colonial buildings were unscathed save for the ravages of neglect. The Ho Chi Minh Mausoleum was built like the one the Soviets had built for Lenin. He lay encased in glass, perfectly preserved. A continuous file of devoted followers in black cotton clothes paid silent respects. Uncle Ho had lived in a two-storeyed bamboo house overlooking a lake with water lilies and ducks. It was a friendly place, informal and summery.

The guides introduced me to some bureaucrats. In their offices were paintings of the Vietnamese Navy junks attacking and sinking the Chinese. That hostility was historic. Their military victories were spoken of with the same pride as an Englishman describing the Armada, Trafalgar, or the Normandy Landings. How could anyone imagine that Vietnam would be a domino to be pushed around by the Chinese, yet that is precisely what the American Secretary of State McNamara got wrong. He failed to see that Ho Chi Minh's struggle was for independence from the West. It was not in the name of

Communism but of nationalism. General MacArthur would have known better.

The Central Bank was the ultimate in French colonial grandeur. Around the spacious main hall were executive offices. While the Vietnamese hatred of the Chinese is vaunted in the paintings, their contempt for France is more recent. At the outset of my meetings with the Deputy Governor I was about to say how much I looked forward to speaking French, but he stopped me mid-sentence. He turned to his interpreter who bowed and said I was to speak in English, the Deputy Governor and Finance Director were to speak in Vietnamese, while he would interpret. I suggested that French would save days of time. They said it was now a forbidden language. The Deputy Governor left me with the Finance Director, an engineer, the interpreter and two secretaries noting everything down. The Director and the engineer knew exactly what they wanted to discuss, machine by machine, process by process, staffing tasks, skills and training.

At the end of the first week the Deputy Governor told us how pleased they all were, and that for the weekend as a reward they were giving me a car with driver, an interpreter and an East German-trained lady economist. We would be accommodated in a rest centre near the Chinese border: Ha Long.

Staying with the Pikes was a pleasure. The building was, as he pointed out, bizarre. The main hall was a tall octagon with naughty little rooms leading off. They had been for ladies of easy virtue. One was my bedroom which had richly patterned wallpaper. The plumbing was pre-war French, and Vietnamese-maintained. There was a loo but the flushing water was piping hot, while the shower was cold and delivered small electric shocks. Michael gave a small dinner party and his young Vietnamese housekeeper wore her *oudzhai*. That was the only time I saw one in Hanoi. All the women in the street wore black cotton. One night the Pikes took me to a club to see the ex-pats perform a light comedy which was well done. Afterwards it was good to hear their optimism about the Vietnamese.

The Bank's car and crew collected me on Saturday morning, the only car in the street. Michael accompanied me outside with his manservant carrying a cardboard crate of beer. We fitted the cans in the boot round my suitcase and the spare wheel. He left the corrugated crate on the pavement. 'Don't think I'm a dirty ambassador,' he said. 'That will be useful to someone. It won't be there for more than a minute.'

Bicycles glided by on treadless tyres, their riders' drab cotton clothes all the same, whether men or women. No colour to be seen. Michael handed me a long box of State Express 555 cigarettes, ten packets of twenty. He said they were used as a sort of currency, but only that particular brand. Ten cigarettes could be worth a week's minimum wage. He advised me how and to whom I should dispense them.

Off the car went, heading north. We passed Haiphong Harbour. There the bomb damage was absolute. The steel girders of the bridge were twisted into spaghetti shapes under an iron grey sky, the wharves barely recovered from the multiple hits year after year. Every ten miles or so we had to cross rivers by barge, pulled doggedly by old tugboats. We were crowded round by men and women, many of them clutching bicycles stacked high with kindling twigs and old boxes. Their faces were expressionless, my crew did not speak to them, nor make any gesture of recognition. The war years of extreme sacrifice, killing off their future hopes, the deaths of so many of their family members and the unfair and never-ending pummelling from the sky had crushed all but their grim determination to survive.

Ha Long overlooked a beautiful bay, and beyond were towering limestone islets, thousands of them stretching out to the horizon, like the ones in southern Thailand near Phuket, which featured in a James Bond film. They had an air of being petrified into knotted shapes, the rock escarpments gripped by tumbling greenery. Nearer the shore was an image of timelessness. There were some junks under sail. They were trawling for fish, barely moving.

The Ha Long residential blocks were G-plan and featureless, four storeys high. My crew led me through the eating hall, stuffed with overweight Soviets at dinner in sweat shirts with stained armpits. I supposed this was their final monopoly as foreigners, now that the West had started to return. I asked, through the interpreter, what they thought of Russians, who had been allies. They conferred excitedly as I looked at that most unattractive crowd, munching noisily, mouths often ajar. The East German-trained economist lady had found my question difficult but eventually summarised what they thought: Russians were like Americans without money. I asked my team to dine with me because I did not want to be left alone in that dining hall, but they said it was not possible. So I had a quick supper and traipsed up to a dim but air-conditioned bedroom.

Next day we went down to the landing stage where there was a fifty-foot diesel-powered ship with a large flat deck. They said with pride that it was a gift from East Germany. It was to be mine for the whole day. I could do whatever I liked, on instructions from the Deputy Governor. This impressed them because they had never had to convey such a generous offer. As we stepped on board several dozen school-children walked by in a group, pre-teen boys and girls in uniform, chatting away sing-song. I asked the interpreter what they were studying. Their teacher spoke up. 'English' came his reply, a nice-looking young man. Wonderful, I said, so they can all come on my boat for an hour and I can talk to them in English. I was a writer and spoke it well. He blanched, avoided my glance and only replied via the interpreter.

It was not allowed.

At the start of my final morning in Hanoi the Deputy Governor came to pay his respects. He said that as a rare privilege the Governor himself wanted to shake me by the hand, five minutes at most. The Governor was dignified and forthcoming. He had studied the twenty or thirty pages of neatly typed notes. He explained that certain things did not appear to be consistent. I said that did not surprise me because we had covered a great deal of ground. For two whole weeks I had been talking my head off. He put his questions one by one, through the interpreter. I was able to resolve everything. It took an hour. He made us feel we had all done a good job and shook our hands. The Deputy Governor was amazed. He said that in their constitution the Governor was an executive member of the national Cabinet. A whole hour with him was exceptional.

Twenty-two

Larry rang to say it was years since we had had an outing together, so I suggested we go to Henley Regatta. I put on the requisite uniform: Leander socks, white flannels, blazer and Christ Church Boat Club tie. He and Joan were now living on the corner of St Leonard's Terrace, overlooking Burton Court. He looked dapper coming out in his summer suit. He liked the two guest badges I pinned on his lapel, one for Stewards' Enclosure, one for Leander. We had a glorious sunny day by the river, even though Eton and Christ Church were knocked out of their races. Everyone in Stewards was dressed according to the rules. A whole day without seeing any horrible jeans and trainers, making the wearers look like refugee rejects. There were many young people looking lovely. Summer dresses and high heels. We lunched in the Stewards' tent and had tea in Leander garden. We then drove to Steyning and he slept in the car for much of the journey.

We arrived with him refreshed and dying for his whisky: 'Dada's num-num'. We were alone there, everything laid ready on the dining table. We were caught up in a feeling of togetherness, nourished by the food and wine, even more so afterwards while we had our nightcaps. He took me round the garden in the twilight, and said the herbaceous borders were 'almost as good as Jill's'. His affection for her was enduring, though he did frequently refer to her as a dyke, which was wrong. She had not been bisexual until well after their marriage but I never corrected him. I thought he was trying to shield himself from the guilt he felt at the way he had deserted her.

Love for your parents becomes deeper when you can reach far into them, so far that they can share their sense of shame. Then the truths he spoke about himself were eclipsed by his railing against Joan. How could he have been so blind to her background; he was hurt by her lack of consideration and rudeness to him even in public. Few of his friends liked her. It was quite a jeremiad, capped with his assertion that she had set their children against him. All this was quite true. I had seen it. I reminded him of the years they had been so happy together, with their very young family.

We went inside, recharged our num-nums and sat in the tiny drawing room. He was curious about my love life. I said that I was on the look out for a mutual love sound enough for us to marry. He said: 'Next time make sure it's a good one.'

He asked what I was reading and I said it was a book about Christianity. 'Christ,' he said, 'I thought you were over that one.'

I was. He wondered what I thought happened after death.

'Finality,' I replied. It was the absolute and complete end of consciousness, of any kind. Non-existence, just as non-existent as we were before being conceived by our parents. Birth throws us into life and death throws us out of it. There is no afterlife. Life itself is sacred. That's all there is for us. Why should we be important enough to be 'granted' life everlasting as a reward? Besides, eternal *anything* would be insufferable. How old would you be, or your parents, or Shakespeare or whoever you wanted to meet? The only sorrow over death is with those remaining who loved you.

'Yes, I like that,' he said.

'What do *you* think?' I asked.

'Oh, I'm sure the furies will get me.'

He had never even addressed such matters in so far as they touched himself. He really did not know or really attempt to know himself. He was quite right when he said that he knew the characters he played better than he knew himself. Whatever made him the world's greatest actor, that was surely one key: observation and knowledge of others, at the sacrifice of his own self.

As we were finishing our nightcap he looked over at me in my Henley attire and said: 'Age is descending on you with glamour. I'm sorry I'm only a life peer. You would have made a wonderful lord.'

Next morning after breakfast he swam twenty lengths in his little pool. At one end he marked each length up with beads on an abacus. This helped his heart and circulation, but his vigour was at a low ebb. Even so he could never really relax and dream away. Lin Yu Tang said that a man who can sit a few hours in a garden doing nothing must have learnt how to live. This was something Larry could never do, even at the end of life. His was a restless soul: creativity finally deprived of a target.

Isis stayed with me one weekend and said I should stop looking for love. 'It always breaks your heart, and it breaks ours to see you unhappy.' I took her advice, while continuing to give dinner parties at home, going out all over London, and for the odd weekend in the country, but I was no longer on the hunt.

Within a few months in the summer of 1985 a Turkish girl moved in downstairs. I first saw her on a Saturday morning by the front door, collecting her mail. She was wearing a yellow tracksuit. Despite my not wearing glasses I saw her face in the sharpest possible focus, her intelligent and lovely eyes, fine Ottoman features, the shapeliest hands. She said her name was Zelfa. I realised I was stricken at first sight, for the third time ever. I had not been looking. I had taken Isis's advice. I asked what she was doing. She said she was going for a picnic. That ruined my day.

With work at De La Rue on a downward slope I did not feel that my peacock plumage was all it should have been. I lacked confidence and held off from getting better acquainted with her. I was seeing an outplacement adviser to identify a suitable new job. I was offered a City job in the platinum business, a new market being exhaust catalysts to neutralise carbon fumes. Another was in Sheffield. but I could not bear the thought of living there. Some ugly headhunter said that with my connections I should be an arms dealer. I lividly stormed out of his office. Two headhunting firms asked me to join them but as I hate the telephone I would not have been suitable. A public relations boss offered me a job but those who would have been my colleagues did not like me. He said this might have been because I knew more key people than they did and they were jealous. De La Rue Giori offered me a job selling their printing machines, worldwide, based in Lausanne, but I had done travelling, and Switzerland. Eventually my adviser said that I should go into film production. I had connections, understood enough about finance, could write and should set up a company.

In 1987 I was made redundant, within weeks of Peter Orchard taking over from Gerry Norman as chairman of De La Rue. I went to his London office to say goodbye. It was as if his conscience prevented him from looking me in the face. So he really was a moral coward as well as being a control freak. Within a short space of time of his being chairman the company was bankrupt, its share price dropping from ten pounds to two. He died in shock and his favourite and inappropriate chief executive officer had a nervous breakdown. The company was patched up by Sir Patrick Pickering, new to the business but a miracle worker who was easy to talk to.

I started working at home and set up a little company with Jeremy Saunders, an experienced film executive, as my co-director. One weekday morning, while still in a dressing gown I was by the front door collecting the post. Zelfa came out of her flat.

'Why aren't you at work?' she asked.

I said that I was. I had set up a film company to finance films in Third World countries.

'What about Ataturk?' she said.

That has been my career signal beyond all others, ever since. I have written a book about the ups and downs suffered so far trying to get together an epic feature film on that most fascinating of men, the founder of modern Turkey. Its publication must wait for the movie. The whole rhythm of my life changed. Zelfa and I lived together for two years, our weekdays downstairs with her, weekends upstairs with me. My children took to her immediately. So did my mother and Joy. There were a few displeased lady friends. Marrying a Turk, they asked, what *does* she look like? Turkish I said. And now her circle of friends is even wider than mine. We have been married for twenty-two years,

I took her down to Steyning for lunch. We sat at the end of the table with Larry, while at the far end sat Joan, the children and daughter-in-law. Zelfa was the second girlfriend I had taken there, Julie being the first, with modest success. Zelfa's exotic beauty bowled him over, and her ease of conversation. Larry was as enchanted with her as I was. At the end of lunch we told him we were trying to put together an epic feature film on Ataturk. He was an admirer of Turkey's Gallipoli hero. We were wondering which actor could play such a role.

He punched his chest and cried like a whiplash: 'ME!!!'

He started introducing Zelfa to his friends as my fiancée, before I had proposed to her. Once I had, and been accepted, and announced our engagement in *The Times,* he introduced her as his daughter-in-law, even before we were married.

Then he died.

For the sake of continuity I will repeat the page about his funeral which I wrote in the memoir *My Father Laurence Olivier.*

He tried everybody's patience. The family had continually to leave him to the long-suffering nurse to answer his demands. There was a long time of pain and anguish, years in fact, yet even then he reassembled his energies to do 'Lear' on television.

My mother wrote to me in March 1978:

'I hear Daddy is not well, but still about, and talked to Donald

Sinden at the Garrick till 2.30 a.m., which fascinated Donald and Diana – he had his taxi waiting. I hear of him from Mu Richardson. He has spent hours with Ralphie [Richardson], frail but full of humour, stayed so late he had to be turned out,

'I don't think he will be with us much longer. I haven't seen him much in the last forty years. It's funny after all that time how I can still love him so much.'

The ex-Chairman of De La Rue, Sir Arthur Norman, sent me a wonderful photograph of Larry he had used to promote the World Wildlife Fund. I showed it to her and she burst into tears. 'How beautiful, how old. He has become a beautiful old old man.'

I last saw Larry two days before he died, on Sunday in a room as tiny as the one he was born in. He was lying shrunken, unshaven, face to the wall hardly breathing, his nose 'as sharp as a pen'. I was told he could be peppery so I refrained from touching him, only called him softly: 'Daddy?' He turned and opened his eyes, glanced at me sideways, eyebrows arched to carry his eyelids outwards, a gleam of defiance, rejection and welcome at once, laughter longed for, rage at the fading of the light.

He died on 11 July 1989 aged 82. Before his funeral, as friends of the family were gathering in the garden, I sought out the young male nurse who had been with him in the last stages. I explained how Larry had loved recounting the dying words of King George the Fifth – 'What's on at the Empire' and 'Bugger Bognor'. The nurse then recalled that a day before his death Larry had been lying speechless on his back. His parched mouth was open and the male nurse, to introduce some kind of fluid, cut an orange in half, held it over the parted lips, and squeezed. A few drops fell wide and trickled under his cheek and round to the temple. The eyes opened and the voice crackled: 'This isn't fucking Hamlet, you know. It's not supposed to go in the ear.'

The private funeral was held in the nearby St James's Church in Ashurst village. It was built of flint stone, twelfth century, and tucked under high trees, beside an overgrown graveyard. I sat in the car with Isis behind Joan. Tristan was ice climbing in Peru, and Clavelle was with Riddelle in Spain. My half-brother Richard and his wife Shelley were with their seventeen-month-old baby son, and behind them Richard's sisters Tamsin and Julie-Kate. Zelfa was in the second car with the rest of the Plowrights. My mother was ill in a nursing home.

On arrival Joan and I and our children stood facing a tier of twenty photographers the other side of the road, with security men provided by Joan's brother David Plowright of ATV. We waited for the coffin. It was lifted from the hearse and all the cameras flashed and whined. It was lowered to a trolley and a huge coronet of flowers placed on it. It was wheeled through the old church doorway. The address was given by Gawn Grainger, one of Larry's closest friends in later life, who had helped him write the book *Olivier on Acting*. Tony Hopkins recited the last lines from *King Lear*. Richard and I read the lessons. He had the more difficult one with the emotional lines of 'O Death where is thy sting? O grave, where is thy victory', which he managed well.

I had Ecclesiasticus: 'Let us now praise famous men and our fathers that begat us.' It could not have been more appropriate. Until then I had never really understood the various ways I had heard it read. The clue was of course in the lines. In the middle, like a caesura, was the sentence: 'And some there be who have no memorial, who are perished as though they had never been, and become as though they had never been born.'

I felt that I, unemployed and unemployable, was talking about myself. Over the lectern were faces I knew so well: John and Mary Mills, Susana Walton, Franco Zeffirelli, Tony Hopkins, Ronald Pickup, Alec Guinness, Maggie Smith and, all the way from New York, Douglas Fairbanks, Larry's oldest living friend.

The lines of Ecclesiasticus then go on rather more kindly about nonentities: 'But these were merciful men, whose righteousness hath not been forgotten.' Every reference to 'their seed' or 'these men' should emphasise the 'their' and 'these', so as to differentiate 'them' from the great ones.

We traipsed out of the church behind the coffin. The little choir and comforting organ had done their best. In our car Joan turned to me and said she that never before had she understood the lesson I had read, and thought Larry would have been proud. She went on to say that for the memorial service they ought to have John Gielgud give the address. It was such a pity he could not be at the funeral. I said that would be risky because he was too emotional. At Vivien's memorial service at St Martin-in-the-Fields he had been tearful, agony for everyone. My mention of Vivien *and* embarrassing delivery made her open to my suggestion of Alec Guinness. She liked the idea. She went on to say that St Paul's would be better than Westminster Abbey because it had double the seating capacity, 5,000. I agreed that with

Nelson and Wellington in the crypt, both played on screen by Larry, it had a certain appeal. But many more were his associations with Westminster Abbey: the kings he had played who had been crowned there, Poets' Corner with his heroes David Garrick and Henry Irving; the ground-plaques with my godparents Sybil Thorndike and Noël Coward, and the restored image of Henry V on his tomb to the east of the High Altar, the hands modelled on Larry's. This impressed her. She had not known about the hands. She asked me to organise the memorial service.

The Abbey had an efficient secretariat. They advised that for them and the BBC, Larry's memorial service would be the grandest occasion since the Coronation. They agreed with the music I recommended, much by William Walton, and Alec Guinness for the address, the various readers and who should be in the procession. They suggested that all Larry's orders and decorations should be carried in on cushions, led by Douglas Fairbanks with the Order of Merit. I said no one would know which medals were what and it might make him look like a Latin-American dictator.

Joan asked the well-known theatre director, my old friend Patrick Garland, to take control of the procession and the participants, all actors in need of an experienced director like him. After Douglas Fairbanks with Larry's OM should come Michael Caine with Larry's Oscar for Lifetime Achievement, Maggie Smith with a silver model of Chichester Theatre, Paul Scofield with a silver model of the National, Derek Jacobi with the Richard III crown worn in the film, Dorothy Tutin with Lear's crown on TV, Jean Simmons with the Hamlet film script, Ian McKellen with Coriolanus's laurel wreath, and Frank Finlay with the sword which had been given to Larry by Gielgud to mark his performance as Richard III after the war, with the Old Vic company at the New Theatre, now the Albery. It had been worn by Edmund Kean, then by Sir Henry Irving.

The family sat along the aisle in the south pews, between the transept and the choir, Richard and Shelley nearest the altar, then Tamsin, Joan, Julie-Kate and me. In the second row under the VIP stalls, Zelfa was behind Shelley, then Tristan, Isis, Clavelle, and my mother. A steward guided her into the Abbey in a wheelchair. I helped her up the steps to her seat behind me.

The Abbey was filled to capacity: two thousand with their tickets awarded by the secretariat on a first come first served basis. There were exceptions at our own request for those whom we could not bear to be absent. The lights for the TV cameras blazed down the full length of the clerestory. Many hundreds of people stood outside to watch the arrivals, then hear the service relayed to them. It would have pleased Larry if I had had a notice placed at the west doors saying 'HOUSE FULL'.

The organ began to play. We all stood as the procession came down the nave towards us. First the choir, then the shining Cross. The young male chorister had to tilt the Cross far forward towards us to come under the arch of the organ screen. The Dean and Precentor were in gold copes followed by their hierarchy.

The organ music and the sight of the Cross seized me, from my guts to my head with all the strength of remembered belief. I had played the organ, and at the height of my religious passion as Keeper of the Lower Chapel Choir I had carried the Cross. It had taken me years to climb out of the definitive and attractive simplicities of religion. It now gave me a bursting sense of outrage that I had ever found it so beguiling. But on the other hand, my early faith had been a comfort, a constant rock during those years of such hastening and categorical changes, of body, mind and soul. That sense of belonging then was axiomatic to a sense of stability. My recollection gave me a sense of gratitude.

Douglas Fairbanks followed with Larry's OM laid on a cushion, with the others and their offerings in pairs behind him. In the east he mounted the steps to the sacrarium. He handed the cushion with the OM to the Dean who placed it on the High Altar and eventually the sword; the other pieces were placed on blue covered tables each side. They took their seats up there. John Gielgud sat nearby like an icon, with Peggy Ashcroft opposite.

In the silence the Dean read out the bidding in a mellow voice, echoed gently by the loudspeakers.

He said: 'On Friday 20 October 1905 Sir Henry Irving was buried in Poets' Corner. Eighty-four years later to the day we come to honour the greatest actor of our time, and next year the ashes of Laurence Olivier will lie beside those of Irving and Garrick, beneath the bust of Shakespeare, and within a stone's throw of the graves of Henry V and the Lady Anne, Queen to Richard III.

'Laurence Olivier received from God a unique and awesome talent which he used to the full. We come then to give thanks ...'

Later in the service again were words thanking God for Laurence Olivier. Alec Guinness delivered his address. At the end of it we all felt we knew Larry just that bit better. Peggy Ashcroft gave a reading from

Milton's 'Lycidas', John Gielgud from John Donne's sonnet 'Death be not proud'. He finished with words from *Hamlet*: 'There is a special providence in the fall of a sparrow. If it be now, 'tis not to come; if it be not to come, it will be now, if it be not now, yet it will come; the readiness is all.'

The climax of the service was the recorded voice of Larry as Henry V, inspiring his troops with the Crispin's Day Speech, crying out: 'We few, we happy few, we band of brothers ... upon St Crispin's Dayeeee ...' echoing round the Abbey.

After the Blessing the Dean led from the High Altar and passed us, followed by the Cross, lowered again under the organ screen, then the choir. Joan and her family. My mother's wheelchair took some time to arrive, attended by the steward. I helped her down the steps. She sat and then he moved her slowly forward. When we came under the organ screen I saw Joan and her family hurrying out, through the great west doors.

I put my hand on my mother's arm, Zelfa and my family behind me, at the speed of a slow march. This, with the sustained splendour of the Abbey's full organ, gave rise to further emotions. My mother had done so much to create Larry in his early years. We were watched by hundreds of people on either side, come to pay their last respects to my father, for whom they had all thanked God.

Then through the soles of my shoes I felt the relief shapes of some brass letters. They were the words on the tomb of Livingstone. My hero. Retracing his footsteps in the Zambezi region of Central Africa had altered the entire course of my life. It had led me to working in eighty countries, hoping to create or at least sustain wealth in one way or another. His was one of the noblest hearts ever produced by the British Empire, embodying the highest ideals in the service of man.

Then we came to the poppies, stretching in a line across our approach, surrounding the Grave of the Unknown Warrior, representing the world's most terrible tragedies in the fall of millions, laying down their lives that we might live in freedom. This place was a core of the whole purpose of human existence. We wheeled my mother to one side of the grave, to the glorious bass diapason notes, and wended our way outside.

Twenty-three

Zelfa and I were married on Monday 30 October 1989 at the Kensington Registry Office. We had been there several months before, each clutching copies of our divorce certificates. We went into the vestibule, sat down and waited. A woman opened the office door and looked down at us, a large municipal woman.

'So you've come to give notice?'

'Yes,' we said, feeling like domestic staff.

We sat in front of her desk.

I explained that we would like to get married on a Monday because that was a convenient day for my club to hold a reception.

'That should be all right,' she said. 'Monday is usually a bad day.'

I said we had both been married before and brought copies of our divorce papers.

'Let me see.'

She rubbed them between finger and thumb. I felt as if she was feeling a sensate part of me. She found the copies unworthy and said they would not do. She had to see the originals.

We went a week later when we knew someone else would be in charge. It turned out to be a man who had worked for Larry as a travel agent in the early days of the National Theatre. The date was fixed, the Garrick Morning Room reserved for an evening reception, and Zelfa immersed herself with her dressmaker.

On the day my children were there and my half-brother Richard as a witness. Zelfa's dress was a trim fit of embossed silk, cream coloured. It was topped with a bridal touch of tulle stretched across her collar bones, with a chic little jacket and no hat. Whenever her name had to be read out our officiating man in the Registry had to ask for help. Understandably. She stated her name: 'Sahnebat Zelfa Salihoglu'. When it came to the marriage certificate her late father's profession was far grander than mine: 'landowner'.

The reception at the Garrick was a success. There were tons of flowers from Turkey, tons of Turks, outnumbered by dozens of English friends my mother had not seen for years. Afterwards the actor Robert

Hardy gave dinner for the two of us and Zelfa's mother at Buck's Club. We flew to Bordeaux for our honeymoon in the Bas-Pyrenées. I wanted her to see Nay, between Pau and Lourdes, where the Oliviers came from.

My mother had set her heart on surviving to be at Larry's memorial service. She had made it but within a year she died. Joy stayed on in the house until she felt that she should go to a home to be nearer to her son, who lived in Great Missenden.

There were many things to go through, all well ordered. In the attic among folded curtains, rolled carpets and various boxes there was a pile of letters stacked in bundles on its own. They went back to her earliest days with Larry: weekly letters she had written to her mother. They gave a first-hand account of how she had been the prime influence on his developing career. It was she who had signed his first contract with Hollywood. He had not dared. His own autobiography *Confessions of an Actor* had fallen far short of the truth in terms of his professional and his personal life.

It was obvious to me that the whole purpose of my mother's keeping those letters would be fulfilled if I included them in a book. I wrote it between many film-related activities in Turkey and Los Angeles. Having been a radio journalist I could write anywhere no matter what interruptions. The first draft even smells of sun lotion from my writing it lying down by a swimming pool. One afternoon at the Hilton a curvaceous model in a bikini was being photographed. One picture shows her stooped over me, her cleavage within my grasp and I never noticed, scribbling away.

My old friend Andrew Sinclair, now married to Sonia Melchett, introduced me to his literary agent Gillon Aitken who gave it to Hodder Headline. They published *My Father Laurence Olivier* at the end of summer 1992. The first review was by Alexander Walker, the film critic of the London *Evening Standard*. It announced the book above the headline on the front page with my picture. He wrote two supportive pages. All the reviews were good. There was relief that I had written generously because I had loved Larry, Vivien and my mother. The book had been produced with wonderful pictures and was reprinted a number of times. It sold more than 15,000 copies in hard cover and paperback, but there were no translations.

I had a powerful agent in New York. My previous publisher William Morrow and a number of others turned the book down despite saying how much they admired it. The writing had made them laugh, and added depth of understanding and insights and so forth, but no, they could not sell it States side. When Zelfa and I were next there we went to see the agent. He looked less than the top class, authoritative agent we had expected.

'Ya sure,' he said, 'liked the book. It made me laugh. I was even a bit moved. Clearly you loved your father right through and held him in high regard.'

'Yes, most certainly,' I said.

'C'mon,' he jeered. 'This is America. That won't wash.'

I digested that for a moment. His was not the America I had grown up in and loved. I took aim and fired back: 'There's something you should know.'

'Aha, what's that?'

'It's something I have never written about.'

'Okay.'

'In fact I have never even talked about it.'

'Yeah, so, fine. Go ahead."

'You should know that my father buggered me.'

A yelp of delight: 'He did!? Wow. *Now* you're talking.'

As if.

In England I received more than a hundred letters about the memoir, all positive. Three listed some errors which should have been picked up by the editor. Two were from old Coldstreamers who had been in my platoon. They said I had been a bit of a disciplinarian but that they had trusted me. Not too bad – it was the Brigade of Guards after all. Several people implored me to write a screenplay.

For me the difference between writing a book and a script is categorical. Work on a book can withstand interruption. A screenplay can't, because it is almost entirely dialogue and you have to key instinctively into the tones of voice, the moods, expressions and even eye language, visualisation of the most precise kind. I suppose you could call it 'method writing'. God forbid the association. I had written several scripts before, taken seriously but not made into movies. With 'Larry and Viv', not surprisingly, I became carried away on a surge for the three deceased people I had most loved in the world. I started writing at 5 a.m. and worked straight through with a quick breakfast and lunch, until 7 p.m. It went wonderfully. If the phone rang in the next room I ignored it. Page followed page on the right hand side of an A4 hard cover writing book, any extraneous ideas or inserts on the left page. In a tearing hurry, spelling mistakes galore, I was flying. Even after writing the memoir, further memories came back for the script, they showed their faces, gave me their voices as if I were unfolding a palimpsest. The retentiveness of memory is one of the mysteries which everyone would find rewarding to explore. As there was no research required, that script took less than the usual year I needed, including all the rewrites.

When the first draft was only a day or two from the end I wanted it never to finish, like a mother weaning her baby. I eased off a bit. The telephone rang in the next room. I decided to go and answer it.

'Hello, is Zelfa there?'

'Who?' I asked.

'Zelfa. I'm returning her call,'

'No one here by that name,' I hung up and went back to Larry and Viv.

It had been one of Zelfa's girlfriends. She called that evening and demanded to know what the hell was going on with Tarquin. Zelfa, of course, understood and explained: 'You see he's writing a script. He's in 1958.'

Her friend found that difficult to credit. Zelfa's understanding brought us ever closer.

The dinner parties we gave with her at the helm were all wonderful. She was an instinctive and fabulous cook, taking infinite care to create original dishes, often guided by recipes she cut from magazines and pasted away in scrapbooks.

One dinner party stands out. We had Robin Day, the one time Grand Inquisitor of the TV Panorama programmes, and still larger than life, and for the lady opposite him we had the ex-wife of Asil Nadir, one time of Polly Peck; she was called Ayşegül, with emerald green eyes, the most beautiful face and fine hands. The other guests were the playwright and screenplay writer Ronald Harwood and his wife Natasha, and the actor Derek Nimmo and Pat.

The evening went well from the start. Robin was very taken by Ayşegül. Half way through dinner he leant over the table to her and asked, in his loud perfunctory way everyone knew so well; 'Tell me. Have you had a nose job?'

I nearly died.

'Yes', she said directly.

Now with Robin there was such a tonnage of kinetic energy that you couldn't make him change track. He was like a speeding freight train.

He went on: 'Are you pleased with your nose job?'

'Oh very.'

Luckily Derek Nimmo spoke up, with his slight stammer: 'I had a nose job too.'

We all turned to him with relief.

'I was born with an Ottoman proboscis. That was wrong for the sort of universal actor I wanted to be. I needed a straight nose. So I had the nose job. Unfortunately they left me with a turned up button of a nose. So I was con-con-condemned to com-comedy.'

Only he could have saved the moment.

Lunch at the Garrick Club on Thursdays was usually with Robin Day, the theatre critic Milton Shulman, Ed Pickering, vice-chairman of Times Newspapers, William Rees-Mogg, one-time editor of *The Times*, Alistair McAlpine, of the construction company family, and one or two others. We were joined by Michael, Earl of Onslow, a gregarious man with a wonderful sense of humour. We had such a good time that I asked him and his wife Robin to have dinner at home with me and Zelfa, just the four of us. Zelfa surpassed even her high standard of food and our foursome made for the most stimulating evening. Robin's letter said she had never known anything like it.

One Saturday they invited us for a lunch they were giving for Dennis and Margaret Thatcher a few years after she had retired. On a table of a dozen I sat opposite Denis, while the ex-Prime Minister sat on Michael's right and Zelfa on his left. Lunch started at one o'clock and continued until six. Margaret Thatcher held forth strongly at her end of the table. She complained about the corruption in Brussels, the stultifying bureaucracy, our having to adhere to their directives without their being approved in Parliament, all the usual euro-sceptic points, and the appointment of commissioners like Neil Kinnock who were no more than superannuated politicians with no experience in power. She made a point of criticising the German Chancellor Helmut Kohl for signing up for the unification of East and West Germany without even advising her of the timing.

The conversation drifted towards the euro. I suggested that few seemed to consider the immense damage done by the unified currency in the United States: the American dollar. This caught her attention. Her blue eyes focused on mine with their full voltage, so I continued. I said there were many different economies in that country, separated by hundreds, even thousands of miles: Alaska with its own unique needs, Seattle with Boeing and internet media, the High Sierras, Los Angeles the one industry town and Silicon Valley nearby, the South with its backwardness, Texas and oil, the 'Fly-over' states' so heavily subsidised by billions of food stamps paid for by everybody else, the Rust Belt,

New York and so forth, all needing their own monetary and fiscal policies. All of them were compromised and some damaged for want of them. Amid the unified fixity something had to be flexible. It's the *people* that have to give. Forty million Americans move house every year. In the United States one of the first questions any American asks another is: 'Where are you from?' The only reason the system works at all is because of their common language, their unity under the Stars and Stripes, and a federal government which dictates the common monetary and fiscal policy.

The countries in the Eurozone have none of that, and with the addition of every new member less well off than the original six the inevitable implosion comes closer. I ended by saying that England should never join the euro. We had always been islanders, and had never been continentals. Margaret Thatcher's face radiated goodwill for a full few seconds. Ours was a reverse position. Although it was I who was speaking she bound me with the strength of her absorption rather than me her with my delivery.

For several summers Zelfa and I were invited by Haldun and Çigdem Simavi for a week aboard their boat *Halas* on the Mediterranean coast of Turkey. Haldun had been a leading newspaper proprietor and she, with her many cultural and charitable deeds, was in all but name the country's First Lady. The boat was a sixty-metre long old ferry with walls of mahogany, and plenty of deck space above all the cabins. If she had had a paddle wheel she would have looked at home on the Mississippi a century before.

We joined the boat when she was moored at one of the many fir-forested islands near Göçek. As we climbed on board Çigdem introduced us to Princess Margaret and her two ladies-in-waiting. They were regular summer guests on board. As I gave a courteous little bow to Princess Margaret I sensed her *frisson* on seeing me, perhaps remembering our last encounter.

During the daytime she sunbathed on deck, reading Dante's *Inferno*. I ventured: 'Isn't it marvellous.' 'What's marvellous?' she asked. 'That there's no music being played.' 'Oh,' she said with relief in her voice, 'you're so right!'

She took a great shine to Zelfa and was constantly asking her to swim with her; rather too constantly but Zelfa always did. After a few days as they swam towards the shore she said how she had worshipped Larry and Vivien. In 1951 she had seats to see them together in *Caesar and Cleopatra* and the following evening in *Antony and Cleopatra*. Unfortunately she had to go to the London Clinic for an operation. She was heartbroken and sent a devastated message of regret. Next day when she was being visited by the Queen Mother and the Queen two large bouquets of roses were brought in to her. One had an enchanting hand-written note from Larry and the other an even more enchanting one from Vivien. She said their being delivered while 'my mother and my sister' were with her made the pleasure even more exquisite. Larry and Vivien's thoughts were for *her*.

She was friendly and a good storyteller. She enjoyed talking about the Queen, whom she always referred to as her sister; which the rest of us knew we should never do. The only real constraint was that we had to keep hidden any newspapers we bought. The red-top press was licking its chops over the affair Princess Diana was having with Dodi Fayed on his father's yacht.

The only time I had met Princess Diana was at the Goldsmiths' Hall when she appeared at her first public function with Prince Charles. Her glorious body was flattering a low-cut black taffeta evening dress, which one tabloid justifiably referred to as a 'Di-version'. She looked wonderful, tall and with brilliant good-humoured blue eyes.

When I next saw her it was at the British Museum for a gala opening of the Suleyman the Magnificent Exhibition. The money for this had been raised by Zelfa, who also arranged the finance and the production of BBC2's excellent documentary. For the occasion the Turkish Prime Minister's wife, Semra Özal, gave a speech in English. She delivered it well. Meanwhile Princess Diana was whispering to her friends and let out a giggle. This was mortifying for Semra Özal who thought she was being laughed at for her English. It was reprehensible bad manners.

Thereafter we had Princess Diana going public on television, a long one-to-one interview at her instigation, and we read about her affair with James Hewitt, who collaborated in a book about it, tried to sell her love letters, then produced his own memoir. I wrote to *The Times*:

> Sir, Now that they are breeding more rapidly than ever, and in both sexes, we should sub-divide the word 'bimbo' into the component parts of 'bimbeau' and 'bimbelle'.

I was commissioned by the Turkish Prime Minister to make a TV documentary on Kemal Ataturk. They knew of my serious and years-long involvement in the subject for a feature film which was killed off temporarily by the Greek and Armenian diaspora in New York. Those objectors had written angry letters, none too threatening, all signed and on headed paper, to the director Bruce Beresford, who quite rightly ignored them, and to the star. His agent withdrew him and the finance so far contrived fell apart. As I had no experience of making documentaries I was advised in London to use a company specialising in the genre. They did a terrible job and I had at my own expense to redo the whole thing before it was accepted. It was broadcast on Turkish Radio Television and in England on the History Channel.

In 2005 the so-called 'Authorised Biography' of Larry, by Terry Coleman, was published. Joan authorised it before a word had been written, without insisting on a treatment. When I read it in typescript I was horrified. Coleman seemed determined to provide new evidence, unearthed from Larry's compendious archives in the British Library, to support his thesis that Larry was, shock horror, gay. He quotes extravagantly camp letters to Larry from an old one-time star actor Henry Ainley, so indulging in senile infatuation that it is difficult to see how anyone could have taken them seriously. But Coleman did, and twisted the idiotic non-evidence by leaving out key matters. The facts are these.

Coleman omits to point out that in 1928 Ainley took to drink. He was out of work until 1930. Then there was an all-star production to re-launch his career as *Hamlet*, selected for a Royal Command Performance at the Haymarket Theatre. On the first night he was so drunk he was sacked.

He became broke. We turn to the minutes of the Garrick Club, where the Secretary reported in October 1933 that he owed £27.17.9. This was left in abeyance. A year later the staff were instructed not to serve him until the account was settled. A month or so after that it was decided by the General Committee that his name be erased from the books of the club. In early 1936 he did play in the film *As You Like It* with Elizabeth Bergner and Larry, in the role of the banished Duke. He was terrible.

Coleman fails to describe any of this and takes up the story from 1936, when Ainley was broke, unemployable, washed up and living in exile in Broadstairs, Kent. Fifteen of his louche letters survive in Larry's archive, all with Broadstairs on the letterhead. The first, quoted in Coleman's account, was undated, probably at the end of 1936. Really they are worth no more than a snigger.

Larry darling,

My pretty. Please. This is very serious – who ever told you I was one of those? Have you seen my Osric? Haven't you? ... I have been tossing (now now) about at night thinking about you. No dammit, really, I am serious. I would like to hear from you if you are well and happy. How Jill must hate me taking you away from her.

The second quoted letter is dated 11 January 1937, also from Broadstairs:

Darling, Christ!

You are a lousy pansy. Don't you ever dare write to me again.

This surely indicates to any reader that Larry had told Ainley to get lost. Coleman does not point this out. Ainley goes on:

You are playing Hamlet therefore you are a king. ... You now rank among the greatest. I am proud of you and so is Jill.

Had Ainley seen Larry's Hamlet he would, as an actor, have appraised it, compared it to other performances including his own, and discussed the production. Any biographer of an actor should know *that* much about theatre people. And it is clear that Ainley knew nothing about Larry's marriage to my mother being at an end, nor of his burgeoning affair with Vivien, all too well known by their associates nearer home in London.

It is easier to prove that something happened, if indeed it did, than to prove that something did not happen, even if it didn't. I will do my best.

Ainley was a drunken exiled wreck hiding in Broadstairs. Larry was at the time head over heels in love with Vivien. Their affair had started in August 1936, two weeks before I was born. He visited her in Stanhope Street W1 whenever he could, while her husband Leigh was at work. He still lived with my mother in Cheyne Walk. At the end of 1936, with her help, he learnt the full-length *Hamlet* and rehearsed for it. It ran from 5 January 1937 to 20 February. Vivien went to fourteen performances. Then from 23 February he played Sir Toby Belch, with my mother as Olivia, in *Twelfth Night*, until 3 April. From 6 April to 22 May (his birthday) he played *Henry V*.

These dates are in Coleman's chronology and overlap the letters Ainley wrote from exile. How could Larry have had contact with him?

So much for any affair or homosexual orgies occurring, as Coleman indicates, either in late 1936 or early 1937.

Coleman excludes the letter Ainley wrote on 29 August:

> Darling Larry,
>   ... no gentleman uses the word 'Balls' when writing to a friend as you do in your letters to me.

So the only indication of Larry paying any attention is a reprimand such as this, rejecting Ainley's frustrated perversion.

Given this evidence how could anybody deduce an affair between the two men? Joan authorised this biographer on the disastrous advice she received from Larry's associates. She was tied by the contract handed to her by Coleman's agent. It is inconceivable that she would have authorised Coleman's work after reading it. When asked by an interviewer on the radio whether Larry was gay she understandably fluffed her lines in shock. As soon as I received Coleman's typescript I wrote on the above lines: to him, his agent, his publisher, Joan, her lawyer and my half-brother Richard. Nothing in the book was changed.

On 5 October 2005 Joan wrote to me:

> Darling Tarquin,
>   I have not commented publicly on the biography as I had no wish to increase the publicity it would inevitably attract. Like you, I believe Ainley's letters could equally well be the work of a fantasist but the author Coleman was unwilling to entertain that possibility. Derek Granger (the original biographer) read the letters when he assembled the archives and dismissed them as 'high camp' – the kind of jokey flirtatiousness that was prevalent in theatre circles at that time. I have since learned that he wrote that kind of letter to a number of other people he fancied. There are no letters [surviving] from LO to Ainley and no proof whatsoever that anything took place between them except in Ainley's imagination. However, I was not around at that time in LO's life and the letters are in his files. But I do know that during our thirty years together his needs were exclusively heterosexual. And I believe all the people, gay and straight, with whom we worked at the National Theatre would confirm that opinion.
>   Coleman's book is not, as its publishers claim, a definitive portrait. It ignores the testimony available of friends who recall the sheer fun of being with LO. And it fails to capture his huge

capacity for enjoyment of the moment despite trouble and suffering – and his utter relish of the work however hard and taxing. Missing too is any sense of the wit, charm and warmth which inspired such deep affection in so many people.

'Oh, I do miss him, he made me laugh so' is a sentiment I've often heard expressed. And oh yes, he made me laugh so much too.

    With love
    Joan

Larry was true, as I set out in my speech at the unveiling of his statue: sometimes without thought for consequences. He vehemently stated to me: 'Christ no. I have never been queer.' His has to be the ultimate authority.

Articles and books will persist in stating that Larry was homosexual and they really shouldn't be taken seriously. It is a load of baloney. He was more heterosexual than most heterosexuals. He adored women. In these days when being gay is no longer something to hide, saying that he 'was one' would not matter in any other profession than his. Acting is different. He never played gay roles such as Shakespeare's Richard II or Prospero. He could not imagine transmuting characters such as theirs within himself. While many of his friends were gay and he adored their company and their talent, many of them being more talented than the rest of us, he hated the whole idea of homosexuality.

Twenty-four

22 May 2007 was the centenary of Larry's birth. Two years before then I contacted institutions which I thought were sure to realise or at least sponsor a suitable project to commemorate him. The National Theatre liked my idea for a bronze statue, life size, of him as Hamlet, climbing the steps of Elsinore Castle to meet the ghost of his father's spirit, holding his sword in front of him like a crucifix. They also suggested a site for it. Beyond that, no organisation would step up to start the project, even though 2005 was a year of continuing prosperity. I had to take responsibility for the whole thing.

Lord Attenborough, universally referred to as 'Dickie', agreed to unveil the statue. With this prestigious information I wrote the first of four hundred letters to people and institutions. Some I wrote to two or three times so as to shame them. Eventually two hundred did reply with a donation made out to the National Theatre Statue Account. Dickie Attenborough's input, with his close relationship with the National's Chairman Sir Hayden Phillips, opened up a way of avoiding payment of VAT because the National was a charity, which saved £25,000.

I had to commission the sculptor long before I had raised sufficient money, so I was personally liable to meet any shortfall. I wondered about the worst case, of my having to sell my flat. If Zelfa had been worried she hid it well. At the end I raised the capital required, plus just more than £5,000 which I gave to the National for upkeep and so forth.

It was a dry and sunny day, 23 September, selected by Nick Hytner the Director of the National. Zelfa was looking lovely, a red silk suit, black jacket with a diamond leaf spray brooch and large dark glasses. About five hundred people stood in Theatre Square including Riddelle and her daughter, facing the South Bank, the Olivier Fly Tower behind them, and Joan Plowright, nearly blind with macular degeneration, led devotedly by Maggie Smith. She recognised me only by my voice. Her three children and grandchildren were there, so were my three and at that stage eight grandchildren.

After Sir Hayden's introduction I made a speech:

Larry was true, he was magnetic, gloriously funny, he is still a part of what makes life worth living, as is his creation the National Theatre. It took much more than a century for this to happen. The third time Queen Elizabeth the Queen Mother laid the foundation stone, in yet another place, she said 'You really ought to put some wheels on this thing.' It took his leadership to bring it to fruition. Harold Wilson implored him to accept a life peerage but he refused until the entire cash commitment for the National was signed and sealed, the heroine in Cabinet being Jennie Lee, Minister for the Arts.

I am not the first Tarquin to erect a statue of his father. But it is a rarity. The last one was two and a half thousand years ago, the last King of Rome, whose son Tarquinius Sextus caused the dynasty's downfall with 'his ravishing strides', to use the lines in *Macbeth*, and what nowadays would be called his unfortunate involvement with Lucrece. A young Roman general, heir to the throne, in a scarlet toga. Irresistible. I am sure she was dying for it.

Together with the generosity of the many more than two hundred contributors, thankfully with so many of you here, we have brought about the creation of an iconic, romantic and most exciting image which is recognised around the world. Many of you wrote wonderful letters regaling me with stories of Larry. Many sent helpful lists of people I could approach for contributions, here, and from the United States and Australia. Where there were no addresses I am most grateful to Anne McGuire of Equity for forwarding many dozens of letters to the addresses she had.

For the many who would have liked to contribute but were never asked I can only ask their forgiveness. All the contributions were entirely voluntary from individuals or independent institutions. They include not one penny from commercial sponsors nor any government-affiliated organisation. This statue is a gift to the National Theatre and future generations from *us*.

All contributors' names are printed in the programme for this evening's celebratory performance. All those who contributed a thousand pounds or more will have their names engraved on the brass plaque which will be placed in front of the statue, once that list has been finalised.

I chose the image of Hamlet because it was one of the few great roles where Larry actually used his own face. In the reception area you can see his Romeo, painted by Marshall, with the first of many false noses; a facsimile of Salvador Dali's Richard the Third personifying the irresistible charm of his brand of evil, and the Ruskin Spear sketch for the full-length portrait of Macbeth, at Stratford. I know of no greater portrayal of every unimaginable pain in any painting than that exhibited by this painting of Larry's Macbeth, even in any Crucifixion.

These roles were recognised as great because they totally absorbed the world's greatest actor into themselves, and transformed his body language, his speech, his mental physical and spiritual energy into becoming them. Obliterating himself. As a profession it demands more discipline and creates more exhaustion than any other kind of artistry. What supreme energy. He really was tapped into some source.

Hamlet, using his own face, is completely different. Of *Hamlet* he said it was set apart from any other play; it is unique, because with Hamlet you cannot cheat. You have to give your complete self, as your own self and no one else's, no role-playing there, no defence: the difference between being a lover and a husband.

I went to tender to three extremely well-known sculptors with photographs from his film of *Hamlet*. The Garrick Club agreed with these images and my selection of Angela Conner's offer. Hers was the only one which answered the terms I asked for: a full-length life-size statue and plinth, with the possibility of two complete copies and three busts of the head taken from the original. These would be made for any suitable institution or collector. Her price, much reduced from her norm, meant that there was no real decision to be made. She was passionate about the subject.

However, she had serious reservations about the iconic image I had chosen. It reflected photographic reference material which did not originate in her own heart and head. It is out of keeping with her own modern thinking. Nonetheless she made a once-in-a-lifetime exception, against the dictates of all her artistic instincts. She indeed remained true to the iconic image of Hamlet, climbing the battlement steps of Elsinore to meet his father's spirit, sword held high in front of him like a crucifix.

Here it also symbolises his utter belief in the creation of the National Theatre. It is far out of keeping with current fashion, but unlike fashion it is an everlasting classic, known and recognised the world over. Many believe it would have been the people's choice. I very much hope it's yours. Although it is life size it seems smaller, perhaps because on stage he looked such a giant. We thought that if it were larger it would make his face too far away.

It was on the basis of Angela Conner's supreme reputation and on this image that I made my appeal. At the outset, everyone I saw in the Lambeth Council expressed their excitement and support, and advised whom I should approach in the National and the South Bank Centre. I would like first to thank the Chairman of the National, Sir Hayden Phillips, and his colleagues the Director Nick Hytner, the Executive Director Nick Starr, and especially the Theatre Manager John Langley and Laura Hough. We all met last February, attended by Lord Attenborough and Angela Conner, whose CV greatly impressed them, and the image of Hamlet they found thrilling.

The site originally selected was where the two enormous Festival of Britain ladies, by Dobson, and called *London Pride* now are. The Appeal would have had to pay for their relocation. Another disadvantage was that that place, between the bookshop and the trees, is not spacious. So after our meeting we measured the ground. They agreed to my suggestion that the statue of Larry should be here, on the north-west corner of Theatre Square, looking across it, towards the National's Main Entrance, and the Olivier Fly Tower above, bang next to the National Film Theatre and in full view of Waterloo Bridge.

The selection of this site made all the difference. It added excitement to the Appeal and it really began to look as if it might succeed. This was unlike anything I had attended to in forty years as a businessman. It would have failed any feasibility study, there was no return for any of us except the hope of fulfilling our shared feelings of love and admiration for Larry, and our determination that his memory should be properly honoured, and the National adorned with this wonderful image of him.

I would also like to thank the South Bank Centre's Director of Partnership and Policy, Mike McCart and his assistant Frances, and the Director of the British Film Institute, Amanda Nevill. This site is actually just on their land.

I would now like to thank our closest associates: Mandip Dhillon the senior planning officer of RPS Planning, Transport and Development, who guided our planning application through its oft amended vicissitudes; Rob Nilsson of the engineering company Price and Myers; and the architects Peter Culley and Owen Jones of Rick Mather who did such beautiful drawings.

Most of all, apart from Angela Conner, I must congratulate her boundlessly skilled Simon Stringer who did all the rubber moulding, made the waxes, poured the silicon bronze at eleven hundred degrees Celsius into his casts, and then welded every single hand, foot, limb, the head and the huge cape together into one piece. Thick stainless-steel stanchions from the calves and deep into the stone plinth lock the complete work into place for keeps.

To illustrate the collaborative atmosphere we all developed as individuals with very different tasks, we often emailed each other as 'Dear All', with copies everywhere, This was a wonderful indication that England is becoming what I call a 'Yes' country. The supportive fellow feeling saved acres of time.

Here I must thank Lisa Burger, the National's Director of Finance, and Chris Walker, Head of Finance, for being Trustees of the Appeal and for accepting my accountancy and banking submissions, and for their acceptance now of this statue, on behalf of the National Theatre, as a gift from all of us.

In his lifetime he was universally referred to as Larry. This is the finest compliment that can be paid to a great artist. So now with immense pride I hand you over to one of our greatest filmmakers whose support for the Appeal has been stupendous. Ladies and gentlemen: Dickie.

In his speech Lord Attenborough proclaimed how Larry had utterly dominated the theatre and the screen as well, marking him out as unique. As he himself was only associated with the screen, and this was the National Theatre, he had asked members of the original theatre company to assist in the unveiling of the statue, which they did with aplomb, Joan Plowright, Maggie Smith, Anna Carteret and about ten others. Once unveiled there was a heart-warming round of applause. That evening both the Olivier and the Lyttelton Theatres were filled to capacity for an informal show by a couple of dozen actors, interspersed with excerpts from Larry's films. It was excellent. Then we had a well-presented buffet supper. The day and the statue were a success. I was affected most by the congratulations of Nick Hytner and Peter Hall, Larry's successor as Artistic Director of the National.

Apart from that I have nothing to show for the efforts of the last few years. I believe some of the films I have written will be made. My children and grandchildren have grown very fond of Zelfa. Our circle of friends is wider and more interesting. These were magnified by journeys we put together for friends and friends of friends; a dozen or so at a time. This was not commercial, save for the economics she negotiated because we were a group. We just shared the cost between all of us. In various late summers we took them to south-east Turkey along the Syrian border, north-east Turkey including Noah's Ark and Mount Ararat, Central Turkey for the Hittite civilisation, Edirne, Rumelia, Istanbul several times and a number of boat trips on the Mediterranean Coast, then Libya, Uzbekistan and plans now lapsed for Syria where she had been born.

In her work she represents the Aman Resort Hotel Group, the supremacy of beauty and service, and after quite a number of years of effort the first project, called Amanrüya, came to completion on 15 December 2011, in a fabulous coastal site near Bodrum, with other projects in the pipeline. We have stayed in their exquisite hotels in Bali, Java, Thailand, Rajasthan and Marrakech.

We have lived together and are living to the full. I'm not as old as I'm going to be, and as long as there is hope there is life.

Low Cost Coinage

A mint master can relax if the face value, the purchasing power of a coin is, say, double the intrinsic value of the metal plus costs of production. This difference is called seigniorage. If, with inflation, the intrinsic metal value plus production cost becomes more than the purchasing power, that is called negative seigniorage. Intrinsic value can of course be reduced by making smaller coins but the limits are obvious. There can be no smaller coin that the five pence. When this negative seigniorage is bigger than the intrinsic value of the metal alone, ignoring the manufacturing costs, the coins can be bought in bulk for cash, melted down and profitably sold as simple metal.

The effects of inflation, as an example, at ten percent compound, will double the price of an object in seven years, as shown in Table 1. The

GRAPH ONE
% Price increase at different rates of inflation

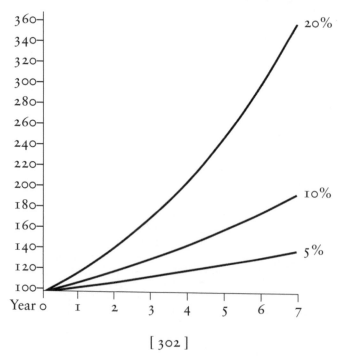

Unit price rises at different inflation rates: 5% 10% 20%

5%	100	105	110	116	122	128	134	141
10%	100	110	121	133	146	161	177	195
20%	100	120	144	173	207	249	299	358

effect on that coin's purchasing power is the reciprocal. It will halve, as in Table 2.

These numbers are reflected in the graphs. For the sake of simplicity the production costs are ignored, as are a number of other factors included in my presentation to the Royal Mint. We concentrate here on intrinsic metal value.

Graph two introduces the intrinsic metal value as fifty percent of the purchasing power, and shows how only seven years of inflation at ten percent will lead to negative seigniorage. With inflation at twenty percent that coin will start to disappear in four years. During the Wilson-Heath regimes we had inflation well above that.

GRAPH TWO

Purchasing power reduced by different rates of inflation

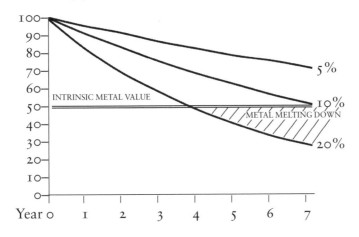

TABLE TWO

Purchasing power = reciprocal of inflation

Inflation rate

5%	1.0	0.95	0.91	0.86	0.82	0.78	0.75	0.71
10%	1.0	0.91	0.83	0.75	0.68	0.62	0.56	0.51
20%	1.0	0.83	0.69	0.58	0.48	0.40	0.33	0.28

There is nothing new here, but the graphic representation, which for the sake of simplicity excludes production costs and shows only the metal value, highlights the dynamic horror. Suppose the cost of metal had increased fifty percent in those years, the coin would have started to disappear in eighteen months. Then what?

The Royal Mint ceased our solid alloy bronze one and two pence coins in 1982, and issued successors containing a ninety percent core of mild steel with a five percent coating all round of bronze; identical in appearance. These electro-plated coins will never be worth anyone's effort to melt down for their intrinsic worth, not to mention the technical difficulty of separating the bronze from the mild steel core. This saved one million pounds in the first year. Retaining our white metal coins as solid cupro nickel in the thirty years since 1982 must have cost tens of millions of pounds.

The era of solid alloy coins has to be ended, all over the world.

Index

Ada, housekeeper in Hong Kong, 218, 228, thinks author pays her too much, 234, 235
Africa, author in, 44–71, 174–8, 180–1; and Francophone countries, 183ff; 189, 191–2, 192–4, 195–7
Ahidjo, Ahmadou, President of Cameroon, rejects banknote designs, 195
Ainley, Henry, and homosexuality issues, 292–4
Aitken, Gillon, 286
Allen, Adrienne, 25, 105,
Amis, (later Sir) Kingsley, 271
Annersley, John, 219
Apia, Western Samoa, author visits, 237
Apple Porch, Esmond grandparents' cottage, 1, 2, 18, 21, 25, 26, 144
Ashcroft, Dame Peggy, 42, 283
Attenborough, Richard (later Baron) and wife Sheila Sim, 73–4; and statue of Larry, 296, 299, 300
Auden, W.H., 42
Aumont, Jean-Pierre and wife Marisa Pavan, 241–2

Bali, author visits, 207
Bancroft, Anne, 241
Bangladesh, author's De La Rue dealings with, 162–72, 173; author visits, 175, 187
Banks, Charles, to be De La Rue new MD, 233; interview with author not a success, 234; improves salary scales, 234; with wife Peggy, dinner organised by Mike Nicholas a disaster, 237–8; author takes to Melbourne to see Australian Printing Works, 238
Bata'an, 222
Battle of Britain Museum, Hendon, 238–40
Beacham, Richard, in CDC's Regional Office for Asia and the Pacific, 219
Benin, 195
Benitez, Tom, 75, 76; and wife Nena, 77; 79, 80, party in Nena's garden, 225; Nena widowed, 249
Bennett, Louise, 'Miss Lou', and husband Eric Coverley, 155
Beresford, Bruce, 292
Blake, Robert (later Baron Blake of Braydeston), 38, 72
Boase, T.S.R., President of Magdalen College, Oxford, 42; entertains author, 42; dinner guest at Notley, 42
Botswana, planning new currency, 189–90
Bowers, Faubion, and wife Santha Rama Rau, 74–5, 81, author sees in New York, 125; split from wife, 125; biography of Scriabin, 125, 201; 208
Bowra, Sir Maurice, 42
Bradley, Tom, Mayor of Los Angeles, 243

[305]

incorporating Thomas De La Rue, author works for, 162ff; collapses under chairmanship of Peter Orchard, but patched up by Sir Patrick Pickering, 278

Deans, Mickey, married to Judy Garland, 149

Dhillon, Mandip, 299

Diana, HRH Princess, 291

Dowling, Alan, Royal Mint Services consultant, advice alarming, 263

D'Urso, Mario, 217, 220–1, author joins for dinner with President and Imelda Marcos, 225–6; introduced to Rowe-Beddoe, 227; travels in special bus through poverty-stricken area with author, Rowe-Beddoe, and Imelda, 227; drinks party and Annabel's, 255–6

Edwards, Alan, solicitor, 220

Edwards, David, sculls with author, 42–3

Esmond, Henry Vernon, author's maternal grandfather, 1

Esmond, Jill (author's mother), 1–2; three West End appearances, 1, and Broadway and film successes, 3–4; divorce, 2; takes author to New York, 3, to Los Angeles, 4ff; screen reputation, 4; and her mother's arrival in California, 8ff; returns to England 1945, 14; part in film *Escape*, 15; 17, at Apple Porch, 18; 20, and gardening, 21; skiing with author, 23; and Eve Brierly, 24; 25, and Jenny, 40; visits Notley with author, 40–1; support for author's travel and writing plans, 75–6; author lives with in London on return from South-East Asia, 101; tour in France with author, 111; comes

out to Trinidad for Carnival, 122–3; helps with author's house purchase in Holland Park, 142; goes with author to see Judy Garland at London Palladium, 148; grand piano and Balinese painting, 179; and ring-tailed lemur, 201; comfort in Stravinsky's music after Larry had left her, 201; author persuades to move to smaller house, 233; and Battle of Britain, 238–9; on Larry, March 1978, 278–80; at Larry's memorial service, 282, 284; at reception after author's marriage to Zelfa, 285; death of, 286; stacks of letters in the attic, going back to her earliest days with Larry, 286

Evans, Dame Edith, 1

Fairbanks, Douglas, Jr, at Larry's private funeral, 281; at memorial service, 282, 283

Farrer, David, 270

Farrer, Lance, 72

Fenner, Sir Claude, Commissioner of Police in Malaya, 91–2, 219; author lunches with and wife Joan, 226; 228

Fenninger, Claude, President of Sheraton International, wants author to work for the company in Brussels, 156

Fichter, Bert, in charge of production, Royal Mint, then with De La Rue's minting department, 262; and wife, 265

Fiji, author visits, 251; to choose between De La Rue and Bradbury for new banknote designs, author's meeting with Fijian Minister of Finance, 258–9

Howlett, Ernie, director of Royal
Mint Services, 262
HSBC and Bradbury Wilkinson:
unauthorised printing of
banknotes in Switzerland, 231
Hunter, Sir Ian, 158
Hutton, Barbara, and husband Cary
Grant, 9–11
Hytner, (Sir, 2010) Nick, 296, 299,
300

Igorots, 77–8
India, author in, 187
Irving, Sir Henry, 1, 282, 283
Ismail, Tan Sri, Malaysian Central
Bank, 260
Issa, Pehin, Brunei, 211

Jacobi, (later Sir) Derek, at Larry's
memorial service, 282
Jamaica, 149–57
Jaya, Agus, 87–8
John Peartree Gallery, Kingston,
Jamaica, 151; Ridelle's exhibition
at, 156
Johnson, Dame Celia, 1
Jonathan, Leabua, Prime Minister of
Lesotho, 176
Jones, Owen, 300

Kelly, Bryan, author's piano teacher,
42
Kennedy, Senator Edward, reception
in Dhaka, 187
Kenyatta, President Jomo, 135
Keynes, Quentin, at Notley, 33;
heads expedition to Africa,
44–71; collection of historical
manuscripts and books, 44–6
Khama, Sir Seretse, President of
Botswana, 189
Khrushchev, President Nikita, 85–7,
108; and Mrs K, see Habib

Kilombero Sugar Company,
author's posting, 135; in dire
straits, 136; subsequent recovery,
142
Kinnock, Neil (Baron, life peer
2005), 289
Kissinger, Henry, US Secretary of
State, 222
Kohl, Chancellor Helmut, 289
Kwan, Nancy, 247

Langley, John, 299
Laos, author attends annual regatta,
210–11
Leander Club, 21
Lee, Jennie (life peeress Baroness Lee
of Asheridge), 297
Lee Kuan Yew, Prime Minister, in
Singapore, 212
Legarda, Ben and Lita, 248
Leigh, Vivien. author's stepmother,
2, 3, 22, 15–16, *Caesar and
Cleopatra*, 16; miscarriage, 16;
and manic depression, 16, 26,
32; in *The Skin of Our Teeth*,
18; with author in South of
France, 23; encourages author
to play piano, 27; invites
Quentin Keynes to Notley, 33;
40, marriage deteriorates, 73;
80, in letter to author reports
she is starting to feel herself
again, 97; living with Jack
Merivale at house near
Uckfield, 102; author stays
there, 102; 108, gives party
for author and Riddelle, 130;
131, 132, 133, death from
TB,141–2; at memorial service
John Gielgud over-emotional,
281; and Princess Margaret,
291
Lesley, Cole, 105, 151

drawing, 182; 200, 220, stays
with author in Hong Kong and
Manila 223–6; 233, 234, 248,
249; 255, 261, cautions author on
looking for love, 277; 280, 282,
285, 296
Olivier, Hon. Julie-Kate, author's
half-sister, at father's funeral, 280;
282, 284,296, and see under entry
following
Olivier, Sir Laurence (as Baron
Olivier of Brighton, life peer,
1970), author's father, 2, 3, 14,
15, buys Notley Abbey, 16ff;
distinguished friends, 16; 18, 22,
with author in South of France,
23; exchange of letters with
author, 25–6; spoof letter to
Jenny's foster-mother, 40; and
Joan Plowright, 75; unable to
continue living with Vivien, 75;
opposed to author's travel plans,
75–6; now married to Joan
Plowright, buys house in
Brighton, 101; son Richard's
christening, 104; and Chichester
productions, 109; and children
Richard and Tamsin, 130;
reproved by Riddelle's mother,
132; author and Riddelle to stay
in Brighton, 134; and Vivien's TB,
141; advice to author, 145;
domestic life under stress, 159;
buys cottage near Steyning,
Sussex, 160; gift of wine to
author, 162; dinner in Victoria
with author and Riddelle, suggests
name 'Clavelle', 173; health
seriously deteriorating, 178;
advice to author on how to
recover Balinese painting from
Jill, 179; in hospital with
dermatomyositis, 180–1, 182;

recovery against all expectations,
182; relationship with wife Joan
increasingly strained, rumoured
affairs, children gang up against
him, 197; stays with author in
Hong Kong, 241; to Hollywood
and *The Betsy*, 241; asks author
to join him, 241; they dine with
Robert Wagner and wife Natalie
Wood, Juliet Mills and her
husband Michael Micklanda,
241; week's filming in Detroit,
241; back to Malibu and
congenial routine with author,
246; to Henley Regatta with
author, then on to Steyning, 276;
affection still for Jill, less for Joan,
276; discussion with author on
after-life, 277; takes to Zelfa, 279;
dies, 279; quote from author's *My
Father Laurence Olivier* on his
funeral, 279–80; private funeral at
St James's, Ashurst, 280–1; and
memorial service at Westminster
Abbey, 281–4; and Princess
Margaret, 291; Terry Coleman's
allegations of homosexuality in
*Olivier: The Authorised
Biography*, 292–5; statue,
296–300
Olivier, Richard (Hon. 1970),
author's half-brother, christening,
104; and wife Shelley at father's
funeral, reads lesson, 280–1; and
Shelley, 282, 284, witness at
author's marriage to Zelfa, 285;
294, 296
Olivier, Sydney, 1st Baron Olivier,
Governor of Jamaica, 150;
Secretary of State for India,
187
Olivier, Hon. Tamsin, author's half-
sister, at father's funeral, 280;

education for developing countries, financing collapses, job-seeking again, 159; basement flat in Holland Park, Riddelle and children miserable there, 159; cruise with David Mitchell-Innes, then joins Riddelle and children in Scotland, 160–1; November 1971 starts working for De La Rue, 162; Riddelle pregnant, 162; dealings with Bangladesh, 162–72; birth of Clavelle, 173; Johannesburg and Cape Town, 174; Swaziland, 174–6; Lesotho, 176–7; Botswana, 177–8; South Africa, 180–1; reads in newspaper Larry in Brighton Hospital with dermatomyositis, 180; visits, 181; and UN sanctions against South Africa, 181–2; Riddelle 'restless', 182; African Francophone countries, 183–6; and French language, 183–4; Bombay and New Delhi, 187; and Edward Kennedy's visit to Dhaka, 187; starts work on a novel, 188; Riddelle assesses it chapter by chapter, 188; and Swazi banknotes, 188–9; in Botswana, 189; Madagascar, 190–1; to Tunisia with three lady banknote examiners from Gateshead factory, 191–2; and Guinea-Conakry, 193–4; and Aeroflot flight, 194–5; Cameroon, 195; Liberia and Sierra Leone, 195–7; holiday in Norfolk, 197; weekend with Larry and Joan, 197; appointed regional manager for South-East and South Asia, 198; in Singapore, then Djakarta, 198–9; leaves Riddelle and children in Mills's house in London, finds house in Singapore, 199–200; Riddelle arrives with children, tells author marriage is over, 200; resites himself in high-rise block, 201; acute sorrow, finds some solace in Scriabin's music, 201; to Saigon, 201–5; and US troops, 202–3; and De La Rue's Vietnamese agent, and wife, 203, 204–5; confrontation with Central Bank over payment terms, 203–4; interview with Governor, 204; resolved to De La Rue's advantage, 204; lunch with agent and guest Annie, 204–5; Embassy urge author to get out of country at once, 205; diagnosed with Reiter's Syndrome, 296; to Chinatown, Singapore, 206–7; treatment in London, briefly sees Riddelle and children, 207; Djakarta meetings with directors of State Printing Works, then to Bali, 207–8; to Kathmandu, numbering errors on banknotes, 208–9; Bangkok, Laos, 209–10; Brunei, 211; Singapore, flies to Sydney, 212; New Zealand, 213–14; Hong Kong, 214–15; Hong Kong race meeting, 215–16; to Manila with Julian Wethered, 216; and Mario D'Urso, 217; Hong Kong flat with housekeeper Ada, 218ff; Riddelle and divorce, 219–20; back to Manila over factory project, 220; invited to State Dinner for President Ford and to visit Corregidor on Marcos's yacht for commemoration of General MacArthur and Second World War, 220–3; two elder children come to stay in Hong Kong and

Manila, 223–6; and banknote contracts, 225–6; dines with President and Imelda Marcos, 225–6; to Malaysia to settle banknote order, 226; takes children to see *The World of Suzie Wong*, 226; joined in Manila by Rowe-Beddoe, 226–7; introduces him to D'Urso, 227; trip through poverty-stricken area with Rowe-Beddoe, D'Urso and Imelda, 227; taken over State Printing Works, 227; to Hong Kong with Rowe-Beddoe to meet Commissioner of Banking, 227; Karachi, 227; and assassination of Sheikh Mujibar Rahman, 227–8; home to Hong Kong via Singapore, 228; loss of weight and arthritis, 228; daily water-skiing, 228; celebrates Chinese New Year, 229; Charles Hoare and wife Felicity, 229; meets Rino Giori, 229; Kuala Lumpur, Kathmandu, 229–30; Singapore, Australia and New Zealand, 230; entertains actors on Derek Nimmo's tours, 231; and Michael Sandberg, 232; persuades Jill to move into smaller house, 233; sales conference in Basingstoke, 233; called in for meeting with Charles Banks, 234; three-month course at London Business School, 234; leaves for Hong Kong, 234; to Honiara, Solomon Islands, 235; Fiji problem with counterfeits, 235–6; author's explanation that certain crises elsewhere must take priority not well received by Governor, 236; meets King of Tonga, 236–7; to Apia, Western Samoa, 237; meets Orchards and Bankses in Sydney, disastrous dinner organised by Mike Nicholas, 237–8; Orchard and Banks put off by technical head of Australian State Printing Works, 238; Orchard calls author by unacceptable nickname, author organises cocktail party in Wellington, 238; and money-raising for Battle of Britain Museum in Hendon, 238–40; to Hollywood to join Larry, 241; Jean-Pierre Aumont and wife Marisa Pavan, 241–2; Joan Collins (then Mrs Kass), 242; reading John Cottrell's biography of Larry, 242; celebrities and childhood memories, 242–4; and Brooke Hayward, 244–5; on Wagners' yacht, 245–6; copper bracelet for arthritic state of hands, 246–7; England and family, 247; problems of possible promotion to sales director, 248; children to Hong Kong, 248; on Marcos's yacht, 249–50; lands banknote order in Western Samoa, 251; row over competitors Bradbury building banknote factory in New Zealand, 251; author has to go to London to be briefed for further meetings in New Zealand, 252; to New York and Los Angeles, 252; confronts chief executive of bank of New Zealand, 253; to Tahiti and Bora Bora, 254–5; Annabel's with Princess Margaret and Imelda Marcos, 255–6; flies to New York with Imelda, on way to New Zealand, gift of cufflinks, 256–7; and Fijian Minister of Finance, 258–9; at Manila seminar on 'The

WITHDRAWN

ACC. No: 02845341

WITHDRAWN